RIGHTS, JUSTICE, AND THE BOUNDS OF LIBERTY

Princeton Series of Collected Essays

This series was initiated in response to requests from students and teachers who want the best essays of leading scholars available in a convenient format. Each book in this series serves scholarship by gathering in one place previously published articles representing the valuable contribution of a noted authority to his field. The format allows for the addition of a preface or introduction and an index to enhance the collection's usefulness. Photoreproduction of the essays keeps costs to a minimum and thus makes possible publication in a relatively inexpensive form.

Rights, Justice, and the Bounds of Liberty

Essays in Social Philosophy

by
JOEL FEINBERG

Princeton University Press
Princeton, New Jersey

For Ben and Melissa

Contents

Preface

I am very pleased that this book is the first to be published in a series of photographically reproduced collections launched by Princeton University Press. It has become increasingly difficult in this period of rapidly increasing costs to justify the use of printing facilities for republication of materials that have already appeared elsewhere. Princeton University Press wisely prefers to devote the major part of its resources to the publication of books hitherto unpublished. Since it is becoming harder and harder for original philosophical works to find a decent publisher, if the Press were to expend anything more than a minimum to republish already available material, it could only be at the cost of leaving some good books unpublished. The main purpose of republishing essays like those in this book is to provide a convenient packaging of widely scattered materials that have been much discussed, and fortunately this purpose can be served through direct reproduction, and distribution in relatively inexpensive paperback form.

The only drawback of this mode of production is that it makes rewriting impossible. For that reason I should like to indicate here what improvements I would try to make if I had the opportunity, and also where the leading critical discussions of these essays can be found. Very likely I would change the title of the first essay to expunge any suggestion of male chauvinism. The word "man," in the title, does not mark the contrast with "woman," but rather the distinction between persons and various other subjects of freedom, such as actions and institutions. Sometimes persons are said to be *free to do* something or other, or to be *free from* some unwelcome condition or other, but on other occasions they are said to be free *tout court*, and that is the sense of "free" this essay is primarily meant to illuminate.

"The Interest in Liberty on the Scales" was written several years after "The Idea of a Free Man" and departs from the earlier essay in at least one respect. In the later work I am no longer as impressed with the theoretical difficulty of comparing different degrees of freedom without bringing in standards external to freedom. There may

still be some unavoidable incommensurability between the situations
of different persons in respect to freedom, but the notion of the
"fecundity of an option" is meant to show how that incommensurability can be substantially reduced.

The third part of "Harm and Self-Interest," which is devoted to the
question of whether death is a harm, has been subjected to heavy
criticism from Ernest Partridge in "Posthumous Interests and Posthumous Respect," *Ethics*, Vol. 89 (1979) and George Pitcher in "The
Misfortunes of the Dead" (unpublished). It is also discussed critically
in a recent interesting article by André Gombay, "What You Don't
Know Doesn't Hurt You," *Aristotelian Society Proceedings*, Vol. 79
(1978-79). If I were to rework the essay now, I would try to soften
much of the sense of paradox which I seem to relish in the original,
by acknowledging more explicitly the costs to common sense in the
view I seem to be advocating, while claiming at most that these costs
may be less than those of alternative views. In discussions of "the
harmfulness of death," no analysis can leave common sense wholly
unscathed.

In my "Reply" to Michael Bayles' astute criticisms of " 'Harmless
Immoralities' and Offensive Nuisances," I accept some of his suggestions, and as a result, my original position is much strengthened.
Even that improved composite view is strongly criticized, however, in
an important recent article by Donald Vandeveer, "Coercive Restraint
of Offensive Actions," *Philosophy and Public Affairs*, Vol. 8 (1979). I
would now be inclined to complicate my position further in ways
Vandeveer suggests, although I would stubbornly resist his suggestion
that I regard offense as a kind of harm. I agree with Vandeveer, however, that the "Standard of Universality" with its *ad hoc* exception for
racial and ethnic slurs is unworkable. I would replace it altogether
with a "balancing" model derived from the law of torts. There is some
suggestion of how this would work in the "Reply" to Bayles. It is
worked out in more detail in my "Pornography and the Criminal
Law," *The University of Pittsburgh Law Review*, Vol. 40 (1979).

The main change I would make in "Legal Paternalism" would be
to state in the first paragraph in the strongest terms that I take a stand
in this essay *against* legal paternalism. My highly qualified and tentative style of exposition has misled even some normally careful readers
in this regard. No doubt misleading to some was my unfortunate
labelling of the view I endorse as "weak paternalism." In fact, my
argument led me to a liberal doctrine which in its immediate effects
can be confused with paternalism but which is essentially quite different from it, namely, that the state has the moral right to prevent
wholly self-regarding harmful conduct when, but only when, it is substantially nonvoluntary, or when temporary intervention is necessary

to establish whether it is voluntary or not (when it is of a sort that can be presumed nonvoluntary unless shown otherwise). My thesis in this article is that *wholly voluntary* actions that have no serious other-regarding consequences may never rightly be prohibited by law. The argument then puts a great burden on the notion of voluntariness and requires a full explication of that critical concept. The essay reprinted here can be interpreted as a preliminary programmatic outline of a fuller account that would come to terms with the notions of fraud and coercion (both of which prevent actions and agreements from being voluntary) as well as exploitation. (Some wholly voluntary transactions may nevertheless be exploitative of one of the parties, and these may at first sight seem to be counterexamples to my thesis.) The best statement, I think, of a view alternative to mine is that of Jonathan Glover in his *Causing Death and Saving Lives* (Penguin Books, 1977). Glover argues that autonomy (the right of self-determination) and personal well-being are equally fundamental moral claims, and that when they are in conflict, a lawmaker can only try to balance them intuitively. For the view that autonomy is more basic than well-being, see my "The Child's Right to an Open Future" in *Children's Rights*, edited by Hugh LaFollette (Littlefield & Adams, 1980).

"The Nature and Value of Rights" has been widely reprinted and widely criticized. Among the more important criticisms are those expressed in the following articles: Bertram Bandman, "Rights and Claims" in *Bioethics and Human Rights*, edited by B. and E. Bandman (Little, Brown, 1978), Rex Martin, "Human Rights as Morally Valid Claims" (A.P.A. paper, 1979, unpublished), Rex Martin and James Nickel, "Recent Work on the Concept of Rights," *American Philosophical Quarterly* (1979), Phillip Montague, "Two Concepts of Rights," *Philosophy and Public Affairs*, Vol. 9 (1980), and Carl Wellman in various of his important articles on rights. In reply to Martin and Wellman, I should emphasize that I intended my essay to be an account of the "nature and value" of only one of the four concepts of a right distinguished by Wesley Hohfeld, namely, that which Hohfeld called "claim-right." I must concede that a full theory of rights would also deal with "powers" and "immunities."

Well after the publication of "The Rights of Animals and Unborn Generations," I learned that the essentials of my view were anticipated by the German philosopher Leonard Nelson in his *A System of Ethics*, first published in 1926. Leading opponents of the thesis that animals can have rights are Martin Golding, "Towards a Theory of Human Rights," *Monist*, Vol. 52 (1968), and John Passmore, *Man's Responsibility for Nature* (Chas. Scribner's Sons, 1974). Tom Regan is strongly committed to the view that animals *do* have rights, but criticizes my account of how such rights are possible in his "Feinberg on What Sorts

of Beings Can Have Rights," *Southern Journal of Philosophy*, Vol. 15
(1977). See also Robert Elliot's rejoinder, "Regan on the Sorts of
Beings That Can Have Rights," *Southern Journal of Philosophy*, Vol.
16 (1978).

The primary flaw in "Human Duties and Animal Rights" is its
suggested answer to the question "why an animal should have any
underivative claim to life-as-such at all." I invoke (albeit tentatively)
the James-Santayana-Perry theory of value as satisfaction of demand,
and suggest that the biological impulse to self-preservation is a "demand," and that it therefore establishes the "value" of every animal
life. As an argument, however, that reasoning is a flagrant *ignoratio
elenchi*. The conclusion that was to be established is not that animal
lives have value but that all animals have a *claim*, amounting in some
circumstances to a right, to continue living, and that is quite another
thing.

My essay "Is There a Right to be Born?" is brief, and thus unavoidably fails to pursue some of its subtleties as far as I should have liked.
Many critics have pointed out the extreme difficulty of denying that
fetuses have "noncontingent rights" based on "actual interests" while
holding that neonates *do* have such rights and interests. The logic of
my argument drives me to withhold noncontingent rights from infants,
too, in the manner of Michael Tooley in his "A Defense of Abortion
and Infanticide" in *The Problem of Abortion* edited by J. Feinberg
(Wadsworth, 1973) and Mary Ann Warren in her "On the Moral and
Legal Status of Abortion," *The Monist*, Vol. 57 (1973). I would then
base the case for prohibiting infanticide on reasons other than that it
would violate the infant's rights, much as Stanley Benn does in his
"Abortion, Infanticide, and Respect for Persons" in *The Problem of
Abortion* (*op. cit.*). My more detailed views about the moral justi-
fiability of abortion can be found in my article "Abortion" in *Matters
of Life and Death*, edited by Tom Regan (Random House, 1979).

The argument in the second paragraph of the discussion of "Alienating vs. Forfeiting" in my "Voluntary Euthanasia and the Inalienable
Right to Life" now strikes me as muddled. If the law treats my right
to life as both forfeitable and inalienable, it does not encourage me
to kill another person if I find my own right to be "burdensome
baggage." It does of course put me in a "Catch-22 situation," for I can
do nothing to bring about the end of my life without committing *some*
legal wrong (i.e., without violating *someone's* rights), and if my conscience forbids me to commit a legal wrong, then I have no choice but
to go on living. But if I am determined to end my life in any case,
then I am no more "encouraged" to commit murder than to commit
suicide, and I will no doubt choose suicide as being quicker, more
certain, and involving smaller moral cost.

That part of the disjunctive conclusion of "Noncomparative Justice" which holds that a false judgment about a person may be unfair to him even though it is not truly derogatory seems to conflict with an earlier claim in the essay that undeservedly favorable criticism of a person cannot be unfair *to him*. Fortunately this inconsistency is easily remedied. The case of the nonderogatory judgment that severely misrepresents a person in a way that is basic to his own conception of himself can be treated as a qualification of the earlier thesis, the one small exception to its universality. For a penetrating criticism of "Noncomparative Justice," see Phillip Montague's "Comparative and Noncomparative Justice" in *The Philosophical Review*, April 1980.

Once more I am indebted to my former colleague Josiah S. Carberry for his help with these essays, but given his proven unreliability, I am not inclined to thank him for it.

J. F.
Tucson, Arizona
September 1979

Sources and Acknowledgments

1. "The Idea of a Free Man" was originally read at a conference on the philosophy of education sponsored by the Council for Philosophical Studies in St. Louis in 1971. The papers presented at that conference were published in *Educational Judgments*, edited by James F. Doyle (London: Routledge & Kegan Paul, 1973). In the book, as at the conference, this essay was paired with the paper "Freedom and the Development of the Free Man" by R. S. Peters of the University of London. That explains the reference in the first sentence to "Professor Peters' admirable essay." "The Idea of a Free Man" is reprinted here by permission of Routledge & Kegan Paul, Ltd.

2. "The Interest in Liberty on the Scales" was published originally in *Values and Morals: Essays in Honor of William K. Frankena, Charles L. Stevenson, and Richard B. Brandt*, edited by Alvin I. Goldman and Jaegwon Kim (Dordrecht: Reidel, 1978), pp. 21-35. Copyright © 1978 by D. Reidel Publishing Company, Dordrecht, Holland. Photographically reproduced by permission of D. Reidel Publishing Company.

3. "Harm and Self-Interest" is from *Law, Morality, and Society: Essays in Honour of H.L.A. Hart*, ed. by P.M.S. Hacker and J. Raz (Oxford: Clarendon Press, 1977), pp. 289-308. It is reprinted here by permission of the Oxford University Press.

4. " 'Harmless Immoralities' and Offensive Nuisances" was presented as part of a symposium at the 1971 Oberlin Colloquium in Philosophy. Comments ("Offensive Conduct and the Law") delivered by Michael Bayles were published along with it in the Proceedings of the Colloquium, *Issues in Law and Morality*, edited by Norman S. Care and Thomas K. Trelogan (Cleveland: Case Western Reserve University Press, 1973), pp. 83-109 and 111-26. My "Reply" (to Bayles), though not delivered orally at Oberlin, appears in the same volume. Both the "Reply" and " 'Harmless Immoralities' and Offensive Nuisances" are reprinted here by permission of Oberlin College.

5. "Legal Paternalism" first appeared in the *Canadian Journal of Philosophy*, Vol. 1, No. 1 (1971), pp. 105-24. It is reprinted here by permission of the *Canadian Journal of Philosophy*.

6. "Duties, Rights, and Claims" was first presented orally as a comment on a lead paper by Richard A. Wasserstrom ("Rights, Human Rights, and Racial Discrimination") in the Symposium on Human Rights at the meeting of the Eastern Division of the American Philosophical Association in Boston, Mass., December 27, 1964. It was subsequently published in the *American Philosophical Quarterly*, Vol. 3, No. 2, April 1966, pp. 1-8. It is reprinted here by permission of the *American Philosophical Quarterly*.

7. "The Nature and Value of Rights" was the Isenberg Memorial Lecture at Michigan State University, January 10, 1969. It was first published in *The Journal of Value Inquiry*, Vol. 4 (1970), pp. 243-57, and is reprinted here by permission of *The Journal of Value Inquiry*.

8. "The Rights of Animals and Unborn Generations" was presented to the Fourth Annual Conference in Philosophy at the University of Georgia on February 18, 1971. It was published with the other papers from that conference in *Philosophy and Environmental Crisis*, edited by William T. Blackstone (Athens: University of Georgia Press, 1974), pp. 43-68. It is reprinted here by permission of the University of Georgia Press.

9. "Human Duties and Animal Rights" is from *The Fifth Day: Animal Rights and Human Ethics*, edited by Richard K. Morris and Michael W. Fox (Washington, D.C.: Acropolis Books, 1978), pp. 45-69. It is reprinted here by permission of The Humane Society of America and Acropolis Books, Ltd.

10. "Is There a Right to be Born?" is from *Understanding Moral Philosophy*, edited by James Rachels, © 1976 by Dickenson Publishing Company, Inc. Reprinted by permission of Wadsworth Publishing Company, Belmont, California 94002.

11. "Voluntary Euthanasia and the Inalienable Right to Life" first appeared in *Philosophy and Public Affairs*, Vol. 7 (Winter 1978), pp. 93-123. It was originally delivered as the 1977 Tanner Lecture on Human Values at the University of Michigan and at Stanford University. Reprinted by permission of the Tanner Lecture Trust. Copyright © 1977 by the Tanner Lecture Trust.

12. "Duty and Obligation in the Non-Ideal World" is a discussion-review of John Rawls' *A Theory of Justice*. It was published in *The Journal of Philosophy*, Vol. 70 (1973), pp. 263-75. It is reprinted here by permission of *The Journal of Philosophy*.

13. "Noncomparative Justice" is from *The Philosophical Review*, Vol. 83 (1974), pp. 297-338. It is reprinted here by permission of *The Philosophical Review*.

14. "Wollaston and His Critics" first appeared in the *Journal of the History of Ideas*, Vol. 38 (April 1977), pp. 345-52. It is reprinted here by permission of the *Journal of the History of Ideas*.

RIGHTS, JUSTICE, AND THE BOUNDS OF LIBERTY

The Idea of a Free Man

Professor Peters's admirable essay has two primary aims: (1) to articulate more clearly a widely prized ideal of character and (2) to consider how that particular personal excellence can be 'learned,' or at least fostered by a certain kind of institutional environment. The character trait in question is one that shares the glittering name of 'freedom' with a puzzling variety of other things that are *not* virtues of character, among them, a certain class of institutional arrangements and control systems. By analyzing the ideal of the free man, on the one hand, and the nature of a free social system, on the other, Peters hoped to be in a better position to illuminate the connection between the two in a way that will be useful for the purposes of educational policy and congruent with the results of psychological learning theory. I think that these purposes of Peters's have been largely achieved by his essay, and therefore I will restrict my comments to a related topic that he had to pass over.

When Peters writes that an examination of 'what is meant by "freedom" in a social context, like that of a school, and what is meant by a "free man," ' can lead to 'some suggestions . . . about the connection between the two,'[1] he has in mind a connection of an instrumental kind. He is concerned to tell us how a free institutional environment can help *bring about* freedom as a trait of individual character. My intention is to complement his essay by considering the conceptual, rather than the instrumental, connection between the two kinds of freedom. I shall proceed by surveying the various things we might mean when we say of an individual person that he is free.

I Free from . . . and free to . . .

'He is free' might, first of all, be an elliptical expression of a singular judgment that someone is, happily, without impediment or constraint to a desire that he has or might have to do, or omit, or be, or have something in particular. It is useful to interpret these singular judgments in terms of a single analytic pattern with three blanks in it:

————————————is free from——————————to do
(or omit, or be, or have)——————————

Sometimes it is perfectly clear from the context *whose* freedom is under discussion. On other occasions, especially when we talk grandly about 'economic' or 'religious' freedom, relying on the adjective in the absence of any names or pronouns, the first blank in the schema will have to be filled in for the sake of clarity and the prevention of equivocation. On other occasions the speaker will be quite clear in his own mind what the subject of his assertion is free *to* do, but will be quite vague about what constraint he is now free *from*. Perhaps all he means to convey in his enthusiasm is that *nothing* now prevents him from doing X, in which case the whole intended emphasis of his remark is on the new option now open to him, and no specific descriptions of missing constraints are necessary to fill out his meaning. If, however, the X in question is something most of us are normally free to do anyway, we may be puzzled by the speaker's remark until he specifies more narrowly which constraint to his desire to do X, formerly present, has now been removed. But when this puzzlement does not arise, no description of specific missing constraints is required for clarity.

On other occasions, the primary or exclusive emphasis of a speaker's assertion of freedom may rest on a specific missing constraint. He may, for example, claim to 'be free' simply because one hated barrier to a given desire has been lifted, even when other barriers to that very same desire admittedly still remain. In that case, all of the emphasis of his remark is on the removed constraint, and his newly asserted freedom does not imply that he can yet *do* any more than he formerly could. He is free *from* one barrier to his doing X, and that may seem to be blessed relief from an oppressive burden, but he may still be unable to do X. In an extreme limiting case, a speaker may have no concern with future *actions* whatever, and the existence of new alternatives for choice may be no part of his intended meaning when he asserts that he is free *from C*. He may be exclusively preoccupied with the removal of some odious condition quite apart from any effect that removal might have on his *other* desires or options. He may simply hate his chains and conceive his 'freedom' to consist entirely in their removal.[2] In this not uncommon limiting case, freedom from . . . implies no new freedom to . . . other than the freedom to be without the thing one is said to be free from.

More typically, however, when we use the language of missing-constraint, we imply that there is something we want to do (or might come to want to do) that the constraint prevents us from doing, and that to be free from that constraint is to be able to do that which the constraint prevents us from doing. In the typical case, then, 'freedom from' and 'freedom to' are two sides of the same coin, each involved with the other, and not two radically distinct kinds of freedom, as some writers have suggested. Indeed, it is difficult fully to characterize a given constraint without mentioning the desires it does or can constrain (that is, desires other than the exclusive desire to be relieved of *it*). The man outside a divorce court who tells us that he is now free (presumably *from* the woman who was his wife) has not communicated much to us until he specifies which desires he can satisfy now that he could not satisfy when he was married. (It might be very bad public relations on his part to leave this entirely up to our ill-informed imaginations.) Without further specification, we know only that he is now without a wife and quite happy about it; but then, as we have seen, that *may* be all that he had in mind when he said that he was free.

It has often been said that there are two main concepts, or types, or ideals of freedom, one positive and the other negative, and that ideologies conflict in so far as they employ, or give emphasis to, the one, or the other, or both of them. The writers who have attached great importance to this distinction have often had an important insight, but even when that has been so, their insight can be preserved and expressed with greater economy in terms of the 'single concept' analysis given here. The writers to whom I refer argue that only one of the two allegedly distinct concepts of freedom, namely the 'negative' one, is to be analyzed as the absence of constraints. We may be free of all constraints to our desire to do X, these philosophers maintain, and still not be free *to* do X. Hence, they conclude, 'positive freedom' (freedom to . . .) is something other than the absence of constraint.

This way of making out the distinction between positive and negative freedom will seem plausible, I think, only if the idea of a constraint is artificially limited. In fact, however, two important distinctions between kinds of constraints, each cutting across the other, can be made, and once these distinctions are recognized, the apparent ground for the 'two concept' analysis vanishes. The distinctions I have in mind are between positive and negative constraints and between internal and external constraints. There is no doubting that some constraints are negative—the lack of money, or strength, or skill, or knowledge, can quite effectively prevent a person from doing, or having, or being something he might want. Since these conditions are absences, they are 'negative,' and since they can be preventive causes, they are constraints.

How we make the distinction between 'internal' and 'external' constraints depends, of course, on how we draw the boundaries of the self. If we contract the self sufficiently so that it becomes a dimensionless non-empirical entity, then *all* causes are external causes. Other narrow conceptions of the self would attribute to its 'inner core' a set of ultimate principles or 'internalized values,' or ultimate ends or desires, and relegate to the merely 'empirical self' or even to a world altogether external to the self, all lower-ranked desires, whims, and fancies. If the distinction between internal and external constraints is to be given a *political* use, however, then perhaps the simplest way of making it out is by means of a merely spatial criterion: external constraints are those that come from outside a person's body-cum-mind, and all other constraints, whether sore muscles, headaches, or refractory 'lower' desires, are internal to him. This would be to use a wide 'total self' rather than the specially intimate 'inner core' self in making the distinction.

The two distinctions described above cut across one another creating four categories. There are *internal positive* constraints such as headaches, obsessive thoughts, and compulsive desires; *internal negative constraints* such as ignorance, weakness, and deficiencies in talent or skill; *external positive constraints* such as barred windows, locked doors, and pointed bayonets; and *external negative constraints* such as lack of money, lack of transportation, and lack of weapons. Freedom from a negative constraint is the absence of an absence, and therefore the presence of some condition that permits a given kind of doing. The presence of such a condition when external to a person is usually called an opportunity, and when internal, an ability. Not every absent condition whose presence would constitute an opportunity or ability, however, is a negative constraint. Only those whose absence constitutes a striking deviation from a norm of expectancy or propriety, or whose absence is in some way an especially important consideration for some practical interest either of the subject or of some later commentator can qualify as constraints.

If only positive factors are counted as constraints, then a pauper might be free of constraints to his (actual or possible) desire to buy a Cadillac, and yet, of course, he is not free *to* buy a Cadillac. Similarly, if constraints are restricted to external factors, then the chronic alcoholic and the extremely ill man in a fever or a coma are both free from constraints to go about their business, but of course, neither is free *to* do so. Once we acknowledge, however, that there can be internal and negative constraints, there is no further need to speak of two distinct kinds of freedom, one of which has nothing to do with constraint. A constraint is something—anything—that prevents one from doing something. Therefore, if nothing prevents me *from* doing X, I am free *to* do X; and conversely, if I am free *to* do X, then nothing prevents me *from* doing X. 'Freedom to' and 'freedom from' are in this way logically linked. Thus, there can be no special 'positive' freedom *to* which is not also a freedom *from*.

Still, there is no harm, I suppose, in characterizing 'positive freedom' as the absence of negative constraints, and 'negative freedom' as the absence of positive constraints, *provided* (1) that both positive and negative freedom are held to be necessary, and equally necessary, to a man's freedom all told (without any adjective), and (2) neither is held to be 'higher' or 'lower' or intrinsically more worth having than the other, and (3) neither is analyzed as totally different in kind from the absence of constraints.

A final distinction between types of constraints can obviate still other difficulties in interpreting singular judgments of the form 'Doe is free *to* do X.' A speaker might mean by this judgment either of the following:

(i)   X is something Doe *may* do, i.e. something he is *permitted* (but not required) to do by someone in authority over him, or by moral or legal rules to which he is subject. (Another way of saying all of this is that Doe is *at liberty* to do X.)

(ii)   X is something that Doe *can* do, i.e. something he is *not in fact prevented* from doing (or required to do) by coercion (direct or indirect) from others or by other kinds of constraints. (In this kind of case, talk of 'liberty' is not always interchangeable with talk of 'freedom.')

When commands or rules are not effectively enforced a person might well be able to do something that he is not permitted to do. Similarly, a person might be permitted to do something that he is unable to do because he is prevented from doing it by constraints other than rules backed by sanctions. Again, a person might be incapable of doing some act simply because the act is prohibited by commands or rules that *are* very effectively enforced. In that case, the enforced rule is itself a constraint.

Corresponding to the distinction between what may be done and what can be done is that between two perspectives from which singular freedom-judgments are made, namely, the *juridical* and the *sociological*. The former is the perspective of a system of legal or legal-like regulations itself. When I say that no one in New York State is free to play poker for money in his own home, I am simply reciting what the New York legal codes prohibit. My judgment is confirmable or discomfirmable by reference to those codes. In fact, of course, thousands of persons play poker for money in private homes in New York every night with little or no risk of apprehension by the indifferent police. When I speak from the sociological perspective, I might well say that everyone in New York, in effect, is free to play poker if he wishes. This judgment is subject to a different kind of confirming or disconfirming evidence, namely, an account of how effectively a law is enforced by the police, how intimidated poker players actually feel by the law, and how many of them in fact are willing to run the risk of detection and conviction.

From the juridical perspective, what I am free to do in a given case is not a matter of degree. For any given act or omission, either it is permitted or it is not; I am at liberty (entirely) to do it or I am not at liberty to do it at all. There are, of course, more subtle forms of legal control which employ variable constraints that permit talk of 'degrees' of freedom. If there is a $100 tax on conduct of type A and a $500 tax on type B, I am left by authority, in a quite intelligible sense, more free to do A than to do B. In the case of the criminal law, however, and all other regulations that control conduct by enjoining, permitting, and prohibiting, my freedom to do any act is, from the law's point of view, either entire or non-existent. On the other hand, from the sociological perspective, it is always intelligible to speak of degrees of freedom or unfreedom even of a particular person to do some one given act, and even when that act is unconditionally prohibited by law, if only because the probabilities of being detected and/or convicted vary from offense to offense.[3]

Most of us, of course, do not *feel free* to do acts that are forbidden by rules or authorities that we have accepted, even when there are no effective external hindrances to our doing so and we stand to profit by disobedience. We are constrained from disobedience not by external barriers and threats but by internal inhibitions. Whether the internal constraint is taken to be a restriction of the self's freedom to act depends upon how we model the self, that is, upon which of the elements of the 'total self' we identify most intimately with, upon where in the internal landscape we take ourselves to live. If we are prevented from doing that which, upon reflection, we think is the best thing on the whole to do, by some internal element—an impulse, a craving, a weakened condition, an intense but illicit desire, a neurotic compulsion, or whatever—then the internal inhibitor is treated as an alien force, internal or not: a kind of 'enemy within.' On the other hand, when the inhibitor is some higher-ranked desire and that which is frustrated is a desire of lesser importance albeit greater momentary intensity, we identify with the desire that is higher in our personal hierarchy, and consider ourselves to be the subject rather than the object of constraint. *A fortiori*, when the desire to do that which is forbidden is constrained by conscience, that is, by the 'internalized authority' of the prohibiting rules themselves, we take ourselves to live where our consciences are, and to be repelling the threat to our personal integrity posed by the refractory lower desire which we 'disown' no matter how 'internal' it may be.

A person who had no hierarchical structure of wants, and aims, and ideals, and no clear conception of where it is within him that he really resides, would be a battlefield for all of his constituent elements, tugged this way and that, and fragmented hopelessly. Such a person would fail of autonomy not because he is a mere conformist whose values are all borrowed second-hand, for his wants and ideals and scruples could be perfectly authentic and original in him, but they would fail of autonomy because they lack internal order and structure. This defective condition Durkheim called 'anomie,' a condition which in its extreme form tends to be fatal. It is interesting to note in passing why, on the unitary 'absence of constraint' theory of freedom, it is intelligible to speak of anomie as a kind of unfreedom. Our picture of the undisciplined or anomic man is not that of a well-defined self with a literal or figurative bayonet at its back, or barriers, locked doors, and barred windows on all sides. Rather it employs the image of roads crowded with vehicles in the absence of traffic cops or traffic signals to keep order: desires, impulses, and purposes come and go at all speeds and in all directions, and get nowhere. The undisciplined person, perpetually liable to internal collisions, jams, and revolts, is unfree even though unrestrained either by the outside world or by an internal governor. To vary the image, he is a man free of external shackles, but tied in knots by the strands of his own wants.[4] When he may 'do anything he wants,' his options will overwhelm his capacity to order them in hierarchies of preference; he will therefore become confused, and disoriented, haunted by boredom and frustration, eager once more simply to be told what he must do. To be unfree is to be constrained, and in the absence of an internal traffic cop, and internal traffic rules, desires will constrain each other in jams and collisions. Surely it is more plausible to construe such a state as unfreedom than as an illustration of the dreadfulness of too much freedom.

II Free on balance

A speaker may intend nothing so precise as our schema with the three blanks suggests when he asserts that he or some other person is free; but the second kind of thing he might mean presupposes and builds upon the singular non-comparative judgments discussed above. He may be saying either that he is *generally* free or *relatively* free in the above sense of 'free.' He may intend to convey that he is on the whole free, or at liberty, to do a great many things, or perhaps to do most of the things that are worth doing, or perhaps to do a greater percentage of the worthwhile things than are open to most people; or he might be emphasizing that he is free *from* most of the things that are worth being without in their own right (disease, poverty, etc.) or freer from those things than are the members of some comparison class. 'On balance judgments' of freedom are of necessity vague and impressionistic, and even the comparative judgments that they sometimes incorporate are usually incapable of precise confirmation.

Suppose that John Doe is permitted by well enforced rules to travel only to Chicago, Houston, and Seattle, but may make adverse criticism of nothing he sees in those cities, whereas Richard Roe may go only to Bridgeport, Elizabeth, and Jersey City and may criticize anything he wishes; or suppose that Doe can go anywhere at all but must not criticize, whereas Roe cannot leave home but may say anything he pleases. In reply to the question, 'Which of the two is more free?' it appears that the only sensible answer is that Doe is more free in one respect (physical movement) and Roe in another (expression of opinion). If the questioner persists in asking who is the more free 'on balance' and 'in the last analysis,' we can only interpret him to be asking which of the two respects is more important. If we are then to avoid a vitiating circularity, our standard of 'importance,' I should think, must be something other than 'conducibility to freedom.'

When two or more properties or 'respects' are subject to precise mathematical comparison, there will always be some quantitative element that they have in common. The difficulty in striking resultant totals of 'on balance freedom' derives from the fact that the relation between the various 'areas' in which people are said to be free is not so much like the relation between the height, breadth, and depth of a physical object as it is like the relation between the gasoline economy, styling, and comfort of an automobile.[5] Height times breadth times depth equals volume, a dimension compounded coherently out of the others; but freedom of expression times freedom of movement yields nothing at all comparable. Still, limited comparisons even of incommensurables are possible. If the average American has greater freedom in *every* dimension than his Ruritanian counterpart, it makes sense to say that he has greater freedom on balance; or if they are equally free in some dimensions but the American is more free in all the others, the same judgment follows. More likely, what we mean when we say that one subject is freer on balance than another is that his freedom is greater in the more valuable, important, or significant dimensions, where the 'value' of a dimension is determined by some independent standard.

There seems to follow from this analysis a result of considerable interest. Since 'maximal freedom' (having as much freedom on balance as possible) is a notion that can be made sense of only by the application of independent standards for determining the relative worth or importance of different sorts of interests and areas of activity, it is by itself a merely formal ideal, one that cannot stand on its own feet without the help of other values. One person's freedom can conflict with another's; freedom in one dimension can contrast with unfreedom in another; and the conflicting dimensions cannot meaningfully be combined on one scale. These conflicts and recalcitrances require that we put types of subjects, possible desires, and areas of activity into some order of importance; and this in turn requires supplementing the political ideal of freedom with moral standards of other kinds. The supplementary values, however, are not external to freedom in the manner of such independently conceived rival ideals as justice and welfare, but rather are 'internally supplementary'—a necessary filling-in of the otherwise partially empty idea of 'on balance freedom' itself.

III 'Free' as a legal status word

The third use of the word 'free' does not fit our analytic paradigm, and therefore, can be conceded to be a distinct 'concept of liberty'; but this use, important as it once was, has declined since the fall of feudalism and slavery, and is now almost archaic. The old English word 'free,' like its ancient counterparts, the Greek '*eleutheros*' and the Latin '*liber*,' had as its original meaning, according to C. S. Lewis,[6] simply 'not a slave,' so that to call a man 'free' in this earliest sense was merely to identify his legal status. To be a freeman was to be a full-fledged member of one's political community with all the rights and privileges, usually including various participatory voting rights, that derived from that membership.[7] In societies with two distinct legal statuses—freeman and slave—to call a man 'free' was simply to describe his legal rights and contrast them with those of a slave. (In the extreme limiting case of irrevocable chattel slavery, the slave had no rights at all.) Such judgments were easily verified by examinations of legal documents, branding marks, and the like.

It was a natural and useful extension of this original sense of 'free' to mean 'unconstrained in one's physical movements,' for the freeman was one who could come and go as he pleased. The statuses of slave and freeman, however, were not defined by the presence or absence of *de facto* or *de jure* constraints, but rather by the possession or non-possession of *rights*, which is quite another matter. The slave whose master was benevolent or motivated by *noblesse oblige* might well be free *to* do a great many important things and free *from* most

of the conditions whose absences are universally desired for their
own sakes. If the benevolent or dutiful master happened also to be
rich, the 'on balance freedom' of the slave might even compare
favorably with that of most freemen. The permissive master might
even leave his slave *at liberty*, within a wide range, to do as he pleased,
so that even from a kind of juridical viewpoint, the freedom of the
slave might be considerable. There is, however, one crucial difference
between the *de jure* liberties of the freeman and those 'permitted'
the slave. The freeman enjoys some of his legal liberties as a matter
of right: no one else is permitted to nullify or withdraw them. When
they are slow to be acknowledged, or where they appear to be
withheld, he may lay claim to them and demand them as his due.
If others violate them he will properly feel not merely hurt but
wronged. Some of his *de jure* liberties are correlated logically with
other people's duties of action and forebearance, and even with the
state's duties of enforcement and support. They are, in short, *rights*.
The liberties permitted the slave, on the other hand, are granted at
the mere pleasure of his owner and may also be withdrawn at his
mere displeasure. He owes his slave nothing and has no legal duty to
'permit' him any 'liberties' at all. When the owner, then, is benevolent, it is fitting that the slave be grateful, and when permissions
are arbitrarily withdrawn, it is expected that the slave might be
disappointed or hurt, but not that he be resentful or aggrieved. The
slave's liberties, in short, are at best what we now call 'mere privileges.' There is no reason in principle, however, why a slave should
not be in many respects 'on balance free,' both from the sociological
and juridical points of view, even though his non-possession of
rights entails an unfree legal status.

IV 'Free' as a status-associated virtue word

By still another easy extension, the word 'free' (and its older Indo-
European counterparts as well) became the name not only of a
status but also of a set of virtues of character, namely, those taken
to be especially becoming to a man of free status. 'Free' in this
sense is opposed to 'servile' which was used to refer to those qualities
characteristic of slaves, and hence inappropriate in a freeman. A
servile person is 'alternately fawning and insolent';[8] a free man,
having nothing to fear, is dignified and deliberate, and can look
any man in the eye. In asking what freedom truly is, we might be
asking for a fuller account of these qualities, and in describing a
given man as free, we may be simply ascribing such virtues to him,
whatever his legal status might be, or however 'free on balance' we
may take him to be.

The linguistic phenomenon exemplified by this extension of the sense of 'free' is that which C. S. Lewis called the 'moralization of status-words':[9]

> Words which originally referred to a person's rank—to legal, social, or economic status and the qualification of birth which have often been attached to these—have a tendency to become words which assign a type of character and behavior. Those implying superior status can become terms of praise; those implying inferior status, terms of disapproval. *Chivalrous, courteous, frank, gentle, generous, liberal,* and *noble* are examples of the first; *ignoble, villain,* and *vulgar,* of the second.

The association of virtues and vices with social classes has probably had some unfortunate effects on the formation of attitudes, but the process that Lewis describes is not without its advantages too. Lewis defends it vigorously against the charge that it reflects the 'inveterate snobbery of the human race,' and at the same time he explains more fully how it has worked:[10]

> A word like nobility begins to take on its social-ethical meaning when it refers not simply to a man's status but to the manners and character which are thought to be appropriate to that status. But the mind cannot long consider those manners and that character without being forced on the reflection that they are sometimes lacking in those who are noble by status and sometimes present in those who are not. Thus from the very first the social-ethical meaning, merely by existing, is bound to separate itself from the status-meaning. Accordingly, from Boethius down, it becomes a commonplace of European literature that the true nobility is within, that *villanie,* not status, makes the villain, that there are 'ungentle gentles' and that 'gentle is as gentle does.' The linguistic phenomenon we are considering is therefore quite as much an escape from, as an assertion of, that pride above and servility below, which in my opinion, should be called snobbery.

How is a philosopher, then, to decide which are the qualities that form the character of a 'free man' in the present sense? Is the philosopher free to select whichever qualities he likes and assign them to a free man's character, thus giving those qualities the benefit of 'freedom's' glitter? Or is he bound strictly to honor the assignments of qualities that have become so traditional that they might plausibly be said even to form part of the meaning of the word 'free' when it refers to a set of virtues? Without opening the technical question of distinguishing between those qualities suggested by a word and those strictly meant by the word, I think we can lay down some rough ground rules. First of all, the philosopher does have some leeway to promote his own favorite qualities. Proposed definitions of 'the free man' are understood by one and all to be attempts to appropriate the phrase for one set of contestable moral conceptions as opposed to others. They mean to be 'persuasive' in Stevenson's sense and 'tactical' in C. S. Lewis's. There is nothing disreputable about this so long as it is frankly acknowledged, and so long as the acknowledgement is not taken to confer a license to avoid the giving of reasons. The best tactical definition, the most persuasive conception, should be the one supported by the best reasons. The character of the free man is not a question forever closed by 'usage.'

But neither is the question wide open. The philosopher, of course, cannot be arbitrary; he must make out a reasonable case that the qualities he favors deserve to be regarded as virtues. Moreover, they cannot be just *any* praiseworthy qualities but only those that are 'appropriate to the status' of freeman (a legal status, incidentally, which is now virtually universal). The key word is 'appropriate.' Part of the description of the freeman's legal status, at least, is clear enough to be beyond cavil. He is, after all, a man who has certain rights, and if he acts *as if* he did not have those rights, he acts inappropriately. Because of common conceptions of the freeman's condition that derive simply from accurate descriptions of his typical circumstances, there have emerged various traditional conceptions of the freeman's 'appropriate' qualities that are relatively fixed in usage, each fastening on an aspect of the freeman's accepted description. While these conceptions are not so fixed as to form part of the very sense of the expression 'free man,' they are sufficiently conventional to require critical examination, at least, before any revisions of outlook are advocated.

As an example of how fluid the game is, consider John Ruskin's celebrated paean to the fly:[11]

> I believe we can nowhere find a better type of a perfectly free creature than in the common house fly. Nor free only, brave; and irreverent to a degree which I think no human republican could by any philosophy exalt himself to. There is no courtesy in him; he does not care whether it is king or clown whom he teases; and in every step of his swift mechanical march, and in every pause of his resolute observation, there is one and the same expression of perfect egotism, perfect independence and self-confidence, and conviction of the world's having been made for flies. Strike at him with your hand; and to him, the mechanical fact and external aspect of the matter is, what to

you it would be, if an acre of red clay, ten feet thick, tore
itself up from the ground in one massive field, hovered over
you in the air for a second, and came crashing down with an
aim. That is the external aspect of it; the inner aspect, to his
fly's mind, is of quite natural and unimportant occurrence—
one of the momentary conditions of his active life. He steps
out of the way of your hand, and alights on the back of it.
You cannot terrify him, nor govern him, nor persuade him,
nor convince him. He has his own positive opinion on all
matters; not an unwise one, usually, for his own ends; and will
ask no advice of yours. He has no work to do—no tyrannical
instinct to obey. The earthworm has his digging; the bee her
gathering and building; the spider her cunning network;
the ant her treasury and accounts. All these are comparatively
slaves, or people of vulgar business. But your fly, free in the
air, free in the chamber—a black incarnation of caprice—
wandering, investigating, flitting, flirting, feasting at his will,
with rich variety of choice in feast, from the heaped sweets in
the grocer's window to those of the butcher's backyard, and
from the galled place on your cab-horse's back, to the brown
spot in the road, from which, as the hoof disturbs him, he
rises with angry republican buzz—what freedom is like his?

There is too much in this remarkable passage to analyze here, and
much sly charm that would vanish if subjected to the indignity of
analysis. But several points are worth notice. Ruskin's portrayal of
the fly is a mixed description, partly an account of the fly's alleged
'on balance freedom to . . . and from . . . ,' partly an account of the
fly's 'appropriate traits,' or virtues. These two accounts are not
clearly separated and there is much to quarrel with in both; but
they are not entirely arbitrary. Amidst many differences, they share
a common character with some traditional conceptions of the free
man as enabled by his circumstances, or indeed by the human
condition itself and his understanding of it, to be self-reliant, self-
sufficient, and self-confident. Ruskin slyly carries conventional
notions of on-balance freedom to an absurd extreme when he
speaks of the 'perfectly free creature' as an 'incarnation of caprice,'
free not only of external direction, compulsion, and constraint, but
also of inner drives, purposes, life plans, controls, scruples, worries,
and 'tyrannical instincts,' a condition that would more closely
resemble anomie than autonomy in a human being. Yet Ruskin
does draw back from this abyss by ascribing to the fly 'his own
ends' and rational means and plans for achieving them. The
anthropomorphic ascription to the fly of 'an angry republican

buzz' when he is disturbed at his dinner implies a consciousness in the fly of its own rights: servile creatures do not show indignation on their own behalfs, nor even plain anger except in the counterfeit of 'cheekiness,' or in the role of insolent bullies with their peers or other weaklings. There is more genuine pride and self-respect in the fly's angry buzz!

The 'free status' that occasions Ruskin's irony was by his time becoming a general and 'equal' condition, a 'republican status,' and Ruskin has described the traits he thinks appropriate to it not only as free but *as* republican. His 'embodiment of caprice,' he thinks, is naturally cocky, dogmatic, and contemptuous. He takes no orders and no lip from anyone. He has no respect for tradition or for authority. He enjoys his freedom from all of that as a matter of right, not just personal or family rights, but general inalienable rights that he shares with everyone. There are no more masters and slaves, says the liberated republican; now we flies are as much masters as anyone else. The kind of creature who would claim such a life as a matter of right, in a world in which there is no longer a place for authority, says Ruskin, would be 'the perfect egoist.' Ruskin's argumentative purpose is evident: Where the trait in question is clearly not a virtue, he suggests, the condition to which it is 'appropriate' is a poor ideal.

We need not linger over Ruskin's caricature except to describe briefly the traditional ideals of which it is a parody. The common tie is the idea of being one's own man, not having to fear persons of superior power, and having no need to please others as a condition of one's well-being. The man of free legal status and high social and economic position did not enjoy his liberty at the sufferance of any one else. Hence, he could be open and natural, rather than guarded and suspicious, with *every one*. He need not flatter nor cringe before any one. He had an easy and unaffected dignity about him. Perfectly secure in respect both to his sense of worth and his feeling of safety, he need not constantly to be calculating his own advantage and plotting his own advancement. There is nothing small-minded or petty about him. Nor will he be haughty and superior, 'putting on airs,' for he needs not the regular reassurance of others' obeisance and respect. He can get along without it. These are the natural and characteristic virtues (and indeed they *are* virtues) of the man of free status.

In contrast:[12]

The true servile character is cheeky, shrewd, cunning, up to every trick, always with an eye to the main chance, determined 'to look after number one' . . . Absence of disinterestedness,

lack of generosity, is the hall-mark of the servile. The typical
slave always has an axe to grind.

The character flaws of the slave (or the man of lowly social or
economic status under feudalism or capitalism) are in their own
way natural to his status, for they are forms of adaptation to a
difficult and insecure position. They are not in the same way
appropriate to the free man because, his position being easier, he
doesn't *need* them. And yet there are other ways for insecure men to
adapt: Epictetus would display all the virtues of the free man in
confronting, as a mere slave, the terrible tyrant. But then, Epictetus
tells us that he has this astonishing virtue only because he is *not*
insecure even in the presence of what others take to be great
power.

The freeman in the ancient two-status societies had not only his
characteristic virtues but also his peculiarly appropriate interests
and occupations. The 'liberal arts,' or pursuits appropriate to a
man of free and secure status, were 'leisure occupations, things
done for their own sakes and not for utility,'[13] not even for money,
or for the sake of plaudits and esteem. They include painting,
composing, contemplating, and philosophizing. 'Only he who is
neither legally enslaved to a master nor economically enslaved by the
struggle for subsistence, is likely to have or to have the leisure for
using, a piano or a library. That is how one's piano or library is
more *liberal*, more characteristic of one's position as a freeman, than
one's coal-shovel or one's tools.'[14]

Aristotle, of course, is the philosopher who has made the most of
the idea of self-sufficient and intrinsically valuable studies and
pursuits, and their unique appropriateness in the life of the man of
free status. C. S. Lewis, in a brilliant speculative passage, associates
Aristotle's doctrine with Aristotle's circumstances:[15]

In *Metaphysics* we learn that the organization of the universe
resembles that of a household, in which 'no one has so little
chance to act at random as the free members. For them
everything or almost everything proceeds according to a fixed
plan, whereas the slaves and domestic animals contribute
little to the common end and act mostly at random.'[16] The
attitude of any slave-owning society is and ought to be
repellent to us, but it is worth while suppressing that revulsion
in order to get the picture as Aristotle saw it. Looking from his
study window he sees the hens scratching in the dust, the pigs
asleep, the dogs hunting for fleas; the slaves, any of them who
are not at that very moment on some appointed task, flirting,
quarrelling, cracking nuts, playing dice, or dozing. He, the

master, may use them all for the common end, the well-being
of the family. They themselves have no such end, nor any
consistent end, in mind. Whatever in their lives is not
compelled from above is random—dependent on the mood of
the moment. His own life is quite different; a systematized
round of religious, political, scientific, literary and social
activities; its very hours of recreation . . . deliberate, approved
and allowed for; consistent with itself. But what is it in the
structure of the universe that corresponds to this distinction
between Aristotle, self-bound with the discipline of a freeman,
and Aristotle's slaves, negatively free with a servile freedom
between each job and the next? I think there is no doubt of
the answer. . . . In the world, as in the household, the higher
acts to a fixed plan; the lower admits the 'random' element.

Thus the freedom of Ruskin's houseflies is that which Aristotle
'permits' his slaves 'between jobs,' and their virtues and interests,
those Aristotle finds appropriate only to the servile condition.
There is no doubt, I think, which of the two conceptions is the more
persuasive.

V Free as independent, self-governing, autonomous

The final use of the word 'free' that I shall consider has its primary
and probably original[17] application not to individuals but to states
and other institutions. Its inevitable extension to apply to individual
human beings was as part of that elaborate parapolitical metaphor
which since the time of Plato has so colored our conception of the
human mind. To understand its extended use we would be well
advised to consider first its literal application to states, which is a
great deal clearer. When one nation is the colony of another, it is
not said to be free until it gains its independence. Formerly, it was
governed from without; now it is governed from within. Hence,
freedom in this sense, and independence, and self-government all
come to the same thing. Freedom in the sense of independence, as
applied to states, does not at first sight seem to fit the unitary
absence-of-constraint model (though, as we shall see, it can be
made to fit with a little tugging, pulling, and squeezing). The 'free
state' may be an impoverished tyranny with minimal on-balance
freedom for its citizens and also for itself *vis-à-vis* other states and
nature. Self-government might turn out to be more repressive
even than foreign occupation. Yet, for all of that, the state might
still be politically independent, sovereign, and governed from
within, hence free.

Analogously, it is often said that the individual person is 'free' when his ruling part or 'real self' governs, and is subject to no foreign power, either external or internal, to whose authority it has not consented. Now suppose that John Doe wants nothing more than to have all his desires, actual and potential, free of constraints. He wants as many options left open as possible and especially the options that are most important to him. He believes that Richard Roe knows best how to arrange this state of affairs. Hence, he puts himself under Roe's control, obeying as if commanded every piece of advice Roe gives him. The example becomes even more forceful if Doe makes this arrangement irrevocable. Now Doe is no longer self-determined, but he gets rich dividends of satisfaction, having found a more effective way of getting all the particular things he wants or may one day come to want. (Self-direction is *not* one of the particular things he wants, nor is it important to him to keep open the option of one day repossessing it.) He may also want 'breathing space' and 'genuine options,' in which case his benevolent director, Roe, arranges his life with these goals in mind, making key decisions for him always in such a way that his own room to maneuver will be most effectively maximized. Now if this picture is coherent, the situation is analogous to that of the nation which gains freedom from constraint by becoming a colony of a wiser benevolent power. In each case, the subject of freedom can increase its freedom from constraint by relinquishing some of its power to govern itself. Both examples then tend to show that self-government is a different kind of freedom from the absence of constraint.[18]

I think we can continue to speak of self-government as 'freedom,' however, without committing ourselves to the view that it is a kind of freedom unanalyzable in terms of the constraint model. Putatively distinct 'concepts' of freedom frequently turn out to be different estimates of 'the importance of only one part of what is always present in any case of freedom'[19]—the importance of one class of subjects as opposed to another, or of one class of desires or open options as opposed to another, or of one class of missing constraints as opposed to another. The point of calling individual self-direction *freedom*, I think, may be to emphasize the overriding importance of one particular kind of desire or option, namely, that to decide for oneself what one shall do. Even wise and benevolent external direction is a constraint to the desire, actual or possible, to decide for oneself. Hence there is a point in calling the absence of *that* constraint (or the presence of self-direction) freedom.

Of course, almost anything at all can, in a similar way, be made out to be a constraint to *some* desire, actual or possible.[20] Hence the absence of anything-at-all (e.g. cloudy skies) can be identified with 'true' or 'positive' freedom. The point, however, of signaling out the desire to govern oneself for this special status is to acknowledge its supreme and special importance among desires. For those to whom the desire to govern themselves for better or worse is so important that few other desires can yield significant satisfactions so long as it is constrained, there is every reason to pre-empt the word 'freedom' for the absence of constraint to *it*. Nor is this singling out of a supreme desire a purely arbitrary or subjective thing. A powerful case can be made to show that other acknowledged values have self-government as their pre-condition, in particular, that dignity, self-esteem, and responsibility are impossible without it.

I come finally to the problem of applying the political metaphor of self-government to the individual, the question which Peters has so effectively illuminated for us in his discussion of autonomy. In my concluding remarks I can only hope to fill out a little more the picture he has accurately traced, and to anticipate some stubborn philosophical perplexities he had no time to dispel.

The individual self

Just as in the case of 'on balance freedom,' the clear application of the concept of autonomy presupposes an adequate conception of the self that is the subject of freedom: a self that is narrow enough so that we can contrast it with other *internal* elements of the total self over which it is said to rule, but also wide enough to include constitutive elements or properties of its own—basic convictions, allegiances, life plans, ultimate objectives, moral principles, etc. The attributes of the inner-core self that rules the wider self include not only 'Reason,' but materials for Reason to work with, and the latter will be the convictions, ideals, and purposes that are most deeply entrenched in an hierarchical network of similar principles, those which, because of their logically central position in the network, are the last to be tampered with when changes of mind or heart must be made. These are the attributes which are often said to 'define the person' or to provide him with his own sense of 'identity.'[21] If we strip our conception of the governing self of all its standards and values, leaving only a bare impersonal Reason imprisoned in its own royal palace, the notion of autonomy becomes empty and incoherent. In order for the word 'free,' in any sense, to have intelligible application, its subject must be an entity with tendencies of its own that can be blocked or fulfilled, 'obeyed' or rebelled against. The human subject of freedom, then, must have some substance, some normative flesh and blood.

There are necessarily two aspects of autonomous self-government.

The governing self must be neither a colony of some external self, or 'foreign power,' nor powerless to enforce its directives to its own interior subjects. If we appropriate William James's usage (modified for our own purposes) and call the 'inner core self' the I and the rest of the comprehensive self over which it rules its Me, then we can put the dual aspect of personal autonomy felicitously: *I am autonomous if I rule me, and no one else rules I.*[22] The absence of dictation from outside the total self is a much desired ideal situation (although *total* absence of external control is not a realistic hope), but since the fulfillment of this ideal of circumstance is largely a matter of luck, it would be odd to consider it also to be a virtue or ideal of character. A man should get credit for his independence of others only to the extent that he doesn't *need* external control (being perfectly in control of himself) and hence, doesn't *allow* it. If it is imposed on him anyway by superior power, that circumstance obviously is no flaw in his character. External control is the sign of a character defect (or should we say 'mental illness'?) only if it is a consequence of a failure of self-government because of the rebellion of ungovernable internal components, or because the inner-core self, lacking cohesion or direction, is incapable of governing.

Authenticity

It is hard to avoid perplexity about the application of that criterion of autonomy that Peters calls 'authenticity.' When *are* we governing ourselves, making or accepting our *own* rules, deciding for genuine not 'artificial' and 'second-hand'[23]) reasons of our *own*? I have always regarded this as a tough personal problem and not merely a theoretical one. Peters, following Piaget, restricts his discussion of authenticity to moral *rules*, but that is only one facet (and I think a relatively easy one) of the problem. Authenticity is a notion that applies also to tastes, opinions, ideals, goals, principles, values, and preferences. We can ask, after all, how we can know when we are choosing in accordance with our *own* preferences or forming our *own* opinions, as opposed to being unknowingly manipulated or self-deceived. When we add these further questions to the problem of authenticity, our personal doubts quicken and philosophical puzzlement deepens. I think these questions are instances of a general problem about knowing one's own *motives* (as opposed to intentions, which are much easier to know): we cannot always know for sure what it is about one object of choice that makes it attractive to us and about another that makes *it* repellent, or what it is about one opinion that 'moves us' to adopt it, and so on. Not uncommonly we are plainly wrong about the basis of appeal to us in some attractive prospect. Sometimes our choices seem over-determined so that it is not evident whether it is the 'good reason' or the prospect of gain that really moves us. When my decisions please others, have I made them because I expected them to please, or for 'genuine' reasons of my own? And when is the desire to please others itself a 'genuine reason' of one's own?

In addition to the general problem of knowing one's own motives, there is the conceptual problem of characterizing the elusive motive of disinterestedness that is the mark of the authentic man. Our standards must be high enough to exclude subtle counterfeits of authenticity, yet not so high as to render authenticity an empty or unrealizable ideal. In particular, we must not demand total transcendence of the culture of one's time and place, for the autonomous Reason even of the authentic man will be at the service of some interests and ways of perceiving the world that are simply 'given' him by the *Zeitgeist* and his own special circumstances. A former colleague of mine, a sensitive and gifted analytical philosopher, once announced to me that after many years of teaching the philosophy of religion he had gradually come to believe in God. My friend had prepared an elaborate and complex rationale for his important new conviction such that I could not doubt the authenticity of his reasonings. Months later he told me that he had joined the local Methodist church. I asked him whether he had done this after a careful examination of the claims to truth of the various Protestant sects against one another, or of Catholicism against Protestantism generally, or of Christianity against the other world religions. Of course, he had not, and my question struck him as merely impertinent. When I asked him what the religious affiliation of his parents and grandparents had been, he answered, of course, Methodist. I took this at the time as strong evidence of inauthenticity, of the acquisition of convictions and commitments in an 'artificial' and 'second-hand' way. But now I'm not so sure. Perhaps my standards of authenticity were pegged unrealistically high. My friend could not even consider becoming (say) a Buddhist or a Roman Catholic. These were, in James's phrase, absolutely dead options to him. After all, if one is a Burmese and finds God one becomes a Buddhist, and if one is Italian or Irish one becomes a Catholic. My friend was not shopping for a different nationality or ethnic identity; his own was too well fixed to be questioned. So he became a Methodist. Was he a 'mere slave' to his time and place in this selection? I think not. We may all be, in some respects, irrevocably the 'products of our culture,' but that is no reason why the self that is such a product cannot be free to govern the self it is.

Contrasts with autonomy

There are a variety of familiar ways of falling short of the ideal of
autonomy, a noting of which might be useful for strengthening our
grasp of the concept. When the *I* is incapable of governing its *Me*,
the result is anomie, a condition which is not control from without,
but rather being virtually 'out of control' altogether. Autonomy is
also contrasted with forms of passive mindless adjustment (the
pejorative term is 'conformity') to the requirements of one's
culture. In a book that made a great splash two decades ago,[24]
David Riesman and his associates described in detail three 'types of
social character,' each one characteristic of human societies at a
given stage of their economic and demographic development. In the
period of 'tradition-direction' the ideal of autonomy would hardly
even occur to anyone. Individuals were 'governed' by rituals and
operating procedures worked out by their ancestors. Social and
technological change was very slow, so that the dominant character
type fits the social conditions well, and such traits as personal
ambition, initiative, and flexibility, are not required. Everyone
does the same thing without question, if only from fear of being
publicly shamed.

Tradition-direction was succeeded in the Western countries by
what Riesman called the 'inner-directed' type. The centuries
following the decline of feudalism were characterized by 'increased
personal mobility . . . constant expansion . . . vast technological
shifts . . . exploration, colonization. . . .' Needed to meet these
challenges was a new type 'who can manage . . . without strict and
self-evident tradition-direction,' a type with a 'rigid but highly
individualized character.'[25] Early in life, a set of 'generalized but
nonetheless inescapably destined goals'[26] and standards are implanted in the child, by his parents, their authoritative source
internalized, so that they become inescapably his forever more. The
inner-directed man thus has within him a kind of 'psychological
gyroscope'[27] that keeps him steadily on his course on pain of
powerful guilt-feelings, and also permits him to 'receive signals'
from authorities who resemble his parents, as well as from his
governing internalized ideal.

So much has been written in adulation of our inner-directed
forebearers that Riesman is obliged to go to great pains to show
how far they too fail to satisfy any reasonable model of autonomy:[28]

First, the gyroscopic mechanism allows the inner-directed
person to appear far more independent than he really is: he is
no less a conformist to others than the other-directed person,

but the voices to which he listens are more distant, of an older generation, their cues internalized in his childhood.

He becomes capable of impersonal relations with people and sometimes incapable of any other kind. This is one of the prices he pays for his relative impermeability to the needs and wishes of his peers, and helps account for his ability, when in pursuit of some end he values, to steel himself against their indifference or hostility.

The social utility of inner-directedness declines, according to Riesman, as industrialization and the population boom run their courses, and an affluent society becomes oriented more toward consumption than production. The other-directed man, characteristic of our own times, is brought up in such a way that he has no inner gyroscope but rather a psychological 'radar-set' extremely sensitive to signals from his own age-group, current fashions, and popular 'media' of communication. In an age when manipulation of persons is a greater economic preoccupation than conquest of the material environment, 'gyroscopic control is no longer sufficiently flexible.'[29] Non-productive consumers form a high proportion of the population and 'they need both the economic opportunity to be prodigal and the character structure that allows it . . . children are made to feel guilty not so much about violation of inner standards as for failure to win social approval.'[30] Extremely sensitive attunement to the wishes of others is implanted early, and the need to be accepted by others becomes the major impetus to thought and action, on pain, not of shame, or guilt, but a 'diffuse anxiety.'

The inauthenticity of the well-adjusted other-directed man is easily shown. If he is plump, he looks better in vertical stripes than in horizontal ones; but if his peers are wearing horizontals this season, so will he, aesthetic considerations be damned. And if inherited temperament inclines him to a life style that is currently out of favor with his peers, he will adopt a different life style instead, even if it ill-fits and ill-becomes his temperament. Even his opinions and 'convictions' he will choose in the way he chooses his clothes for their conformity to the public 'image' he wishes to present for the approval of his peers.

If these are the ways of missing the target, what do they tell us about the target itself? A human being must have a capacity for self-regulation, otherwise he suffers anomie; but if his internal regulator is itself an unregulable gyroscope or radar set, he cannot be autonomous, no matter how happily adjusted (or 'attuned') he is. Yet all of us presumably were given our gyroscopes or radar sets or some combination of the two as children. How then can autonomy be possible for us? Riesman says that autonomous men may be maladjusted to their societies, but that they differ from other dissidents and misfits in that they are capable of conforming if they choose. That is to say, they are 'free to choose whether to conform or not,'[31] and if they choose not, they are not subject to immobilizing guilt or pervasive anxiety. They will conform when and only when there are good reasons for doing so; and they can attend to reason free from the interfering static of 'signals' from other voices. They can control the speed and direction of their gyroscopes, if they have them, or rotate their radar apparatus, or turn it off. The autonomous man will buy his clothes in part to match his purse, his build, and his functions; he will select his life style to match his temperament, and his political attitudes to fit his ideals and interests. He cannot be indifferent to the reactions of others, but he *can* be moved by other considerations too.

If 'other-direction' is becoming the prevalent mode of ensuring conformity in our time, as Riesman maintained, then the autonomous man will have to exercise his autonomy by overcoming or outwitting, somehow, his own deeply implanted radar receptor. One can see today how difficult that problem can be, as youths, eager to be authentic, still keep cultishly attuned to one another. Perhaps the best hope of educators is to utilize the inevitable radar sets, when by-passing them is not possible, by feeding 'rationalistic' signals into the transmission system. Suppose that the schools and the media cooperated in creating images of rationality that would be immediately picked up by the sensitive receivers of the young and made part of their own network of signals, so that the 'in' way of buying commodities, for example, would be to check *Consumer's Union* tests and evaluations, rather than responding to the polished images of the advertising men. Suppose that *that* kind of prudent rationality were taken to be characteristic not of egg-heads and other alien groups merely, but also of what real swingers generally do, so that teenagers would lose standing with their peers for acting out of their assigned judicious roles. The practice of independent deliberative judgment might then begin as a kind of other-directed play acting, but if constantly reinforced by incoming signals from peers (not 'authorities') it could become a fixed and functionally autonomous habit.[32] Perhaps the product of such arrangements would not be perfectly pure autonomy, since the basic motive in people would still be to win the approval of their peers, but it would surely be a closer approximation than most people have ever achieved, and how many of *us* have achieved anything 'purer'?

Rational reflection

I wish my final emphasis to be on the danger of taking autonomy too seriously as a goal of education either in the home or the school. One can do this either by conceiving of autonomy in such an exalted way that its criteria can never be satisfied, or else by promoting the ideal prematurely in a self-defeating way. To reflect rationally, in the manner of an autonomous man, is to apply some already accepted principles in accordance with the rules of rational procedure, to the test of more tentative principles or candidates for principles, or to possible judgments or decisions. Rational reflection thus presupposes some relatively settled convictions to reason from and with. If we take autonomy to require that all principles are to be examined afresh in the light of reason on each occasion for decision, then nothing resembling rational reflection can ever get started.

Ten years after the publication of *The Lonely Crowd* Riesman wrote that autonomy presupposes 'the power of individuals to shape their own characters by their selection among models and experiences'[33]—a power, I might add, that we find more and more college age youths bent on exercising in the current variegated search for 'identity.' My modest point is simply that a person must already possess at least a tentative character before he can hope to *choose* a new one. The other side of that point is that if a child needs to 'learn to be autonomous,' it must be the case that he is not already autonomous when he starts. There can be no magical *ex nihilo* creation of the habit of rational reflection. Some principles, and especially the commitment to reasonableness itself, must be implanted in a child, if he is to have a reasonable opportunity of growing in the proper direction.

The rough equivalent of 'anomie' in the realm of beliefs and ideals is that corruption of the ideal of open-mindedness, where everything is always 'up for grabs,' and every conviction or allegiance is to be examined afresh each time it comes up, as if past confirmations counted for nothing. The 'cognitively anomic' man thus has no firm direction in his reasonings, nothing unquestioned with which to compare and test the questionable. This description begins to resemble Ruskin's picture of 'the embodiment of caprice.' If *that* is what autonomy is, then it is neither an ideal state nor a virtue appropriate to free status, and the comprehensive ideal of *a free man all-told* must be incoherent. But to conceive of autonomy in that way is a mistake which Piaget, Kohlberg, and Peters, with their careful attention to stages in the gradual progression up to autonomy, do not make.

Summary

My aim has been to probe for conceptual linkages between the idea of a free man and the idea of a free society, by considering how the word 'free' has come to apply to both. I have divided the inquiry into five parts corresponding to the five alternative ways of interpreting the sentence 'I am free.' The results are not easy to summarize. The idea of an *absence of constraint* is essential to one pattern of usages, the idea of a *status-right* to another, the idea of *appropriateness to a status* to another, the political metaphor of *self-rule* to another. Much unity can be seen to underlie this diversity if we accept internal and negative factors as constraints, and allow the desire simply to be rid of something for its own sake and the desire to decide for oneself what one will do to be among the possible objects of constraint. Even the idea of general or relative freedom from constraint, however, requires supplementation by normative standards for determining the relative worth of conflicting wants and interests. Indeed, three of the patterns discussed above (on-balance freedom, the virtue of freedom, and autonomy) have been penetrated at several points by standards and values of other kinds: standards of worthiness, fittingness, and reasonableness are of necessity built into them. But that in no way detracts from their coherence or importance. *A free man all-told* will be free on-balance *to* do what is most worth doing and *from* those constraints most worth being without. The characteristic images of on-balance *unfreedom* are the barrier or locked room (external constraint), the bayonet at one's back (compulsion) and the internal traffic jam or hang-up. The free man all-told will also be fortunate enough to be a freeman, but he will show his worthiness of this legal status by his possession of virtues appropriate to it: a secure sense of his own worth, generosity, high-mindedness, disinterestedness, and self-sufficiency. Finally, he will 'govern' himself rather than be directed in all his choices and preferences by unexamined traditions, or signals from an unmodifiable gyroscope or radar-set within him. Most of these components of the composite ideal, it can readily be seen, presuppose for their intelligibility, an acquaintance with social systems to which the word 'free' or its antonyms can also have application.

Notes

1 R. S. Peters, 'Freedom and the Development of the Free Man', p. 120.
2 Cf. Isaiah Berlin, *Four Essays on Liberty*, O.U.P., 1969, 'Introduction', p. xliii n.

3 According to Felix Oppenheim, if we know that only 70 per cent of the parking violations in a given city are detected and penalized, then, given certain other assumptions, we can predict with 70 per cent probability that a given overparker will be fined, and this entitles us to say (from the sociological perspective, of course!) that 'drivers in that city are officially unfree to a degree of 0.7 to overpark and their freedom to do so is 0.3'—*Dimensions of Freedom*, New York: St Martin's Press, 1961, p. 187.

4 To vary the image still again, he is subject to 'hang-ups,' and even 'hoist with his own petard.'

5 Cf. Oppenheim, *op. cit.*, p. 200.

6 C. S. Lewis, *Studies in Words*, Cambridge University Press, 1961, p. 114.

7 In the ancient world, says Lewis, 'Freedom can mean simply "citizenship," and when the centurion tells Saint Paul that he had paid a lot of money to acquire Roman citizenship (*politeia*), the Authorized Version says "At a great price obtained I this freedom" ... This meaning is fossilized in the surviving English use of *franchise* to mean the power of voting, conceived as the essential mark of full citizenship.'—*Studies in Words*, p. 125.

8 *Ibid.*, p. 114.

9 *Ibid.*, p. 21.

10 *Ibid.*, p. 22.

11 John Ruskin, *The Queen of the Air*, ch. 3.

12 C. S. Lewis, *op. cit.*, p. 112.

13 *Ibid.*, p. 126.

14 *Loc. cit.*

15 *Op. cit.*, pp. 128–9.

16 Aristotle, *Metaphysics*, 1075b.

17 C. S. Lewis, *op. cit.*, pp. 124–5.

18 Compare Isaiah Berlin, *op. cit.*, p. 130: 'The answer to the question—"Who governs me?"—is logically distinct from the question— "How far does government interfere with me?" It is in this difference that the great contrast between the two concepts of liberty in the end consists.'

19 Gerald C. MacCallum, Jr, 'Negative and Positive Freedom', *Philosophical Review*, vol. 76, 1967, p. 318.

20 An unconstrained possible but unactual desire is an 'open option.'

21 What social scientists call the 'problem of identity,' if I understand them correctly, is that of selecting out of the class of true descriptions of a person (e.g. he is male, young, brown-eyed, poor, American, Catholic, a philosopher, a ball player, a liberal, a flutist, a father) those that are to be in some way *essential* to his own conception of himself, as opposed to those that are trivial, dispensable, and accidental; the status as essential, in the normal case, being partly chosen by the not-fully-formed young person himself in accordance with whatever 'inner-core' principles he already has (or is).

22 This account of autonomy also satisfies John Austin's famous

definition of *sovereignty*. Perhaps the two concepts come to the same thing in their political application. Perhaps the expression 'personal sovereignty,' which we do not use, would be preferable to 'personal autonomy,' which we do use, in that its character as a political metaphor would be less concealed.

23 Peters, *op. cit.*, pp. 123–4.
24 David Riesman, *et al, The Lonely Crowd*, New Haven, Yale University Press, 1950. My references will be to the abridged edition (Yale Paperbound, 1961).
25 *Ibid.*, p. 14.
26 *Ibid.*, p. 15.
27 *Ibid.*, p. 16.
28 *Ibid.*, p. 31, p. 56.
29 *Ibid.*, p. 18.
30 *Ibid.*, pp. 19, 21.
31 *Ibid.*, p. 242.
32 In similar ways, in an inner-directed period, parents who are dedicated to autonomy might 'instill' it in their children by means of a psychological gyroscope whose unswerving aim is in the direction of the parental ideal. The voices to which the child would listen would be his parents', but their only message would be: Think for yourself!
33 *Op. cit.*, 'Preface', p. xlviii.

The Interest in Liberty on the Scales

There is one version of John Stuart Mill's famous 'harm principle' for determining the moral limits of state coercion that is virtually beyond controversy.
Few would deny that it is always a morally relevant reason in support of a
proposed criminal prohibition that it is reasonably necessary (that is, that
there are reasonable grounds for taking it to be necessary) to prevent harm
or the unreasonable risk of harm to parties other than the persons whose
conduct is to be constrained. Some might deny that the necessity to prevent harm to others is a *sufficient* reason for state coercion on the grounds
that prevention of minor harms may not be worth the social costs of state
intervention. Others might deny. that the prevention of harm to others is
a *necessary* condition of justified interference on the grounds that there are
other reasons for coercion (e.g. the prevention of mere offense, or the enforcement of morality as such) that can apply even to harmless behavior.
But hardly anyone would deny that the need to prevent harm to others is
always *a* reason in support of state coercion even if it is not always a conclusive reason, and even if it is not the only kind of reason that can apply.

Whatever this weakened version of the harm principle gains in plausibility, however, it loses in practical utility as a guide to legislative decisions.
Legislators must not only decide *whether* to use the weakened harm principle, but also *how* to use it in cases of merely minor harms, moderately
probable harms, reasonable and unreasonable risks of harm, aggregative
harms, competitive harms, accumulative harms, and so on.[1] Solutions to
these problems cannot be provided by the harm principle in its simply stated
version, but absolutely require the help of supplementary principles, some of
which represent controversial moral decisions and maxims of justice. In this
paper, I shall consider some of those problems involved in the legislative
application of the harm principle that require that classes of personal interests
be compared and ranked in importance. The process of ranking interests in
order to determine how to minimize social 'harms' is invariably described in
terms of the metaphor of a scales: interests are 'balanced' in order to determine which has the greater 'weight.' Specifically, I shall be concerned to
characterize the balancing process when one of the interests to be weighed
is the generalized interest in liberty which the law presumes to be shared

(like the interests in health and economic sufficiency) equally by all citizens.

I

Typically the interests that must be compared and graded ('weighed and balanced') by a legislature do not include, or include only to a minor degree, the interest in liberty. I have in mind cases of the following kind: a certain kind of activity has a tendency to cause harm to the people who are affected by it, but effective prohibition of that activity would tend to cause harm to those who have an interest (that is, a stake) in engaging in it, and not merely in the often trivial respect in which *all* restrictions of liberty (even the liberty to murder) are *pro tanto* harmful to the persons whose alternatives are narrowed, but rather because other substantial interests of these persons are totally thwarted. In all such cases, to prevent A from harming B's interest in Y would be to harm A's interest in X (as well as his general interest in liberty, for whatever that is worth). The legislator therefore must decide whether B's interest in Y is more or less important — more or less worth protecting — in itself (questions of degree of risk aside) than A's interest in X. And the legislator must think not merely of some specific persons A and B, but of *all* persons of types A and B, that is, of standard A's and B's. The harm principle, without further specification, is a largely empty formula. It tells him that protecting B's interest from harm is a good and relevant reason for restraining A, but that is *all* it tells him. It doesn't tell him *how* good a reason it is compared with the obvious reason, itself derived from the need to minimize harms, for permitting A to pursue *his* interest untrammeled. If A has a genuine stake in the promotion or achievement of X, then any constraint to his pursuit of X will set back or thwart that interest, and thus in the relevant sense cause *him* 'harm.'

To be sure, we should protect an interest that is certain to be harmed in preference to one whose liability to harm is only conjectural, other things being equal, and we should deem it more important to prevent the total thwarting of one interest than the mere invasion to some small degree of a conflicting interest, other things being equal. Harm (in the relevant legal sense) is the invasion of an interest, and invasions do differ in degree, but when interests of quite different kinds — for example a motorcyclist's interest in speed, excitement, and economical transport, and the interests of the professional scholar residing in the suburbs in the peace and quiet of his neighborhood — are invaded to the same degree, where is the greater harm?

That depends, of course, on which of the two kinds of interest is the more important.

The 'importance' of interests other than the interest in liberty is normally measured by at least three different indices: their importance to their possessor, that is, their 'vitality' within his total system of personal interests; the degree to which they are reinforced by other interests, private and public; and perhaps (this is more controversial) their inherent moral quality. The standard of vitality is applied to a particular interest when we consider the extent to which the thwarting of that interest is likely to harm the whole economy of one's personal interests. The interests of a 'standard person' of a given type in X may be more important than his interests in Y in that harming his interest in X will do less harm on balance to his net personal interest (in the singular) than would harming his interest in Y, just as harm to one's heart or brain will do more damage to one's bodily health than an 'equal degree' of harm to less vital organs. Where a standard person's interest of high vitality in his system conflicts with another standard person's interest of relatively low vitality in *his* system, then, other things being equal, the former interest can be deemed more important than the latter.

The most vital interests in a personal system of interests are those I choose to call 'welfare interests' in the indispensable means to one's ulterior goals whatever the latter may be, or later come to be. In this category are the interests in one's own physical health and vigor, the integrity and normal functioning of one's body, the absence of distracting pain and suffering or grotesque disfigurement, minimal intellectual acuity, emotional stability, the absence of groundless anxieties and resentments, the capacity to engage normally in social intercourse, at least minimal wealth, income, and financial security, a tolerable social and physical environment, and a certain amount of freedom from interference and coercion. These standard interests are in conditions that are generalized means to a great variety of possible goals and whose joint realization, in the absence of very special circumstances, is necessary for the achievement of more ultimate goals. In one way, then, they are the very most important interests a person has, for without their fulfillment a person (the 'standard person' who is always before the eyes of the legislator) is lost.

In various other ways, however, welfare interests are likely to seem rather trivial goods, necessary but grossly insufficient for a good life. They are the 'basic requisites of a man's well-being'[2] but by no means the whole of that well-being itself. Moreover, as I shall understand them, welfare interests share the common character of bare minimality. One can achieve one's more ulterior goals and thus one's 'higher good' in most cases even if one is in poor health, or has little money, or lives in an unattractive environment, but one has no chance at all if one's health is totally broken, or one is totally and irretrievably destitute, or lives in a pestilential sink. One can threaten another person's welfare interests by weakening his health or diminishing his wealth, but one does not actually invade those interests until one brings them below a tolerable minimum.

Corresponding to many of the basic welfare interests are possible ulterior interests, which some of us do and some of us do not have, in achieving a much higher level of a particular element of welfare than is actually required. Thus the interest in becoming prosperous or affluent resembles the welfare interest in having enough money for a decent life in that both of them are economic interests, and would be so categorized in a different system of classification. But an interest in affluence, while differing from the welfare interest in financial sufficiency only in degree, is by no means itself a welfare interest. Similarly, the interest in putting oneself in vibrant, blooming health and the very best athletic condition is a kind of physical interest like the welfare interest in not being sick, but is not itself a welfare interest.

Any given welfare interest when considered entirely by itself may at first sight seem a trivial and obvious component of a wider and genuinely important structure of welfare interests, one whose singular violation could easily be compensated for by gains in other sectors of welfare. This impression ceases, however, when one notices that welfare interests, unlike more ulterior interests, are linked together so that they are no stronger than their weakest link. Nicholas Rescher traces the medical analogy: "Deficiencies in one place are generally not to be compensated for by superiority in another; there are few, if any trade-offs operative here — just as cardiovascular superiority does not make up for a deficient liver so added strengths in one sector of welfare cannot cancel our weaknesses in another."[3] All the money in the world won't help you if you have a fatal disease, and great physical strength will not compensate for destitution or imprisonment.

Despite these various respects in which any given welfare interest is likely to seem a trivial thing, there is no doubt that the welfare interests severally and collectively are the most vital and therefore in one clear sense, at least, the most important, in a person's interest-system. When they are blocked or damaged, a person is very seriously harmed indeed, for in that case his more ultimate aspirations are defeated too; whereas setbacks to a given higher goal do not necessarily inflict damage on the whole network of his interests. To be sure, one cannot live on bread alone, but without bread one cannot live at all.

While welfare interests are the most vital ones, non-welfare interests too can be ranked in terms of relative vitality, just as the hand can be deemed a more vital appendage than the little toe even though neither is an essential organ, and harm to one's hand can be deemed more serious than harm to the little toe. Determining which of two non-welfare interests is the more vital is no easy task, especially when we are restricted to a consideration of the interest systems of various types of 'standard men;' but even if we could settle this matter, there would remain difficult complexities. Interests tend to pile up and reinforce one another. My interest (as a professional scholar residing in the suburbs in peace and quiet) may be more vital in my system than the motorcyclist's interests in speed, excitement, and economy are in his, but there is also the interest of the cyclist's employer in having workers efficiently transported to his factory, and the economic interest of the community in general (including me) in the flourishing of the factory owner's business; the interest of the motorcycle manufacturers in their own profits; the interest of the police and others (perhaps including me) in providing a relatively harmless outlet for adolescent exuberance, and in not having a difficult rule to enforce. There may be nowhere near so great a buildup of reinforcing interests, personal and public, in the quietude of my neighborhood. For that reason, the motorcyclist's interest may be a more vital component of the system of *community interests* than mine, though when we also consider the effects of his noise on property values and on the attractiveness of the community to peace-loving outsiders who would otherwise be tempted to move into it and contribute their talents, the question can be seen in its full complexity as a close and difficult one.[4]

The final consideration that may complicate the delicate task of interest-balancing invokes the inherent moral worth of the compared interests themselves quite apart from their vitality or their relation to other interests. At most this factor is considered only in extreme cases, in respect to interests that are thought to be unworthy of any protection at all. If there are such things as 'sick,' 'morbid,' 'sadistic,' or 'depraved' *interests* (as opposed to mere desires) — and in the absence of an agreed-upon detailed analysis of the concept of an interest philosophers can be expected to disagree about this — then such interests could plausibly be found to be without 'weight' or importance, and thus easily counterbalanced by *any* legitimate conflicting interest.

II

Two intertwined questions can arise when interest-balancers turn their attention to the interest in liberty. Whenever a person's interest in X is thwarted, say by a legal prohibition against anyone's doing, pursuing, or possessing Xs, an interest in liberty is also impeded, namely, the interest in having a choice whether to do, possess, or pursue X or not. We can ask, then, how important generally speaking is the interest in being free to choose, and also in a given case of legal coercion, how great an invasion has been made of that general interest. The latter question presupposes that we can make sense of quantitative expressions about 'greater' and 'lesser' depletions of liberty.

If our personal liberties were totally destroyed by some ruthlessly efficient totalitarian state, most of us would be no more able to pursue the ultimate interests that constitute our good than if the sources of our economic income were destroyed or our health ruined. For that reason our interest in liberty is best understood as a basic welfare interest. When some specific kind of conduct is made illegal, every citizen's liberty is diminished in at least one respect: no one is at liberty to engage in the newly prohibited conduct. But it does not follow by any means that everyone's welfare interest in liberty has been thwarted by new legal prohibitions any more than a new tax, as such, is an invasion of the welfare interest in economic sufficiency. These welfare interests, as we have seen, are not violated until they are brought below a tolerable minimum level. There may also be a non-welfare, trans-minimal interest in liberty analogous to the interest some people have in possessing as much money as possible, though the image of the 'liberty-miser' is sufficiently blurred to weaken the analogy somewhat. Invasions of the interest in having as much money (or liberty) as possible, of course, are much less harmful than invasions of the interest in having *enough* money (or liberty) for a decent life, and possess correspondingly less weight on the interest balancing scales.

Everyone has a derivative interest, however, in possessing more money or liberty than he actually needs, as a 'cushion' against possible future invasions of his welfare interest in having enough to get along. Consequently, the closer are one's assets (in money, liberty, or health) to the minimum line, the more harmful are depletions of them above the minimum line. For all welfare interests there is some analogue of the principle of the diminishing marginal utility of money. The legislative interest-balancer then will ascribe some weight to all legitimate interests including all interests in liberty, but he will ascribe greater weight to the welfare interest in liberty than to the security interest in cushioning that welfare interest, and greater weight to the interest in securing minimal liberty than to the interest in accumulating extensive trans-minimal liberty or 'as much liberty as possible.'

III

There is a standing presumption against all proposals to criminalize conduct that is derived simply from the interest 'standard persons' are presumed to have in political liberty, but the strength of this presumption varies not only with the type of interest in liberty (welfare, security, or accumulative) but also with the degree to which that interest is actually invaded by the proposed legislation. Invasions of the interest in liberty are as much a matter of degree as invasions of the interest in money, though we lack clear-cut conventional units for measuring them, corresponding to dollars, pounds, and francs. The interest in liberty *as such* — as opposed to the various interests we have in doing the things we may be free or unfree to do — is an interest in having as many *open options* as possible with respect to various kinds of action, omission, and possession. I have an open option with respect to a given act X when I am permitted to do X and I am also permitted to do *not-X* (that is to omit doing X) so that it is up to me entirely whether I do X or not. If I am permitted to do X but not permitted to do *not-X*, I am not in any usual sense at liberty to do X, for if X is the only thing I am permitted to do, it follows that I am compelled to do X, and compulsion, of course, is the plain opposite of liberty. The possession of a liberty is simply the possession of alternative possibilities of action, and the more alternatives, the more liberty. Some criminal statutes reduce our alternatives more than others, though as Isaiah Berlin reminds us, "possibilities of action are not discrete entities like apples which can be exhaustively enumerated,"[5] nor like shillings and pence (we might add) which can be accurately counted. Counting and evaluating options, therefore, "can never be more than impressionistic,"[6] but there are better and worse ways of gathering one's impressions, and some persons' impressions may be more accurate than others', for all that.

We can think of life as a kind of maze of railroad tracks connected and disjoined, here and there, by switches. Wherever there is an unlocked switch which can be pulled one way or the other, there is an 'open option;' wherever the switch is locked in one position the option is 'closed.' As we chug along our various tracks in the maze, other persons are busily locking and unlocking, opening and closing switches, thereby enlarging and restricting our various possibilities of movement. Some of these switchmen are part of a team of legislators, policemen, and judges; they claim *authority* for their switch positionings. Other switchmen operate illicitly at night, often undoing what was authoritatively arranged in the daylight. This model, of course, is simpler than the real world where the 'tracks' and 'switches' are not so clearly marked; but it does give us a sense for how some closed options can be more restrictive of liberty than others. When a switchman closes and locks a switch, he forces us to continue straight on, or stop, or back up. What we cannot do is move on to a different track heading off in a different direction from the one we are on. Before the switch was locked we had the option of continuing on or else moving to the new track, but now that particular option is closed to us. If the track from which we are barred is only a short line leading to a siding, and coming to a dead end in a country village, then our liberty has not been *much* diminished. We are not at liberty to go to one precise destination, but the whole network of tracks with all its diverse possibilities may yet be open before us. If, on the other hand, the closed switch prevents us from turning on to a trunk line, which itself is connected at a large number of switching points with branch lines heading off in many directions, then our liberty has been severely diminished, since we are debarred not only from turning at this one point, but also from enjoying a vast number of (otherwise) open options at points along the trunk line and its branches. In this case, one locked switch effectively closes dozens of options further up the line. Options that lead to many further options can be called 'fecund;' those that are relatively unfecund can be called 'limited.' The closing of fecund options, then, is more restrictive of liberty, other things being equal, than the closing of limited options, and the more fecund the option closed, the more harm is done to the general interest in liberty.

The railroad model is inadequate in a number of respects. It is an approximate rendering of our idea of liberty of movement, but it is difficult to apply to liberty of expression and opinion, or to 'passive liberties' like the freedom to be let alone, and the like. Moreover, it needs many complications before it can adequately render the full complexity of choices designated by the single word 'options.' Free men are often faced with choices of the form 'to X or not to X': to vote or not to vote, to buy a car or not to buy a car, to travel or to stay at home. Even our more complicated decisions can be crammed into this logical form, but the form in which they present themselves to our minds is often many sided: to vote for candidate A or B or C or D? to buy a Ford or Chevrolet or a Datsun or a Volkswagen or a Renault? to travel to England or France or Holland or Sweden or Spain or Italy? to marry Tom or Dick or Harry or . . . ? Our options in these cases are shaped more like tuning forks than wedges, and a barrier at the base of the fork restricts our liberty more than one at the base of a single prong. Other options disjoin conjunctions of alternatives rather than single possibilities. When the highwayman sticks his gun in one's ribs and says "your money or your life," he allows one the option of giving or not giving one's money, and the option of staying or not staying alive, but he closes the option of keeping *both* one's money *and* one's life – a most fecund option indeed.

The 'open option' theory of liberty is to be preferred, I think, to its main rival, the theory of liberty as the absence of barriers to one's actual desires, whatever they should happen to be.[7] Suppose that Martin Chuzzlewit finds himself on a trunk line with all of its switches closed and locked, and with other 'trains' moving in the same direction on the same track at his rear, so that he has no choice at all but to continue moving straight ahead to destination D. On the 'open option' theory of liberty, this is the clearest example of a total lack of liberty: all of his options are closed, there are not alternative possibilities, he is forced to move to D. But now let us suppose that getting to D is Chuzzlewit's highest ambition in life and his most intensely felt desire. In that case, he is sure to get the thing in life he wants most. Does that affect the way the situation should be described in respect to liberty? According to the theory that one is at liberty to the extent that one can do what one wants, a theory held by the ancient Stoics and Epicureans and many modern writers too, Chuzzlewit enjoys perfect liberty in this situation because he can do what he wants, even though he can do nothing else. But since this theory blurs the distinction between liberty and compulsion, and in this one extreme hypothetical case actually identifies the two, it does not recommend itself to common sense.

Common sense may seem to pose difficulties for the 'open option' theory too. The problem for that analysis of liberty is to explain why we attach so great a value to liberty if it is understood to have no necessary connection to our actual desires. Suppose Tom Pinch's highest ambition in life (again speaking in the terms of the railroad metaphor) is to go to destination E, a small siding at a warehouse on a dead end line of a minor branch. Suppose further that the switch enabling trains to move on to that track is unalterably locked in the position barring entry, and is, furthermore, the only locked switch in the entire network of tracks. It may be a small consolation indeed to our frustrated traveler that he is perfectly free to go everywhere except to the one place he wants most to go. The problem for the open-options account is to explain why Chuzzlewit, who *can* do what he wants most to do, but nothing else, *lacks* something of value, and also why Pinch, who *cannot* do what he wants most to do but can do everything else, *possesses* something of value (his liberty).

There are two moves open to a theorist who accepts this challenge. The first is to compromise his open-option theory (as Berlin apparently does) by admitting other elements. Berlin, in a qualifying footnote, suggests that the total amount of liberty enjoyed by a given person at a given time is a function not only of the number and fecundity of his open options, but also "the value [that] not merely the agent, but the general sentiment of the society in which he lives, puts on the various possibilities."[8] If we accept Berlin's suggestion some strange consequences follow. Chuzzlewit, who in our example is compelled to go to D whatever he might wish, is not really unfree after all, provided D is considered a desirable destination both by Chuzzlewit and "the society in which he lives." I fail to see how the desirability of D affects one way or the other the question whether Chuzzlewit has any choice about going there. If Chuzzlewit is allowed no alternative to D, it follows that he is forced willy-nilly to go to D. His situation pleases him, no doubt, but that simply shows that persons can do quite willingly what they are compelled to do, that they can be contented in their unfreedom, a fact of experience that has been much observed and long known. As for our poor frustrated traveler Pinch, Berlin's suggestion can take away his last consolation. If his preferred destination is deemed a desirable place to be both by himself and by the 'general sentiment' of his society, then he is not very free after all, even though his options to move through the system of tracks are almost completely open. He may in fact be no freer, or even less free, than Chuzzlewit, although this is hard to determine since Berlin, who accepts both the number and the value of open possibilities as liberty-determining factors, gives us no clue as to their relative importance. If society at large does not agree with Pinch's eccentric estimate of the desirability of his destination (a fact that Pinch might be expected to find irrelevant to the question of how free he is) and thus finds the barriers to his desire not only singular and limited, but also of no great disvalue, it will tell him that he is 'truly free' no matter how frustrated he feels.

A more plausible way of accounting for the value of liberty will make firm but more modest claims on its behalf. As Berlin himself says many times in his main text, liberty is a thing of solid value, but not the only thing that is valuable. In particular, it is implausible to identify liberty with happiness or contentment, other states to which most persons attach high value. Chuzzlewit may be contented with his heart's desire in the absence of alternative possibilities; indeed he may even be better off, on balance, contented and unfree, than he would be free and uncontented. And Pinch might understandably be willing to trade a great amount of unneeded liberty for the one thing that is necessary to his contentment. But what these examples show is not that 'true freedom is contentment' or that compulsion and freedom are compatible (when one is contented with the compulsion), but rather that freedom is one thing and contentment another, that they are both valuable, but sometimes in conflict with one another so that one cannot have both.

IV

What then is the basis of our interest in liberty? Why should it matter that we have few 'open-options' if we have everything else we want and our other interests are flourishing? Our welfare interest in having a tolerable bare minimum of liberty is perhaps the easiest to account for of the various kind of interests persons have in liberty. If human beings had no alternative possibilities at all, if all their actions at all times were the *only* actions permitted them, they might yet be contented provided their desires for alternative possibilities were all thoroughly repressed or extinguished, and they might even achieve things of value, provided that they were wisely programmed to do so. But they could take no credit or blame for any of their achievements, and they could no more be responsible for their lives, in prospect or retrospect, than are robots, or the trains in our fertile metaphor that must run on 'predestined grooves.' They could have dignity neither in their own eyes nor in the eyes of their fellows, and both esteem for others and self-esteem would dwindle. They could not develop and pursue new interests, nor guide the pursuit of old interests into new and congenial channels, for their lack of key to life's important switches would make it impossible for them to maneuver out of their narrow grooves. Only a small number of kinds of ultimate interests would be consistent with what is permitted, and there would be no point in wanting to develop new ones more harmonious with one's temperament or natural propensities. There would be no point, in fact, in thinking of changing in any important way, in changing one's mind, one's purposes, one's ambitions, or one's desires, for without the flexibility that freedom confers, movements in new directions would be defeated by old barriers. The self-monitoring and self-critical capacities, so essential to human nature, might as well dry up and wither; they would no longer have any function. The contentment with which all of this might still be consistent would not be a recognizably human happiness.

Most of us have fallen into fairly settled grooves by middle life, so the enjoyment of a vast number of open options beyond the requirements of the welfare interest in liberty may not seem very urgent to us. There is no particular comfort in the thought that if I should happen to change my desires or ambitions there will be no externally imposed barrier to my pursuit of the new ones, when the probability of such change seems virtually nil. Still there is something very appealing in the realization that just in case there should be changes in me or my circumstances (contrary to my present expectation), the world will not frustrate and defeat me. The 'breathing space' conferred by alternative possibilities then is an important kind of security.

Another source of the interest in liberty is quite independent of security. Enjoyment of open options is valued by many persons for its own sake, in quite the same way as the enjoyment of a pleasing natural and social environment. There is a kind of symbolic value in possessing a library with more books than one will ever read, or having access to a museum with more exhibits than one can ever see, or eating in a restaurant which offers more dishes than that which one wants most to choose. It is good to have a choice to exercise even when one would be content anyway without it. Alternative options not only secure a person against the possibility of changes of preference, they also permit an appreciation of the richness and diversity of the world's possibilities, and form themselves an environment in which it is pleasant to live.

For young persons whose characters are not fully formed, however, and even for older persons who have not become fixed in their ways, the primary base of the interest in liberty is the necessity to experiment with modes and styles of life, and to search among as large as possible a stock of possible careers for the one that best fits the shape of one's ideals, aptitudes, and preferences. For such persons, open options may be more a vital need than a luxury. But for others, the accumulation of open-options well beyond necessity or security may be itself a kind of ulterior interest, one of those focal aims[9] whose joint advancement constitutes a person's well-being. For some persons an accumulative interest in liberty may have the same status and footing as the interests others may have in the beauty of their surroundings, or in blooming health beyond mere instrumental utility, or in vast wealth or power.

V

Two points about the interest in liberty should be re-emphasized before we conclude. The first is that the interest in liberty is not derived simply from the prior interests we have in things we may or may not be at liberty to do. The motorcyclist's interest in getting to his job quickly and inexpensively is not the same as his interest in having a choice among alternative ways to get to his job, and the suburban scholar's interest in the peace and quiet of his neighborhood is not the same as his interest in having various alternative places where he might study. When we come to 'weigh' and 'balance' the conflicting interests of the motorcyclist and the scholar, their interests in speed, economy, and quiet will go directly and entirely on the scales, but their respective interests in liberty are only fractionally involved. The person against whose interests the legislature or court decides will still have left a great deal of liberty in other respects even though one of his options, in the case at hand, will be authoritatively closed. The weight to be ascribed to the respective interests in liberty, then, will be only part of the total weight of interests each party puts on the scale, and whether it is greater or lesser than the rival's interest in liberty will depend on their respective degrees of fecundity.[10] Criminal proscriptions sometimes infringe our interest in doing the thing prohibited, though this is not frequently the case, since most of us have no interest in the prohibited conduct to begin with, but the interest in open options is something of quite independent value, and is *always* invaded to some degree by criminalization even when no other actual interest is. That fact has little moral bearing, however, except when the options closed by criminal statutes are relatively fecund, in which case it is a fact of high moral importance.

The second point about the interest in liberty derives from the fact that options can effectively be closed by illicit actions of private individuals as well as by the authoritative decrees of legislators as enforced by the police, the courts, and the prisons. Criminal laws are designed to protect interests, including the interest in having open options, from such private incursions. Contemplating criminal legislation, therefore, always involves appraisals of the 'trade-off' between diminished political liberty and enlarged *de facto* freedom. When the statute is clearly justified by the harm principle, most of us *usually* make a gain in *de facto* freedom that more than compensates us for any loss of liberty to engage in the proscribed conduct.

Since legislators normally have interests other than the interest in liberty in mind when they prohibit or discourage certain kinds of conduct, it is difficult to think of clear examples of criminal statutes that enlarge freedom on balance. The clearest cases, of course, are laws prohibiting false imprisonment, kidnapping, high-jacking, forcible detention, and other direct incursions of the liberty of victims to come and go as they wish. When a person is wrongfully locked in a room, for example, it is as if he were an engine on a siding when the only switch connecting to the main track-network is locked against his entry. The option thus closed is therefore an extremely fecund one. On the other side, no matter how circumstances may have brought the 'false imprisoner's' interest in his own liberty into the situation, that interest will surely not sit on the legislative scales with anywhere near so great a weight, since the option closed by the prohibition against false imprisonment, in all but the most exceptional cases,[11] will not be as fecund as the options protected.

Most criminal prohibitions, however, are designed primarily to protect interests in life and limb, health, property, privacy, and the like, and protect liberty only incidentally. Even these statutes often find some justification in their net enlargement of liberty, though they would be fully justified by the harm principle in any case because of their protection of other interests. The law forbidding rape, for example, while designed to prevent women from psychological trauma and physical harm, and fully justified on those grounds, also protects the interest in liberty to whatever minor extent that interest sits on the scales. That law closes one relatively unfecund option of most adult males while depriving females of no liberty whatever.[12] At the same time it not only protects the interest that all females have in the absence of harmful and offensive bodily contacts (an independent merit that looms much larger than liberty in the law's rationale), it protects various of their relatively fecund open options from forcible closure by private individuals. All females, therefore, gain protection of fecund open options with no sacrifice of any other liberty, while most males suffer the closure of one small limited option − a clear net gain for liberty. Criminal legislation, however, is not always and necessarily so good a trade from the point of view of liberty.[13] And in any case, it is the weights of affected interests other than liberty that are likely to be decisive when interests conflict.

NOTES

[1] In a forthcoming book I discuss these problems in detail. The problem of *aggregative harms*, as I use the term, arises when specific instances of generally harmful activities (e.g. drinking alcoholic beverages, possessing firearms) are often, or even usually, socially harmless in themselves. Blanket permission leads to an increase of harm in the aggregate, but blanket prohibition would interfere with harmless and beneficial as well as harmful instances of the activity. The middle road, a system of licensure, often has severe difficulties of its own. *Competitive harms* are incurred by competitive interests, those aimed at achieving a certain position relative to others: priority, victory, or ascendance. The persons harmed are losers in structured competitions. The problem of *accumulative harms* is that which stems from the familiar phenomenon where single occurrences of

certain activities are harmless up to a threshold, but general performance of those activities would be harmful. Again, blanket prohibitions would necessarily ban harmless and beneficial, as well as harmful, actions.

² Nicholas Rescher, *Welfare, The Social Issue in Philosophical Perspective* (Pittsburgh: The University of Pittsburgh Press), p. 6.

³ *Ibid.,* p. 5.

⁴ Much of the material in this paragraph is drawn from my essay, 'Limits to the Free Expression of Opinion', in J. Feinberg and H. Gross (eds.), *Philosophy of Law* (Encino, CA: Dickenson Publishing Co., 1975), pp. 141–42.

⁵ Isaiah Berlin, 'Two Concepts of Liberty'. in *Four Essays on Liberty* (London: Oxford University Press, 1969), p. 130 n.

⁶ *Loc. cit.*

⁷ I discuss these rival theories in a not altogether satisfactory fashion in 'The Idea of a Free Man', in James F. Doyle, ed., *Educational Judgments* (London: Routledge & Kegan Paul, 1973), pp. 149–151, and in *Social Philosophy* (Englewood Cliffs, N.J.: Prentice-Hall, 1973), pp. 5–7 and 18–19.

⁸ Berlin, *op. cit.,* p. 130. I think that this passage in a long footnote is an aberration from arguments in the main text with which I am largely in agreement.

⁹ This term is from C.L. Stevenson, *Ethics and Language* (New Haven: Yale University Press, 1944), p. 203. Stevenson's formal definition is as follows: "an end which is also such an exceptionally important means to so many divergent ends that if anything else is not, in its turn, a means to this, it will be without predominating value." Since a person may have more than one focal aim, the definition should be amended as follows: "... if anything else is not a means to this, *or to another focal aim*, it will be without predominating value."

¹⁰ Strictly speaking, the conflicting interests are: one party's interest in a specific open option and another party's interest in another specific open option. These are 'interests in liberty' only in the sense that they are interests in the 'liberty category,' as opposed, for example, to the 'life,' 'property,' or 'privacy' categories. Fecundity is a property, strictly speaking, of the options themselves, not of the interests.

¹¹ In many of these 'most exceptional cases,' the party who is tempted to capture, detain, kidnap, or highjack, is driven to such desperate means by threats to his own fecund liberties that are ultimately of his own making, or the consequences of his own wrongdoing, e.g. his need to escape arrest and eventual incarceration for some earlier crime. In some other very exceptional cases, the detainer may have the justification of 'necessity' or forced choice of the lesser evil, as when one 'borrows' another's automobile in an emergency leaving the owner at least temporarily stranded and immobile. The 'lesser evil' in this case could be an infringement of a less fecund liberty.

¹² Except insofar as a woman is legally capable of committing rape herself as an accomplice to the main perpetrator who must, legally speaking, be male. This is a trivial qualification of the point in the text, and deserves at most a footnote.

¹³ Consider, for example, mandatory curfew laws, ordinances forbidding minors from purchasing alcoholic beverages or from lingering in places where they are sold, statutes prohibiting the sale of obscene books or the showing, even to audiences of willing and eager adults, of pornographic films. If such laws are justified, it is because they protect interests other than the interest in liberty, for they open nowhere near as many or as fecund options as they close.

Harm and Self-Interest

THE study of *kakapoeics*, or the general theory and classification of harms, should be a central enterprise of legal philosophy. Most writers agree, after all, that the prevention of harms is a legitimate aim of both the criminal law and the coercive parts of the civil law, though of course there is much disagreement over whether it is the *sole* proper concern of coercive law, over *whose* harms are properly considered, and over which types of harm have priority in cases of conflict. There are also conceptual riddles concerning the scope of the term 'harm', three of which provide the excuse for this essay, namely, whether there can be such things as purely *moral harms* (harm to character), *vicarious harms* (as I shall call them), and *posthumous harms*. My discussion of these questions will assume without argument the orthodox juris-prudential analysis of harm as invaded interest, not because I think that account is self-evidently correct or luminously perspicuous, but rather because I wish to explore its implications for the borderline cases of harm, the better to test its adequacy, and to determine the respects in which the concept of self-interest still needs clarification.

The theory of the nature of harms assumed here can be sketched quickly. A person is harmed when someone invades (blocks or thwarts) one of his interests.[1] A person has an interest in Y when he has a *stake* in Y, that is, when he stands to gain or lose depending on the condition or outcome of Y.[2] A person's interest in the singular

---

[1] Interests can be blocked or defeated by events in impersonal nature or by plain bad luck. But they can only be 'invaded' by human beings, either oneself, acting negligently or perversely, or by others, singly or in groups and organizations. It is only when an interest is invaded by self or others that its possessor is harmed in the usual legal sense, though obviously an earthquake or a plague can cause enormous harm in the ordinary sense.

[2] Strictly speaking, this definition is circular since a person would probably have to know what it is to have an interest in something before he could know what it is to

(his personal interest or self-interest) consists in the harmonious advancement of all his interests in the plural. We speak not only of the things a person 'has an interest in' but also of the various things that are 'in his interest', that is, the things that promote his interests as a group. 'Welfare interests' are interests in the indispensable means to one's ulterior goals, whatever the latter may be. These include health, financial sufficiency, and the like. 'Ulterior interests' are based on stable, long-range objectives, achievements of goals valued at least partly as ends in themselves—for example producing a book, raising a family, building a dream house, advancing a cause. Characteristically human well-being consists in the advancing of such interests.

Welfare and ulterior interests bear somewhat different relations to wants or desires. Anything we believe we have a stake in, whether it be mere minimal health or ultimate achievement, we will desire to some degree, in so far at least as we are rational. But we have some welfare interests in conditions that are good for us even if we should not want them (for example, health), whereas in respect to our more ultimate goals, we have a stake in them because we desire their achievement, not the other way round. In these instances, if our wants were to change, our interests would too. It is not true, however, that wants, even strong wants, are *sufficient* to create interests. Few non-betting football fans, for example, have ulterior interests in their favourite team's victory, though many may have very intense desires for that outcome. As a psychological generalization, it is probably true that few persons can 'invest' enough in a wanted outcome to create a stake in it unless promoting that outcome becomes a personal goal or objective. Surely, no mere 'desire of the moment', like a desire to go to the cinema,[3] can generate an ulterior interest, but only a relatively deep-rooted and stable want whose fulfilment can be both reasonably hoped for (mere idle wishes won't do) and influenced by one's own efforts.[4]

'gain or lose' as well as vice versa. But even a circular definition can have some practical utility in providing an equivalent expression for the *definiendum* that is more easily manipulated to good purpose, or which is more suggestive, or productive of insight. The word 'stake', e.g. brings out with intuitive vividness the connection between interests and risks. The word 'stake' has its primary or literal use to refer to 'the amount risked by a party to a wager, or match, or gambler, a thing whose existence, or safety, or ownership depends on some issue'.

[3] Cf. Brian Barry, *Political Argument* (Routledge & Kegan Paul, London, 1965), p. 183.

[4] There is, I suppose, a respect in which anyone who has a strong desire for anything

1. *Moral harm*. Is interest, then, a wholly 'want-regarding' concept, or does the analysis sketched in the preceding paragraphs leave out something important? The label 'want-regarding' comes from Brian Barry[5] who contrasted it with what he called 'ideal-regarding' concepts and principles. A concept is want-regarding if it can be analysed entirely in terms of the 'wants which people happen to have', whereas it is ideal-regarding if reference must also be made to what would be ideal, or best for people, their wants notwithstanding, or to the wants they ought to have whether they have them in fact or not. The ideal-regarding theory of interest holds that it is in a person's interest ultimately not only to have his wants and goals fulfilled, but also (and often this is held to be more important) to have his tastes elevated, his sensibilities refined, his judgment sharpened, his integrity strengthened: in short to become a better person. On this view, a person can be harmed not only in his health, his purse, his worldly ambition, and the like, but also in his character. One's ultimate good is not only to *have* the things one wants, but (perhaps more importantly) to *be* an excellent person, whatever one may want. We not only degrade and corrupt a man by making him a worse man than he would otherwise be; on this view, we inflict serious *harm* on him, even though all his other interests flourish. Socrates and the Stoics even went so far as to hold that this 'moral harm' is the *only* genuine harm. Epictetus was so impressed with the harm that consists simply in having a poor character that he thought it redundant to punish a morally depraved person for his crimes. Such a person is punished enough, he thought, just by being the sort of person he is.

To a certain extent, the conflict between the two accounts of interest is entirely academic. That is because most forms of excellence, most of the time, tend to promote want-based interests. If there is an antecedent desire for excellence, as there often is, then the achievement of excellence is want-fulfilling, and even in the absence of such a

---

at all stands to 'gain' or 'lose' depending on whether it is satisfied. The pleasant state of mind we call satisfaction is itself a kind of reward or form of 'gain' (although it does not come automatically when we get what we desire) and intense disappointment is a kind of 'loss'. But one cannot do without the inverted commas. There is a distinction, crucial for our present purposes, between being disappointed *because* one has suffered a personal loss, and the 'loss' that consists entirely in disappointment, and between the 'gain' that consists entirely in satisfaction at some outcome, and the satisfaction that occurs *because* there has been some personal gain. The 'losses' and 'gains' in inverted commas have no direct connection with interests or with harms. We are commonly enough disappointed, dissatisfied, even frustrated without suffering harm.

[5] Barry, op. cit., pp. 38 ff.

desire, personal excellence is likely to contribute to the joint satisfaction of other wants. But contrary to Plato and many other ancient
sages, there is no necessity that excellence and happiness always
coincide, no impossiblity that morally inferior persons can be happy,
and excellent persons miserable. There is still room for controversy
then over what is truly good for persons in the latter two cases. In
particular, philosophers have disagreed over whether it is *in the
interest* of the contented moral defective to become a better person.
This disagreement can persist even when it is agreed on all sides that
it is desirable that the defective's character improve. Desirable, yes;
a good thing, to be sure; but in *his* interest? That is another thing.

The source of the appeal of the ideal-regarding theory, I think, is
evident: Few of us would wish to exchange places with people we
regard as morally flawed, no matter how content they seem to be. It
is easy to understand and sympathize with Epictetus' attitude toward
the morally depraved criminal. We would not want to be *him* even if
he escaped punishment, indeed even if he profited richly from his
crime and suffered no remorse for it. Neither would we wish to be
contented and vulgar, contented and dull, contented and stupid. We
would in fact be prepared to sacrifice a good deal of our (other)
want-fulfilments to avoid becoming flawed in these ways. But that is
surely because we already have *desires* for excellences of character
construed in accordance with our own standards. It is because we
have such wants that we think it in our *interest* to be excellent, or at
least not defective. Without those antecedent wants, it would not be
in our interest to be excellent at all, except of course indirectly through
the happy effects (not always to be relied upon) of excellent character
on popularity and material success. By the same token, it is not in the
interest of the contented moral defective to have *our* idea of virtue,
which he doesn't share, imposed on him, unless, of course, we speak
of thrift, prudence, diligence, etc., all of which could improve his
chances of fulfilling his *other* ulterior wants. But if he is clever enough
to make a 'good thing' in material terms out of dishonesty and
unscrupulousness, even while he is cold-hearted, mean, vulgar,
greedy, and vain, then it can hardly be in his interest to become warm,
sensitive, cultivated, and generous; much less witty, perceptive,
tactful, disinterested, and wise. We would not trade places with him
to be sure, for it would not be in *our* interests to do so in so far as we
have a stake, through the investment of our wants, in excellent
character. We think, and rightly so in most cases, that we could only

lose by becoming worse persons, and that the change itself would constitute a loss, whatever further losses or gains it caused to our other interests.

Partisans of the ideal-regarding theory often rest their case on the example of child raising. Surely, it is said, we do not educate our children simply to become good want-fulfillers; rather we wish them to have the right wants in the first place, and to acquire the traits of character from which right wants emerge. Thus Stanley Benn claims that we are promoting the interests of the child when, at a time before he has achieved a good character, we commence with 'educating him to be a person of a certain sort'.

His desires are beside the point [Benn writes], for it is often a question of whether he is to be encouraged to have desires of some approved sort instead of undesirable ones. It might be in the child's interests to deny him satisfaction of some of his desires to save him from becoming the sort of person who habitually desires the wrong thing.[6]

Benn's example supports an important point, but not the one he claims to be making. The point of moral education at the time it is undertaken is not simply to serve the child's interests either as they are or as they might one day become; not simply to promote his gain, profit, or advantage, his happiness or well-being. The aim is rather to lead the child, through creating new wants in him, to seek his happiness *by* pursuing personal excellence: to give him a *stake* in having a good character. The parent who values good character will want to give the child his own interest in it, so that the child's pursuit of his own interests will necessarily involve seeking and preserving virtues of character. The effect of making goodness one of a person's ulterior interests is to make the achievement of happiness impossible without attention to it. So, far from showing that a good character is in a person's interest even if it does not promote want-satisfaction, Benn's example shows instead that good character can be something that is directly in a person's interest only when the person has a want-based interest in *it*.

One of the advantages of the want-regarding theory is that it enables us all the more forcibly to praise personal excellence. Good character would be a good thing to have even if it didn't advance a person's self-interest. Self-interest, after all, isn't everything. It is no aid to clarity to insist that everything that is good *in* a person must be

[6] S. I. Benn, ' "Interests" in Politics', *Proceedings of the Aristotelian Society* 60 (1960), 130–1.

good *for* the person. Nor does it help to say that the evil in a person must be harmful to him. The contented moral defective is an ineligible model for emulation even though his faults cause no harm to himself. He is both evil and well off, and his evil character does not detract from his well-offness. Epictetus's 'pity' for him then is ill-placed. Vice is its own punishment, just as virtue is its own reward, only to the person who has a stake in being good.

It is not merely useful but morally important to preserve in this way the distinction between being good and being well off, for it saves us from speaking as if, and perhaps really believing, that well-offness is the sole good. It is important to be a good person and not merely a happy or fulfilled one. That is why we train children to seek their happiness in part through seeking their goodness. In that way we ensure that they will not be completely happy unless they are good.

Morally corrupting a person, that is, causing him to be a worse person than he would otherwise be, can *harm* him, therefore, only if he has an antecedent interest in being good. (It may in fact harm no one to corrupt him if he is corrupted in a way that does not make him dangerous to others.) The moral corruption or neglect of an unformed child, then, is no direct harm to him, provided that he has the resources to pursue his own interests effectively anyway, but it can be a very real harm to his parents if *they* have a powerful stake in the child's moral development.

2. *Other-regarding wants and vicarious harms.* There are two ways in which one person can have an interest in the well-being of another. In the one case, *A* may be dependent upon the help of *B* for the advancement of his own (*A*'s) interests, so that if *B*'s fortunes should decline, *B* would be less likely to help *A*. What promotes *B*'s interest, in this case, indirectly promotes that of his dependent *A* as well. It is therefore in *A*'s interest that *B*'s interest be advanced. In the extreme version of this case, where *A* is *wholly* dependent on *B*'s help, and so long as *B*'s personal interest flourishes the help is sure to continue, *B*'s good is, in effect, one of *A*'s welfare interests, the advancement of which (like his own health) promotes the whole economy of his ulterior interests and is absolutely essential to his well-being, whatever his ulterior interests happen to be.

In the second kind of case, *C* has 'invested' a desire so strong, durable, and stable in *D*'s well-being, that he comes to have a personal stake in it himself. It becomes, therefore, one of his ulterior interests or 'focal aims'.[7] This should be contrasted with the more common phenomenon of spontaneous sympathy, pity, or compassion which can be directed at total strangers. It may make *A* very unhappy to see *B* (a stranger) suffer, and *A* may do what he can to help *B*, from genuinely disinterested, compassionate motives. But the harm that has been done *B*, say, by a hit-and-run motorist who knocked him down, is not *also* harm done *A*. The interests of *A* have not been invaded by the harm done *B*; he has only suffered sōme vicarious unhappiness on *B*'s behalf which will leave his own personal interests largely unaffected. In the case of genuinely other-regarding interest that I have in mind, *C* has an abiding interest of his own in *D*'s well-being which is not merely an episodic 'passing desire'. Further, he desires *D*'s good not simply as a means to the promotion of the other ulterior aims that are components of his own good, but quite sincerely as an end in itself. Such cases are, of course, rare, but no rarer than disinterested love. Indeed, there is one sense of 'love' (that which the New Testament writers called *agape*) which is well defined by the presence of purely other-regarding interest. Ralph Barton Perry once defined 'love' in this sense as an interest in the advancement of someone else's interests.[8] When *C* has a loving interest in *D*'s personal interest, then anything that harms *D* directly *ipso facto* harms *C* indirectly. Can anyone doubt that one harms a loving parent by maiming his child (or as in the previous example, by corrupting his child) or that one harms a loving husband or wife by causing a disappointment that plunges his or her spouse into despair?

The separation of the two kinds of cases distinguished in the preceding paragraphs is somewhat artificial. The distinction is clearly enough conceived, but in real life psychological elements rarely separate so neatly. Most of the things we desire for their own sakes we *also* desire as means to other things. Harm to a child may itself be harm to its loving parent in that it directly violates the parent's 'purely' other-regarding interest, but it may also be instrumentally damaging to various self-regarding interests of the parent, in that it creates a drain on his funds, a burden on his time and energy, and a strain on his emotional stability. Similarly, when one spouse sinks into despair, this not only harms the other person's wholly other-regarding interest in the ailing mate's well-being; it also

[7] This phrase is C. L. Stevenson's. See his account in *Ethics and Language* (Yale U.P., New Haven, 1944), p. 203.

[8] Ralph Barton Perry, *General Theory of Value* (Longmans, Green, & Co., New York, 1926), p. 672. His exact words: '. . . a favourable interest in the satisfaction of the interest of a second person'.

deprives him or her of the myriad services and pleasures that a cheerful partner would contribute.

Loving interests are so commonly intertwined with, and reinforced by, instrumental, essentially self-regarding interests, that many observers are led to discount the former, or even deny altogether their existence in given cases. Others have embraced the apparently cynical view that there are no purely other-regarding interests at all, that human nature being what it is, no one 'really cares' about the well-being of other persons, except in so far as it affects his own self-regarding interests. All interests in the well-being of others, on this view, are of the first type distinguished above. This extreme form of psychological egoism rules out not only disinterested love, but episodic sympathy and compassion as well. Egoism of this sort can never be persuasive to those who are deeply impressed by the genuine purity of their own love for others, so its advocates must posit a good deal of self-deception in their opponents. Since the purity of people's motives is not readily subject to careful scrutiny, the egoistic theory, as a matter of empirical psychology, is not easily refuted, though the stronger philosophical arguments *for* the view are invariably muddled.

Some types of apparently other-regarding interests are so familiar, however, that the burden of explaining them away should be placed on the egoist. One common example is the case of pooled interest, where, either through design or accident, separate persons are so related that they share a common lot. Such common interests, 'all for one and one for all', are found wherever parties are led (or forced) by circumstances to act in concert and share the risk of common failure or the fruits of an indivisible success.[9] Whatever the ultimate truth of the matter, common sense reports that persons with pooled or inter-dependent interests are sometimes drawn even closer by bonds of sentiment directed toward common objects or reciprocal affection (of an *apparently* disinterested kind) between the parties. And when this happens, as it sometimes seems to in marriages and family groups, each has a genuine stake of a not merely instrumental kind in the well-being of the others, a stable ulterior goal, or focal aim, that the others flourish, partly as an end in itself, partly as a means to a great diversity of other ends.

Despite the familiarity of these observations, some very able philosophers have chosen to exclude purely other-regarding wants

[9] See my 'Collective Responsibility' in *Doing and Deserving* (Princeton U.P., Princeton, N.J., 1970), pp. 233–41.

altogether from their otherwise want-regarding analyses of interest. The writers in question do not necessarily deny that there are purely other-regarding wants. Professor Barry, for example, admits that some of us, some of the time, genuinely want other persons as well as ourselves to enjoy increased opportunities to satisfy ulterior wants. Indeed, he concedes that some persons, some of the time, even voluntarily suffer a diminution of their opportunities for want-satisfaction in order to increase the opportunities of other persons to satisfy *their* wants. But the latter cases, Barry insists, are best described as cases where our *principles* are allowed to override out interests.[10] Barry is right about the cases he seems to be considering, where persons voluntarily sacrifice their own interests for others out of a sense of justice, or for ideal-regarding reasons, or for charity. But he doesn't even consider cases of the kind discussed above where help to others is not thought to be a *sacrifice* at all, but a direct promotion of one's own other-regarding interest in the advancement of the interests of another party.

I think the theoretical motives of writers who exclude other-regarding wants from their analyses of self-interest are clear enough, and worthy of respect. They are simply taking the easiest way out of a kind of linguistic muddle. They are afraid that inclusion of purely other-regarding aims as eligible constituents of a person's own self-interest would commit them to saying various odd-sounding things. They fear that we would have to say when Jones gives his last cent to promote the cause of his favourite political party, or to finance his child's education, or to secure the very best doctor for his sick wife, that he is advancing his own interest *merely* (treacherous word, 'merely'). Hence, we must think of his act as 'selfish', since it was done in his own self-interest, after all. The less paradoxical alternative, they think, is to deny that the act is in the actor's own interest at all, and to say instead that Jones was acting from conscience, or out of principle, or for charity, and against his own interest. After all, how could his act be at once disinterested and self-interested, unselfish yet self-advancing?

There is, however, a more satisfactory, if less direct, way out of the muddle. That is simply to consider very carefully what it means to call an act 'unselfish' and 'disinterested', and to come by this route to appreciate how unselfish and disinterested conduct, without affecting any of the actor's interests other than those he has in the well-being

[10] Barry, op. cit., p. 77

of others, can nevertheless be in his own personal interest. A person who has such a stake in the happiness of other people that his own well-being depends on the advancement of their interests is not the proper model of a selfish person. A selfish person is one who pays insufficient attention to the interests of other people, and thus comes to pursue his own self-regarding interests at the expense of, or in disregard of, the interests of others. That is quite another thing than pursuing one's own interest in *promoting* the interests of others. The loving parent or spouse and the public-spirited zealot can make no distinction between their own interests and that of their children, or spouse, or party. Far from indicating their selfishness, that identity of interests shows how unselfish they probably are. They might yet be blamably selfish, however, if they pursue those of their own interests which include the interests of *some* other people (for example, a daughter and a son) at the expense of the interests of still *other* people (for example, their neighbours' children). It is in fact an advantage of our analysis (as opposed to Barry's) that it enables us to explain why conduct of the latter kind is selfish. On Barry's analysis, neither want—that for the well-being of my children nor that for the well-being of my neighbours' children—is one of my own interests. Hence, when I promote the interests of some of these parties at the expense of those of the others, I am acting neither for nor against my own interests. I can be acting oddly or wrongly in that case, but not specifically selfishly. That judgment, however, seems plainly false. It surely *is* selfish wrongly to benefit one's own loved ones at the expense of others.

The best way, it seems to me, to conceive of the relation between self-interested, selfish, unselfish, and disinterested acts is that indicated in a chart with two genera, one of which is further sub-divided (see diagram 1 on p.295).

The generic distinction in the chart is that on the top line between self-interested acts and acts that are not self-interested, particularly those that concerned Barry, namely, conscientious or charitable acts that are not predominantly in the actor's interest. Self-interested acts are then divided into self-regarding and other-regarding species. Depending on our purposes, of course, we would classify the acts in this motley category in various alternative ways, but it is especially useful for our present purposes to divide them into these mutually exclusive and jointly exhaustive categories. The self-regarding class is then further divided into directly and indirectly self-regarding subclasses. For an example of directly self-regarding activity (A1a) consider an unmarried home-owner's labour at improving his property so that he can take more enjoyment and pride in it, impress those in a

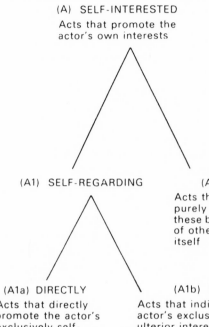

(A) SELF-INTERESTED
Acts that promote the actor's own interests

(B) NOT SELF-INTERESTED
Acts done from principle or charity that are not done in order to promote the actor's interests and can even be against his interests on balance

(A1) SELF-REGARDING

(A2) OTHER–REGARDING
Acts that directly promote the actor's purely other-regarding interests, these being desires for the well-being of others, at least partly as an end in itself

(A1a) DIRECTLY
Acts that directly promote the actor's exclusively self-regarding ulterior interests

(A1b) INDIRECTLY
Acts that indirectly promote the actor's exclusively self-regarding ulterior interests by directly promoting the well-being of others, the latter being desired as means only

position to help, and disproportionately increase its resale value in a rising market. Such a person is promoting his own purely self-regarding ulterior interests in material possession, career advancement, and capital accumulation. An example of indirectly self-regarding activity (A1b) is found in the story of the gambler, A, who bets B $50,000 that C will recover from a serious illness. Thus C's health is in A's interest, and A has a stake (in a literal sense) in C's recovery. To protect that stake he works hard to promote C's recovery, providing at his own expense, the best medical and nursing care that he can find. He thus promotes the well-being of another as ardently as a lover or a saint would, though the other's well-being, his immediate goal, is desired only as a means to the advancement of his own self-regarding interest.

In contrast, acts in the genuinely other-regarding species of the self-interested genus (A2) aim at the promotion of another's good at least partly as an end in itself. An example would be that of a parent whose stake in the well-being of his child is derived from his love for the child simply, and not from any incidental service to his other (self-regarding) interests that the child might contribute. If such a parent depletes his own life savings to advance or protect his child, his act would fall in the other-regarding species of the self-interested genus. This is the species which is thought to be empty, for quite different reasons, by psychological egoists and Brian Barry. The egoists deny that any acts are genuinely other-regarding (that is, motivated by a desire to promote or retard the good of another as an end in itself), while Barry denies that any other-regarding acts are self-interested. But if any person ever does 'really care' whether another person is harmed or benefited, and not simply as a means to his own gain but at least in part for the other's own sake, then the egoists are wrong. And if any person ever does have a genuine stake in the happiness of another person—an independent ulterior interest not wholly derived from its service to other ulterior interests—such that he himself gains or loses directly depending on the condition of the other person, then the view suggested by Barry is wrong.

The chart enables us to distinguish several senses of 'disinterested action' and also two kinds of selfish action. A disinterested act can be defined in a first approximation, as one not done simply to advance the actor's interests.[11] One class of disinterested actions, then, consists of those in the chart's second genus: those not done to advance *any* of the actor's interests, self-regarding or other-regarding. These are actions done from conscience, or out of a sense of justice, or from charity, or from a spontaneous benevolent impulse, often with the conscious expectation that they will be against the actor's own interest. A second kind of disinterested action is one which meets a stricter test; it is neither done to promote the actor's own interest or to favour the interests of any second parties unfairly at the expense of third parties when the actor's own interests simply aren't involved one way or the other. Thus, a judge's decision is disinterested when it is unbiased and impartial. These related senses of the word 'disinterested' are well established in usage. A third sense

[11] Cf. *Webster's New International Dictionary*, 2nd edn. (1954): 'not influenced by regard to personal advantage . . .' and *The Oxford English Dictionary*: 'not influenced by self-interest . . .'

(one which is suggested by our chart) is not so clearly established and may in fact be somewhat extended beyond what is recognized in ordinary usage. I am not sure. Still, it stands for an important category that deserves to be distinguished from the others, whatever name it bears. I refer to actions in the other-regarding species of the self-interested genus (A2), acts done out of the perfectly genuine desire to help another whose well-being is actually a constituent of the actor's own good. When a person promotes the well-being of a loved one in a self-sacrificing or otherwise 'selfless' way, it may be misleading to call his act disinterested since he does have a personal stake, even a predominant ulterior interest, in the outcome. But it can be equally misleading to deny that his act is disinterested since apart from the well-being of the loved one that is his goal, there may be no 'personal advantage' in his action, and no trace of self-interest in his motivation. In an extreme case, he might even sacrifice all his other interests for the good of another person or cause in which he has 'invested' everything. The least misleading thing to say about such conduct is that it is not disinterested in one very familiar sense of the term, but that it is disinterested in another, less familiar, sense. In any event, extreme psychological egoists are likely to deny that there are disinterested acts of either kind, and sometimes put that view by saying that all voluntary actions are 'selfish'.

Now a selfish act, whatever else it may be, is one that is morally defective. A person acts selfishly when he pursues his own interests (or the satisfaction of transitory desires and appetites) *wrongly* at the expense of others. Sometimes, of course, there is nothing blamable in the pursuit of self-interest at the expense of others, as for example, in legitimately or unavoidably competitive contexts. An act is selfish only when its pursuit of self-interest is somehow in excess of what is right or reasonable in the situation.

The more familiar kind of selfish act is a defective specimen of those in the self-regarding species of self-interested actions (A1a and b). The father who refuses to spend money on his children for anything beyond their minimal needs, and uses his surplus instead to buy fine clothes and wines for himself is selfish in this way. But as we have seen, defective specimens of acts in the other-regarding species of the self-interested genus (A2) can also be selfish, as when a parent with a genuinely independent stake in his own children's advancement (an 'other-regarding interest') pursues that interest wrongly at the expense of his neighbour's children. We would be reluctant, I think, to call the latter actions 'disinterested' in *any* sense, since it would be intolerably odd to think of an act as both disinterested and selfish. Hence I am forced to qualify the account given above of the self-interested acts that can also be, in an 'unfamiliar sense', disinterested, as follows: an act is disinterested in that third sense provided that (i) it is done in order to advance the good of another party, but (ii) not merely as a means to the advancement of the actor's own self-regarding interests, *and* (iii) it is not done to promote the actor's other-regarding interest in the well-being of one party wrongly at the expense of still another party. (This third condition amends the definition, in effect, by requiring that a disinterested act not be a selfish act of the second kind.)

Selfish actions, then, can be defined as those which pursue the actor's self-interest *wrongly* at the expense of, or in disregard of, other people, and the two main types of selfish actions are those which are appropriately defective instances of category A1 on the chart, and those which are appropriately defective instances of A2. (Morally defective instances of B, as we shall see, are not called 'selfish'.) It is best, I think, to define 'selfish' and 'unselfish' as logical contraries rather than contradictories, in recognition of a large and motley class of actions that are neither selfish nor unselfish. An unselfish act then can be defined as one which pursues the interests of others (or the fulfilment of their transitory wants or appetites) *rightly* at the expense of, or in praiseworthy disregard of, the actor's own interests (or wants and appetites).[12] Voluntary actions in the middle group that qualify neither as selfish nor as unselfish include those which pursue the actor's own self-regarding wants or interests (A1) in a non-defective way (not wrong or blamable, not deficient in concern for others) as well as those whose motivation does not include concern for self-interest one way or the other, as in the case of the judge in a controversy between two persons who are strangers to him.

There are blamably defective specimens of acts even in the non-self-interested genus (B on the chart), but these characteristically bear names other than 'selfish'. Acting entirely out of principle, for example, a person might be rigid, cruel, or intolerant. A person might, in another case, act honestly in accord with a dictate of his

---

[12] Two kinds of unselfish actions then can be distinguished in terms of the categories in the chart: those in category B and those actions in category A2 that are not done wrongly at the expense of, or in blamable disregard of, the interests (or passing wants) of third parties.

own mistaken or confused conscience. Another person might act unjustly or imprudently out of spontaneous compassion. All of these morally defective acts can be against the actor's interest and known to be such, yet deliberately chosen anyway. They may be blameable, but they are not selfish.

According to our provisional definition of 'harm', a violation of an interest in any of the categories in the chart is a harm to its possessor. Any action, omission, or rule that interferes with a person's self-interested action, thus thwarting his interest, causes him harm. But does it follow from the definition that interferences with voluntary acts in the non-self-interested genus (B) are *not* harms? That would seem at first sight to be the case. Since acting out of conscience or benevolence is not acting to advance one's own interest, interference with such action does not violate one's interest, and therefore is not, by definition, a harm to one. Moreover, such interference, when it prevents a person from acting contrary to his own interest, actually *serves* his interest, and would seem therefore to be beneficial to him. Any interference, however, with a voluntary action, even with a non-self-interested one, is an invasion of a person's interest in *liberty*, and is thus harmful to him to that extent. If that seems too trivial a harm in the case at hand to be the basis of a powerful claim to non-interference, the liberal will have to retreat from the harm principle and seek a stronger defensive position, perhaps in the principle that infringements of an actor's *autonomy* are seriously wrongful even when they do him, at most, only trivial harm.

3. *Death and posthumous harms.* If a murderer is asked whether he has harmed his victim, he might well reply: 'Harmed him? Hell no; I killed him outright!' The victim's mourners too might feel that it is something of an understatement to describe the death of their loved one as a harm (to him). The death of the victim, it would seem, is not merely a 'harmed condition' he is put in; it is no 'condition' of him at all, but rather his total extinction. Consider the purest possible hypothetical case of the infliction of death, where all extraneous and distracting harms have been excluded from the example. A man in the prime of his life, with many on-going projects and enterprises, but with no dependents or friends close enough to mourn him, is shot by an unseen assailant in the back of the head. Without ever being aware even that he was in danger, much less that he has been fatally wounded, he dies instantly. Right up to the very instant he was shot, he was unharmed; then at that very moment, perhaps one second

after the killer squeezed the trigger, he was dead. At the very most, he was in a 'harmed condition' for the one half-second, or so, before he died. As for death itself, one might agree with the ancient Epicureans: 'Where he was, death was not, and where death was, he was not'.

Yet for all of that, it seems clear that the murderer did violate his victim's interest in remaining alive. One second before the trigger was pulled, it was true of the victim (as it is now true of both the author and reader of these words) that continued life was something *in his interest*. Indeed, there is nothing a normal person (in reasonable health and tolerable circumstances) dreads more than his own death, and that dread in the vast majority of cases, is as rational as it is unavoidable, for unless we continue alive, we have no chance whatever of achieving the goals that are the ground of our ultimate interests. Some of these goals perhaps might be achieved for us by others after our deaths, publicly oriented and other-regarding goals in particular. But most of our interests require not simply that some result be brought about, but rather that it be brought about *by* us, or if not by us, then *for* us. My interest in producing an excellent book, or a beautiful art object, is not fully satisfied by another person's creation of such objects. My interest was not simply that such objects exist, but that *I* bring them into existence. Similarly my aim to build a dream house, or to achieve leisure in security, is not satisfied when such a house or such leisure comes into existence, but only when I am present to enjoy and use it. Our interest in avoiding death is a supreme welfare interest, an indispensable condition for the advancement of most, if not all, of the ulterior interests that constitute our good. There is something bare minimal about it on the one hand, yet something supremely important on the other. Apart from the interests it serves, it has no value in itself; yet unless it is protected, hardly any of a person's ulterior interests will be advanced. To extinguish a person's life is, at one stroke, to defeat almost all of his self-regarding interests: to ensure that his on-going projects and enterprises, his long-range goals, and his most earnest hopes for his own achievement and personal enjoyment, must all be dashed.

There is a case then both for saying that death is not a harm and that it *is* a violation of an antecedent interest in staying alive. That makes death a very hard case indeed for the analysis of harm as invaded interest. There may be no way out of this for the writer who has strong theoretical incentives for saving the invaded interest theory other than to stipulate an admittedly extended sense of 'harm' broad enough to include death as a harm.[13] This would be a minor and quite excusable departure from the conventions of ordinary language for the sake of theoretical economy; still, it would make things tidier all around if we could *show* that, ordinary language to the contrary—and not as a matter of mere arbitrary stipulation—death *is* a harm.[14] It would be unreasonable to expect that this conclusion could be demonstrated, and indeed, there are various common sense considerations other than the oddness of its sound to the ear that militate against it. But there is also a way of conceiving death (even without the assumption of survival or immortality) that mitigates its paradox and lends it some plausibility. That is all that can be claimed, at best, for the view that death can be a harm to the one who dies.

To be sure, death is not always and necessarily a harm to the one who dies. To the person in hopeless, painful illness, who has already 'withdrawn his investments' in all ulterior interests, there may be nothing to lose, and cessation of agony or boredom to be 'gained', in which case death is a blessing. For the retired nonogenarian, death may not exactly be ardently desired, but still it will be a non-tragedy. Those who mourn his death will not think of themselves as mourning *for him*, but rather for his dependants and loved ones, if any, or simply in virtue of the capacity of any *memento mori* to evoke sadness. In contrast, when a young vigorous person dies, we think of *him* as chief among those who suffered loss.

One way of saving the 'invaded interest' theory of harm, at minimal cost to common sense, is to think of all harm as done to interests themselves, and interpret talk of harm done to men and women as convenient elliptical references to, and identification of, the interest that was thwarted or set back. Thus, when Cain harms Abel by punching him in the nose, it is Abel's interest in the physical integrity of his nose that is the immediate object of the harm, and

[13] For the writer who is interested in formulating a more precise and defensible version of Mill's 'harm principle' there is another alternative. He can simply amend his statement of that principle so that it restricts interferences with liberty to those necessary to prevent *harm or death* (implying that they are not the same thing). The cost of this amendment, however, would be the abandonment of the analysis of harm as 'any invasion of interest', for there *is* an interest in avoiding death, yet the amendment implies that death is not a harm.

[14] Thomas Nagel has argued ingeniously but inconclusively that death is an 'evil' or a 'misfortune' to the one who dies. This is not quite the same perhaps as saying that a person is *harmed* when he is killed, but it is close. See his article 'Death' in its expanded form in *Moral Problems*, edited by James Rachels (Harper & Row, New York, 1971), pp. 361–70.

Abel himself is harmed in the derivative sense of being the owner of a harmed interest. This is perhaps a step beyond (but only a small step beyond) saying what is obviously true: that it is only in virtue of having interests that people can be harmed, and that the only way to harm any person is to invade his interests. If Abel had no interest of the usual welfare kind in the integrity and normal functioning of his body, then Cain could not have harmed him by punching him in the nose, but at most only hurt, annoyed, or disappointed him. The next step is to point out that most of a person's self-regarding interests, at least, are thwarted permanently, and thus harmed, by his death. Although *he* no longer exists, we can refer to his earlier goals (as a matter of identification) as *his* interests, and *they* were the interests directly harmed by his death.

What then does it mean to say that an *interest* has been harmed? Our answer to this question will depend on which of two conceptions of interest enhancement and impairment we adopt. As we have seen, interests are 'stakes' that are derived from and linked to wants, in the case of ulterior interests to more ulterior goals or focal aims. Now we can apply to these wants W. D. Ross's distinction between want-fulfilment and want-satisfaction.[15] The *fulfilment* of a want is simply the coming into existence of that which is desired. The *satisfaction* of a want is the pleasant experience of contentment or gratification that normally occurs in the mind of the desirer when he believes that his desire has been fulfilled. When the object of a want does not come into existence, we can say that the want has been *unfulfilled* or *thwarted*; the experience in the mind of the desirer when he believes that his desire has been thwarted is called *frustration* or *disappointment*. Notoriously, fulfilment of desire can fail to give satisfaction. There is no more melancholy state than the disillusionment that comes from getting what we wanted and finding it disappointing. Such dis-illusionment can usually be explained as the consequence of a rash or ill-considered desire and unrealistic expectations. On other occasions, the original desire will bear up under retrospective scrutiny, and yet its fulfilment gives no pleasure. Indeed, the occurrences of subjective satisfaction is a highly contingent and unreliable phenomenon. Sometimes when our goals are achieved, we don't experience much joy, but only fatigue and sadness, or an affective blankness. Some persons, perhaps, are disposed by temperament normally to receive their achievements in this unthrilled fashion. Still, even in these cases,

[15] W. D. Ross, *Foundations of Ethics* (Clarendon Press, Oxford, 1939), p. 300.

re-examination of the goal whose fulfilment failed to satisfy may disclose no hidden defects, no reasons for regret, in a word, no disillusionment. Not only can one have fulfilment without satisfaction; one can also have satisfaction of a want in the absence of its actual fulfilment, provided only that one is led to believe, falsely, that one's want has been fulfilled. Similarly, pleasant states of mind resembling 'satisfaction' can be induced by drugs, hypnosis, and other forms of manipulation that have no relation whatever to prior wants.

Similarly, one's wants can be thwarted without causing frustration, or disappointment, and one can be quite discontented even when one's wants have in fact been fulfilled. These negative cases are perfectly parallel with the positive ones. Non-fulfilment of a want yields no disappointment when the want was ill advised in the first place. In such a case, the want can happily be renounced after rational reassessment. Disillusionment, however, is often not involved. A perfectly genuine and well-considered goal may be thwarted without causing mental pain when the desirer has a placid temperament or a stoic philosophy. And discontent does not presuppose thwarting of desire any more than satisfaction presupposes fulfilment. One can have feelings of frustration and disappointment caused by false beliefs that one's wants have been thwarted, or by drugs and other manipulative techniques.

For these reasons, harm to an interest is better defined in terms of the objective blocking of goals and thwarting of desires than in subjective terms; and the enhancement or benefiting of an interest is likewise best defined in terms of the objective fulfilment of well-considered wants than in terms of subjective states of pleasure. Most persons will agree, I think, that the important thing is to get what they want, even if that causes no joy.[16] The pleasure that normally attends want-fulfilment is a welcome dividend, but the object of our efforts is to fulfil our wants in the external world, not to bring about states

[16] This judgment is probably too confident if understood to extend to cases where what is wanted is expected to cause actual *disappointment*. Derek Parfit has reminded me of the distinction between cases where fulfilment *can't possibly* produce satisfaction because the person will never be in a position to know that his want has been fulfilled, and cases where fulfilment can produce satisfaction but in fact won't. In the former case, all would agree that the important thing is that what we want to happen will happen (our desire will be fulfilled). But in the latter case, if people know or confidently expect that fulfilment will not only 'not cause joy' but will actually produce disappointment, it is not so clear, as Parfit points out, that the important thing is 'to get what one wants'. There is some question, however, whether the existence of the want could even survive such conditions.

of our own minds. Indeed, if this were not the case, there would be no way to account for the pleasure of satisfaction when it does come; we are satisfied only because we think that our desires are fulfilled. If the object of our desires were valuable to us only as a means to our pleasant inner states, those inner glows could never come.

The object of a focal aim that is the basis of an interest, then, like the object of any want, is not simply satisfaction or contentment, and the defeat of an interest is not to be identified with disappointment or frustration. Hence, death can be a thwarting of the interests of the person who dies, and must be the total defeat of most of his self-regarding interests, even though, as a dead man, he can feel no pain.

This account helps explain, I think, why we grieve for a young, vigorous 'victim of death' himself, and not *only* for those who loved him and depended on him. We grieve for him in virtue of his unfulfilled interests. We think of him as one who has invested all his energies and hopes in the world, and then has lost everything. We think of his life as a whole as not as good a thing as it might have been had he lived on. In some special circumstances, death not only does its harm in this wholly 'negative' way, preventing the flowering of the interests in which a person's lifetime good consists, it also does direct and 'positive' harm to a person by undoing or setting back important interests that were already prospering. Death, in these cases, leads to the harming of surviving interests that might otherwise have been prevented.[17]

Because the objects of a person's interests are usually wanted or aimed-at events that occur outside of his immediate experience and at some future time, the area of a person's good or harm is necessarily wider than his subjective experience and longer than his biological life. The moment of death is the terminating boundary of one's biological life, but it is itself an important event within the life of one's future-oriented interests. When death thwarts an interest, the interest is harmed, and the harm can be ascribed to the man who is no more, just as his debts can be charged to his estate.

The interests that die with a person are those that can no longer be helped or harmed by posthumous events. These include most of his self-regarding interests, those based, for example, on desires for personal achievement and personal enjoyment, and those based on 'self-confined' wants that a person could have 'if he were the only

[17] The most vivid example I know in literature of a 'positively harmful' death is that foreseen by Pip at the hands of the villainous Orlick in Dickens's *Great Expectations*.

person that had ever existed',[18] for example, the desire to be a self of a certain kind, or the desire for self-respect. Other self-regarding wants, in contrast, seem more like other-regarding and publicly oriented wants, in that they can be fulfilled or thwarted after the death of the person whose wants they are. I refer to some of a person's desires to stand in certain relations to other people where 'the concern is primarily with the self . . . and with others only as objects or as other terms in a relation to me'.[19] These desires can be called 'self-centred', and include as a class such wants as the desire to assert or display oneself before others, to be the object of the affection or esteem of others, and so on. In particular, the desire to maintain a good reputation, like the desire that some social or political cause triumph, or the desire that one's loved ones flourish, can be the basis of interests that survive their owner's death, in a manner of speaking, and can be promoted or harmed by events subsequent to that death. Fulfilment and thwarting of interest, after all, may still be possible, even when it is too late for satisfaction or disappointment.

The above account might still contain elements of paradox, but it can be defended against one objection that is sure to be made. How can a man be harmed, it might be asked, by what he can't know? Dead men are permanently unconscious; hence they cannot be aware of events as they occur; hence (it will be said) they can have no stake one way or the other, in such events. That this argument employs a false premiss can be shown by a consideration of various interests of *living* persons that can be violated without them ever becoming aware of it. Most of these are 'possessary interests' whose rationality can be doubted, for example, a landowner's interest in the *exclusive* possession and enjoyment of his land—an interest that can be invaded by an otherwise harmless trespasser who takes one un-observed step inside the entrance gates; or the legally recognized 'interest in domestic relations' which is invaded when one's spouse engages in secret adulterous activity with a lover. The latter is an interest in being the exclusive object of one's spouse's love, and has been criticized by some as implying property in another's affections. But there is no criticizing on such grounds the interest every person has in his own reputation, which is perhaps the best example for our present purposes. If someone spreads a libellous description of me,

---

[18] C. D. Broad, 'Egoism as a Theory of Human Motives' in *Ethics and the History of Philosophy* (Routledge and Kegan Paul, London, 1952), p. 220.
[19] Op. cit., p. 221.

without my knowledge, among hundreds of persons in a remote part of the country, so that I am, still without my knowledge, an object of general scorn and mockery in that group, I have been injured in virtue of the harm done my interest in a good reputation, even though I *never* learn what has happened. That is because I have an interest, so I believe, in having a good reputation *as such*, in addition to my interest in avoiding hurt feelings, embarrassment, and economic injury. And *that* interest can be seriously harmed without my ever learning of it.

How is the situation changed in any relevant way by the death of the person defamed? If knowledge is not a necessary condition of harm before one's death why should it be necessary afterward? Suppose that after my death, an enemy cleverly forges documents to 'prove' very convincingly that I was a philanderer, an adulterer, and a plagiarist, and communicates this 'information' to the general public that includes my widow, children, and former colleagues and friends. Can there be any doubt that I have been harmed by such libels? The 'self-centred' interest I had at my death in the continued high regard of my fellows, in this example, was not thwarted by my death itself, but by events that occurred afterward. Similarly, my other-regarding interest in the well-being of my children could be defeated or harmed after my death by other parties overturning my will, or by thieves and swindlers who cheat my heirs of their inheritance. None of these events will embarrass or distress me, since dead men can have no feelings; but all of them can harm my interests by forcing non-fulfilment of goals in which I had placed a great stake.

This liability, to which we are all subject, to drastic changes in our fortune both before and after death was well understood by the Greeks. Aristotle devotes a chapter of his *Nicomachean Ethics* to a saying already ancient in his time, and attributed by some to Solon, that we can 'call no man fortunate before his death'.[20] On one interpretation, this dark saying means that 'only when he is dead is it safe to call a man ... beyond the arrows of outrageous fortune'. On the day before he dies, his interests can be totally smashed and his life thus ruined. But as Aristotle shrewdly observes (attributing the point to the general popular wisdom), some of a person's interests are not made safe even by his death, and we cannot call him fortunate with perfect confidence until several more decades have passed; 'For a dead man is popularly believed to be capable of experiencing both

[20] Aristotle, *Nicomachean Ethics*, I. 10.

good and ill fortune—honour and dishonour, and prosperity and the
loss of it among his children and descendants generally—in exactly
the same way as if he were alive but unaware or unobservant of what
was happening'.[21]

Three hypothetical cases can illustrate the 'popular belief' mentioned by Aristotle, and the case for posthumous harm must rest
with them.

Case A. A man devotes thirty years of his life to the furtherance of
certain ideals and ambitions in the form of one vast undertaking. He
founds an institution dedicated to these ends and works single-
mindedly for its advancement, both for the sake of the social good he
believes it to promote, and for the sake of his own glory. One month
before he dies, the 'empire of his hopes' collapses utterly as the
establishment into which he has poured his life's energies crumbles
into ruin, and he is personally disgraced. He never learns the unhappy
truth, however, as his friends, eager to save him from disappointment,
conceal or misrepresent the facts. He dies contented.

Case B. The facts are the same as in Case A, except that the
institution in which the man had so great an interest remains healthy,
growing and flourishing, until the man's death. But it begins to
founder a month later, and within a year, it collapses utterly, while
at the same time, the man and his life's work are totally discredited.

Case C. The facts are the same as in Case B, except for an additional surmise about the cause of the decline and collapse of the man's
fortune after his death. In the present case, a group of malevolent
conspirators, having made solemn promises to the man before his
death, deliberately violate them after he has died. From motives of
vengeance, malice, and envy, they spread damaging lies about the
man and his institution, reveal secret plans, and otherwise betray his
trust in order to bring about the ruin of his interests.

It would not be very controversial to say that the man in Case A
had suffered grievous harm to his interests although he never learned
the bad news. Those very same interests are harmed in Case B to
exactly the same extent, and again the man does not learn the bad
news, in this case because he is dead, and dead men hear no news at
all. There seems no relevant difference between Case A and Case B

---

[21] Ibid., first paragraph. Aristotle's primary concern in this chapter, however, was
not to show that a person's interests can be affected after his death, but rather that
well-being, whether before or after death, cannot be destroyed by the caprice of events,
but at worst, only somewhat tarnished. The point about interests surviving death he
simply assumed as beyond need of argument.

except that in Case B there might seem to be no subject of the harm, the man being dead. But if we consider that the true subjects of harms are interests, and that interests are harmed by thwarting or non-fulfilment rather than by subjective disappointment, we can think of posthumous harms as having subjects after all. But if that point is not convincing, the argument must depend on its reinforcement by Case C. In that example, the man is not *merely* harmed (if he is harmed at all); rather he is exploited, betrayed, and wronged. When a promise is broken, someone is wronged, and who if not the promisee? When a confidence is revealed, someone is betrayed, and who, if not the person whose confidence it was? When a reputation is falsely blackened, someone is defamed, and who, if not the person lied about? If there is no 'problem of the subject' when we speak of wronging the dead, why should there be, when we speak of harming them, especially when the harm is an essential ingredient of the wrong?

To summarize then: Death can thwart a person's ulterior, self-regarding interests in personal achievement and enjoyment, by totally defeating the welfare interest that is necessary for fulfilment of the goals and focal aims that are their bases. It is for this reason alone that death is a harm to the one who dies suddenly, in the prime of life, never knowing what hit him, and unmourned by loved ones or dependents. We grieve for such a person (as opposed to grieving for our own loss) because of his unfulfilled interests. Events after death can thwart or promote those interests of a person which may have 'survived' his death. These include his publicly oriented and other-regarding interests, and also his 'self-centred' interests in being thought of in certain ways by others. Posthumous harm occurs when the deceased's interest is thwarted at a time subsequent to his death. The awareness of the subject is no more necessary than it is for harm to occur to certain of his interests at or before death.

"Harmless Immoralities" and Offensive Nuisances

I am not at all sure that there are any private immoral actions that do not cause harm, but I am quite sure that *if* there are such things, there is no justification for their suppression by the state and especially not for their proscription by the criminal law. On the other hand, there clearly are such things as actions that are very offensive to others, and I think the state is justified in preventing at least some of these when certain strict conditions have been satisfied. In coming to these conclusions (which I shall defend in what follows) I appear to have endorsed one and rejected another of the principles commonly proposed as justifications for political restriction of private liberty. Preventing offense, I maintain, is at least sometimes a ground for limiting liberty, whereas the "enforcement of morality as such" is never a valid ground.

I

There are perhaps as many as seven liberty-limiting principles that are frequently proposed by leading writers. It has been held that restriction of a person's liberty may be justified:[1]

1. to prevent injury to others (the *private harm principle*);
2. to prevent impairment of institutional practices and regulatory systems that are in the public interest, such as the collection of taxes and custom duties (the *public harm principle*);

This is an expanded version of the material from Chapters 2 and 3 of *Social Philosophy* by Joel Feinberg, copyright © 1973 by Prentice-Hall, Inc., Englewood Cliffs, N.J. By permission of the publishers.

3.   to prevent offense to others (the *offense principle*);
4.   to prevent harm to self (*legal paternalism*);[2]
5.   to prevent or punish sin, i.e. "to enforce morality as such" (*legal moralism*);
6.   to benefit the self (*extreme paternalism*);[3]
7.   to benefit others (the *welfare principle*).

The private harm principle, which of course is indissolubly associated with the name of John Stuart Mill, is virtually beyond controversy. Hardly anyone would deny the state the right to make criminal, on this ground, such harmful conduct as willful homicide, aggravated assault, and robbery. Mill often wrote as if the prevention of private harm were the *sole* valid ground for state coercion, but this must surely not have been his considered intention. He would not have wiped from the books such crimes as tax evasion, smuggling, and contempt of court, which need not injure to any measurable degree any assignable individuals, except insofar as they weaken public institutions in whose health we all have a stake, however indirect. I assume then that Mill held both the private and the public versions of the harm principle.

In some sections of *On Liberty*, Mill suggests that harm of one kind or another is the *only* valid ground for coercion, so that the prevention of mere offensiveness, as opposed to harmfulness, can never be sufficient ground to warrant interference with liberty. Yet in the final chapter of *On Liberty*, Mill seems to retreat on this issue too. There he refers to public acts that are "a violation of good manners and, coming thus within the category of offenses against others, may rightly be prohibited. Of this kind," he continues, "are offenses against decency, on which it is unnecessary to dwell. . . ."[4] Mill's view about offensiveness can be made consistent, however, in the following way. One subclass of actions, on his view, has a very special social importance. These actions are instances of expressing orally or in print opinions about matters of fact and about historical, scientific, theological, philosophical, political, and moral questions.[5] The free expression of opinion is of such great importance to the well-being and progress of the community, that it can be validly restricted only to prevent certain very clear harms to individuals, such as libel, slander, incited violence, and, perhaps, invasions of privacy. The importance of free expression is so great and so special that only the necessity to prevent direct and substantial harm to assignable persons can be a sufficient reason for overriding the presumption in its favor. Mere shock to tender sensibilities can never be a weighty enough harm to counterbalance the case for free expression of opinion. But Mill did not consider public nudity, indecency, public displays of "dirty pictures," and the like, to be forms of "symbolic speech," or expressions of *opinion* of any kind. The presumption in favor of liberty is much weaker in the case of conduct that does not have the "redeeming social importance" peculiar to assertion, criticism, advocacy, and debate; and hence, even "mere offensiveness" in the absence of harm may be a valid ground for suppressing it.[6]

II

What is offensiveness and how is it related to harm? If we follow some legal writers and define "harm" as the violation of an interest, and then posit a universal interest in not being offended, it will follow that to suffer offense is to suffer a kind of harm. But there are some offenses that are (in a narrow sense) "harmless" in that they do not lead to any *further* harm, that is, they do not violate any interests other than the interest in not being offended. Thus, there is a sense of "offense" which is contrasted with harm, and in the interest of clarity, that is the sense we should employ.

Offensive behavior is such in virtue of its capacity to induce in others any of a large miscellany of mental states that have little in common except that they are unpleasant, uncomfortable, or disliked. These states do not necessarily "hurt," as sorrow and distress do. Rather the relation between them and hurt is analogous to that between physical unpleasantness and pain. There are, after all, a great variety of unpleasant but not painful bodily states—itches, shocks, and discomforts—that have little in common except that they don't hurt but are nevertheless universally disliked.

No complete catalog of the unpleasant states caused by offensiveness is possible here, but surely among the main ones are: irritating sensations (e.g. bad smells and loud noises); unaffected disgust and acute repugnance as caused, for example, by extreme vulgarity and filth; shocked moral, religious, or patriotic sensibilities; unsettling anger or irritation as caused, for example, by another's "obnoxious, insulting, rude, or insolent behavior"; and shameful embarrassment or invaded privacy, as caused, for example, by another's nudity or indecency.

Nuisance law protects people from loud noises, noisome stenches, and other direct and inescapable irritants to the senses, usually by providing civil remedies. An evil smell, of course, even when not harmful (in the narrow sense) can still be an annoyance, inconvenience, or irritation. Something like "unaffected disgust" is often evoked by behavior that is neither harmful nor in any ordinary sense "immoral," but is rather vulgar, uncouth, crass, boorish, or unseemly to an extreme. Normally, bad manners are considered beneath the attention of either morals or law, but when they are bad enough, some have plausibly argued, we can demand "protection" from them. Imagine a filthy and verminous man who scratches himself, spits, wipes his nose with the back of his hand, slobbers, and speaks in a raucous voice uttering mostly profanities and obscenities. If such a person spoke freely to passers-by on the public street, he just might be subject to arrest as a public nuisance, whether he harms anyone or not.

Still other offensive behavior tends to arouse outrage and indignation more than "unaffected disgust." Because the connection between open displays of disapproved conduct and indignation is so well known, engaging in such conduct is frequently a deliberate way of issuing a symbolic insult to a group of people. Sometimes open flaunting is in itself a kind of taunting or challenging and is well understood as "an invitation to violence." The flaunter deliberately arouses shocked anger and revulsion just as if he were saying with contempt, "That's what I think of you and your precious values!" The wearing and displaying of Nazi emblems in

New York would enrage and challenge in this manner. So, alas, would a racially mixed couple strolling harmlessly, hand in hand, down the streets of Jackson, Mississippi. The latter kind of behavior, of course, can have a point and a motive independent of the desire to flaunt and taunt. Engaging in such behavior in public must be known to affront the sensibilities of those regarded as benighted; but its motive may not be to taunt so much as to display one's independence and contempt for custom while boldly affirming, and thus vindicating, one's rights.

When there is no point to the flaunted conduct independent of the desire to offend, still another model is sometimes appropriate, namely, that of desecration or sacrilege. The sacred, whatever else it may be, is no laughing matter. A person to whom "nothing is sacred" is a person able to mock or ridicule anything. But most of us are so constructed that some things are beyond mockery to us. It is difficult then to tolerate swastikas (with their symbolic suggestions of barbarity and genocide) or public flag burnings, or dragging venerated religious symbols in the mud. These things are so widely and intensely resented that some find it hard to think of reasons why they should be tolerated.

Still another kind of offensive behavior is that usually called "indecent." Indecency can have any of the motives and intended effects discussed above. Its distinctive feature is the public exhibition of that which, because of its extremely personal or intimately interpersonal character, had best remain hidden from view, according to prevailing mores. To be offended by indecency is not to be insulted or angered so much as to be acutely and profoundly embarrassed. Indecency, like other offensiveness, may be indirectly harmful when it exacerbates guilt, leads to incapacitating shock, sets a bad example, or provokes violence; but when the law forbids even "harmless indecency," its primary purpose is simply to protect the "unwilling witness of it in the streets."[7]

I have little doubt than that the offense principle should supplement the private and public harm principles in any full statement of the grounds for justifiable constraint. That principle, however, is as dangerous as it is necessary, and, as I shall argue in the section on obscenity below, it must be hedged in with careful qualifications.[8]

III

Are there any harmless immoralities? According to the utilitarian conception of ethics, harmfulness is the very ground and essential nature of immorality; but there is no doubt that our moral code is not (yet) wholly utilitarian. Certain actions are still widely held to be immoral even though they harm no one or, at most, only the actor himself. The question is whether the law should be used to force people to refrain from such conduct.

The central problem cases are those criminal actions generally called morals offenses. Offenses against morality and decency have long constituted a category of crimes (as distinct from offenses against the person, offenses against property, etc.). These have included mainly sex offenses—adultery, fornication, sodomy, incest, and prostitution, but also a miscellany of nonsexual offenses including cruelty to animals, desecration of the flag or other venerated symbols, and mistreatment of corpses. In a very useful article, Louis B. Schwartz maintains that what sets these crimes off as a class is not their special relation to morality (after all, murder is also an offense against morality, but it is not a "morals offense") but rather the lack of an essential connection between them and social harm. In particular, their suppression is not required by the public security.[9] Some morals offenses may harm the perpetrators themselves, but there is rarely harm of this sort the risk of which was not consented to in advance by the actors. Offense to other parties, when it occurs, is a consequence of the perpetration of the offending deeds *in public* and can be prevented by "public nuisance" laws or by statutes against "open lewdness" or "solicitation" in public places. That still leaves "morals offenses" when committed by consenting adults in private: should they really be crimes?

Some arguments in favor of the statutes that create morals offenses are drawn from the private and public harm principles. There might be no direct unconsented-to harm caused by discreet and private, illicit sex relations, it is sometimes conceded; but indirectly harmful consequences to innocent parties or to society itself invariably result. The socially useful institutions of marriage and the family can be weakened, and the chaste life made more difficult. Such indirect and diffuse consequences, however, are highly speculative, and there is no hard evidence that penal laws would prevent them in any case. On the other hand, the harm principles might be used to argue *against* such laws on the grounds that some of the side effects of the laws themselves are invariably harmful. Laws against homosexuality, for example, lead to the iniquities of selective enforcement and to enhanced opportunities for blackmail and private vengeance. Moreover, "the criminal law prevents some deviates from seeking psychiatric aid. Further, the pursuit of homosexuals involves policemen in degrading entrapment practices, and diverts attention and effort that could be employed more usefully against the crimes of violent aggression, fraud, and government corruption, which are the overriding concerns of our metropolitan civilization."[10]

Indeed, the essentially utilitarian argument based on the need for prudent allocation of our social energies in fighting crime may, by itself, be a conclusive argument against the use of the criminal sanction to prevent private (and therefore inoffensive) conduct whose harmfulness is indirect and speculative at most. While seriously harmful crimes against person and property are everywhere on the rise, our police stations, criminal courts, and prisons are flooded with persons charged with drunkenness or marijuana possession, and other perpetrators of "crimes without victims," and if their numbers are not joined by swarms of fornicators, pornographers, and homosexuals, it is only because detection of such "criminals" is so difficult. Only an occasional morals offender is swept into the police nets out of the tens of millions who must violate some part of our sex laws, and these are usually members of economically deprived classes and minority races. Herbert Packer gives sound advice, then, when he cautions the rational legislator that "every dollar and every man-hour is the object of competition among uses," and that "he should not only put first things first, but also, what is perhaps harder, put last things last."[11] From the point of view of resource allocation in the fight against crime, "*merely* moral offenses," that is, those disapproved acts that neither harm nor offend (if there are such) are indeed "last things."

It is another matter to use the criminal law to prevent the offense caused to disgusted captive observers by unavoidable public behavior. In such cases, the offense principle can justify a statute forcing the offending parties to restrict their offensive conduct to private places. This would be to use the law to prevent indecency, however, not immorality as such.[12] Such a statute would be very little more restrictive of liberty than similarly grounded statutes against public nudity. Some conduct may be so offensive as to amount to a kind of "psychic aggression," in which case, the private harm principle would allow its suppression on the same grounds as that of physical assault. But even when all this is said and done, the harm and offense principles together will not support all "enforcement of morality as such," for they do not permit interference with the voluntary conduct of consenting adults in the privacy of their own rooms behind locked doors and drawn blinds.

For these reasons many writers have argued for the repeal of statutes that prohibit private immorality; but not surprisingly the same considerations have led others to abandon the view that the harm and offense principles provide an adequate guide to legislative policy. The alternative principle of "legal moralism" favored by the latter writers has several forms. In its more moderate version, it is commonly associated with the views of Patrick Devlin.[13] Lord Devlin's theory, as I understand it, is really a form of utilitarianism or, more exactly, an application of the public harm principle. The proper aim of the criminal law, he holds, is the prevention of harm, not merely harm to individuals but also, and primarily, harm to society itself. A shared moral code, Devlin argues, is a necessary condition for the very existence of a community. Shared moral convictions function as "invisible bonds" or a kind of "social cement" tying individuals together into an orderly society. Moreover the fundamental unifying morality (to switch the metaphor) is a kind of "seamless web":[14] To damage it at one point is to weaken it throughout. Hence, society has as much right to protect its moral code by legal coercion as it does to protect its equally indispensable political institutions. The law cannot tolerate politically revolutionary activity; nor can it accept activity that rips asunder its moral fabric. Thus, "The suppression of vice is as much the law's business as the suppression of subversive activities; it is no more possible to define a sphere of private morality than it is to define one of private subversive activity."[15]

   H. L. A. Hart finds it plausible that some shared morality is necessary to the existence of a community, but criticizes Devlin's further contention "that a society is identical with its morality as that is at any given moment of its history, so that a change in its morality is tantamount to the destruction of a society."[16] Indeed a moral critic might admit that we can't exist as a society without some morality or other, while insisting that we can perfectly well exist without *this* morality (if we put a better one in its place). Devlin seems to reply to this criticism that the shared morality *can* be changed even though protected by law, and when it does change, then the emergent reformed morality in turn deserves *its* legal protection.[17] The law then functions to make moral reform difficult, but there is no preventing change where the reforming zeal is fierce enough. How then does one bring about a change in prevailing moral beliefs when they are enshrined in law? Presumably one advocates conduct which is in fact illegal; one puts into public practice what one preaches; one demonstrates one's sincerity by marching proudly off to jail for one's convictions:

> there is . . . a natural respect for opinions that are sincerely held. When such opinions accumulate enough weight, the law must either yield or it is broken. In a democratic society . . . there will be a strong tendency for it to yield—not to abandon all defenses so as to let in the horde, but to give ground to those who are prepared to fight for something that they prize. To fight may be to suffer. A

willingness to suffer is the most convincing proof of sincerity. Without the law there would be no proof. The law is the anvil on which
the hammer strikes.[18]

In this remarkable passage, Devlin has discovered another argument for enforcing "morality as such," and incidentally for principled civil disobedience as the main technique for initiating and
regulating moral change. A similar argument, deriving from Samuel Johnson, and applying mainly to changes in religious doctrine,
was well known to Mill. Religious innovators deserve to be perse-
cuted, on this theory, for persecution allows them to prove their
mettle and demonstrate their disinterested good faith, while their
teachings, insofar as they are true, cannot be hurt, since truth will
always triumph in the end. Mill regarded this method of testing
truth to be uneconomical, as well as ungenerous:

> To discover to the world something which deeply concerns it, and of
> which it was previously ignorant, to prove to it that it had been mis-
> taken on some vital point of temporal or spiritual interest, is as impor-
> tant a service as a human being can render to his fellow creatures.
> . . . That the authors of such splendid benefits should be requited by
> martyrdom, that their reward should be to be dealt with as the vilest
> of criminals, is not, upon this theory, a deplorable error and misfor-
> tune for which humanity should mourn in sackcloth and ashes, but the
> normal and justifiable state of things. . . . People who defend this
> mode of treating benefactors cannot be supposed to set much value
> on the benefit.[19]

If self-sacrificing civil disobedience, on the other hand, is not the
most efficient and humane remedy to grant to the moral reformer,
what instruments of moral change are available for him? This question is not only difficult to answer in its own right, it is also the
rock that sinks Devlin's favorite analogy between harmless immorality and political subversion.

Consider what subversion is. In most modern law-governed
countries there is a constitution, a set of duly constituted authorities, and a body of statutes, or "positive laws," created and enforced by the duly constituted authorities. There will be ways of
changing these things that are well known, orderly, and permitted

by the constitution. For example, constitutions are amended; new legislation is introduced; legislators are elected. On the other hand, it is easy to conceive of various sorts of unpermitted and disorderly change, for example, through assassination and violent revolution, or through bribery and subornation, or through the use of legitimately won power to extort and intimidate. Only these illegitimate methods of change, of course, can be called "subversion." But here the analogy between positive law and positive morality begins to break down. There is no "moral constitution," no well-known and orderly way of introducing moral legislation to duly constituted moral legislators, no clear convention of majority rule. Moral subversion, if there is such a thing, must consist in the employment of disallowed techniques of change instead of the officially permitted "constitutional" ones. It consists not simply of change as such, but of illegitimate change. Insofar as the notion of legitimately induced moral change remains obscure, "illegitimate moral change" can do no better. Still, there is enough content to both notions to preserve some analogy to the political case. A citizen works *legitimately* to change prevailing moral beliefs when he publicly and forthrightly expresses his own dissent; when he attempts to argue, and persuade, and offer reasons; when he lives according to his own convictions with persuasive quiet and dignity, neither harming others nor offering counterpersuasive offense to tender sensibilities. On the other hand, a citizen attempts to change mores by *illegitimate* means when he abandons argument and example for force and fraud. If this is the basis of the distinction between legitimate and illegitimate techniques of moral change, then the use of state power to affect moral belief *one way or the other*, when harmfulness is not involved, would be a clear example of illegitimacy. Government enforcement of the conventional code is not to be called "moral subversion," of course, because it is used on behalf of the *status quo*; but whether conservative or innovative it is equally in defiance of our "moral constitution"—if anything is.

The second version of legal moralism is the pure version, not some other principle in disguise, but legal moralism properly so called. The enforcement of morality as such and the attendant punishment of sin are not justified as means to some further social aim (such as the preservation of social cohesiveness) but are ends in themselves. Perhaps J. F. Stephen was expressing this pure moralism when he wrote that "there are acts of wickedness so gross and outrageous that self-protection apart they must be prevented at any cost to the offender and punished if they occur with exemplary severity."[20] (From his examples it is clear that Stephen had in mind the very acts that are called "morals offenses" in the law.) That the act to be punished is truly wicked and outrageous must be the virtually unanimous opinion of society, Stephen goes on to add; and the public condemnation of acts of its kind must be "strenuous and unequivocal."[21]

Adequate discussion of Stephen's view requires that a distinction be made between the moral code actually in existence at a given time and place, and some ideal rational code. The former is often called "conventional" or "positive" morality, and the latter "rational" or "critical" morality. Whether or not a given type of act is wicked according to a given positive morality is a matter of sociological fact; whether or not it is "truly wicked" is a question for argument of a different kind and notoriously more difficult to settle. Stephen apparently identified critical morality in large measure with the Victorian positive morality of his time and place. A century later we can be pardoned, I think, for being somewhat skeptical about that. Once we grant that there is no necessary and self-evident correspondence between some given positive morality and the true critical morality, it becomes plain that the pure version of legal moralism is one or another of two distinct principles, depending on which sense of "morality" it employs.

Consider first, then, the view that the legal enforcement of positive morality is an end in itself. This means that it is good for its own sake that the state prohibit and punish all actions of a kind held wicked by the vast majority of citizens, even when such acts are harmless and done in private with all deference to the moral sensibilities of others. It is hard to argue against propositions that derive their support mainly from ethical intuition, but when one fully grasps the concept of a *positive morality*, even the intuitive basis of this moralistic proposition begins to dissolve. What is so precious, one wonders, about public opinion as such? Let us suppose that public opinion about moral questions is wrong, as it so often has been in the past. Is there still some intrinsic value in its legal enforcement derived from the mere fact that it *is* public opinion? This hardly seems plausible, much less intuitively certain, especially when one considers that enforcement would make it all the more difficult to correct the mistake. Perhaps it gives the public some satisfaction to know that conduct it regards (rightly or wrongly) as odious or sinful occurs very rarely even behind drawn blinds and that when it occurs, it is punished with "exemplary severity." But again it is hard to see how such "satisfaction" could have any intrinsic value; and even if we grant it intrinsic value for the sake of the argument, we should have to weigh it against such solid intrinsic evils as the infliction of suffering and the invasion of privacy.

The more plausible version of pure moralism restricts its scope to critical morality. This is the view that the state is justified in enforcing a truly rational morality as such and in punishing deviations from that morality even when they are of a kind that is not harmful to others. This principle too is said to rest on an intuitive basis. It is often said that the universe is an intrinsically worse place for having immoral (even harmlessly immoral) conduct in it. The threat of punishment (the argument continues) deters such conduct. The actual instances of punishment not only back up the threat, and thus help keep future moral weeds out of the universe's garden, they also erase the past evils from the universe's temporal record by "nullifying" them, or making it as if they never were. Thus punishment contributes to the net intrinsic value of the universe in two ways: by cancelling out past sins and preventing future ones.[22]

There may be some minimal plausibility in this view when it is applied to ordinary harmful crimes, especially those involving duplicity or cruelty, which really do seem to "set the universe out of

joint." It is natural enough to think of repentance, apology, or for-
giveness as "setting things straight," and of punishment as a kind
of "payment" or a wiping clean of the moral slate. But in cases
where it is natural to resort to such analogies, there is not only a
rule infraction, there is also a *victim*—some person or society of
persons who have been harmed. When there is no victim—and especially where there is no profit at the expense of another—"setting
things straight" has no clear intuitive content.

Punishment may yet play its role in discouraging harmless private immoralities for the sake of "the universe's moral record."
But if fear of punishment is to keep people from illicit intercourse
(or from desecrating flags or mistreating corpses) in the privacy of
their own rooms, then morality must be enforced with a fear-
some efficiency that shows no respect for anyone's privacy. There
may be some, like Stephen, who would derive great satisfaction
from the thought that no harmless immoralities are being perpe-
trated behind anyone's locked doors (to the greater credit of the
universe as a whole); but how many of these would be willing to
sacrifice their *own* privacy for this "satisfaction"? Yet if private
immoralities are to be deterred by threat of punishment, the de-
tecting authorities *must* be able to look, somehow, into the hidden
chambers and locked rooms of anyone's private domicile. And
when we put this massive forfeiture of privacy into the balance
along with the usual costs of coercion—loss of spontaneity, stunt-
ing of rational powers, anxiety, hypocrisy, and the rest—the price
of securing mere outward conformity to the community's moral
standards (for that is all that can be achieved by the penal law) is
exorbitant.

In an extremely acute article,[23] Ronald Dworkin suggests (without fully endorsing) a version of pure legal moralism that shares
some of the features of both versions discussed above. He distinguishes between genuine moral convictions and mere prejudices,
personal aversions, arbitrary dogmas, and rationalizations. The actual moral convictions of a community, providing they constitute
a genuine "discriminatory morality," Dworkin suggests, might well

be enforced by the criminal law; but the "morality" that consists in mere emotional aversion, no matter how widespread, is a morality only in a weak "anthropological sense" and is undeserving of legal enforcement. Indeed, "the belief that prejudices, personal aversions, and rationalizations do not justify restricting another's freedom itself occupies a critical and fundamental position in our popular morality."[24] The consensus judgment in our community that homosexuality is wicked, in Dworkin's view, is not a genuine moral judgment at all, and "what is shocking and wrong is not [Devlin's] idea that the community's morality counts, but his idea of what counts as the community's morality."[25]

Dworkin's point is a good one against Devlin's position on sexual offenses, but I would go much further still. Even if there is a *genuine* moral consensus in a community that certain sorts of "harmless" activities are wrong, I see no reason why that consensus should be enforced by the criminal law and at least one very good reason why it ought not to be enforced: even a genuine "discriminatory" popular morality might, for all of that, be *mistaken*, and legal enforcement inhibits critical dissent and prevents progressive improvement.

Among the nonsexual morals offenses, cruelty to animals is the most interesting hard case for the application of liberty-limiting principles. Suppose that John Doe is an intelligent, sensitive person with one very neurotic trait—he loves to see living things suffer pain. Fortunately, he never has occasion to torture human beings (he would genuinely regret that) for he can always find an animal for the purpose. For a period he locks himself in his room every night, carefully draws the blind, and then beats and tortures a dog to death. The sounds of shrieks and moans, which are music to his ears, are nuisances however to his neighbors; and when his landlady discovers what he has been doing, she is so shocked she has to be hospitalized. Distressed that he has caused harm to human beings, Doe leaves the rooming house, buys a five-hundred acre ranch, and moves into a house in the remote unpopulated center of his own property. There in the perfect privacy of his own home, he spends every evening maiming, torturing, and beating to death his own animals.

What are we to say of Doe's bizarre behavior? We have three alternatives. First we can say that it is perfectly permissible consisting as it does simply in a man's destruction of his own property. How a man disposes in private of his own property is no concern of anyone else providing he causes no nuisance such as loud noises and evil smells. Second, we can say that this behavior is patently immoral even though it causes no harm to the interests of anyone other than the actor; and further, since it obviously should not be permitted by the law, that this is a case where the harm and offense principles are inadequate and must be supplemented by legal moralism. Third, we can extend the harm principle to animals and argue that the law can interfere with the private enjoyment of property in this case not to enforce "morality as such" but rather to prevent harm to the animals. The third alternative is the most inviting, but it is not without its difficulties. We *must* control animal movements, exploit animal labor, and in many cases, deliberately slaughter animals. All these forms of treatment would be "harm" if inflicted on human beings, but cannot be allowed to count as harm to animals if the harm principle is to be extended to animals in a realistic way. The best compromise is to recognize one supreme interest of animals, namely the interest in freedom from cruelly or wantonly inflicted pain, and to count as "harm" all and only invasions of *that* interest.

IV

Up to this point we have considered the harm and offense principles together in order to determine whether between them they are sufficient to regulate conventional immoralities, or whether they need help from some further independent principle (legal moralism). Morals offenses were treated as essentially private so that the offense principle could not be stretched to apply to them. Obscene literature is quite different in this respect. It is material deliberately published for the eyes of others, and its existence can bring partisans of the unsupplemented harm and offense principles into head-on conflict.

"Obscenity" has both an ordinary and a technical legal sense. In the untechnical pre-legal sense, it refers to material dealing with nudity, sex, or excretion in an offensive manner. Such material becomes obscene in the legal sense when either because of its offensiveness or for some other reason (this question had best be left open in the definition), it is or ought to be without legal protection. The legal sense then incorporates the everyday one, and essential to both is the requirement that the material be *offensive*. One and the same item may offend one person and not another. "Obscenity," if it is to avoid this subjective relativity, must involve an interpersonal objective sense of "offensive." For material to be offensive in the requisite sense it must be so by prevailing community standards that are public and well known, or be such that it is apt to offend virtually everyone.

The American Civil Liberties Union, adopting an approach characteristic of both the friends and the foes of censorship in an earlier period, insists that the offensiveness of obscenity is much too trivial a ground to warrant prior restraint or censorship.[26] The A.C.L.U. argument for this position treats literature, drama, and painting as forms of expression subject to the same rules as expressions of opinion. The power to censor and punish, it maintains, involves risks of great magnitude that socially valuable material will be repressed along with the "filth"; and the overall effect of suppression, it insists, can only be to discourage nonconformist and eccentric expression generally. In order to override these serious risks, the A.C.L.U. concludes, there must be in a given case an even more clear and present danger that the obscene material, if not squelched, will cause even greater harm; and evidence of this countervailing kind is never forthcoming (especially when "mere offense" is not counted as a kind of harm).

The A.C.L.U. stand on obscenity seems clearly to be the position dictated by the unsupplemented harm principles and their corollary, the clear and present danger test. Is there any reason at this point to introduce the offense principle into the discussion? Unhappily, we may be forced to do just that if we are to do justice to all of our particular intuitions in the most harmonious way. Consider an example suggested by Louis B. Schwartz. By the provisions of the new Model Penal Code, he writes, "a rich homosexual may not use a billboard on Times Square to promulgate to the general populace the techniques and pleasures of sodomy."[27] If the notion of "harm" is restricted to its narrow sense that is contrasted with "offense," it will be hard to reconstruct a rationale for this prohibition that is based on a harm principle. It is unlikely that there would be evidence that a lurid and obscene public poster in Times Square would create a clear and present danger of injury to those unfortunate persons who fail to avert their eyes in time as they come blinking out of the subway stations. And yet it will be surpassingly difficult even for the most dedicated liberal to advocate freedom of expression in a case of this kind. Hence, if we are to justify coercion in this case, we will likely be driven, however reluctantly, to the offense principle.

There is good reason to be "reluctant" to embrace the offense principle until driven to it by an example of the above kind. People take offense—perfectly genuine offense—at many socially useful or harmless activities, from commercial advertisements to inane chatter. Moreover, as we have seen, irrational prejudices of a very widespread kind can lead people to be disgusted, shocked, even morally repelled by perfectly innocent activities, and we should be loath to permit their groundless repugnance to override the innocence. The offense principle, therefore, must be formulated in a very precise way so as not to open the door to wholesale and intuitively unwarranted repression.

It is instructive to note that a strictly drawn offense principle would not only justify prohibition of public conduct and publicly pictured conduct that is in its inherent character repellent (e.g., buggery, bestiality, sexual sado-masochism), but also conduct and pictured conduct that is inoffensive in itself but offensive only when it occurs in inappropriate circumstances. I have in mind so-called indecencies such as public nudity. One can imagine an advocate of the harm principle more extreme (and perhaps more consistent) even than J. S. Mill who argues against the public nudity prohibition on the grounds that the sight of a naked body does no one any harm and that the state has no right to impose any given standards of dress or undress on private citizens. How one chooses to dress, after all, is a form of self-expression. If we do not permit the state to bar clashing colors, or bizarre hair styles, by what right does it prohibit total undress? Perhaps the sight of naked people could lead to riots or other forms of anti-social behavior, but that is precisely the sort of contingency for which we have police. If we don't take away a man's right of free speech for the reason that its exercise may lead others to misbehave, we cannot in consistency deny his right to dress or undress as he chooses for the same reason.

There may be no answering this challenge on its own ground; but the offense principle provides a special rationale of its own for the nudity prohibition. There is no doubt that the sight of nude bodies in public places is for almost everyone acutely *embarrassing*. Part of the explanation, no doubt, rests on the fact that nudity has an irresistible power to draw the eye and focus the thoughts on matters that are normally repressed. The conflict between these attracting and repressing forces, between allure and disgust,[28] is exciting, upsetting, and anxiety-producing. In most persons it will create a kind of painful turmoil at best and at worst, that experience of exposure to oneself of one's "peculiarly sensitive, intimate, vulnerable aspects"[29] which is called *shame*. When one has not been able to prepare one's defenses, "one's feeling is involuntarily exposed openly in one's face. . . . We are . . . caught unawares, made a fool of."[30] For many people the result is not mere "offense," but a kind of psychic jolt that can be a painful wound. Those better able to cope with their feelings might well resent the necessity to do so and regard it as an irritating distraction and a bore, much the same as any other nuisance.[31]

V

If we are to accept the offense principle as a supplement to the harm principles, we must accept two mediating norms of interpretation which stand to it in a way similar to that in which the clear and present danger test stands to the harm principles. The first is the *standard of universality* which has already been touched upon. The interracial couple strolling hand in hand down the streets of Jackson, Mississippi, without question cause shock and mortification, even shame and disgust, to the overwhelming majority of white pedestrians who happen to observe them; but we surely don't want our offense principle applied to justify preventive coercion on that ground. To avoid that consequence let us stipulate that in order for "offense" (repugnance, embarrassment, shame, etc.) to be sufficient to warrant coercion, it should be the reaction that could reasonably be expected from almost any person chosen at random, taking the nation as a whole, and not because the individual selected belongs to some faction, clique, or party.

That qualification should be more than sufficient to protect the interracial couple, but, alas, it may yield undesirable consequences in another class of cases. I have in mind abusive, mocking, insulting behavior or speech attacking specific subgroups of the population—especially ethnic, racial, or religious groups. Public cross-burnings, displays of swastikas, "jokes" that ridicule Americans of Polish descent told on public media, public displays of banners with large and abusive caricatures of the Pope[32] are extremely offensive to the groups so insulted, and no doubt also offensive to large numbers of sympathetic outsiders. But still, there will be many millions of people who will not respond emotionally at all, and many millions more who may secretly approve. Thus, our amended offense principle will not justify the criminal proscription of such speech or conduct. I am inclined, therefore, simply to patch up that principle in an *ad hoc* fashion once more. For that special class of offensive behavior (only one of several distinct kinds of offensiveness distinguished in Part II above) that consists in the flaunting of abusive, mocking, insulting behavior of a sort bound to upset, alarm, anger, or irritate those it insults, I would allow the offense principle to apply, even though the behavior would *not* offend the entire population. Those who are taunted by such conduct will understandably suffer intense and complicated emotions. They might be frightened or wounded; and their blood might boil in wrath. Yet the law cannot permit them to accept the challenge and vent their anger in retaliatory aggression. But again, having to cope with one's rage is as burdensome a bore as having to suffer shame, or disgust, or noisome stenches, and the law might well undertake to protect those who are vulnerable, even if they are—indeed, precisely because they are—a minority.[33]

The second mediating principle for the application of the offense principle is the standard of reasonable avoidability. No one has a right to protection from the state against offensive experiences if he can easily and effectively avoid those experiences with no unreasonable effort or inconvenience. If a nude person enters a public bus and takes a seat near the front, there may be no effective way whatever for the other patrons to avoid intensely shameful embarrassment (or other insupportable feelings) short of leaving the bus themselves, which would be an unreasonable inconvenience. Similarly, obscene remarks over a loudspeaker, homosexual billboards in Times Square, pornographic handbills thrust into the hands of passing pedestrians all fail to be reasonably avoidable.

On the other hand, the offense principle, properly qualified, can give no warrant to the suppression of *books* on the grounds of obscenity. When printed words hide decorously behind covers of books sitting passively on the shelves of a bookstore, their offensiveness is easily avoided. The contrary view is no doubt encouraged by the common comparison of obscenity with "smut," "filth," or "dirt." This in turn suggests an analogy to nuisance law, which governs cases where certain activities create loud noises or terrible odors offensive to neighbors, and "the courts must weigh the gravity of the nuisance [substitute "offense"] to the neighbors against the social utility [substitute "redeeming social value"] of the defendant's conduct."[34] There is, however, one vitiating disanalogy in this comparison. In the case of "dirty books," the offense is easily avoidable. There is nothing like the evil smell of rancid garbage oozing right out through the covers of a book whether one looks at it or not. When an "obscene" book sits on a shelf, who is there to be offended? Those who want to read it for the sake of erotic stimulation presumably will not be offended (else they wouldn't read it), and those who choose not to read it will have no experience of it to be offended by. If its covers are too decorous, some innocents may browse through it by mistake and then be offended by what they find, but they need only close the book again to escape the offense. Even this offense, minimal as it is, could be completely avoided by a prior consulting of trusted book reviewers. Moreover, no one forces a customer to browse randomly, and if he is informed in advance of the risk of risqué passages, he should be prepared to shoulder that risk himself without complaint. I conclude that there are no sufficient grounds derived either from the harm or offense principles for suppressing obscene literature, unless that ground be the protection of children; but I see no reason why selective prohibitions for children could not work as well in the case of books as in the cases of cigarettes and whiskey.

Two further restrictions on the offense principle are necessary. The first is implicit in the universality principle but is important enough to be made fully explicit and emphatic. In applying the offense principle, no respect should be shown for *abnormal susceptibilities*. Here again the law of nuisance provides a fitting model. In one typical tort case, for example, the court ruled that "it is not a nuisance to ring a church bell merely because it throws a hypersensitive individual into convulsions."[35] In deciding what kind of conduct is sufficiently annoying to qualify as a nuisance, says Prosser, "some other standard must obviously be adopted than the personal tastes, susceptibilities, and idiosyncrasies of the particular plaintiff. The standard must necessarily be that of definite offensiveness or annoyance to *the normal person in the community.*"[36]

A similar standard in the criminal law would protect us all from homosexual billboards in Times Square, but not from billboard pictures of fully clothed heterosexual lovers. There is one kind of offended sensibility that can certainly not satisfy such a standard, namely the shock or disappointment occasioned by the bare knowledge (no pun intended) that other persons are, or may be, doing immoral things in private. The offense principle cannot be used as a life-raft to save the shipwrecked legal moralist. It is conceivable, I suppose, that there be a person whose moral sensibilities are so tender that bare knowledge of the existence of private "harmless immoralities" would lead to severe mental distress; but in such a case, it would be more plausible to attribute the distress to abnormal susceptibilities than to the precipitating cause. If a sneeze causes a glass window to break, we should blame the weakness or brittleness of the glass and not the sneeze. The offense principle is not different from the private harm principle in this respect: the application of both requires some conception of *normalcy*. It is the person of normal vulnerability whose interests are to be protected by coercive power; the person who, figuratively speaking, can be blown over by a sneeze, cannot demand that other people's vigorous but *normally* harmless activities be suspended by government power for his protection. He can demand protection only against conduct that would harm or offend the normal person in his position. The further protection he needs he must provide for himself—and of course he must be *permitted* to provide for himself—by noncoercive methods.[37]

The final condition for the safe use of the offense principle is that the person constrained by the law from being offensive to others must be granted an allowable alternative outlet or mode of expression, perhaps on analogy with temporary restrictions on free speech based on anti-littering statutes, public expense, or public inconvenience. The public interest in clean streets, perhaps, can justify a municipal restraining order against the distribution of political handbills, but the restraint obviously goes too far if it prevents handouts even by persons willing themselves to clean up the debris or pay for the job, or if it prevents mailings of handbills, and all other modes of dissemination. Similarly, an exhibition of

naked love-making or its depiction on the city streets can be banned
by the offense principle, but the restraint goes too far if it prevents
the same conduct or represented conduct from being shown in a
private home or rented theatre to an eager and willing voluntary
audience. The offense principle cannot justify the prohibition of
"offensive" conduct even where it does not offend, without under-
going metamorphosis into the unpalatable principle of legal moralism.

NOTES

1. I use the word "justified" in the formulation of these principles in
such a way that it does not follow from the fact that a given limitation on
liberty is justified that the state has a duty to impose it, but only that the
state *may* interfere on the ground in question if it should choose to do so.
Cf. Ted Honderich, *Punishment: Its Supposed Justifications* (Hutchinson
of London, 1969), p. 175. Moreover, as these principles are formulated
here, they state sufficient but not necessary conditions for "justified" (that
is, permissible) coercion. Each states that interference is permissible *if* (but
not *only if*) a certain condition is satisfied. Hence the principles are not
mutually exclusive; it is possible to hold two or more of them at once, even
all of them together. And it is possible to deny all of them. In fact, since
all combinations and permutations of these principles are (logically) possible, there are 2^7 or 128 possible positions (and more) about the legitimacy of coercion represented by the list.

2. For recent detailed discussions of the principle of legal paternalism,
see Gerald Dworkin, "Paternalism" in *Morality and the Law*, ed. Richard
Wasserstrom (Belmont, Cal.: Wadsworth, 1971), and Joel Feinberg, "Legal Paternalism," *Canadian Journal of Philosophy* 1 (1971): 105–24.

3. I shall not discuss the merits and defects of extreme paternalism and
the welfare principle in this paper. Both principles presuppose that sense
can be made out of the difficult distinctions between benefitting and not
harming, and harming and not benefitting.

4. J. S. Mill, *On Liberty*, Chapter 5, paragraph 7.

5. These are the matters discussed collectively under the rubric "Of
the Liberty of Thought and Discussion" in Chapter II of *On Liberty*. As
Harry Kalven points out, Mill neglects to include "the novel, the poem,
the painting, the drama, or the piece of sculpture" among those expressions that have an extreme social value. The emphasis in Mill, as in Chafee
and Meiklejohn, is "all on truth winning out in a fair fight between competing ideas." See Kalven's "Metaphysics of the Law of Obscenity," in

1960: The Supreme Court Review, ed. Philip B. Kurland (Chicago: University of Chicago Press, 1960), pp. 15–16.

6. Mill's view, then, as I have interpreted it, is strikingly similar to that expressed in the majority opinion by Mr. Justice Brennan in *United States vs. Roth* (1957) except that the latter has a conception of "social value" broad enough to include works of art.

7. H. L. A. Hart, *Law, Liberty, and Morality* (Stanford, Cal.: Stanford University Press, 1963), p. 45.

8. Traditionally, offensiveness has tended to arouse even more extreme penalties than harmfulness. The New York Penal Law, for example, until recently provided a maximum sentence of ten years for first degree assault and twenty years for sodomy; Pennsylvania's Penal Code provides a maximum of seven years for assault with intent to kill and ten years for pandering; California provides a maximum of two years for corporal injury to wife or child but fifteen years for "perversion." Mayhem and assault with intent to commit a serious felony get fourteen and twenty years, respectively, in California, but statutory rape and incest get fifty years each. Zechariah Chafee gives the best example I know of perverse judicial zeal to avenge mere offense: "The white slave traffic was first exposed by W. T. Stead in a magazine article, 'The Maiden Tribute.' The English law did absolutely nothing to the profiteers in vice, but put Stead in prison for a year for writing about an indecent subject" (Z. Chafee, *Free Speech in the United States* [Cambridge, Mass.: Harvard University Press, 1964], p. 151). It is worth noting, finally, that the most common generic synonym for "crimes" is neither "harms" nor "injuries," but "offenses."

9. For example, "One has only to stroll along certain streets in Amsterdam to see that prostitution may be permitted to flourish openly without impairing personal security, economic prosperity, or indeed the general moral tone of a most respected nation of the Western world" (Louis B. Schwartz, "Morals Offenses and the Model Penal Code," *Columbia Law Review* 63 [1963]: 670).

10. *Ibid.*, p. 672.

11. Herbert Packer, *The Limits of the Criminal Sanction* (Stanford, Cal.: Stanford University Press, 1968), p. 260.

12. The distinction between immorality and indecency is well put by H. L. A. Hart: "Sexual intercourse between husband and wife is not immoral, but if it takes place in public, it is an affront to public decency. Homosexual intercourse between consenting adults in private is immoral according to conventional morality, but not an affront to public decency, though it would be if it took place in public" (*Law, Liberty, and Morality*, p. 44).

13. Patrick Devlin, *The Enforcement of Morals* (London: Oxford University Press, 1965).

14. The phrase is not Devlin's but rather that of his critic, H. L. A.

Hart, in *Law, Liberty, and Morality*, p. 51. In his rejoinder to Hart, Devlin writes: "Seamlessness presses the simile rather hard, but apart from that, I should say that for most people morality is a web of beliefs, rather than a number of unconnected ones" (Devlin, *Enforcement*, p. 115).

15.   Devlin, *Enforcement*, pp. 13–14.

16.   Hart, *Law, Liberty, and Morality*, p. 51.

17.   Devlin, *Enforcement*, pp. 115ff.

18.   *Ibid.*, p. 116.

19.   Mill, *On Liberty*, Chapter 2, paragraph 14.

20.   James Fitzjames Stephen, *Liberty, Equality, Fraternity* (London, 1873), p. 163.

21.   *Ibid.*, p. 159.

22.   Cf. C. D. Broad, "Certain Features in Moore's Ethical Doctrines," in *The Philosophy of G. E. Moore*, ed. P. A. Schilpp, (Evanston: Northwestern University Press, 1942), pp. 48ff.

23.   Ronald Dworkin, "Lord Devlin and the Enforcement of Morals," *Yale Law Journal*, 75 (1966).

24.   *Ibid.*, p. 1001.

25.   *Loc. cit.*

26.   "Obscenity and Censorship" (New York: American Civil Liberties Union, March, 1963). The approach that was characteristic of the late fifties and early sixties was to assimilate the obscenity question to developed free speech doctrine requiring a showing of a "clear and present danger" of substantive harm to justify government suppression. Obscene materials pertaining to sex (but not excretion!) were taken to be dangerous, if at all, because they are *alluring* and thus capable of tempting persons into antisocial (harmful) conduct. As Herbert Packer points out (*Limits of Criminal Sanction*, p. 319) the clear and present danger test is virtually certain to be passed by even the most offensive materials. Of proposals made in the fifties that such a test be used, he writes: "It is difficult to know whether these suggestions were advanced seriously or tongue in cheek. It seems clear that, conscientiously applied, they would lead to exoneration in all but the most bizarre cases. I prefer to regard them as, in effect, calling the bluff of proponents of the traditional tests. 'If you really are concerned with dangerous tendencies rather than with immorality as such, then put up or shut up.' " In most cases, as it turned out, the arch enemies of obscenity were indeed concerned with "immorality as such." Even the Model Penal Code rule that so influenced the U.S. Supreme Court in the famous *Roth* and *Ginsburg* decisions seems to imply that the existence of sexual thoughts of a "prurient" kind is an inherent evil, and appeal to "prurient interests" a form of wickedness, apart from consequences.

27.   Schwartz, "Morals Offenses," p. 681.

28.   Use of the word "filthy" to express disgust and revulsion at vulgar treatments of sexual matters, according to Harry Kalven, "points to an

evil of obscenity which is the exact opposite of that usually recognized: the obscene is bad because it is revolting, not because it is alluring." Kalven then goes on to chide the courts for an apparent inconsistency: "Since it [obscenity] cannot be both [revolting and alluring] at the same time for the same audience, it would be well to have more explicit guidance as to which objection controls." Kalven here misses the most important (and elusive) point about obscenity: it *can* be both alluring and revolting at the same time to the same person. Attraction and disgust are often both involved in the complex mechanism of shameful embarrassment, the most distinctive mode of offensiveness produced by obscenity. The quotations are from Kalven's otherwise excellent and very helpful article, "The Metaphysics of the Law of Obscenity," pp. 41–42.

29. Helen Lynd, *On Shame and the Search for Identity* (New York: Science Editions, 1961), p. 33.

30. *Ibid.*, p. 32.

31. There are, of course, those who apparently *enjoy* the tension between allure and disgust, who find its inner turmoil and excitement "thrilling" and actively seek it out, very much as youngsters seek out roller coasters and other exciting rides at amusement parks for the thrill of sensations that are normally alarming and generally taken to be disagreeable. The analogy, I think, is close. In both cases, persons should be permitted to seek and "enjoy" the thrilling sensations, but no person should ever have such sensations imposed upon him without his consent.

32. For a penetrating discussion of an actual case of this description see Zechariah Chafee, *Free Speech in the United States* (Cambridge, Mass.: Harvard University Press, 1964), p. 161.

33. As indeed the laws in many states do. Section 722 of the New York Penal Law, for example, specifies punishment for "disorderly, threatening, insulting language or behavior in public places, and acts which annoy, obstruct, or are offensive to others." A showing of a clear and present danger of substantive harm is presumably not required. In 1939, in a typical prosecution, one Ninfo, a Christian Front street orator, was convicted under this statute for saying "If I had my way, I would hang all the Jews in this country. I wish I had $100,000 from Hitler. I would show those damn Jews what I would do, you mockies, you damn Jews, you scum." See David Riesman, "Democracy and Defamation: Control of Group Libel," *Columbia Law Review*, 42 (1942): 751ff. Reisman discusses not only offensive insults to groups, but the more complex question of group defamation.

34. William L. Prosser, *Handbook of the Law of Torts* (St. Paul: West Publishing Co., 1955).

35. *Rogers v. Elliott* (Massachusetts, 1888).

36. Prosser, *Handbook*, pp. 395–96. Emphasis added.

37. On the other hand, the abnormally vulnerable person should be protected from deliberate and malicious attempts to seek him out, pursue and harass him, and exploit his vulnerability for no respectable purpose.

Reply

Bayles' comments illuminate most of the matters they touch and advance the discussion to a higher level of clarity. Formulating adequate normative principles to govern the political control of private conduct, we both agree, can be construed as a task for a philosophical "ideal legislator." Bayles has my vote for that office, despite the minor disagreements that persist between us. Here I can only comment briefly on some of the issues he raises.

1. *The status of liberty-limiting principles.* Bayles' interpretation of various proposed grounds for justified state interference in private affairs is a definite improvement over my own, and I am grateful to him for it. Liberty-limiting principles are best understood as stating neither necessary nor sufficient conditions for justified coercion, but rather only specifications of the *kinds* of reasons that are always relevant or acceptable in support of proposed coercion even though in a given case they may not be conclusive. As defined in my article, these principles are not mutually exclusive, since it is possible to hold two or more of them at once, even all of them together. Hence, a liberty-limiting principle states considerations that are always good reasons for coercion, though neither exclusively nor, in every case, decisively good reasons.

This improved interpretation is especially welcome in that it protects my highly qualified "offense principle" from quick and facile counter-examples. Some critics (but not Bayles) have argued that my position would justify the prohibition of minor eccentricities of fashion or taste, for example, extremely long hair on men or crew cuts on women, provided only that they cause the most exiguous irritation to the overwhelming majority of onlookers. But all that my re-interpreted principle declares about these cases is that the fact of irritation is relevant to the question of the permissibility of the conduct in question, and relevant only if (or only because) it is nearly universal. Nevertheless, a relevant consideration can be outweighed by relevant reasons on the other side, and a merely exiguous irritation does not have much weight of its own. The necessity for balancing conflicting considerations is not peculiar to the offense principle. The harm principle, for example, does not justify state interference to prevent a tiny bit of inconsequential harm merely. The prevention of minor harm always counts in favor of proposals (say, in a legislature) to restrict liberty, but in a given instance it might not count *enough* to outweigh the general presumption against interference, or it might be outweighed by the prospect of practical difficulties of enforcement, excessive costs, forfeitures of privacy, and the like.

Moreover, when a legislature considers whether it should protect one set of private interests by interfering with still other private interests, obviously it must weigh those conflicting interests against one another to determine which are more "worthy" or "important" in general, and how heavily the general interests sit on the scale in cases of the kind under consideration. Like Herbert Packer, I hold that obscenity should be treated more as a nuisance than as a menace, and nuisance law, with its various tests for the balancing of interests, provides a model for how this might be done. (Indeed, nuisance law seems to be the model for the Supreme Court's *Roth* formula which Bayles chides me for neglecting.)

William L. Prosser, in his justly famous and philosophically rewarding text on the law of torts,[1] tells us that "nuisance" is a term with two distinct uses in the law: " 'Public nuisance' is a term applied to a miscellaneous group of minor criminal offenses . . . and 'private nuisance' is . . . applied to unreasonable interference with the interest of an individual in the use or enjoyment of land. . . . The reasonableness of the interference [Prosser continues] is determined by weighing the gravity of the harm to the plaintiff against the utility of the defendant's conduct."[2] So long as the interference is substantial and "such as would be offensive or incon-

venient to the normal person,"[3] the law will protect landowners
from it, provided it is not the unavoidable consequence of socially
important activities. But such interferences are not nuisances
where the annoyance is slight and the offending conduct reasonable.[4] Weighing the gravity of the "harm" to the plaintiff requires
the consideration of numerous factors: the extent and duration of
the interference and its precise character, the social value the plaintiff makes of his land, and the ease or difficulty of the means of
avoiding the harm are among them.

On the defendant's balance pan, still other factors must be
weighed:

> the utility of his conduct is always affected by the social value which
> the law attaches to its ultimate purpose. The world must have fac-
> tories, smelters, oil refineries, noisy machinery, and blasting even at
> the expense of some inconvenience to those in the vicinity, and the
> plaintiff may be required to accept and tolerate some not unreason-
> able discomfort for the general good. . . . On the other hand, a
> foul pond, or a vicious or noisy dog will have little if any social val-
> ue, and relatively slight annoyance from it may justify relief.[5]

Moreover, the defendant's conduct is unreasonable if it has a malicious or spiteful *motive*, or if alternative modes of conduct less
annoying to his neighbors are reasonably open to him. Finally,
Prosser concludes, "the interest of the community or the public at
large must also be thrown into the scale along with those of the
contending parties. . . ."[6]

It is not difficult to see how the interest-balancing model would
apply to the interracial couple in Mississippi. The interests of the
couple in free association and movement are of a kind considered
so fundamentally important to everyone that their protection is
commonly included in lists of inalienable human rights. The normal, spontaneous, joint comings and goings of the couple, free of
fear and anxiety, can plausibly be regarded by each of them as indispensable to a decent life. On the other side of the scale, there is
mere momentary repugnance in the eye of the casual beholder,
hardly as "weighty" a matter. Similarly, the state is ready to protect travelers on public buses or trains from severe offense or an-

noyance caused by the conduct of their fellow passengers, e.g. from shrill noises, overt sexual play, nudity, and so on; but the state will not prevent passengers from engaging in fatuous idle chatter in the presence of neighboring passengers, no matter how severe the annoyance, or the sheer boredom, induced in the unwilling auditor; for the interest in relaxed and spontaneous talk is deemed far more worthy of protection, on grounds both of private preference and public utility, than the interest in freedom from boredom. But that is not to say that the auditor's interest has no weight at all.

2. *Criminal and noncriminal prohibitions.* I also wish to acknowledge Bayles' important point that the criminal law is only one of numerous alternative devices for the control of undesirable conduct, and the one which carries the heaviest social costs. Some offensive conduct, no doubt, can be prevented more economically by reliance on individual suits for injunctions, or by court orders initiated by police to cease and desist on pain of penalty, or by licensing procedures that rely on administrative suspension of license as a sanction. These alternatives would not entirely dispose of the need for punishment as a back-up threat (or "sanction of last resort"), as Bayles admits, but punishment would not be inflicted for offending others so much as for defying authority by persisting in prohibited conduct. I doubt very much, however, whether all properly prohibitable offensive conduct could be controlled by such techniques. In some cases, we can know very well in advance that conduct of a certain kind will offend, that is, we don't have to wait for the particular circumstances to decide the question. Moreover, in some cases, there will not be time to get an injunction or an administrative hearing. By the time that sort of relief is forthcoming, the annoyance has come and gone, and the "harm," such as it is, has been done. In cases of that kind, the "interest-balancing" is done in advance by legislators, and the state issues a kind of blanket protection instead of a specific restraining order addressed to a specific person. In any case, I agree with Bayles that the penalty for merely offensive "harmless" conduct ought always to be less than that for conduct that threatens injury to individuals or harm to public institutions and practices.

3. *Offensive conduct and free speech*. Bayles regrets that I did not find time in my original paper to discuss more thoroughly the connection between the offense principle and the right of free speech. In particular, he criticizes me for failure to bring my brief early discussion of free expression to bear on the examples of obscene billboards and speech abusive of minorities. Let me try to remedy things here. I emphatically agree with Mill, Chafee, Meiklejohn, and Bayles that there is a greater presumption in favor of free expression than for freedoms of most other kinds, partly because the individual interest in free expression is so strong, and partly because unimpeded general discussion is vitally necessary to the general search for truth, which in turn is indispensably important to a myriad of public interests. I am so impressed by the case that Mill and other libertarians have made for the personal and social value of free expression that I would *never* permit the state to restrict or punish the expression of opinion[7] on the grounds of mere offensiveness. But it is crucial at this point in the discussion to make a distinction among the possible *sources* of offense in an offensive utterance. (Such a distinction will inevitably raise perplexities about the classification of difficult borderline cases, but, alas, that difficulty seems to attend most of the distinctions that lawyers and legislators must make.) One can be offended by the *opinion* expressed or implied by an utterance, as a devout Christian, for example, might be offended by the bare assertion of atheism, or one might be offended by something other than an expressed opinion, for example, an obscene poster of Jesus and Mary. The offending conduct might not involve the use of language at all; or it might be an utterance with no clear propositional content at all; or the expressed opinion might be only incidental to the cause of offense which is located in the manner and context of expression.

A recent Supreme Court case conveniently illustrates the distinction made above (and its difficulty). It was a hard case for the court because it involved the expression of political opinion in obscene language:

> WASHINGTON (Gannett News Service)—"Dissent by its nature involves the right to be offensive" said a lawyer, defending the public

use of "one of the most notorious four-letter words in the English language" before the U. S. Supreme Court.

A basic purpose of the U. S. Constitution's First Amendment (guaranteeing freedom of speech) is to protect offensive statements, argued attorney Melville B. Nimmer. His client, a California man, had been arrested for appearing in public wearing a jacket emblazoned with "F— The Draft."

The First Amendment, said Nimmer, protects the writings of Josef Stalin and Adolf Hitler, which are "more offensive than this word."

The appellant, Paul Robert Cohen, had worn the jacket in the corridor of the Los Angeles Municipal Court. Women and children were present.

Cohen was convicted of engaging in "tumultuous and offensive conduct" and sentenced to 30 days in county jail.

As the one-hour long argument opened Monday Chief Justice Warren E. Burger seemed to be implying that he'd just as soon the word itself weren't uttered in the courtroom: "The court is thoroughly familiar with the facts of the case and it will not be necessary for you to dwell on them," he said.

But Nimmer managed to utter the word—an Anglo-Saxon one meaning sexual intercourse—the one time it was spoken during the argument.

The court will probably rule on the case within a month or two. (*Mamaroneck Daily Times*, Feb. 23, 1971)

I will not venture an opinion about the constitutional issues in this case, but I can point out how Mill's kind of liberal principles, which I attempted to clarify in my article, would apply. Mill would argue that no political opinion whatever can rightly be banned merely on the ground that it is offensive. Thus one can shout to a crowd, or carry a sign or words on one's back, to the effect that we should abandon democracy for Nazism or Communism, that our troops should invade Thailand or bomb China, that sexual intercourse in public should be permitted, or that the Catholic Church should be nationalized—offensive as these opinions may be to many people. Similarly, one can condemn the draft and advocate its repeal, and do this in the imperative or exclamatory moods. But to forbid the public display of the sentence "Fuck the draft" is not to ban the expression of a political opinion because *it* (the opinion) is offensive; rather it is to ban the public use of a single word whose offensiveness, such as it is, has nothing to do with political opinion. If twins had appeared in the corridor of the Los Angeles Municipal Court, one wearing a jacket emblazoned with the single word "Fuck" and the other with the words "Down with the draft," only the former could rightly be banned on Mill's principles.[8]

It should be clear, then, how my qualified offense principle would handle "thematic obscenity." It would permit public *advocacy*, whether on billboards, or soap boxes, or in magazines, of *any* "values" whatever, pertaining to sex, religion, politics, or anything else; but it would not permit graphic portrayals on billboards of homosexual (or heterosexual) couplings. So precious is free speech on questions of public policy, however, that public *advocacy* of laws permitting graphically obscene billboards should be permitted. Indeed, public advocacy even of the legalization of homicide should be permitted provided the manner of advocacy itself is not offensive in one of the ways recognized by the qualified offense principle.

4. *My use of examples.* Bayles writes that there are "essentially three types of cases" which drive me, reluctantly, to the offense principle, namely, "obscene billboards, speech abusive of minorities, and public nudity." I did employ these examples prominently in my argument, but they are by no means the only kinds of examples I might have used. I might very well have discussed other examples of indecency and "flaunting and taunting," and examples of the other major categories of offense that I listed (irritating sensations, disgust and repugnance, shocked sensibilities) and still other categories not included in my miscellaneous and open-ended list of types of "offended mental states," e.g. acute boredom. So there was nothing "essential" in the examples that I did use. I selected them simply for their familiarity, vividness, and (I hoped) special persuasiveness.

I should like to take this opportunity to try one final example and to rest my case on it. It is an example that illustrates not just one but virtually all the categories of offensiveness mentioned in my article; and if the reader fails to concede that it provides a legitimate occasion for legal interference with a citizen's conduct on grounds other than harmfulness, then I must abandon my effort to convince him at all, at least by the use of examples. Consider then the man who walks down the main street of a town at mid-day. In the middle of a block in the central part of town, he stops, opens his briefcase, and pulls out a portable folding camp-toilet. In the prescribed manner, he attaches a plastic bag to its under side, sets it on the sidewalk, and proceeds to defecate in it, to the utter amazement and disgust of the passers-by. While he is thus relieving himself, he unfolds a large banner which reads "This is what I think of the Ruritanians" (substitute "Niggers," "Kikes," "Spics," "Dagos," "Polacks," or "Hunkies"). Another placard placed prominently next to him invites ladies to join him in some of the more bizarre sexual-excretory perversions mentioned in Kraft-Ebbing and includes a large-scale graphic painting of the conduct he solicits. For those who avert their eyes too quickly, he plays an obscene phonograph record on a small portable machine, and accompanies its raunchier parts with grotesquely lewd bodily motions. He concludes his public performance by tasting some of his own excrement, and after savouring it slowly and thoroughly in the manner of a true epicure, he consumes it. He then dresses, ties the plastic bag containing the rest of the excrement, places it carefully in his briefcase, and continues on his way.

Now I would not have the man in the example executed, or severely punished. I'm not sure I would want him punished at all, unless he defied authoritative orders to "move along" or to cease and desist in the future. But I would surely want the coercive arm of the state to protect passers-by (by the most economical and humane means) from being unwilling audiences for such performances. I assume in the example (I hope with some plausibility) that the offensive conduct causes no harm or injury either of a public or a private kind. After all, if the numerous tons of dog dung dropped every day on the streets of New York are no health hazard, then surely the fastidious use of a sanitary plastic bag cannot be seriously unhygienic.

5. *The problem of change.* Bayles is quite right again when he observes that the offense principle is dependent on "cultural standards that constantly and rapidly change." Even public defecation is common and inoffensive in many parts of the world, and there are many examples of conduct that was once universally offensive in our country but is now commonplace. I must grant these facts, but as a "reluctant" advocate of the offense principle, I needn't be embarrassed by them. One can imagine similar changes in the conditions for the application of the harm principle, but they don't weaken any one's confidence in that principle. Conduct which is banned at a given time because it spreads disease ought not to be banned at a subsequent time when that disease is rendered harmless by universal vaccination. Similarly, conduct which causes universal offense at a given time, ought not to be banned at a later time when many people no longer are offended, whatever the cause of the change. The two cases seem to me to be on precisely the same footing in this respect.

The fact of cultural change does cause me some embarrassment in another way, however. I now suspect that I was somewhat self-righteous in my criticism of Devlin's treatment of the analogous problem (for him) of moral change. Devlin might well have a *tu quoque* response to make to me. He could ask me a question precisely parallel to the one I asked him, and I would have to give an answer uncomfortably similar to the one he gave that I criticized as "uneconomical and ungenerous." How do the *sensibilities* of people (as opposed to their moral judgments) come to change? Surely one of the more common causes of such change is a steady increase in the number of offending cases. What once caused spontaneous horror, revulsion, shame, or wrath, as it becomes more common, becomes less horrifying and revolting. We become accustomed to it, and hardened against it, and then invulnerable to it, and finally (even) tolerant of it. But what of those offending persons who have the misfortune to engage in a given type of behavior during the transition period between the stage when the qualified offense principle clearly applies and the stage when it clearly no longer can apply? Some of them, no doubt, will be punished for what may be done a year later with impunity—and on my principle, rightly so. These unfortunate chaps are in a way like the last soldiers to be killed in a war. They are treated no worse than those of their predecessors in an earlier period who were punished in the same way for the same thing, but their punishment, coming near the end of an earlier stage of cultural history, is somehow more poignant. To a later tolerant age, they will inevitably appear to be martyrs punished for exercising their rightful liberties a trifle prematurely. More to the point, their conduct had a direct causal influence on the attitudes and sensibilities they were punished for offending. Their punishment was for conduct that helped destroy the very conditions that rendered that kind of conduct criminal in the first place.

Thus, I am in the uncomfortable position of justifying the punishment of, say, anti-war demonstrators in 1965 for parading a Viet-Cong flag (shocking!) while denouncing the punishment of other protestors in 1970 for doing the same thing (yawn). Rapid cultural change will always claim some victims in this way, and perhaps I should sadly conclude that some unfair martyrdom in the transitional stages is simply inevitable, a tragic fact of life. My discomfort in this position is at least mitigated by the thought that martyrs to the cause of cultural change, on my view, should never be subject to more than very minor penalties or coercive pressure. So the "tragedy" of their punishment is not at all that lamentable. Furthermore, "martyrs" of the offense principle are not as repressed as the victims of legal moralism, for they are not deprived of the option of engaging in the offensive behavior in private.

6. *Reasonable and unreasonable offense.* At several places in his comments, Bayles points out that I do not require that universal taking of offense be *reasonable*. Providing only that the offense taken be *genuine* offense and that it be near universal, I allow it substantial weight in legislative deliberations. Others have joined Bayles in insisting that unreasonable offense should have no weight whatever. Sometimes the argument for the latter position deploys

a hypothetical example against me. Suppose (fortunately contrary to fact) that the sight of an interracial couple *did* satisfy my qualifying conditions on the offense principle. Suppose, contrary to fact, that virtually everybody found such a sight intensely and profoundly offensive, and that such a reaction would equally be that of young and old, male and female, liberal and conservative, northerner and southerner, even white and black. Under those imaginary conditions, my principle might (subject to the reservations expressed in section 1, above) justify legal prohibition of the conduct in question, and that consequence is supposed to be embarrassing to me. This sort of example usually disturbs me for a moment until I fully grasp what the imagined circumstances would actually be like, and then invariably, the example begins to lose its intuitive persuasiveness. "What if . . . ," the question always begins: "What if something perfectly innocuous and inoffensive to any reasonable person, say, long hair, or white shirts, or eating chocolate candy in public, were to affect onlookers in some hypothetical society in precisely the way the public eating of excrement affects onlookers in our society?" In response, I am expected to recant and admit that there would be no justification, even in that imaginary community, for legal interference with the eccentric conduct. But as soon as I focus hard on the example and take it seriously on its own terms, it quickly loses all force. If the sight of a person eating chocolate affects all onlookers in that society in *precisely the same way* as the sight of a person eating excrement affects all onlookers in our society, then why should one want the hypothetical law to treat that hypothetical case any differently from the way in which the actual law treats the actual case? The example derives its initial plausibility from the difficulty of imagining that chocolate *could* be as revolting as excrement; but that difficulty, of course, is logically irrelevant.

I am resistant to Bayles' suggestion that I restrict the offense principle to cases of reasonable offense in part because so many of the forms of offense discussed in my article seem to have nothing to do with reasonableness. It is neither reasonable nor unreasonable but simply "nonreasonable" to be bothered by the sight of nude bodies, public defecation, disgusting "food," and the like. One can no more give "reasons" for these culturally determined reactions than one can for the offensiveness of "evil smells." Yet the offended states are real, predictable, unpleasant, and unmodifiable by argument; and these characteristics seem to me clearly to ground *prima facie* claims against the state for protection, claims that *can* be outweighed by stronger claims in the opposing balance pan, but which nevertheless do have some weight of their own.

Other offended states, I must concede, *are* subject to rational appraisal and criticism. It is perfectly reasonable to be offended by the word "nigger," and profoundly contrary to reason to be offended by the sight of an interracial couple. My principles would protect people, in certain circumstances, from reasonable offense, so that category raises no problem. As for most forms of *unreasonable* offense, the very unreasonableness of the reaction will tend to keep it from being sufficiently universal to warrant preventive coercion. As for the handful of remaining cases, there is still a claim for protection, it seems to me, even though offense is taken unreasonably. Providing that very real and intense offense is taken predictably by virtually everyone, and the offending conduct has hardly any countervailing personal or social value of its own, prohibition seems reasonable even where the protected interests themselves are not. Again, there may be parallel cases for the harm principle. We can at least imagine that because of some widespread superstitious (and thus "irrational") belief, virtually all persons in a given community react with such horror to a given type of otherwise innocent conduct that they suffer real physical damage, say to their hearts, whenever confronted with such conduct. Harm, of course, is a more serious thing than mere offense, but the point at issue applies in the same way to both harm and offense. The claim of superstitious people to protection from foreseeable harm is in no way weakened by the objective unreasonableness of their response to the offending conduct. Nor does the unreasonableness of the response count against the description of the resultant harm (heart attacks) *as* harm. The same points, I should think, would apply to foreseeable and universal offense when it too is the partial product of unreason.[9]

Perhaps the greatest source of my reluctance to restrict the offense principle to "reasonable offense," however, is that it would require agencies of the state to make official judgments of the reasonableness and unreasonableness of emotional states and sensibilities, in effect closing these questions to dissent and putting the stamp of state approval on answers to questions which, like issues of ideology and belief, should be left open to unimpeded discussion and practice. Much offense, for example, is caused by the obnoxious or aggressive expression of disrespect, scorn, or mockery of things that are loved, esteemed, or venerated. To take offense at expressed scorn for something that is not worthy of respect in the first place is, I suppose, to take offense unreasonably. But when is something truly worthy of love or respect or loyalty? To make *those* questions subject to administrative or judicial determination, I should think, would be dangerous and distinctly contrary to liberal principles.

NOTES

1. William L. Prosser, *The Law of Torts* (St. Paul: West Publishing Co., 1955).

2. *Ibid.*, p. 411.

3. *Ibid.*, p. 407.

4. "As it was said in an ancient case in regard to candle-making in a town, '*Le utility del chose excusera le noisemeness del stink,*' " *ibid.*, p. 399.

5. *Ibid.*

6. *Ibid.*, p. 413.

7. Offensive expression in art and literature is a more difficult and complex case impossible to argue here; but I would come to a similar conclusion.

8. I am forced to admit in this footnote that the United States Supreme Court did not follow my advice in this case. It overturned Cohen's conviction 4 to 3. (*Cohen v. California*, 403, U. S. 15 [1971]).

9. For whatever it is worth, I am cheered by the agreement with this

view of the law of nuisance from which I have derived so much stimulation. Prosser reports a case of private nuisance in which the defendant was a tuberculosis hospital and the plaintiff a home owner in the neighborhood. The plaintiff's suit was successful even though the fear of contagion which was the basis of the nuisance was judged by the court to be "unfounded." Virtually all the home owners in the neighborhood suffered from constant and intense anxiety that interfered with "the enjoyment of their land," and that very real anxiety constituted a nuisance, according to the court, even though unsupported by evidence of danger.

Legal Paternalism[1]

The principle of legal paternalism justifies state coercion to protect individuals from self-inflicted harm, or in its extreme version, to guide them, whether they like it or not, toward their own good. Parents can be expected to justify their interference in the lives of their children (e.g. telling them what they must eat and when they must sleep) on the ground that "daddy knows best." Legal paternalism seems to imply that since the state often can know the interests of individual citizens better than the citizens know them themselves, it stands as a permanent guardian of those interests *in loco parentis*. Put in this blunt way, paternalism seems a preposterous doctrine. If adults are treated as children they will come in time to be like children. Deprived of the right to choose for themselves, they will soon lose the power of rational judgment and decision. Even children, after a certain point, had better not be "treated as children," else they will never acquire the outlook and capability of responsible adults.

Yet if we reject paternalism entirely, and deny that a person's own good is *ever* a valid ground for coercing him, we seem to fly in the face both of common sense and our long established customs and laws. In the criminal law, for example, a prospective victim's freely granted consent is no defense to the charge of mayhem or homicide. The state simply refuses to permit anyone to agree to his own disablement or killing. The law of contracts, similarly, refuses to recognize as valid, contracts to sell oneself into slavery, or to become a mistress, or a second wife. Any ordinary citizen is legally justified in using reasonable force to prevent another from mutilating himself or committing suicide. No one is allowed to purchase certain drugs even for

---

[1] The Phi Beta Kappa lecture at Franklin and Marshall College, 1970; also presented to the Pacific Division of the American Philosophical Association, April, 1970, to the Summer Workshop at the Catholic University of America, June, 1970, and to "Philosopher's Holiday" at Vassar College, November, 1970.

therapeutic purposes without a physician's prescription (Doctor knows best). The use of other drugs, such as heroin, for pleasure merely, is permitted under no circumstances whatever. It is hard to find any plausible rationale for all such restrictions apart from the argument that beatings, mutilations, and death, concubinage, slavery, and bigamy are always bad for a person whether he or she knows it or not, and that antibiotics are too dangerous for any non-expert, and heroin for anyone at all, to take on his own initiative.

The trick is stopping short once we undertake this path, unless we wish to ban whiskey, cigarettes, and fried foods, which tend to be bad for people too, whether they know it or not. The problem is to reconcile somehow our general repugnance for paternalism with the apparent necessity, or at least reasonableness, of some paternalistic regulations. My method of dealing with this problem will not be particularly ideological. Rather, I shall try to organize our elementary intuitions by finding a principle that will render them consistent. Let us begin, then, by rejecting the views both that the protection of a person from himself is *always* a valid ground for interference in his affairs, and that it is *never* a valid ground. It follows that it is a valid ground only under certain conditions, and we must now try to state those conditions.[2]

I

It will be useful to make some preliminary distinctions. The first distinction is between harms or likely harms that are produced directly by a person upon himself and those produced by the actions of another person to which the first party has consented. Committing suicide would be an example of self-inflicted harm; arranging for a person to put one out of one's misery would be an example of a "harm" inflicted by the action of another to which one has consented. There is a venerable legal maxim traceable to the Roman Law that *"Volenti non fit inuria,"* sometimes translated, misleadingly, as: "To one who consents no harm is done." Now, I suppose that the notion of consent applies, strictly speaking, only to the actions of another person

---

[2] The discussion that follows has two important unstated and undefended presuppositions. The first is that in some societies, at least, and at some times, a line can be drawn (as Mill claimed it could in Victorian England) between other-regarding behaviour and behaviour that is primarily and directly self-regarding and only indirectly and remotely, therefore trivially, other-regarding. If this assumption is false, there is no interesting problem concerning legal paternalism since all "paternalistic" restrictions, in that case, could be defended as necessary to protect persons other than those restricted, and hence would not be (wholly) paternalistic. The second presupposition is that the spontaneous repugnance toward paternalism (which I assume the reader shares with me) is well-grounded and supportable.

that affect oneself. If so, then, consent to one's *own* actions is a kind of metaphor. Indeed, to say that I consented to my own actions, seems just a colorful way to saying that I acted voluntarily. My involuntary actions, after all, are, from the moral point of view, no different from the actions of someone else to which I have not had an opportunity to consent. In any case, it seems plainly false to say that a person cannot be *harmed* by actions, whether his own or those of another, to which he has consented. People who quite voluntarily eat an amount that is in fact too much cause themselves to suffer from indigestion; and girls who consent to advances sometimes become pregnant.

One way of interpreting the *Volenti* maxim is to take it as a kind of presumptive principle. A person does not generally consent to what he believes will be, on balance, harmful to himself, and by and large, an individual is in a better position to appraise risks to himself than are outsiders. Given these data, and considerations of convenience in the administration of the law, the *Volenti* maxim might be understood to say that for the purposes of the law (whatever the actual facts might be) nothing is to count as harm to a given person that he has freely consented to. If this presumption is held to be conclusive, then the *Volenti* maxim becomes a kind of "legal fiction" when applied to cases of undeniable harm resulting from behavior to which the harmed one freely consented. A much more likely interpretation, however, takes the *Volenti* maxim to say nothing at all, literal or fictional, about *harms*. Rather, it is about what used to be called "injuries," that is, injustices or wrongs. To one who freely consents to a thing no *wrong* is done, no matter how harmful to him the consequences may be. "He cannot waive his right," says Salmond, "and then complain of its infringement."[3] If the *Volenti* maxim is simply an expression of Salmond's insight, it is not a presumptive or fictional principle about harms, but rather an absolute principle about wrongs.

The *Volenti* maxim (or something very like it) plays a key role in the argument for John Stuart Mill's doctrine about liberty. Characteristically, Mill seems to employ the maxim in both of its interpretations, as it suits his purposes, without noticing the distinction between them. On the one hand, Mill's argument purports to be an elaborate application of the calculus of harms and benefits to the problem of political liberty. The state can rightly restrain a man to prevent harm to others. Why then can it not

---

[3] See Glanville Williams (ed.), *Salmond on Jurisprudence*, Eleventh Edition (London: Sweet & Maxwell, 1957), p. 531.

restrain a man to prevent him from harming himself? After all, a harm is a harm whatever its cause, and if our sole concern is to minimize harms all round, why should we distinguish between origins of harm? One way Mill answers this question is to employ the *Volenti* maxim in its first interpretation. For the purposes of his argument, he will presume conclusively that "to one who consents no *harm* is done." Self-inflicted or consented-to harm simply is not to count as harm at all; and the reasons for this are that the coercion required to prevent such harm is itself a harm of such gravity that it is likely in the overwhelming proportion of cases to outweigh any good it can produce for the one coerced; and moreover, individuals themselves, in the overwhelming proportion of cases, can know their own true interests better than any outsiders can, so that outside coercion is almost certain to be self-defeating.

But as Gerald Dworkin has pointed out,[4] arguments of this merely statistical kind at best create a strong but rebuttable presumption against coercion of a man in his own interest. Yet Mill purports to be arguing for an absolute prohibition. Absolute prohibitions are hard to defend on purely utilitarian grounds, so Mill, when his confidence wanes, tends to move to the second interpretation of the *Volenti* maxim. To what a man consents he may be harmed, but he cannot be wronged; and Mill's "harm principle," reinterpreted accordingly, is designed to protect him and others only from wrongful invasions of their interest. Moreover, when the state intervenes on any other ground, its *own* intervention is a wrongful invasion. What justifies the absolute prohibition of interference in primarily self-regarding affairs is *not* that such interference is self-defeating and likely (merely likely) to cause more harm than it prevents, but rather that it would itself be an injustice, a wrong, a violation of the private

---

[4] See his excellent article, "Paternalism" in *Morality and the Law*, ed. by R. A. Wasserstrom (Belmont, Calif: Wadsworth Publishing Co., 1971).

[5] Mill's rhetoric often supports this second interpretation of his argument. He is especially fond of such political metaphors as independence, legitimate rule, dominion, and sovereignty. The state must respect the status of the individual as an independent entity whose "*sovereignty* over himself" (in Mill's phrase), like Britain's over its territory, is absolute. In self-regarding affairs, a person's individuality ought to "*reign* uncontrolled from the outside" (another phrase of Mill's). Interference in those affairs, whether successful or self-defeating, is a violation of *legitimate boundaries*, like trespass in law, or aggression between states. Even self-mutilation and suicide are permissible if the individual truly chooses them, and other interests are not directly affected. The individual person has an absolute right to choose for himself, to be wrong, to go to hell on his own, and it is nobody else's proper *business* or *office* to interfere. The individual *owns* (not merely possesses) his life; he has *title* to it. He alone is *arbiter* of his own life and death. See how legalistic and un-utilitarian these terms are! The great wonder is that Mill could claim to have foregone any benefit in argument from the notion of an abstract right. Mill's intentions aside, however, I can not conceal my own preference for this second interpretation of his argument.

sanctuary which is every person's self; and this is so whatever the calculus of harms and benefits might show.[5]

The second distinction is between those cases where a person directly produces harm to himself, where the harm is the certain upshot of his conduct and its desired end, on the one hand, and those cases where a person simply creates a *risk* of harm to himself in the course of activities directed toward other ends. The man who knowingly swallows a lethal dose of arsenic will certainly die, and death must be imputed to him as his goal in acting. Another man is offended by the sight of his left hand, so he grasps an ax in his right hand and chops his left hand off. He does not thereby "endanger" his interest in the physical integrity of his limbs or "risk" the loss of his hand. He brings about the loss directly and deliberately. On the other hand, to smoke cigarettes or to drive at excessive speeds is not directly to harm oneself, but rather to increase beyond a normal level the probability that harm to oneself will result.

The third ditinction is that between reasonable and unreasonable risks. There is no form of activity (or inactivity either for that matter) that does not involve some risks. On some occasions we have a choice between more and less risky actions and prudence dictates that we take the less dangerous course; but what is called "prudence" is not always reasonable. Sometimes it is more reasonable to assume a great risk for a great gain than to play it safe and forfeit a unique opportunity. Thus it is not necessarily more reasonable for a coronary patient to increase his life expectancy by living a life of quiet inactivity than to continue working hard at his career in the hope of achieving something important even at the risk of a sudden fatal heart attack at any moment. There is no simple mathematical formula to guide one in making such decisions or for judging them "reasonable" or "unreasonable." On the other hand, there are other decisions that are manifestly unreasonable. It is unreasonable to drive at sixty miles an hour through a twenty mile an hour zone in order to arrive at a party on time, but it may be reasonable to drive fifty miles an hour to get a pregnant wife to the maternity ward. It is foolish to resist an armed robber in an effort to protect one's wallet, but it may be worth a desperate lunge to protect one's very life, or the life of a loved one.

In all of these cases a number of district considerations are involved.[6] If there is time to deliberate one should consider: (1)

---

[6] The distinctions in this paragraph are borrowed from: Henry T. Terry, "Negligence," *Harvard Law Review*, Vol. 29 (1915).

the degree of probability that harm to oneself will result from a given course of action, (2) the seriousness of the harm being risked, i.e. "the value or importance of that which is exposed to the risk," (3) the degree of probability that the goal inclining one to shoulder the risk will in fact result from the course of action, (4) the value or importance of achieving that goal, that is, just how worthwhile it is to one (this is the intimately personal factor, requiring a decision about one's own preferences, that makes the reasonableness of a risk-assessment on the whole so difficult for the *outsider* to make), and (5) the necessity of the risk, that is, the availability or absence of alternative, less risky, means to the desired goal. Certain judgments about the reasonableness of risk-assumptions are quite uncontroversial. We can say, for example, that the greater are considerations (1)—the probability of harm to self, and (2)—the magnitude of the harm risked, the *less* reasonable the risk; and the greater considerations (3) —the probability the desired goal will result, (4)—the importance of that goal to the actor, and (5)—the necessity of the means, the *more* reasonable the risk. But in a given difficult case, even where questions of "probability" are meaningful and beyond dispute, and where all the relevant facts are known, the risk-decision may defy objective assessment because of its component personal value judgments. In any case, if the state is to be given the right to prevent a person from risking harm to himself (and only himself) this must not be on the ground that the prohibited action is risky, or even that it is extremely risky, but rather on the ground that the risk is extreme and, in respect to its objectively assessable components, manifestly *unreasonable*. There are very good reasons, sometimes, for regarding even a person's judgment of personal worthwhileness (consideration 4) to be "manifestly unreasonable," but it remains to be seen whether (or when) that kind of unreasonableness can be sufficient grounds for interference.

The fourth and final distinction is between fully voluntary and not fully voluntary assumptions of a risk. One assumes a risk in a fully voluntary way when one shoulders it while fully informed of all relevant facts and contingencies, with one's eyes wide open, so to speak, and in the absence of all coercive pressure of compulsion. There must be calmness and deliberateness, no distracting or unsettling emotions, no neurotic compulsion, no misunderstanding. To whatever extent there is compulsion, misinformation, excitement or impetuousness, clouded judgment (as e.g. from alcohol), or immature or defective faculties of reasoning, to that extent the choice falls short of perfect voluntariness. Voluntariness then is a matter of degree. One's "choice" is *completely involuntary* either when it is no choice at all, properly speaking—when one lacks all muscular control of one's movements, or when one is knocked down, or pushed, or sent reeling by a blow, or a wind, or an explosion—or when through ignorance one chooses something other than what one means to choose, as when one thinks the arsenic powder is table salt, and thus chooses to sprinkle it on one's scrambled eggs. Most harmful choices, as most choices generally, fall somewhere in between the extremes of perfect voluntariness and complete involuntariness.

Now, the terms "voluntary" and "involuntary" have a variety of disparate but overlapping uses in philosophy, law, and ordinary life, and some of them are not altogether clear. I should point out here that my usage does not correspond with that of Aristotle, who allowed that infants, animals, drunkards, and men in a towering rage might yet act voluntarily if only they are undeceived and not overwhelmed by external physical force. What I call a voluntary assumption of risk corresponds more closely to what Aristotle called "deliberate choice." Impulsive and emotional actions, and those of animals and infants are voluntary in Aristotle's ‹sense, but they are not *chosen.* Chosen actions are those that are decided upon by *deliberation,* and that is a process that requires time, information, a clear head, and highly developed rational faculties. When I use such phrases then as "voluntary act," "free and genuine consent," and so on, I refer to acts that are more than "voluntary" in the Aristotelian sense, acts that Aristotle himself would call "deliberately chosen." Such acts not only have their origin "in the agent," they also represent him faithfully in some important way: they express his settled values and preferences. In the fullest sense, therefore, they are actions for which he can take responsibility.

II

The central thesis of John Stuart Mill and other individualists about paternalism is that the fully voluntary choice or consent of a mature and rational human being concerning matters that affect only his own interests is such a precious thing that no one else (and certainly not the state) has a right to interfere with it simply for the person's "own good." No doubt this thesis was also meant to apply to almost-but-not-quite fully

voluntary choices as well, and probably also even to some substantially non-voluntary ones (e.g. a neurotic person's choice
of a wife who will satisfy his neurotic needs but only at the
price of great unhappiness, eventual divorce, and exacerbated
guilt); but it is not probable that the individualist thesis was
meant to apply to choices near the bottom of the scale of voluntariness, and Mill himself left no doubt that he did *not* intend
it to apply to completely involuntary "choices." Nor should we
expect anti-paternalistic individualism to deny protection to a
person from his own nonvoluntary choices, for insofar as the
choices are not voluntary they are just as alien to him as the
choices of someone else.

Thus Mill would permit the state to protect a man from his
own ignorance at least in circumstances that create a strong
presumption that his uninformed or misinformed choice would
not correspond to his eventual one.

> If either a public officer or anyone else saw a person attempting to cross
> a bridge which had been ascertained to be unsafe, and there were no time
> to warn him of his danger, they might seize him and turn him back, with-
> out any real infringement of his liberty; for liberty consists in doing what
> one desires, and he does not desire to fall into the river.[7]

Of course, for all the public officer may know, the man on the
bridge does desire to fall into the river, or to take the risk of
falling for other purposes. If the person is then fully warned
of the danger and wishes to proceed anyway, then, Mill argues,
that is his business alone; but because most people do *not* wish
to run such risks, there was a solid presumption, in advance of
checking, that this person did not wish to run the risk either.
Hence the officer was justified, Mill would argue, in his original
interference.

On other occasions a person may need to be protected not
from his ignorance but from some other condition that may
render his informed choice substantially less than voluntary.
He may be "a child, or delirious, or in some state of excitement or absorption incompatible with the full use of the reflecting faculty."[8] Mill would not permit any such person to
cross an objectively unsafe bridge. On the other hand, there is
no reason why a child, or an excited person, or a drunkard, or
a mentally ill person should not be allowed to proceed on
his way home across a perfectly safe thoroughfare. Even substantially nonvoluntary choices deserve protection unless there
is good reason to judge them dangerous.

---

[7] J. S. Mill, *On Liberty* (New York: Liberal Arts Press, 1956), p. 117.

[8] *Loc. cit.*

Now it may be the case, for all we can know, that the behaviour of a drunk or an emotionally upset person would be
exactly the same even if he were sober and calm; but when
the behaviour seems patently self-damaging and is of a sort
that most calm and normal persons would not engage in, then
there are strong grounds, if only a statistical sort, for inferring
the opposite; and these grounds, on Mill's principle, would
justify interference. It may be that there is no kind of action
of which it can be said "No mentally competent adult in a
calm, attentive mood, fully informed, etc. would *ever* choose
(or consent to) *that.*" Nevertheless, there are actions of a kind
that create a powerful *presumption* that any given actor, if he
were in his right mind, would not choose them. The point of
calling this hypothesis a "presumption" is to require that it be
completely overridden before legal permission be given to a
person, who has already been interfered with, to go on as before. So, for example, if a policeman (or anyone else) sees John
Doe about to chop off his hand with an ax, he is perfectly
justified in using force to prevent him, because of the presumption that no one could voluntarily choose to do such a thing.
The presumtion, however, should always be taken as rebuttable
in principle; and now it will be up to Doe to prove before an
official tribunal that he is calm, competent, and free, and that
he still wishes to chop off his hand. Perhaps this is too great a
burden to expect Doe himself to "prove," but the tribunal should
require that the presumption against voluntariness be overturned by evidence from some source or other. The existence
of the presumption should require that an objective determination be made, whether by the usual adversary procedures of
law courts, or simply by a collective investigation by the tribunal into the available facts. The greater the presumption to
be overridden, the more elaborate and fastidious should be the
legal paraphernalia required, and the stricter the standards of
evidence. (The law of wills might prove a model for this.) The
point of the procedure would not be to evaluate the wisdom or
worthiness of a person's choice, but rather to determine whether
the choice really is his.

This seems to lead us to a form of paternalism that is so
weak and innocuous that it could be accepted even by Mill,
namely, that the state has the right to prevent self-regarding
harmful conduct only when it is substantially nonvoluntary or
when temporary intervention is necessary to establish whether
it is voluntary or not. When there is a strong presumption that

no normal person would voluntarily choose or consent to the kind of conduct in question, that should be a proper ground for detaining the person until the voluntary character of his choice can be established. We can use the phrase "the standard of voluntariness" as a label for the considerations that mediate the application of the principle that a person may properly be protected from his own folly. (Still another ground for forcible delay and inquiry that is perfectly compatible with Mill's individualism is the possibility that important third party interests might be involved. Perhaps a man's wife and family should have some say before he is permitted to commit suicide—or even to chop off his hand.)

III

Working out the details of the voluntariness standard is far too difficult to undertake here, but some of the complexities, at least, can be illustrated by a consideration of some typical hard cases. Consider first of all the problem of harmful drugs. Suppose Richard Roe requests a prescription of drug X from Dr. Doe, and the following discussion ensues:

> Dr. Doe: I cannot prescribe drug X to you because it will do you physical harm.

> Mr. Roe: But you are mistaken. It will not cause me physical harm.

In a case like this, the state, of course, backs the doctor. The state deems medical questions to be technical matters subject to expert opinions. This entails that a non-expert layman is not the best judge of his own medical interests. If a layman disagrees with a physician on a question of medical fact the layman can be presumed wrong, and if nevertheless he chooses to act on his factually mistaken belief, his action will be substantially less than fully voluntary in the sense explained above. That is to say that the action of *ingesting a substance which will in fact harm him* is not the action he voluntarily chooses to do. Hence the state intervenes to protect him not from his own free and voluntary choices, but from his own ignorance.

Suppose however that the exchange goes as follows:

> Dr. Doe: I cannot prescribe drug X to you because it will do you physical harm.

> Mr. Roe: Exactly. That's just what I want. I want to harm myself.

In this case Roe *is* properly apprised of the facts. He suffers from no delusions or misconceptions. Yet his choice is so odd that there exists a reasonable presumption that he has been deprived somehow of the "full use of his reflecting faculty." It is because we know that the overwhelming majority of choices to inflict injury for its own sake on oneself are not fully voluntary that we are entitled to presume that the present choice too is not fully voluntary. If no further evidence of derangement, or illness, or severe depression, or unsettling excitation can be discovered, however, and the patient can convince an objective panel that his choice is voluntary (unlikely event!) and further if there are no third party interests, for example those of wife or family, that require protection, then our "voluntariness standard" would permit no further state constraint.

Now consider the third possibility:

Dr. Doe: I cannot prescribe drug X to you because it is very likely to do you physical harm.

Mr. Roe: I don't care if it causes me physical harm. I'll get a lot of pleasure first, so much pleasure in fact, that it is well worth running the risk of physical harm. If I must pay a price for my pleasure I am willing to do so.

This is perhaps the most troublesome case. Roe's choice is not patently irrational on its face. He may have a well thought-out philosophical hedonism as one of his profoundest convictions. He may have made a fundamental decision of principle committing himself to the intensely pleasurable, even if brief life. If no third party interests are directly involved, the state can hardly be permitted to declare his philosophical convictions unsound or "sick" and prevent him from practicing them, without assuming powers that it will inevitably misuse disastrously.

On the other hand, this case may be very little different from the preceding one, depending of course on what the exact facts are. If the drug is known to give only an hour's mild euphoria and then cause an immediate violently painful death, then the risks incurred appear so unreasonable as to create a powerful presumption of nonvoluntariness. The desire to commit suicide must always be presumed to be both nonvoluntary and harmful to others until shown otherwise. (Of course is some cases it can be shown otherwise.) On the other hand, drug X may be harmful in the way nicotine is now known to be harmful; twenty or thirty years of heavy use may create a grave risk of lung cancer or heart disease. Using the drug for pleasure merely, when the risks are of this kind, may be to run unreasonable risks, but that is no strong evidence of nonvoluntariness. Many perfectly normal, rational persons voluntarily choose to run precisely these risks for whatever pleasures they find in smoking.[9] The way for the state to assure itself that such practices are truly voluntary is continually to confront smokers with the ugly medical facts so that there is no escaping the knowledge of what the medical risks to health exactly are. Constant reminders of the hazards should be at every hand and with no softening of the gory details. The state might even be justified in using its taxing, regulatory, and persuasive powers to make smoking (and similar drug usage) more difficult or less attractive; but to prohibit it outright for everyone would be to tell the voluntary risk-taker that even his informed judgments of what is worthwhile are less reasonable than those of the state, and that therefore, he may not act on them. This is paternalism of the strong kind, unmediated by the voluntariness standard. As a principle of public policy, it has an acrid moral flavour, and creates serious risks of governmental tyranny.

IV

Another class of hard cases are those involving contracts in which one party agrees to restrict his own liberty in some respect. The most extreme case is that in which one party freely sells himself into slavery to another, perhaps in exchange for some benefit that is to be consumed before the period of slavery begins, perhaps for some reward to be bestowed upon some third party. Our point of departure will be Mill's classic treatment of the subject:

> In this and most other civilized countries... an engagement by which a person should sell himself, or allow himself to be sold, as a slave would be null and void, neither enforced by law nor by opinion. The ground for *thus limiting his power of voluntarily disposing of his own lot in life* is apparent, and is very clearly seen in this extreme case. The reason for not interfering, unless for the sake of others, with a person's voluntary acts is consideration for his liberty. His voluntary choice is evidence that what he so chooses is desirable, or at least endurable to him, and his good is on the whole best provided for by allowing him to take his own means of pursuing it. But by selling himself for a slave, he abdicates his liberty; he foregoes any future use of it beyond that single act. He therefore defeats, in his own case, the very purpose which is the justification of allowing him to dispose of himself. He is no longer free, but is thenceforth in a position which has no longer the presumption in its favour that would be afforded by his voluntarily remaining in it. The principle of freedom cannot require that he should be free not to be free.[10] [my italics]

It seems plain to me that Mill, in this one extreme case,

---

[9] Perfectly rational men can have "unreasonable desires" as judged by other perfectly rational men, just as perfectly rational men (e.g. great philosophers) can hold "unreasonable beliefs" or doctrines as judged by other perfectly rational men. Particular unreasonableness, then, can hardly be strong evidence of general irrationality.

[10] Mill, *op. cit.*, p. 125.

has been driven to embrace the principle of paternalism. The "harm-to-others principle," as mediated by the *Volenti* maxim[11] would permit a competent, fully informed adult, who is capable of rational reflection and free of undue pressure, to be himself the judge of his own interests, no matter how queer or perverse his judgment may seem to others. There is, of course, always the presumption, and a very strong one indeed, that a person who elects to "sell" himself into slavery is either incompetent, unfree, or misinformed. Hence the state should require very strong evidence of voluntariness—elaborate tests, swearings, psychiatric testifying, waiting periods, public witnessing, and the like—before validating such contracts. Similar forms of official "making sure" are involved in marriages and wills, and slavery is even more serious a thing, not to be rashly undertaken. Undoubtedly, very few slavery contracts would survive such procedures, perhaps even none at all. It may be literally true that "no one in his right mind would sell himself into slavery," but if this is a truth it is not an *a priori* one but rather one that must be tested anew in each case by the application of independent, non-circular criteria of mental illness.

The supposition is at least intelligible, therefore, that every now and then a normal person in full possession of his faculties would voluntarily consent to permanent slavery. We can imagine any number of intelligible (if not attractive) motives for doing such a thing. A person might agree to become a slave in exchange for a million dollars to be delivered in advance to a loved one or to a worthy cause, or out of a religious conviction requiring a life of humility or penitence, or in payment for the prior enjoyment of some supreme benefit, as in the *Faust* legend. Mill, in the passage quoted above, would disallow such a contract no matter how certain it is that the agreement is fully voluntary, apparently on the ground that the permanent and irrevocable loss of freedom is such a great evil, and slavery so harmful a condition, that no one ought ever to be allowed to choose it, even voluntarily. Any person who thinks that he can be a gainer, in the end, from such an agreement, Mill implies, is simply wrong whatever his reasons, and can be known *a priori* to be wrong. Mill's earlier argument, if I understand it correctly, implies that a man should be permitted to mutilate

---

[11] That is, the principle that prevention of harm to others is the sole ground for legal coercion, and that what is freely consented to is not to count as harm. These are Mill's primary normative principles in *On Liberty*.

his body, take harmful drugs, or commit suicide, provided only that his decision to do these things is voluntary and no other person will be directly and seriously harmed. But voluntarily acceding to slavery is too much for Mill to stomach. Here is an evil of another order, he seems to say; so the "harm to others" principle and the *Volenti* maxim come to their limiting point here, and paternalism in the strong sense (unmediated by the voluntariness test) must be invoked, if only for this one kind of case.

There are, of course, other ways of justifying the refusal to enforce slavery contracts. Some of these are derived from principles not acknowledged in Mill's moral philosophy but which at least have the merit of being non-paternalistic. One might argue that what is odious in "harsh and unconscionable" contracts, even when they are voluntary on both sides, is not that a man should suffer the harm he freely risked, but rather that another party should "exploit" or take advantage of him. What is to be prevented, according to this line of argument, is one man exploiting the weakness, or foolishness, or recklessness of another. If a weak, foolish, or reckless man freely chooses to harm or risk harm to himself, that is all right, but that is no reason why another should be a party to it, or be permitted to benefit himself at the other's expense. (This principle, however, can only apply to extreme cases, else it will ban all competition.) Applied to voluntary slavery, the principle of non-exploitation might say that it isn't aimed at preventing one man from being a slave so much as preventing the other from being a slave-owner. The basic principle of argument here is a form of legal moralism. To own another human being, as one might own a table or a horse, is to be in a relation to him that is inherently immoral, and therefore properly forbidden by law. That, of course, is a line of argument that would be uncongenial to Mill, as would also be the Kantian argument that there is something in every man that is not his to alienate or dispose of, *viz.*, the "humanity" that we are enjoined to "respect, whether in our own person or that of another." (It is worth noting, in passing, that Kant was an uncompromising foe of legal paternalism.)

There are still other ways of arguing against the recognition of slavery contracts, however, that are neither paternalistic (in the strong sense) nor inconsistent with Mill's primary principles. One might argue, for example, that weakening respect for human dignity (which is weak enough to begin with) can lead

in the long run to harm of the most serious kind to non-consent-
ing parties. Or one might use a variant of the "public charge"
argument commonly used in the nineteenth century against
permitting even those without dependents to assume the risk of
penury, illness, and starvation. We could let men gamble recklessly with their own lives, and then adopt inflexibly unsympa-
thetic attitudes toward the losers. "They made their beds." we
might say in the manner of some proper Victorians, "now let
them sleep in them". But this would be to render the whole
national character cold and hard. It would encourage insensi-
tivity generally and impose an unfair economic penalty on those
who possess the socially useful virtue of benevolence. Realistical-
ly, we just can't let men wither and die right in front our eyes;
and if we intervene to help, as we inevitably must, it will cost
us a lot of money. There are certain risks then of an *apparently*
self-regarding kind that men cannot be permitted to run, if only
for the sake of others who must either pay the bill or turn
their backs on intolerable misery. This kind of argument, which
can be applied equally well to the slavery case, is at least
not *very* paternalistic.

Finally, a non-paternalistic opponent of voluntary slavery
might argue (and this the argument to which I wish to give the
most emphasis) that while exclusively self-regarding and fully
voluntary "slavery contracts" are unobjectionable in principle,
the legal machinery for testing voluntariness would be so cumbersome and expensive as to be impractical. Such procedures,
after all, would have to be paid for out of tax revenues, the
payment of which is mandatory for taxpayers. (And psychiatric
consultant fees, among other things, are very high.) Even expensive legal machinery might be so highly fallible that there
could be no sure way of determining voluntariness, so that some
mentally ill people, for example, might become enslaved. Given
the uncertain quality of evidence on these matters, and the
enormous general presumption of nonvoluntariness, the state
might be justified simply in *presuming nonvoluntariness conclusively in every case as the least risky course.* Some rational
bargain-makers might be unfairly restrained under this policy,
but on the alternative policy, even more people, perhaps, would
become unjustly (mistakenly) enslaved, so that the evil prevented by the absolute prohibition would be greater than the
occasional evil permitted. The principles involved in this argument are of the following two kinds: (1) It is better (say) that
one hundred people be wrongly denied permission to be en-

slaved than that one be wrongly permitted, and (2) If we allow the institution of "voluntary slavery" at all, then no matter how stringent our tests of voluntariness are, it is likely that a good many persons *will* be wrongly permitted.

V

Mill's argument that leads to a (strong) paternalistic conclusion in this one case (slavery) employs only calculations of harms and benefits and the presumptive interpretation of *Volenti non fit inuria*. The notion of the inviolable sovereignty of the individual person over his own life does not appear in the argument. Liberty, he seems to tell us, is one good or benefit (though an extremely important one) among many, and its loss, one evil or harm (though an extremely serious one) among many types of harm. The aim of the law being to prevent harms of all kinds and from all sources, the law must take a very negative attitude toward forfeitures of liberty. Still, by and large, legal paternalism is an unacceptable policy because in attempting to impose upon a man an external conception of his own good, it is very likely to be self-defeating. "His voluntary choice is *evidence* (emphasis added) that what he so chooses is desirable, or at least endurable to him, and his good is *on the whole* (more emphasis added) best provided for by allowing him to take his own means of pursuing it." On the whole, then, the harm of coercion will outweigh any good it can produce for the person coerced. But when the person chooses slavery, the scales are clearly and necessarily tipped the other way, and the normal case against intervention is defeated. The ultimate appeal in this argument of Mill's is to the prevention of personal harms, so that permitting a person voluntarily to sell all his freedom would be to permit him to be "free not to be free", that is, free to inflict an *undeniable* harm upon himself, and this (Mill would say) is as paradoxical as permitting a legislature to vote by a majority to abolish majority rule. If, on the other hand, our ultimate principle expresses respect for a person's voluntary choice *as such*, even when it is the choice of a loss of freedom, we can remain adamantly opposed to paternalism even in the most extreme cases of self-harm, for we shall be committed to the view that there is something more important (even) than the avoidance of harm. The principle that shuts and locks the door leading to strong paternalism is that every man has a human right to "voluntarily dispose of his own lot in life" whatever the effect on his own net balance of benefits (including "freedom") and harms.

What does Mill say about less extreme cases of contracting away liberty? His next sentence (but one) is revealing': "These reasons, the force of which is so conspicuous in this particular case [slavery], are evidently of far wider application, yet a limit is everywhere set to them by the necessities of life, which continually require, not indeed that we should resign our freedom, but that we should consent to this and the other limitation of it."[12] Mill seems to say here that the same reasons that justify preventing the total and irrevocable relinquishment of freedom also militate against agreements to relinquish lesser amounts for lesser periods, but that unfortunately such agreements are sometimes rendered necessary by practical considerations. I would prefer to argue in the very opposite way, from the obvious permissibility of limited resignations of freedom to the permissibility in principle even of extreme forfeitures, except that in the latter case (slavery) the "necessities of life"—administrative complications in determining voluntariness, high expenses, and so on—forbid it.

Many perfectly reasonable employment contracts involve an agreement by the employee virtually to abandon his liberty to do as he pleases for a daily period, and even to do (within obvious limits) whatever his boss tells him, in exchange for a salary that the employer, in turn, is not at liberty to withhold. Sometimes, of course, the terms of such agreements are quite unfavourable to one of the parties, but when the agreements have been fairly bargained, with no undue pressure or deception (i.e. when they are fully voluntary) the courts enforce them even though lopsided in their distribution of benefits. Employment contracts, of course, are relatively easily broken; so in that respect they are altogether different from "slavery contracts." Perhaps better examples for our purposes, therefore, are contractual forfeitures of some extensive liberty for long periods of time or even forever. Certain contracts "in restraint of trade" are good examples. Consider contracts for the sale of the "good will" of a business:

> Manifestly, the buyer of a shop or of a practice will not be satisfied with what he buys unless he can persuade the seller to contract that he will not immediately set up a competing business next door and draw back most of his old clients or customers. Hence the buyer will usually request the seller to agree not to enter into competition with him .... Clauses of this kind are [also] often found in written contracts of employment, the

---

[12] *Loc. cit.*

employer requiring his employee to agree that he will not work for a competing employer after he leaves his present work.[13]

There are limits, both spatial and temporal, to the amount of liberty the courts will permit to be relinquished in such contracts. In general, it is considered reasonable for a seller to agree not to reopen a business in the same neighborhood or even the same city for several years, but not reasonable to agree not to re-enter the trade in a distant city, or for a period (say) of fifty years. The courts insist that the agreed-to-self-restraint be no wider "than is reasonably necessary to protect the buyer's purchase;"[14] but where the buyer's interests are very large the restraints may cover a great deal of space and time:

> For instance, in the leading case on the subject, a company which bought an armaments business for the colossal sum of £287,000 was held justified in taking a contract from the seller that he would not enter into competition with this business anywhere in the world for a period of twenty-five years. In view of the fact that the business was world-wide in its operations, and that its customers were mainly governments, any attempt by the seller to re-enter the armament business anywhere in the world might easily have affected the value of the buyer's purchase.[15]

The courts then do permit people to contract away extensive liberties for extensive periods of time in exchange for other benefits in reasonable bargains. Persons are even permitted to forfeit their future liberties in exchange for cash. Sometimes such transactions are perfectly reasonable, promoting the interests of both parties. Hence there would appear to be no good reason why they should be prohibited. Selling oneself into slavery is forfeiting *all* one's liberty for the rest of one's life in exchange for some prized benefit, and thus is only the extreme limiting case of contracting away liberty, but not altogether different in principle. Mill's argument that liberty is not the sort of good that by its very nature can properly be traded, then, does not seem a convincing way of arguing against voluntary slavery.

On the other hand, a court does not permit the seller of a business freely to forfeit any more liberty than is reasonable or necessary, and reserves to *itself* the right to determine the question of reasonableness. This restrictive policy *could* be an expression of paternalism designed to protect contracters from their own foolishness; but in fact it is based on an entirely different ground—the public interest in maintaining a competi-

---

[13] P. S. Atiyah, *An Introduction to the Law of Contracts* (Oxford: Clarendon Press, 1961), p. 176.

[14] *Ibid.*, pp. 176-77.

[15] *Ibid.*, p. 177.

tive system of free trade. The consumer's interests in having prices determined by a competitive marketplace rather than by uncontrolled monopolies requires that the state make it difficult for wealthy businessmen to buy off their competitors. Reasonable contracts "in restraint of trade" are a limited class of exceptions to a general policy designed to protect the economic interests of third parties (consumers) rather than the expression of an independent paternalistic policy of protecting free bargainers from their own mistakes.

There is still a final class of cases that deserve mention. These too are instances of persons voluntarily relinquishing liberties for other benefits; but they occur under such circumstances that prohibitions against them could not plausibly be justified except on paternalistic grounds, and usually not even on those grounds. I have in mind examples of persons who voluntarily "put themselves under the protection of rules" that deprive them and others too of liberties, when those liberties are unrewarding and burdensome. Suppose all upperclass undergraduates are given the option by their college to live either in private apartment buildings entirely unrestricted or else in college dormitories subject to the usual curfew and parietal rules. If one chooses the latter, he or she must be in after a certain hour, be quiet after a certain time, and so on, subject to certain sanctions. In "exchange" for these forfeitures, of course, one is assured that the other students too must be predictable in their habits, orderly, and quiet. The net gain for one's interests as a student over the "freer" private life could be considerable. Moreover, the curfew rule can be a great convenience for a girl who wishes to "date" boys very often, but who also wishes: (a) to get enough sleep for good health, (b) to remain efficient in her work, and (c) to be free of tension and quarrels when on dates over the question of when it is time to return home. If the rule requires a return at a certain time then neither the girl nor the boy has any choice in the matter, and what a boon that can be! To invoke these considerations is *not* to resort to paternalism unless they are employed in support of a prohibition. It is paternalism to *forbid* a student to live in a private apartment "for his own good" or "his own safety." It is not paternalism to *permit* him to live under the governance of coercive rules when he freely chooses to do so, and the other alternative is kept open to him. In fact it would be paternalism to deny a person the liberty of trading liberties for other benefits when he voluntarily chooses to do so.

VI

In summary: There are weak and strong versions of legal paternalism. The weak version is hardly an independent principle and can be entirely acceptable to the philosopher who, like Mill, is committed only to the "harm to others" principle as mediated by the *Volenti* maxim, where the latter is more than a mere presumption derived from generalizations about the causes of harm. According to the strong version of legal paternalism, the state is justified in protecting a person, against his will, from the harmful consequences even of his fully voluntary choices and undertakings. Strong paternalism is a departure from the "harm to others" principle and the strictly interpreted *Volenti* maxim that Mill should not, or need not, have taken in his discussion of contractual forfeitures of liberty. According to the weaker version of legal paternalism, a man can rightly be prevented from harming himself (when other interests are not directly involved) only if his intended action is substantially nonvoluntary or can be presumed to be so in the absence of evidence to the contrary. The "harm to others" principle, after all, permits us to protect a man from the choices of other people; weak paternalism would permit us to protect him from "nonvoluntary choices," which, being the choices of no one at all, are no less foreign to him.

Duties, Rights, and Claims

Among the questions that still divide philosophers who are concerned with problems about rights are (1) whether, or to what extent, rights and duties are logically correlative, and (2) whether it is theoretically illuminating generally, and in particular, whether in considering question (1) it is strategically useful, to treat rights as *claims*. Although question (1) is in a familiar sense a logical question (Do statements of duties *entail* statements of other people's rights, and do statements of rights *entail* statements of other people's duties?), this paper is more a descriptive or impressionistic study than a formalistic one. Part I consists of an examination of the many kinds of normative relations called "duty" with the aim of distinguishing those that are clearly correlated with other people's rights from those that apparently are not. The second part of the paper shifts the focus to rights and argues that there is at least one kind of talk about rights-as-claims that is neither reducible to, nor in any clear logical relation with, talk about duties. The word "claim" of course is ambiguous. Claims *to* (I shall argue) are not always expressible as claims *against*, and "having a claim to . . ." and "making claim to . . ." are different sorts of things from "claiming that. . . ." The paper concludes, however, that each of the ideas capable of being expressed by the word "claim" is essential either to the understanding or the just appreciation of rights.

I. DUTIES AND RIGHTS

Which of the various kinds of duty are necessarily correlated with the rights of other people? Consider first the relation between a debtor and his creditor. Indebtedness is the clearest example of one person *owing* something to another; and owing, in turn, is a perspicuous model for the interpretation of that treacherous little preposition "to" as it occurs in the phrase "obligation *to* someone." Now it is unquestionably true that when one party *owes* something to another, the latter has a *right* to what he is owed. The debtor's obligation is his creditor's right seen from a different vantage point. A *duty of indebtedness*, moreover, entails a right of a very specific kind, called, in the jargon of jurisprudence, a positive *in personam* right, that is, a right against one specific person requiring him to perform a "positive act," not a mere omission.

A second class of duties, being based on promises, is also more properly called "obligations,"[1] but we can call them (other) *duties of commitment*. In discussing these, we must not be misled by the preposition "to." When a debtor owes money to a creditor, he can be said to have an obligation *to* the creditor; but the preposition here is ambiguous and obscures the distinction between two different offices the creditor occupies. On the one hand he is the one to whom the obligation is *owed*, and the one therefore who can claim it as his due. On the other hand, he is the intended beneficiary of his debtor's promised act. This dual role is also played sometimes by persons owed other kinds of duties of commitment. If Abel promises Baker to meet him at a certain time, or to shine his shoes, or favorably review his book, then Baker is both claimant and intended beneficiary of Abel's duty. There may, of course, be others who stand to gain, if only indirectly, from Abel's discharge of his obligation, but in most cases these so-called "third party beneficiaries" will profit in merely picayune and remote ways.

Sometimes, however, there is a separation of offices, and the intended direct beneficiary is not the promisee, but instead some third party designated by the promisee. This class of transactions can be further subdivided: In some cases, only the promisee is the claimant, or rightholder, while in other cases, both the promisee and the third-party beneficiary have rights to the promisor's performance. If Abel promises Baker to look after Baker's dog Fido, then Fido is the direct beneficiary of the promised services, while Baker himself, and probably only Baker, is the claimant. On the other hand, if Baker designates his wife or mother (or dog?) as beneficiary on his life insurance policy, then *both* Baker as promisee and the designated beneficiary can be said to have a right that the benefit-payment go to the beneficiary. (Even after Baker is dead, it can be said that the insurance company *owes it to him* to pay the beneficiary.)

Philosophers[2] have sometimes found it useful to direct their attention primarily to those cases where third-party beneficiaries do *not* derive rights from promises, for such cases illustrate most clearly that

---

[1] For subtle discussions of the distinction between obligations and duties, see E. J. Lemmon, "Moral Dilemmas," *The Philosophical Review*, vol. 71 (1962), pp. 139-158; and Richard B. Brandt, "The Concepts of Obligation and Duty," *Mind*, vol. 73 (1964), pp. 374-393.

[2] Most notably, H.L.A. Hart, "Are There Any Natural Rights?" *The Philosophical Review*, vol. 64 (1955), pp. 179-182.

promisee and intended beneficiary *are* distinct moral offices. Furthermore, in cases of that kind, the distinction between the two offices is
not totally obscured by ordinary language which distinguishes (sometimes) between duties *to* claimants and duties *toward*, or in respect to,
beneficiaries. But total preoccupation with this kind of case is as dangerous as it is unnecessary. The danger is that it might blind us to
the large class of cases where third-party beneficiaries, both in law[3]
and morals, do have a claim-right against the promisor; and in any
case, the distinction between the offices of promisee and beneficiary
can be equally well made out in the case where the third-party beneficiary and the promisee are both claimants. For in these cases, it does
not *follow necessarily* from the fact that a person is an intended beneficiary of a promised service that he has a right to it, whereas it always
follows necessarily from the fact that a person is a promisee that he
has a right to what is promised. This difference, of course, would not
be possible if beneficiary and promisee were not distinct offices. Another way of putting the point is to say that the rights of third-party
beneficiaries, unlike those of promisees, are not logically correlated
with the obligations of the promisor, but correlated only in virtue of
moral or judicial policies and rules. In those cases where there is some
temptation to say that the right of a third-party beneficiary is logically
correlated with a promisor's duty, the temptation will be at least as
great to say that the promisor made a *tacit promise* to the beneficiary
in addition to the express promise to his promisee. I have in mind
those cases where the parties to the promise allow the promise to be
known to the third-party beneficiary, and the latter acts in reliance on
its performance.

In all of these cases, the important relation for our present purposes is that between promisor and *claimant*, whether the latter be
promisee, or beneficiary, or both. This relation is another proper and
familiar case of owing, although it is already one step removed from
what we might call the "paradigm case" of indebtedness. Duties of
commitment, like the standard cases of owing, are obviously correlated

[3] For a subtle and detailed discussion of this complex topic see *Corbin on Contracts* (St. Paul, Minn., West, 1952), pp. 723-783. Corbin writes on p. 733: "The
following is an attempt at a consistent statement of the generally prevailing law: A
third party who is not a promisee and who gave no consideration has an enforceable
right by reason of a contract made by two others (1) if he is a creditor of the promisee or of some other person and the contract calls for a performance by the promisor
in satisfaction of the obligation; or (2) if the promised performance will be of pecuniary benefit to him and the contract is so expressed as to give the promisor
reason to know that such benefit is contemplated by the promisee as one of the
motivating causes of his making the contract. A third party may be included within
both of these provisions at once, but need not be. One who is included within
neither of them has no right, even though performance will incidentally benefit
him."

with other people's *in personam* rights. The claimant has a right *in personam* against the promisor to either a positive performance, as in the case of feeding Fido, or else a forebearance, as when I promise to waive my right to keep you off my land, giving you thereby a claim to my noninterference, that is, a negative *in personam* right.

Similar remarks can be made about a third class of duties, the *duties of reparation*. When your loss is "my fault," that is, when it was caused by my negligence, recklessness, impulsiveness, carelessness, dishonesty, malevolence, or the like, then I have a duty to you to repair the harm or otherwise make good the loss. I "owe" reparation to you in much the same manner as I would owe you the return of something I borrowed or took from you without your permission. My duty, in these examples, is to return to you what is really your own, or where this is impossible, something of equivalent value; and your correlative right is a claim *in personam* to my positive services.

A fourth class of duties also permits talk of "owing" something to someone, although we are now at least two steps away from the example of indebtedness. "Mr. Churchill feels that he owes this legacy to the world," said a 1964 advertisement for a set of recordings by Winston Churchill of public and private speeches, letters, and reminiscences. Presumably, Sir Winston did not feel that he must simply return what he had borrowed or keep some sort of promise, express or implied. I suspect rather that he felt a duty to give to the world something that it needs, but which he, at age 90, no longer had reason to keep his exclusive possession. I propose to call this, and other more worldly examples of the duty abundance owes to need, *duties of need-fulfillment*. Such duties clearly give rise to positive *in personam* rights, often in many claimants.

A fifth class of duties is related to gratitude, but had better be called *duties of reciprocation*, since gratitude, a feeling, is a less appropriate subject for duty than reciprocation, which is, after all, action. There are, moreover, other confusions commonly infecting the idea of a "duty of gratitude." Many writers speak of duties of gratitude as if they were special instances, or perhaps informal analogues, of duties of indebtedness. But gratitude, I submit, feels nothing at all like indebtedness. When a person under no duty to me does me a service or helps me out of a jam, from what I imagine to be benevolent motives, my feelings of gratitude toward him bears no important resemblance to the feeling I have toward a merchant who ships me ordered goods before I pay for them. The cause of the widespread confusion of gratitude with moral indebtedness, I suspect, is a disposition, allegedly characteristic of but certainly not peculiar to the Japanese, to feel some loss of status when helped by others, and some consequent resentment of the benefactor under the respectable mask of "gratitude." We feel impelled to pay back a benefactor sometimes because we feel that his benefaction has made him "one up" and we want to get even.

The expression "duty of reciprocation" is better used for a different kind of case: My benefactor once freely offered me his services when I needed them. There was, on that occasion, nothing for me to do in return but express my deepest gratitude to him. (How alien to gratitude any sort of *payment* would have been!) But now circumstances have arisen in which he needs help, and I am in a position to help him. Surely, I *owe* him my services now, and he would be entitled to resent my failure to come through. In short, he has a right to my help now, and I have a correlative duty to proffer it to him. Like the other examples, the right in this case is *in personam* and typically positive.

I think I have now enumerated the main classes of duties that permit talk of one person owing something to another. Of course, there may be a very wide sense of "owe" in which it goes with all talk of duty, perhaps as a kind of synonym for the feeling of requirement or "must do" that goes with all duty. But still in respect to the remaining classes of duties, while one must do something, this is not because he *owes* it to someone to do it.

The sixth kind of duty is typified by the duty we all have to stay off a landowner's property. I don't think we would naturally speak of this duty as something "owed" to the landowner, although I admit the law doesn't hesitate to speak that way. In acknowledging a duty not to interfere with another's property, we show our respect for his interest in the exclusive possession and control of it. Such duties of noninterference with the person or (prototypically) the property of another, I propose to call *duties of respect*. This use of the word "respect" is not the only one, but it is, I think, a familiar one. Webster's dictionary puts it thus, ". . . to esteem; value; hence to refrain from obtruding upon or interfering with; as to respect a person's privacy."

The rights correlative with duties of respect are typically negative, that is, rights to other people's abstentions, forebearances, or noninterference, and unlike the rights discussed in our earlier examples, they are what lawyers call *in rem* rather than *in personam* rights. An *in rem* right holds, not against some specific namable person or persons but rather, in the legal phrase, against the world at large. In saying that "the whole world" has a duty to stay off my land, all I can mean, of course, is that any person in a position to enter my property has a duty to stay out. That implies that even General De Gaulle, if I wished to keep him out, would have to stop at my gate. My right *in rem*, in imposing on others a duty of respect, is itself no respecter of persons.

Are all *in rem* rights negative? There is no denying that negative *in rem* rights, modeled after the proprietary right and then extended to cover personal interests as well, have had an enormous influence on political thought, especially in America. They dominated lists of "natural rights," for example, in various eighteenth-century manifestos. Still there are positive *in rem* rights too, whose importance has come to be appreciated anew only in recent decades. Consider, for example, the duty of care that every citizen is said to owe to any and every person in a position to be injured by his negligence. I have this duty to some degree even to the uninvited trespasser on my land. Or consider the duty (not equally recognized in our law) that every citizen has to come to the aid of accident victims. These unfortunates have a right to be assisted that holds against every or any person in a position to help. I propose to call such positive *in rem* rights, *rights of community membership*, because it is their recognition, more than anything else, that molds a society into a cohesive community.

An eighth class of duties, which I shall call *duties of status*, is perhaps the original from which many of the others derive. In the Middle Ages, a "duty" was something *due* a feudal lord, in virtue of his role and its status in the social system, from one of his inferiors, a vassal or a serf, in virtue of *his* status. A person, in being born into his relatively fixed position in the social order, was at the same time born into the duties that went with, and indeed defined, that position. One's duty was conceived as a kind of payment of one's proper share to the general economy of interests, and of course there were different shares to be exacted from different ranks and stations. Doing one's duty might be paying in crops or livestock, or performing assigned tasks at periodic intervals, or for the higher ranks contributing troops, horses, and weapons. Very likely these payments were made in a spirit similar to that in which club members pay their dues, especially in a club whose rules prescribe different types of payment for different types of members.

It was not difficult, in a rigidly hierarchical society, to know *to whom* one's duty was owed, for payments were generally from lower rank to higher, with the occupant of the higher rank always capable of exacting payment, if necessary, by force. With the decline of feudalism, however, it became increasingly difficult to find a specific claimant for every status duty. Offices and roles, of course, still survived, and carried with them their attached duties, but there was no longer a single clear line of direction in which they were owed, or single source of sanctions for their enforcement. To be sure, later when contract came to supplant status as a primary principle of social organization, one could in theory come to think of the duties of one's job as derived from the "employment contract" and therefore *owed as obligations* to the boss, as promisee. This was seldom, however, a convincing myth. Employment contracts were often unfairly bargained, and by the time conditions improved in that respect, the employer was so vast and impersonal he could hardly be conceived as the claimant of a personal obligation. Hence, duties of status have come less and less to be thought of as *owed* to anyone.

The concept of a duty, however, has by no means completely forgotten its past. It still preserves its ancestral connection with offices, stations, and jobs;[4] it is still bound up, however remotely, with the idea of coercion, and it still commonly suggests the idea of a fair share of burdens, imposed on one as a levy, for the promotion of socially shared interests. In group undertakings, it is often said that "if only everybody pitches in and does his *share*, the job will be done." The share we are thereby exhorted to contribute is, of course, the very same as our duty, and it will be greater for the rich than the poor and lesser for the weak than the strong.

Does it still make sense to ask *to whom* one's duty or status is owed? Perhaps, but we can no longer always expect a simple answer mentioning some specific person, such as "one's feudal lord," or "one's employer." To whom does the left tackle on a football team owe his assigned duty to block the player opposing him? In a case like this it is odd to say that the duty is owed to anyone but "the team." And similarly we often hear of status-duties owed "to the company," or "to the university," or "to one's country." And in still other cases, for example the duty of a janitor to sweep the corridors, it might plausibly be urged that the duty is owed to *no one at all*, although it is no less a duty for that.

Perhaps the most important feature of our talk about duties I have only mentioned up to now, and that is the alliance of the idea of duty with the idea of coercion. A duty, whatever else it be, is something *required* of one. That is to say first of all that a duty, like an obligation, is something that *obliges*. It is something we conceive of as *imposed* upon our inclinations, something we must do *whether we want to or not*. Second, a requirement is, in a perfectly good sense, a *liability*, something *we must do or else* "face the consequences" (punishment, firing, guilt feelings). When the coercive element common to duties and obligations is in clear focus, it is likely to seem so centrally important as to dim the various differences between the two conceptions, as when the lawbooks, for example, speak interchangeably of imposing

---

[4] If the phrase "moral duty," unlike "moral obligation," sounds odd in our ears, it is, I submit, because it suggests that there is an office or job of "man as such"—a most dubious metaphysical idea (*pace* Plato and Aristotle). Generally speaking, it is difficult to find plausible analogies between our moral problems as men and our moral problems as office holders. There are no analogies of this kind to compare with the close analogy between our obligations as contract signers and our moral commitments as promisors. Hence, the appropriateness of the phrase "moral obligation" and the oddness of "moral duty."

duties and obligations. Moreover, both terms, "duty" and "obligation," have developed extended senses in which *only* the coercive feature is essential, as when we speak, for example, of an action, fitting
perhaps as a "gesture," or symbolic expression of feeling, as a duty
when it seems to have a "compelling" appropriateness. "Duty" and
"obligation" both tend now to be used for any action we feel we must
(for whatever reason) do.

Duties of compelling appropriateness are perhaps only duties in an
extended sense, but still there is no harm in labeling them and including them in our catalogue.[5] The class probably includes such
philosophically puzzling specimens as "duties of perfection," "duties
of self-sacrifice," "duties of love," "duties of vicarious gratitude," and
so on. It is clear, I think, that people who feel that they have duties of
this kind do not feel them as owed to anyone.[6]

In speaking of a duty as a liability, we should take care to distinguish
it from another kind of liability also imposed by roles and jobs,
namely those that have come to be called *responsibilities*. A responsibility, like a duty, is both a burden and a liability; but unlike a duty
it carries considerable discretion (sometimes called "authority") along
with it. A goal is assigned and the means of achieving it are left to the
independent judgment of the responsible party. Moreover, the liability
to unwanted consequences in the case of a responsibility tends to be
"stricter" than in the case of a mere duty. That a man tried his best
is more likely to be accepted as an excuse for failure to perform one's
duty than for failure to fulfill one's responsibility. Indeed, the more
discretion allowed in the responsibility assignment, the stricter the
liability for failure is likely to be. In general, the closer the resemblance of a task assignment to the purely nondiscretionary cases, where
for example, the officer's command "Fire!" imposes the duty to pull the

---

5 It would be going too far, however, to include "duties of compelling attractiveness," which could be duties in no proper sense, paradigmatic or extended.

6 H. B. Acton gives several examples of persons who act "on a conception of duty
that requires [them] to give benefits to others much in excess of what is [be-
lieved to be] their right." "Thus Celia in Eliot's *The Cocktail Party* must have considered she had duties to savages who certainly had no right to services from her.
The man who, in Malraux's novel, gave all his supply of poison to his fellow-
prisoners to enable them by suicide to escape the burning alive which was to be
their fate and his, probably did not think that they had more right to the poison
than he had, though he thought it his duty to give it to them. Some of these supererogatory acts may be a form of disguised egoism, the agent regarding himself as
worthy of a much stricter code of behaviour than the majority of people. Others are
the result of compassion or benevolence, and in that way, perhaps outside the sphere
of rights and duties. But some of the more impressive acts of moral heroism appear
to be performed at the behest of an exacting sense of duty without their being [I
should add 'any sense of'] corresponding rights on the part of the beneficiaries."
H. B. Acton, "Symposium on 'Rights'," *Proceedings of the Aristotelian Society*, Supplementary Volume 24 (1950), pp. 107-108.

trigger, or where the annual dues notice imposes the duty to pay, the more likely we are to characterize it as a duty, and the less likely to call it a responsibility. A "duty to obey" makes sense; but there could be no such thing as a "responsibility to obey."[7]

This leads us to our final class of duties, the *duties of obedience*. The medieval lord was, in relation to his serf's duty, both beneficiary, claimant, and enforcing authority. In the complication of social roles that followed the collapse of feudalism, the separation of these three offices became common. In particular, the man who can, in some institutions, command the performance of duty from us, and back up his command with sanctions, is not always the same as the person, if there is one, to whom that duty is *owed*. It appears then to be a quite different sense of the preposition "to" in which we have duties *to* a commanding authority. And yet we commonly enough hear talk of "owing obedience" to parents, police officers, and bosses, and these authorities speak readily enough of having a claim to our obedience. Does an authority then have a *right* to be obeyed by his inferiors?

A traffic cop blows his whistle, points and shouts "Stop!" This, of course, imposes a (legal) duty on a motorist to stop. Still it is not true that the policeman can claim the motorist's stopping as *his* due or that the motorist owes it to *him* to stop. Perhaps the policeman has an *official* right, derived from his status *qua* policeman, rather than a *personal* right, that the motorist stop. I suspect, however, that this is simply a roundabout way of saying that the policeman's office confers on him the authority to command motorists to stop, which of course is beyond question, yet does nothing to settle the further question whether authorities can be said to have a right that persons do as they command. In any case, many duties of obedience are "owed" to impersonal authority like "the law," or a painted stop sign. Here it is especially difficult to find an assignable person who can claim another's stopping as his due. Some duties of obedience, then, seem to entail no correlative rights; and if my suspicion is correct, none of them do. For if the preposition "to" in the phrase "duty (of obedience) to one's superior" means the same as it does in the expression "answerable to so-and-so for his failure," and I suspect that this is so, then the authority to whom one "owes" obedience is not a *claimant* in the manner of (say) a creditor, but rather simply the one who may properly command

---

[7] The title of a current paperback book found in most drugstores is *The Sexual Responsibility of Woman*. The book spends several hundred pages describing the many kinds of situations in married life that call for the exercise of intelligence, judgment, and adaptability on the part of the wife. On the other hand, there could be no doubt what might be meant by a book, published say in Victorian England, with the title *The Sexual Duty of Woman*, for the sexual duty of a wife, if there could be such a thing, could only be to submit. There could be no such thing as a "responsibility to submit."

performance of duty and apply sanctions in case of failure. The little preposition "to" then is triply ambiguous when used with "duty." One can have a duty *to* his claimant, *to* (or toward) a mere beneficiary, and be liable for failure *to* an authority; but it is only the claimant who can properly be said to have a right to one's performance.

In summary, duties of indebtedness, commitment, reparation, need-fulfillment, and reciprocation are necessarily correlated with other people's *in personam* rights. Duties of respect and community membership are necessarily correlated with other people's *in rem* rights, negative in the case of duties of respect, positive in the case of duties of community membership. Finally, duties of status, duties of obedience, and duties of compelling appropriateness are not necessarily correlated with other people's rights.

II. RIGHTS AS CLAIMS TO . . .

Having described the various kinds of duties that *are* correlated with rights, have we thereby done all that is necessary to elucidate the concept of a right? Many writers seem to think so.[8] I am inclined, however, to agree with Richard Wasserstrom[9] that we have not until we have said something further about rights as *claims*. It will not help to attempt a formal definition of rights in terms of claims, for the idea of a right is already included in that of a claim, and we would fall into a circle. Nevertheless, certain facts about rights, more easily, if not solely, expressible in the language of claims and claiming, are necessary to a full understanding of what rights are and why they are so vitally important.

There may at first sight be grounds for holding that claims are always *against* someone, and therefore necessarily correlated with the duties of those against whom they hold; but there is a sense of "claim," closely related to "need," in which this is not always so. Imagine a

[8] Howard Warrender speaks of rights as "merely the shadows cast by [other people's] duties" (*The Political Philosophy of Hobbes* [Oxford, Clarendon Press, 1957], p. 19); S. I. Benn and Richard Peters write that "Right and duty are different names for the same normative relation, according to the point of view from which it is regarded" (*Social Principles and the Democratic State* [London, Allen & Unwin, 1959], p. 89); and Richard Brandt writes that "a society with a language that had no term corresponding to 'a right' might still be said to have the *concept* of a right, if it were recognized that people have the *obligations* toward others which are the ones that correspond with rights" (*Ethical Theory* [Englewood Cliffs, N.J., Prentice-Hall, 1959], p. 441). In his sensitive discussion, Professor Brandt does allow, however, that there are important differences in emphasis and "overtone" between talk of rights and equivalent talk of duties.

[9] "Rights, Human Rights, and Racial Discrimination," *The Journal of Philosophy*, vol. 61 (1964), pp. 628-641.

hungry, sickly, fatherless infant, one of a dozen children of a desper-
ately impoverished and illiterate mother in a squalid Mexican slum.
Doesn't this child have a *claim* to be fed, to be given medical care, to
be taught to read? Can't we know this before we have any idea where
correlative duties lie? Won't we still believe it even if we despair of
finding anyone whose duty it is to provide these things? Indeed, if we
do finally *assign* the duty to someone, I suspect we would do so because
there *is* this prior claim, looking, so to speak, for a duty to go with it.

In our time it is commonplace to speak of *needs* as "constituting
claims." William James thought that every interest is a kind of claim
against the world and that the validity of an interest *qua* claim lies
"in its mere existence as a matter of fact."[10] This probably goes too
far. We don't think of every desire or even every need as a claim, but
important needs are another matter. They "cry out," we say, for satisfaction. (Note the etymological connection of "claim" with "clamor.")
And when they cry no proper name but only their own need, we speak
of their claims "against the world"; but this is but a rhetorical way of
saying "claim against no one at all." (Or perhaps a "claim against the
world" is like an explosion in the desert—there is no one to hear it,
but were anyone to get close to it what a commotion he would hear,
and what an impact he would feel! So it is perhaps with my little
Mexican urchin. Perhaps her claim is like a "permanent possibility
of sensation," real enough, though no one comes within its range. Still
note what one does hear, if he is not morally deaf, when he comes
close enough: He hears a *crying need*, a claim *to . . .* that is so strong
it may be felt as a claim *against. . . .*)

The right to education, like other positive *in rem* rights peculiar to
twentieth-century manifestos, has caused much confusion and dissen-
sion, partly because theorists, in their eagerness to provide schematic
translations for all rights in terms of other people's duties, have simply
overlooked the sense of "right" uppermost in the minds of manifesto
writers. Professor Brandt, for instance, says of "my having a right to
an education" that it "implies roughly that each individual in my
community has an obligation to do what he can [in another formulation Brandt says "to cooperate substantially"] in view of his opportunities and capacities and other obligations, to secure and maintain a
system in which I and persons in my position are provided with an
opportunity for education."[11] But surely there is a familiar sense of
"right" that requires more than that others try, or "do what they can"
(considering of course how *busy* they all are) or "cooperate substan-

10 William James, "The Moral Philosopher and the Moral Life," *International
Journal of Ethics* (1891), reprinted in *Essays in Pragmatism*, ed. A. Castell (New
York, Hafner, 1948), p. 73.
11 Brandt, *Ethical Theory, op. cit.,* p. 437.

tially." My right in this sense is *to* the education (there is that preposition again in still a fourth sense) and not simply to other people's dutiful efforts. More likely my right in this case (if I have one) entails not simply a duty to try but a responsibility to succeed; but even this doesn't do the whole job of translation, for there is a MUST HAVE here not wholly translatable into any number of MUST DO's.[12]

III. CLAIMING THAT ONE HAS A RIGHT

I wish finally to emphasize the importance of the verb "to claim," not to the analysis of a right, but to an understanding of why rights are, in Wasserstrom's phrase, such "valuable commodities."[13] To claim that one has a right (or for that matter that one has any of the other things one might claim—knowledge, ability, whatever) is to *assert* in such a manner as to demand or insist that what is asserted be *recognized*. It is my contention that for every right there is a further right to claim, in appropriate circumstances,[14] that one has that right. Why is the right to demand recognition of one's rights so important? The reason, I think, is that if one begged, pleaded, or prayed for recognition merely, at best one would receive a kind of beneficent treatment easily confused with the acknowledgment of rights, but in fact altogether foreign and deadly to it.

There are in general two quite distinct kinds of moral transaction.

---

[12] No doubt this is an extended sense of "right." I insist only that it is a proper and important one. Note that there are parallel extended senses of "claim" and "demand" both in quite general circulation. Webster's gives as its fourth sense of "demand," for example, "to call for or require as necessary or useful; to be in urgent need of, as in the phrase 'the case demands care.'" It is in this sense, *at the very least*, that children require education, sickness calls for medicine, and hunger demands food.

[13] Wasserstrom, *op. cit.*, p. 629.

[14] G. J. Warnock in a useful article ("Claims to Knowledge," *Proceedings of the Aristotelian Society*, Supplementary Volume 36 [1962], p. 21) says that when I claim to others that I *know* something, I am not merely asserting it, but rather I am "obtruding my putative knowledge upon their attention, demanding that it be recognized, that appropriate notice be taken of it by those concerned. . . ." This sounds like the behavior of a perfect boor! I don't wish to contend that all rights confer the additional right to be boorish, but only that one may insist, in the appropriate circumstances and with only an appropriate degree of vehemence, that one's right be recognized.

A list of "appropriate circumstances" would include occasions when one is challenged, when his rights are explicitly denied, when he must make application for them, where his possession seems insufficiently acknowledged or appreciated, etc. There may even be appropriate circumstances for one's demanding recognition of his second-level right to claim ground-level rights; but circumstances would rarely be appropriate for claiming third-level rights, and probably never for levels higher than that. So the contention in the text that for every right there is a right to claim *in appropriate circumstances* that one has that right leads to no kind of vicious regress.

On the one hand there are gifts and services and favors motivated by love or pity or mercy and for which gratitude is the sole fitting response. On the other hand there are dutiful actions and omissions called for by the rights of other people. These can be demanded, claimed, insisted upon, without embarrassment or shame. When not forthcoming, the appropriate reaction is indignation; and when duly done there is no place for gratitude, an expression of which would suggest that it is not simply one's own or one's due that one was given.[15] Both kinds of transaction are important, and any world with one but not the other would—in Wasserstrom's phrase—be "morally impoverished." A world without loving favors would be cold and dangerous; a world full of kindness, but without universal rights, would be one in which self-respect would be rare and difficult. Too much gratitude is a very bad thing, leading donors to be complacent and hypocritical, and doing worse harm still to the recipients. If the rugged individualist who boasts in his blindness that he owes nothing to any man is no moral paragon, neither is he who feels gratitude for everything, for that is a kind of self-abasement; and from men who respect not their own interests nor feel even their most basic needs as claims, little good, and probably considerable mischief, can be anticipated.

[15] The obverse of this point is worth noting too. Gratitude often *is* the appropriate response to a person's deliberate *failure* to press for his rights. I quote from a perceptive editorial in *The New Yorker* (June 3, 1961, p. 23): ". . . Conceivably it is in the national interest to persuade Negro leaders to set a slower pace, but the argument is one that does not permit a high moral tone. One can hardly, with justice, inform a Negro that he has a duty as a citizen to refrain from sharing in the rights of citizenship. We can imagine asking it, under special circumstances, but only as the immense favor that it would be, rather than as the obligation it certainly is not."

The Nature and Value of Rights

1

I would like to begin by conducting a thought experiment. Try to imagine Nowheresville — a world very much like our own except that no one, or hardly any one (the
qualification is not important), has *rights.* If this flaw makes Nowheresville too
ugly to hold very long in contemplation, we can make it as pretty as we wish in
other moral respects. We can, for example, make the human beings in it as attractive
and virtuous as possible without taxing our conceptions of the limits of human
nature. In particular, let the virtues of moral sensibility flourish. Fill this imagined
world with as much benevolence, compassion, sympathy, and pity as it will conveniently hold without strain. Now we can imagine men helping one another from
compassionate motives merely, quite as much or even more than they do in our
actual world from a variety of more complicated motives.

   This picture, pleasant as it is in some respects, would hardly have satisfied
Immanuel Kant. Benevolently motivated actions do good, Kant admitted, and
therefore are better, *ceteris paribus,* than malevolently motivated actions; but no
action can have supreme kind of worth — what Kant called "moral worth" — unless
its whole motivating power derives from the thought that it is *required by duty.*
Accordingly, let us try to make Nowheresville more appealing to Kant by introducing the idea of duty into it, and letting the sense of duty be a sufficient motive for
many beneficent and honorable actions. But doesn't this bring our original thought
experiment to an abortive conclusion? If duties are permitted entry into Nowheresville, are not rights necessarily smuggled in along with them?

   The question is well-asked, and requires here a brief digression so that we might
consider the so-called "doctrine of the logical correlativity of rights and duties."
This is the doctrine that (i) all duties entail other people's rights and (ii) all rights
entail other people's duties. Only the first part of the doctrine, the alleged entail-
ment from duties to rights, need concern us here. Is this part of the doctrine correct?
It should not be surprising that my answer is: "In a sense yes and in a sense no."
Etymologically, the word "duty" is associated with actions that are *due* someone
else, the payments of debts *to* creditors, the keeping of agreements with promises,
the payment of club dues, or legal fees, or tariff levies to appropriate authorities or
their representatives. In this original sense of "duty," all duties are correlated with
the rights of those *to* whom the duty is owed. On the other hand, there seem to be
numerous classes of duties, both of a legal and non-legal kind, that are *not* logically
correlated with the rights of other persons. This seems to be a consequence of the
fact that the word "duty" has come to be used for *any* action understood to be
required, whether by the rights of others, or by law, or by higher authority, or by
conscience, or whatever. When the notion of requirement is in clear focus it is likely
to seem the only element in the idea of duty that is essential, and the other component notion — that a duty is something *due* someone else — drops off. Thus, in this

widespread but derivative usage, "duty" tends to be used for any action we feel we *must* (for whatever reason) do. It comes, in short, to be a term of moral modality merely; and it is no wonder that the first thesis of the logical correlativity doctrine often fails.

Let us then introduce duties into Nowheresville, but only in the sense of actions that are, or believed to be, morally mandatory, but not in the older sense of actions that are due others and can be claimed by others as their right. Nowheresville now can have duties of the sort imposed by positive law. A legal duty is not something we are implored or advised to do merely; it is something the law, or an authority under the law, *requires* us to do whether we want to or not, under pain of penalty. When traffic lights turn red, however, there is no determinate person who can plausibly be said to claim our stopping as his due, so that the motorist owes it to *him* to stop, in the way a debtor owes it to his creditor to pay. In our own actual world, of course, we sometimes owe it to our *fellow motorists* to stop; but that kind of right-correlated duty does not exist in Nowheresville. There, motorists "owe" obedience to the Law, but they owe nothing to one another. When they collide, no matter who is at fault, no one is accountable to anyone else, and no one has any sound grievance or "right to complain."

When we leave legal contexts to consider moral obligations and other extra-legal duties, a greater variety of duties-without-correlative-rights present themselves. Duties of charity, for example, require us to contribute to one or another of a large number of eligible recipients, no one of whom can claim our contribution from us as his due. Charitable contributions are more like gratuitous services, favours, and gifts than like repayments of debts or reparations; and yet we do have duties to be charitable. Many persons, moreover, in our actual world believe that they are required by their own consciences to do more than that "duty" that *can* be demanded of them by their prospective beneficiaries. I have quoted elsewhere the citation from H. B. Acton of a character in a Malraux novel who "gave all his supply of poison to his fellow prisoners to enable them by suicide to escape the burning alive which was to be their fate and his." This man, Acton adds, "probably did not think that [the others] had more of a right to the poison than he had, though he thought it his duty to give it to them."[1] I am sure that there are many actual examples, less dramatically heroic than this fictitious one, of persons who believe, rightly or wrongly, that they *must do* something (hence the word "duty") for another person in excess of what that person can appropriately demand of him (hence the absence of "right").

Now the digression is over and we can return to Nowheresville and summarize what we have put in it thus far. We now find spontaneous benevolence in somewhat larger degree than in our actual world, and also the acknowledged existence of duties of obedience, duties of charity, and duties imposed by exacting private consciences, and also, let us suppose, a degree of conscientiousness in respect to those duties somewhat in excess of what is to be found in our actual world. I doubt that Kant would be fully satisfied with Nowheresville even now that duty and respect for law and authority have been added to it; but I feel certain that he would regard

---

[1]H. B. Acton, "Symposium of 'Rights'," *Proceedings of the Aristotelian Society*, Supplementary Volume 24 (1950), pp. 107–108.

their addition at least as an improvement. I will now introduce two further moral practices into Nowheresville that will make the world very little more appealing to Kant, but will make it appear more familiar to us. These are the practices connected with the notions of *personal desert* and what I call a *sovereign monopoly of rights.*

When a person is said to deserve something good from us what is meant in parts is that there would be a certain propriety in our giving that good thing to him in virtue of the kind of person he is, perhaps, or more likely, in virtue of some specific thing he has done. The propriety involved here is a much weaker kind than that which derives from our having promised him the good thing or from his having qualified for it by satisfying the well-advertised conditions of some public rule. In the latter case he could be said not merely to deserve the good thing but also to have a *right* to it, that is to be in a position to demand it as his due; and of course we will not have that sort of thing in Nowheresville. That weaker kind of propriety which is mere desert is simply a kind of *fittingness* between one party's character or action and another party's favorable response, much like that between humor and laughter, or good performance and applause.

The following seems to be the origin of the idea of deserving good or bad treatment from others: A master or lord was under no obligation to reward his servant for especially good service; still a master might naturally feel that there would be a special fittingness in giving a gratuitous reward as a grateful response to the good service (or conversely imposing a penalty for bad service). Such an act while surely fitting and proper was entirely supererogatory. The fitting response in turn from the rewarded servant should be gratitude. If the deserved reward had not been given him he should have had no complaint, since he only *deserved* the reward, as opposed to having a *right* to it, or a ground for claiming it as his due.

The idea of desert has evolved a good bit away from its beginnings by now, but nevertheless, it seems clearly to be one of those words J. L. Austin said "never entirely forget their pasts."[2] Today servants qualify for their wages by doing their agreed upon chores, no more and no less. If their wages are not forthcoming, their contractual rights have been violated and they can make legal claim to the money that is their due. If they do less than they agreed to do, however, their employers may "dock" them, by paying them proportionately less than the agreed upon fee. This is all a matter of right. But if the servant does a splendid job, above and beyond his minimal contractual duties, the employer is under no further obligation to reward him, for this was not agreed upon, even tacitly, in advance. The additional service was all the servant's idea and done entirely on his own. Nevertheless, the morally sensitive employer may feel that it would be exceptionally appropriate for him to respond, freely on *his* own, to the servant's meritorious service, with a reward. The employee cannot demand it as his due, but he will happily accept it, with gratitude, as a fitting response to his desert.

In our age of organized labor, even this picture is now archaic; for almost every kind of exchange of service is governed by hard bargained contracts so that even bonuses can sometimes be demanded as a matter of right, and nothing is given for nothing on either side of the bargaining table. And perhaps that is a good thing; for consider an anachronistic instance of the earlier kind of practice that survives, at

[2]J. L. Austin, "A Plea for Excuses," *Proceedings of the Aristotelian Society,* Vol. 57 (1956–57).

least as a matter of form, in the quaint old practice of "tipping." The tip was originally conceived as a reward that has to be earned by "zealous service." It is not something to be taken for granted as a standard response to *any* service. That is to say that its payment is a "*gratuity*," not a discharge of obligation, but something given apart from, or in addition to, anything the recipient can expect as a matter of right. That is what tipping originally meant at any rate, and tips are still referred to as "gratuities" in the tax forms. But try to explain all that to a New York cab driver! If he has *earned* his gratuity, by God, he has it coming, and there had better be sufficient acknowledgement of his desert or he'll give you a piece of his mind! I'm not generally prone to defend New York cab drivers, but they do have a point here. There is the making of a paradox in the queerly unstable concept of an "earned gratuity." One can understand how "desert" in the weak sense of "propriety" or "mere fittingness" tends to generate a stronger sense in which desert is itself the ground for a claim of right.

In Nowheresville, nevertheless, we will have only the original weak kind of desert. Indeed, it will be impossible to keep this idea out if we allow such practices as teachers grading students, judges awarding prizes, and servants serving benevolent but class-conscious masters. Nowheresville is a reasonably good world in many ways, and its teachers, judges, and masters will generally try to give students, contestants, and servants the grades, prizes, and rewards they deserve. For this the recipients will be grateful; but they will never think to complain, or even feel aggrieved, when expected responses to desert fail. The masters, judges, and teachers don't *have* to do good things, after all, for *anyone.* One should be happy that they *ever* treat us well, and not grumble over their occasional lapses. Their hoped for responses, after all, are *gratuities,* and there is no wrong in the omission of what is merely gratuitous. Such is the response of persons who have no concept of *rights,* even persons who are proud of their own deserts.[3]

Surely, one might ask, rights have to come in somewhere, if we are to have even moderately complex forms of social organization. Without rules that confer rights and impose obligations, how can we have ownership of property, bargains and deals, promises and contracts, appointments and loans, marriages and partnerships? Very well, let us introduce all of these social and economic practices into Nowheresville, but *with one big twist.* With them I should like to introduce the curious notion of a "sovereign right-monopoly." You will recall that the subjects in Hobbes's *Leviathan* had no rights whatever against their sovereign. He could do as he liked with them, even gratuitously harm them, but this gave them no valid grievance against him. The sovereign, to be sure, had a certain duty to treat his subjects well, but this duty was owed not to the subjects directly, but to God, just as we might have a duty to a person to treat his property well, but of course no duty to the property itself but only to its owner. Thus, while the sovereign was quite capable of *harming* his subjects, he could commit no wrong against them that they could complain about, since they had no prior claims against his conduct. The only party *wronged* by the sovereign's mistreatment of his subjects was God, the supreme

[3]For a fuller discussion of the concept of personal desert see my "Justice and Personal Desert," *Nomos VI, Justice,* ed. by C. J. Chapman (New York: Atherton Press, 1963), pp. 69–97.

lawmaker. Thus, in repenting cruelty to his subjects, the sovereign might say to God, as David did after killing Uriah, "to Thee only have I sinned."[4]

Even in the *Leviathan,* however, ordinary people had ordinary rights *against one another.* They played roles, occupied offices, made agreements, and signed contracts. In a genuine "sovereign right-monopoly," as I shall be using that phrase, they will do all those things too, and thus incur genuine obligations toward one another; but the obligations (here is the twist) will not be owed directly *to* promises, creditors, parents, and the like, but rather to God alone, or to the members of some elite, or to a single sovereign under God. Hence, the rights correlative to the obligations that derive from these transactions are all owned by some "outside" authority.

As far as I know, no philosopher has ever suggested that even our role and contract obligations (in this, our actual world) are all owed directly to a divine intermediary, but some theologians have approached such extreme moral occasionalism. I have in mind the familiar phrase in certain widely distributed religious tracts that "it takes three to marry," which suggests that marital vows are not made between bride and groom directly but between each spouse and God, so that if one breaks his vow, the other cannot rightly complain of being wronged, since only God could have claimed performance of the marital duties as his *own* due; and hence God alone had a claim-right violated by nonperformance. If John breaks his vow to God, he might then properly repent in the words of David: "To Thee only have I sinned."

In our actual world, very few spouses conceive of their mutual obligations in this way; but their small children, at a certain stage in their moral upbringing, are likely to feel precisely this way toward *their* mutual obligations. If Billy kicks Bobby and is punished by Daddy, he may come to feel contrition for his naughtiness induced by his painful estrangement from the loved parent. He may then be happy to make amends and sincere apology to *Daddy;* but when Daddy insists that he apologize to his wronged brother, that is another story. A direct apology to Billy would be a tacit recognition of Billy's status as a right-holder against him, someone he can wrong as well as harm, and someone to whom he is directly accountable for his wrongs. This is a status Bobby will happily accord Daddy; but it would imply a respect for Billy that he does not presently feel, so he bitterly resents according it to him. On the "three-to-marry" model, the relations between each spouse and God would be like those between Bobby and Daddy; respect for the other spouse as an independent claimant would not even be necessary; and where present, of course, never sufficient.

The advocates of the "three-to-marry" model who conceive it either as a description of our actual institution of marriage or a recommendation of what marriage ought to be, may wish to escape this embarrassment by granting rights to spouses in capacities other than as promisees. They may wish to say, for example, that when John promises God that he will be faithful to Mary, a right is thus conferred not only on God as promisee but also on Mary herself as third-party beneficiary, just as when John contracts with an insurance company and names Mary as his intended beneficiary, she has a right to the accumulated funds after John's death, even though

[4]II Sam. 11. Cited with approval by Thomas Hobbes in *The Leviathan,* Part II, Chap. 21.

the insurance company made no promise to her. But this seems to be an unnecessarily cumbersome complication contributing nothing to our understanding of the marriage bond. The life insurance transaction is necessarily a three party relation, involving occupants of three distinct offices, no two of whom alone could do the whole job. The transaction, after all, is defined as the purchase by the customer (first office) from the vendor (second office) of protection for a beneficiary (third office) against the customer's untimely death. Marriage, on the other hand, in this our actual world, appears to be a binary relation between a husband and wife, and even though third parties such as children, neighbors, psychiatrists, and priests may sometimes be helpful and even causally necessary for the survival of the relation, they are not logically necessary to our *conception* of the relation, and indeed many married couples do quite well without them. Still I am not now purporting to describe our actual world, but rather trying to contrast it with a counterpart world of the imagination. In *that* world, it takes three to make almost *any* moral relation and all rights are owned by God or some sovereign under God.

There will, of course, be delegated authorities in the imaginary world, empowered to give commands to their underlings and to punish them for their disobedience. But the commands are all given in the name of the right-monopoly who in turn are the only persons to whom obligations are owed. Hence, even intermediate superiors do not have claim-rights against their subordinates but only legal *powers* to create obligations in the subordinates *to* the monopolistic right-holders, and also the legal *privilege* to impose penalties in the name of that monopoly.

2

So much for the imaginary "world without rights." If some of the moral concepts and practices I have allowed into that world do not sit well with one another, no matter. Imagine Nowheresville with all of these practices if you can, or with any harmonious subset of them, if you prefer. The important thing is not what I've let into it, but what I have kept out. The remainder of this paper will be devoted to an analysis of what precisely a world is missing when it does not contain rights and why that absence is morally important.

The most conspicuous difference, I think, between the Nowheresvillians and ourselves has something to do with the activity of *claiming*. Nowheresvillians, even when they are discriminated against invidiously, or left without the things they need, or otherwise badly treated, do not think to leap to their feet and make righteous demands against one another though they may not hesitate to resort to force and trickery to get what they want. They have no notion of rights, so they do not have a notion of what is their due; hence they do not claim before they take. The conceptual linkage between personal rights and claiming has long been noticed by legal writers and is reflected in the standard usage in which "claim-rights" are distinguished from other mere liberties, immunities, and powers, also sometimes called "rights," with which they are easily confused. When a person has a legal claim-right to X, it must be the case (i) that he is at liberty in respect to X, i.e. that he has no duty to refrain from or relinquish X, and also (ii) that his liberty is the ground of other people's *duties* to grant him X or not to interfere with him in respect to X. Thus, in the sense of claim-rights, it is true by definition that rights logically entail other people's duties. The paradigmatic examples of such rights are the creditor's right to be paid a debt by his debtor, and the landowner's right not to be interfered with by anyone in the exclusive occupancy of his land. The creditor's right against his debtor, for example, and the debtor's duty to his creditor, are precisely the same relation seen from two different vantage points, as inextricably linked as the two sides of the same coin.

And yet, this is not quite an accurate account of the matter, for it fails to do justice to the way claim-rights are somehow prior to, or more basic than, the duties with which they are necessarily correlated. If Nip has a claim-right against Tuck, it is because of this fact that Tuck has a duty to Nip. It is only because something from Tuck is *due* Nip (directional element) that there is something Tuck *must do* (modal element). This is a relation, moreover, in which Tuck is bound and Nip is free. Nip not only *has* a right, but he can choose whether or not to exercise it, whether to claim it, whether to register complaints upon its infringement, even whether to release Tuck from his duty, and forget the whole thing. If the personal claim-right is also backed up by criminal sanctions, however, Tuck may yet have a duty of obedience to the law from which no one, not even Nip, may release him. He would even have such duties if he lived in Nowheresville; but duties subject to acts of claiming, duties derivative from the contingent upon the personal rights of others, are unknown and undreamed of in Nowheresville.

Many philosophical writers have simply identified rights with claims. The dictionaries tend to define "claims," in turn as "assertions of right," a dizzying piece of circularity that led one philosopher to complain — "We go in search of rights and are directed to claims, and then back again to rights in bureaucratic futility."[5] What then is the relation between a claim and a right?

As we shall see, a right *is* a kind of claim, and a claim is "an assertion of right," so that a formal definition of either notion in terms of the other will not get us very far. Thus if a "formal definition" of the usual philosophical sort is what we are after, the game is over before it has begun, and we can say that the concept of a right is a "simple, undefinable, unanalysable primitive." Here as elsewhere in philosophy this will have the effect of making the commonplace seem unnecessarily mysterious. We would be better advised, I think, not to attempt definition of either "right" or "claim," but rather to use the idea of a claim in informal elucidation of the idea of a right. This is made possible by the fact that *claiming* is an elaborate sort of rule-governed *activity*. A claim is that which is claimed, the object of the act of claiming. . . . If we concentrate on the whole activity of claiming, which is public, familiar, and open to our observation, rather than on its upshot alone, we may learn more about the generic nature of rights than we could ever hope to learn from a formal definition, even if one were possible. Moreover, certain facts about rights more easily, if not solely, expressible in the language of claims and claiming are essential to a full understanding not only of what rights are, but also why they are so vitally important.

Let us begin then by distinguishing between: (i) making claim to . . . , (ii) claiming that . . . , and (iii) having a claim. One sort of thing we may be doing when we claim is to *make claim to something*. This is "to petition or seek by virtue of sup-

[5] H. B. Acton, *op. cit.*

posed right; to demand as due." Sometimes this is done by an acknowledged right-holder when he serves notice that he now wants turned over to him that which has already been acknowledged to be his, something borrowed, say, or improperly taken from him. This is often done by turning in a chit, a receipt, an I.O.U., a check, an insurance policy, or a deed, that is, a *title* to something currently in the possession of someone else. On other occasions, making claim is making application for titles or rights themselves, as when a mining prospector stakes a claim to mineral rights, or a householder to a tract of land in the public domain, or an inventor to his patent rights. In the one kind of case, to make claim is to exercise rights one already has by presenting title; in the other kind of case it is to apply for the title itself, by showing that one has satisfied the conditions specified by a rule for the ownership of title and therefore that one can demand it as one's due.

Generally speaking, only the person who has a title or who has qualified for it, or someone speaking in his name, can make claim to something as a matter of right. It is an important fact about rights (or claims), then, that they can be claimed only by those who have them. Anyone can claim, of course, *that* this umbrella is yours, but only you or your representative can actually claim the umbrella. If Smith owes Jones five dollars, only Jones can claim the five dollars as his own, though any bystander can *claim that* it belongs to Jones. One important difference then between *making legal claim to* and *claiming that* is that the former is a legal performance with direct legal consequences whereas the latter is often a mere piece of descriptive commentary with no legal force. Legally speaking, *making claim to* can itself make things happen. This sense of "claiming," then, might well be called "the performative sense." The legal power to claim (performatively) one's right or the things to which one has a right seems to be essential to the very notion of a right. A right to which one could not make claim (i.e. not even for recognition) would be a very "imperfect" right indeed!

Claiming that one has a right (what we can call "propositional claiming" as opposed to "performative claiming") is another sort of thing one can do with language, but it is not the sort of doing that characteristically has legal consequences. To claim that one has rights is to make an assertion that one has them, and to make it in such a manner as to demand or insist that they be recognized. In this sense of "claim" many things in addition to rights can be claimed, that is, many other kinds of proposition can be asserted in the claiming way. I can claim, for example, that you, he, or she has certain rights, or that Julius Caesar once had certain rights; or I can claim that certain statements are true, or that I have certain skills, or accomplishments, or virtually anything at all. I can claim that the earth is flat. What is essential to *claiming that* is the manner of assertion. One can assert without even caring very much whether anyone is listening, but part of the point of propositional claiming is to *make sure* people listen. When I claim to others that I know something, for example, I am not merely asserting it, but rather "obtruding my putative knowledge upon their attention, demanding that it be recognized, that appropriate notice be taken of it by those concerned. . . ."[6] Not every truth is properly assertable, much

[6]G. J. Warnock, "Claims to Knowledge," *Proceedings of the Aristotelian Society,* Supplementary Volume 36 (1962), p. 21.

less claimable, in every context. To claim that something is the case in circumstances that justify no more than calm assertion is to behave like a boor. (This kind of boorishness, I might add, is probably less common in Nowheresville.) But not to claim in the appropriate circumstances that one has a right is to be spiritless or foolish. A list of "appropriate circumstances" would include occasions when one is challenged, when one's possession is denied, or seems insufficiently acknowledged or appreciated; and of course even in these circumstances, the claiming should be done only with an appropriate degree of vehemence.

Even if there are conceivable circumstances in which one would admit rights diffidently, there is no doubt that their characteristic use and that for which they are distinctively well suited, is to be claimed, demanded, affirmed, insisted upon. They are especially sturdy objects to "stand upon," a most useful sort of moral furniture. Having rights, of course, makes claiming possible; but it is claiming that gives rights their special moral significance. This feature of rights is connected in a way with the customary rhetoric about what it is to be a human being. Having rights enables us to "stand up like men," to look others in the eye, and to feel in some fundamental way the equal of anyone. To think of oneself as the holder of rights is not to be unduly but properly proud, to have that minimal self-respect that is necessary to be worthy of the love and esteem of others. Indeed, respect for persons (this is an intriguing idea) may simply be respect for their rights, so that there cannot be the one without the other; and what is called "human dignity" may simply be the recognizable capacity to assert claims. To respect a person then, or to think of him as possessed of human dignity, simply *is* to think of him as a potential maker of claims. Not all of this can be packed into a definition of "rights"; but these are *facts* about the possession of rights that argue well their supreme moral importance. More than anything else I am going to say, these facts explain what is wrong with Nowheresville.

We come now to the third interesting employment of the claiming vocabulary, that involving not the verb "to claim" but the substantive "a claim." What is to *have a claim* and how is this related to rights? I would like to suggest that *having a claim consists in being in a position to claim, that is, to make claim to or claim that.* If this suggestion is correct it shows the primacy of the verbal over the nominative forms. It links claims to a kind of activity and obviates the temptation to think of claims as *things,* on the model of coins, pencils, and other material possessions which we can carry in our hip pockets. To be sure, we often make or establish our claims by presenting titles, and these typically have the form of receipts, tickets, certificates, and other pieces of paper or parchment. The title, however, is not the same thing as the claim; rather it is the evidence that establishes the claim as valid. On this analysis, one might have a claim without ever claiming that to which one is entitled, or without even knowing that one has the claim; for one might simply be ignorant of the fact that one is in a position to claim; or one might be unwilling to exploit that position for one reason or another, including fear that the legal machinery is broken down or corrupt and will not enforce one's claim despite its validity.

Nearly all writers maintain that there is some intimate connection between having a claim and having a right. Some identify right and claim without qualification; some define "right" as justified or justifiable claim, others as recognized claim, still others as valid claim. My own preference is for the latter definition. Some writers, however, reject the identification of rights with valid claims on the ground that all claims as such are valid, so that the expression "valid claim" is redundant. These writers, therefore, would identify rights with claims *simpliciter*. But this is a very simple confusion. All claims, to be sure, are *put forward* as justified, whether they are justified in fact or not. A claim conceded even by its maker to have no validity is not a claim at all, but a mere demand. The highwayman, for example, *demands* his victim's money; but he hardly makes claim to it as rightfully his own.

But it does not follow from this sound point that it is redundant to qualify claims as justified (or as I prefer, valid) in the definition of a right; for it remains true that not all claims put forward as valid really are valid; and only the valid ones can be acknowledged as rights.

If having a valid claim is not redundant, i.e. if it is not redundant to pronounce *another's* claim valid, there must be such a thing as having a claim that is not valid. What would this be like? One might accumulate just enough evidence to argue with relevance and cogency that one has a right (or ought to be granted a right), although one's case might not be overwhelmingly conclusive. In such a case, one might have strong enough argument to be entitled to a hearing and given fair consideration. When one is in this position, it might be said that one "has a claim" that deserves to be weighed carefully. Nevertheless, the balance of reasons may turn out to militate against recognition of the claim, so that the claim, which one admittedly had, and perhaps still does, is not a valid claim or right. "Having a claim" in this sense is an expression very much like the legal phrase "having a *prima facie* case." A plaintiff establishes a *prima facie* case for the defendant's liability when he establishes grounds that will be sufficient for liability unless outweighed by reasons of a different sort that may be offered by the defendant. Similarly, in the criminal law, a grand jury returns an indictment when it thinks that the prosecution has sufficient evidence to be taken seriously and given a fair hearing, whatever counter-vailing reasons may eventually be offered on the other side. That initial evidence, serious but not conclusive, is also sometimes called a *prima facie* case. In a parallel *"prima facie* sense" of "claim," having a claim to X is not (yet) the same as having a right to X, but is rather having a case of at least minimal plausibility that one has a right to X, a case that does establish a right, not to X, but to a fair hearing and consideration. Claims, so conceived, differ in degree: some are stronger than others. Rights, on the other hand, do not differ in degree; no one right is more of a right than another.[7]

Another reason for not identifying rights with claims *simply* is that there is a well-established usage in international law that makes a theoretically interesting

[7]This is the important difference between rights and mere claims. It is analogous to the difference between *evidence* of guilt (subject to degrees of cogency) and conviction of guilt (which is all or nothing). One can "have evidence" that is not conclusive just as one can "have a claim" that is not valid. "Prima-facieness" is built into the sense of "claim," but the notion of a "prima-facie right" makes little sense. On the latter point see A. I. Melden, *Rights and Right Conduct* (Oxford: Basil Blackwell, 1959), pp. 18–20, and Herbert Morris, "Persons and Punishment," *The Monist,* Vol. 52 (1968), pp. 498–9.

distinction between claims and rights. Statesmen are sometimes led to speak of "claims" when they are concerned with the natural needs of deprived human beings in conditions of scarcity. Young orphans *need* good upbringings, balanced diets, education, and technical training everywhere in the world; but unfortunately there are many places where these goods are in such short supply that it is impossible to provision all who need them. If we persist, nevertheless, in speaking of these needs as constituting rights and not merely claims, we are committed to the conception of a right which is an entitlement *to* some good, but not a valid claim *against* any particular individual; for in conditions of scarcity there may be no determinate individuals who can plausibly be said to have a duty to provide the missing goods to those in need. J. E. S. Fawcett therefore prefers to keep the distinction between claims and rights firmly in mind. "Claims," he writes, "are needs and demands in movement, and there is a continuous transformation, as a society advances [towards greater abundance] of economic and social claims into civil and political rights . . . and not all countries or all claims are by any means at the same stage in the process."[8] The manifesto writers on the other side who seem to identify needs, or at least basic needs, with what they call "human rights," are more properly described, I think, as urging upon the world community the moral principle that *all* basic human needs ought to be recognized as *claims* (in the customary *prima facie* sense) worthy of sympathy and serious consideration right now, even though, in many cases, they cannot yet plausibly be treated as *valid* claims, that is, as grounds of any other people's duties. This way of talking avoids the anomaly of ascribing to all human beings now, even those in pre-industrial societies, such "economic and social rights" as "periodic holidays with pay."[9]

Still for all of that, I have a certain sympathy with the manifesto writers, and I am even willing to speak of a special "manifesto sense" of "right," in which a right need not be correlated with another's duty. Natural needs are real claims if only upon hypothetical future beings not yet in existence. I accept the moral principle that to have an unfulfilled need is to have a kind of claim against the world, even if against no one in particular. A natural need for some good as such, like a natural desert, is always a reason in support of a claim to that good. A person in need, then, is always "in a position" to make a claim, even when there is no one in the corresponding position to do anything about it. Such claims, based on need alone, are "permanent possibilities of rights," the natural seed from which rights grow. When manifesto writers speak of them as if already actual rights, they are easily forgiven, for this is but a powerful way of expressing the conviction that they ought to be recognized by states here and now as potential rights and consequently as determinants of *present* aspirations and guides to *present* policies. That usage, I think, is a valid exercise of rhetorical licence.

I prefer to characterize rights as valid claims rather than justified ones, because I suspect that justification is rather too broad a qualification. "Validity," as I

[8]J. E. S. Fawcett, "The International Protection of Human Rights," in *Political Theory and the Rights of Man,* ed. by D. D. Raphael (Bloomington: Indiana University Press, 1967), pp. 125 and 128.
[9]As declared in Article 24 of *The Universal Declaration of Human Rights* adopted on December 10, 1948, by the General Assembly of the United Nations.

understand it, is justification of a peculiar and narrow kind, namely justification within a system of rules. A man has a legal right when the official recognition of his claim (as valid) is called for by the governing rules. This definition, of course, hardly applies to moral rights, but that is not because the genus of which moral rights are a species is something other than *claims.* A man has a moral right when he has a claim the recognition of which is called for − not (necessarily) by legal rules − but by moral principles, or the principles of an enlightened conscience.

There is one final kind of attack on the generic identification of rights with claims, and it has been launched with great spirit in a recent article by H. J. McCloskey, who holds that rights are not essentially claims at all, but rather entitlements. The springboard of his argument is his insistence that rights in their essential character are always *rights to,* not *rights against:*

My right to life is not a right against anyone. It is my right and by virtue of it, it is normally permissible for me to sustain my life in the face of obstacles. It does give rise to rights against others *in the sense* that others have or may come to have duties to refrain from killing me, but it is essentially a right of mine, not an infinite list of claims, hypothetical and actual, against an infinite number of actual, potential, and as yet nonexistent human beings . . . Similarly, the right of the tennis club member to play on the club courts is a right to play, not a right against some vague group of potential or possible obstructors.10

The argument seems to be that since rights are essentially rights *to*, whereas claims are essentially claims *against,* rights cannot be claims, though they can be grounds for claims. The argument is doubly defective though. First of all, contrary to McCloskey, rights (at least legal claim-rights) *are* held *against* others. McCloskey admits this in the case of *in personam* rights (what he calls "special rights") but denies it in the case of *in rem* rights (which he calls "general rights"):

Special rights are sometimes against specific individuals or institutions − e.g. rights created by promises, contracts, etc. . . . but these differ from . . . characteristic . . . general rights where the right is simply a right to . . .11

As far as I can tell, the only reason McCloskey gives for denying that *in rem* rights are against others is that those against whom they would have to hold make up an enormously multitudinous and "vague" group, including hypothetical people not yet even in existence. Many others have found this a paradoxical consequence of the notion of *in rem* rights, but I see nothing troublesome in it. If a general rule gives me a right of noninterference in a certain respect against everybody, then there are literally hundreds of millions of people who have a duty toward me in that respect; and if the same general rule gives the same right to everyone else, then it imposes on me literally hundreds of millions of duties − or duties towards hundreds of millions of people. I see nothing paradoxical about this, however. The

10H. J. McCloskey, "Rights," *Philosophical Quarterly,* Vol. 15 (1965), p. 118.
11*Loc. cit.*

duties, after all, are negative; and I can discharge all of them at a stroke simply by minding my own business. And if all human beings make up one moral community and there are hundreds of millions of human beings, we should expect there to be hundreds of millions of moral relations holding between them.

McCloskey's other premise is even more obviously defective. There is no good reason to think that all *claims* are "essentially" *against,* rather than *to.* Indeed most of the discussion of claims above has been of claims *to,* and we have seen, the law finds it useful to recognize claims *to* (or "mere claims") that are not yet qualified to be claims *against,* or rights (except in a "manifesto sense" of "rights").

Whether we are speaking of claims or rights, however, we must notice that they seem to have two dimensions, as indicated by the prepositions "to" and "against," and it is quite natural to wonder whether either of these dimensions is somehow more fundamental or essential than the other. All rights seem to merge *entitlements to* do, have, omit, or be something with *claims against* others to act or refrain from acting in certain ways. In some statements of rights the entitlement is perfectly determinate (e.g. *to* play tennis) and the claim vague (e.g. *against* "some vague group of potential or possible obstructors"); but in other cases the object of the claim is clear and determinate (e.g. *against* one's parents), and the entitlement general and indeterminate (e.g. to be given a proper upbringing). If we mean by "entitlement" that *to* which one has a right and by "claim" something directed at those against whom the right holds (as McCloskey apparently does), then we can say that all claim-rights necessarily involve both, though in individual cases the one element or the other may be in sharper focus.

In brief conclusion: To have a right is to have a claim against someone whose recognition as valid is called for by some set of governing rules or moral principles. To have a *claim* in turn, is to have a case meriting consideration, that is, to have reasons or grounds that put one in a position to engage in performative and propositional claiming. The activity of claiming, finally, as much as any other thing, makes for self-respect and respect for others, gives a sense to the notion of personal dignity, and distinguishes this otherwise morally flawed world from the even worse world or Nowheresville.

A Postscript to the Nature and Value of Rights

I would like to take this opportunity to supplement the brief account
of the role of rights in human life and to correct some of its emphases. First, it
appears in several places as though *having* rights is what is necessary for self-respect,
dignity, and other things of value. Actually, it is not enough to have the rights; one
must know that one has the rights. In fact, the poor benighted citizens of Nowheresville do have various rights, whether they know it or not. They could not possibly
know − or understand − that they have rights, however, because they do not
even have the *concept* of a personal right. Such a notion has never even been
dreamed of in Nowheresville. The inhabitants are consequently deficient in respect
for self and others, even though, as hypothetical human beings, they have dignity
in the eye of our imaginations.

Second, even knowing that one has rights and being prepared to act accordingly
are not sufficient (but only necessary) for a fully human and morally satisfactory
life. A person who never presses his claims or stands on his rights is servile, but the
person who never waives a right, never releases others from their correlative obligations, or never does another a favor when he has a right to refuse to do so is a
bloodless moral automaton. If such a person fully understands and appreciates
what rights are and invokes that understanding in justification of his rigid conduct,
he is a self-righteous prig as well. If he can also truly testify that he always conscientiously performs *his* duties to others and respects *their* rights, he has then
achieved "the righteousness of the scribes and pharisees."

The point to emphasize here is that (with some rare exceptions mentioned below)
right-holders are not always obliged to exercise their rights. To have a right typically
is to have the discretion or "liberty" to exercise it or not as one chooses. This
freedom is another feature of right-ownership that helps to explain why rights are
so valuable. When a person has a discretionary right and fully understands the
power that possession gives him, he can if he chooses make sacrifices for the sake
of others, voluntarily give up what is rightfully his own, freely make gifts that he is
in no way obligated to make, and forgive others for their wrongs to him by declining to demand the compensation or vengeance he may have coming or by warmly
welcoming them back into his friendship or love. Imagine what life would be like
without these saving graces. Consider Nowheresville II where almost everyone performs his duties to others faithfully and always insists upon his own rights against
others; where debtors are never forgiven their debts, wrongdoers pardoned, gratuitous gifts conferred, or sacrifices voluntarily made, so long as it is within one's
rights to refuse to do any of these things. The citizens of Nowheresville II have
forgotten, if they ever knew, how to exercise rightful discretion. They have but
half the concept of a right; they know how to claim but not how to release, waive,
or surrender.

The point I wish to emphasize is not that the saving graces show that there is a
limit to the moral importance of rights, but rather that rights are even more

important — and important in other ways — than my original article suggests. Knowing that one has rights makes not only claiming (and self-respect) but also releasing (and magnanimity) possible. Without the duties that others have toward one (correlated with one's rights against them) there could be no sense in the notion of one's supererogatory conduct toward other people, for to help others when one has a right to decline is precisely what conduct "above and beyond duty" amounts to. Understanding that one has rights, of course, is not *sufficient* for one to have an admirable character, for one might yet be a mean-spirited pharisee, unwilling ever to be generous, forgiving, or sacrificing. But consciousness of one's rights is *necessary* for the supererogatory virtues, for the latter cannot even be given a sense except by contrast with the disposition always to claim one's rights. Waivers and gratuities can exist only against a background of understood rules assigning rights and duties. Forgiving debts obviously would not be possible without the prior practice of loaning and repaying with its rule-structured complexes of rights and correlative duties. Even in Nowheresville I, I suppose, one person can give a useful thing to another, but he cannot make a *gift* or *gratuity*, since giving more than the recipient can rightly claim (a gift) presupposes that others *can* make rightful claims in some circumstances and that there is such a concept and such a practice.

One final point. Some familiar political rights appear to be exceptions to the assertion above that rights confer liberty or discretion upon their possessors who may always choose, if they wish, not to exercise them. The "right to education," for example, seems to be a kind of "mandatory right" in that children who possess it have no choice whether to go to school or not. Similarly, the legal right of schoolchildren to be vaccinated against certain contagious diseases is entirely coincident (except for the exemption on religious grounds) with their legal *duty* to be vaccinated. I suggest that when we use the language of rights in this way to refer to duties, we do so because we think that some of our duties are so beneficial that we can make *claim* against others to provide the opportunity for, and to abstain from interference with, our performance of them.

Textbooks frequently say that to have a claim-right to do X is (1) to be at liberty with respect to X and (2) for others to have a duty to one to provide or (as the case may be) not to interfere with X. When a claim-right is analyzed in this fashion, its component liberty is then said to be simply the absence of a duty *not* to X. But this characterization of a liberty, I submit, is misleading. To be at liberty to do X in ordinary speech is to have *discretion* in respect to X, to be free *both* of a duty not to do X *and* of a duty to do X. To be free of a duty not to do X is to have only a "half-liberty" with respect to X if one should at the same time have a duty *to do X*. Thus schoolchildren have "no duty" to stay away from school (a half-liberty with respect to school attendance), though they do have a duty to go to school. They are, therefore, deprived of the other "half-liberty" that would add up to full liberty, or the discretion to decide whether to attend school or not. Most rights to do X are full liberties to do X or not to do X as one chooses, conjoined with duties of other people not to interfere with one's choice. But so-called "mandatory rights" to do X confer only the half-liberty to do X without the other half-liberty not to do X. Why then are they called "rights" at all?

The answer is that the rights in question are best understood as ordinary duties with associated half-liberties rather than ordinary claim-rights with associated full liberties, but that the performance of the duty is presumed to be so beneficial to the person whose duty it is that he can *claim* the necessary means from the state and noninterference from others as *his* due. Its character as claim is precisely what his half-liberty shares with the more usual (discretionary) rights and what warrants his use of the word "right" in demanding it.

The Rights of Animals and Unborn Generations

EVERY PHILOSOPHICAL PAPER must begin with an unproved assumption. Mine is the assumption that there will still be a world five hundred years from now, and that it will contain human beings who are very much like us. We have it within our power now, clearly, to affect the lives of these creatures for better or worse by contributing to the conservation or corruption of the environment in which they must live. I shall assume furthermore that it is psychologically possible for us to care about our remote descendants, that many of us in fact do care, and indeed that we ought to care. My main concern then will be to show that it makes sense to speak of the rights of unborn generations against us, and that given the moral judgment that we ought to conserve our environmental inheritance for them, and its grounds, we might well say that future generations *do* have rights correlative to our present duties toward them. Protecting our environment now is also a matter of elementary prudence, and insofar as we do it for the next generation already here in the persons of our children, it is a matter of love. But from the perspective of our remote descendants it is basically a matter of justice, of respect for their rights. My main concern here will be to examine the concept of a right to better understand how that can be.

THE PROBLEM

To have a right is to have a claim[1] *to* something and *against* someone, the recognition of which is called for by legal rules or, in the case of moral rights, by the principles of an enlightened

---

1. I shall leave the concept of a claim unanalyzed here, but for a detailed discussion, see my "The Nature and Value of Rights," *Journal of Value Inquiry* 4 (Winter 1971): 263–277.

conscience. In the familiar cases of rights, the claimant is a competent adult human being, and the claimee is an officeholder in an institution or else a private individual, in either case, another competent adult human being. Normal adult human beings, then, are obviously the sorts of beings of whom rights can meaningfully be predicated. Everyone would agree to that, even extreme misanthropes who deny that anyone in fact has rights. On the other hand, it is absurd to say that rocks can have rights, not because rocks are morally inferior things unworthy of rights (that statement makes no sense either), but because rocks belong to a category of entities of whom rights cannot be meaningfully predicated. That is not to say that there are no circumstances in which we ought to treat rocks carefully, but only that the rocks themselves cannot validly claim good treatment from us. In between the clear cases of rocks and normal human beings, however, is a spectrum of less obvious cases, including some bewildering borderline ones. Is it meaningful or conceptually possible to ascribe rights to our dead ancestors? to individual animals? to whole species of animals? to plants? to idiots and madmen? to fetuses? to generations yet unborn? Until we know how to settle these puzzling cases, we cannot claim fully to grasp the concept of a right, or to know the shape of its logical boundaries.

One way to approach these riddles is to turn one's attention first to the most familiar and unproblematic instances of rights, note their most salient characteristics, and then compare the borderline cases with them, measuring as closely as possible the points of similarity and difference. In the end, the way we classify the borderline cases may depend on whether we are more impressed with the similarities or the differences between them and the cases in which we have the most confidence.

It will be useful to consider the problem of individual animals first because their case is the one that has already been debated with the most thoroughness by philosophers so that the dialectic of claim and rejoinder has now unfolded to the point where disputants can get to the end game quickly and isolate the crucial point at issue. When we understand precisely what *is* at issue in the debate over animal rights, I think we will have the key to the solution of all the other riddles about rights.

INDIVIDUAL ANIMALS

Almost all modern writers agree that we ought to be kind to animals, but that is quite another thing from holding that animals can claim kind treatment from us as their due. Statutes making cruelty to animals a crime are now very common, and these, of course, impose legal duties on people not to mistreat animals; but that still leaves open the question whether the animals, as beneficiaries of those duties, possess rights correlative to them. We may very well have duties *regarding* animals that are not at the same time duties *to* animals, just as we may have duties regarding rocks, or buildings, or lawns, that are not duties *to* the rocks, buildings, or lawns. Some legal writers have taken the still more extreme position that animals themselves are not even the directly intended beneficiaries of statutes prohibiting cruelty to animals. During the nineteenth century, for example, it was commonly said that such statutes were designed to protect human beings by preventing the growth of cruel habits that could later threaten human beings with harm too. Prof. Louis B. Schwartz finds the rationale of the cruelty-to-animals prohibition in its protection of animal lovers from affronts to their sensibilities. "It is not the mistreated dog who is the ultimate object of concern," he writes. "Our concern is for the feelings of other human beings, a large proportion of whom, although accustomed to the slaughter of animals for food, readily identify themselves with a tortured dog or horse and respond with great sensitivity to its sufferings."[2] This seems to me to be factitious. How much more natural it is to say with John Chipman Gray that the true purpose of cruelty-to-animals statutes is "to preserve the dumb brutes from suffering."[3] The very people whose sensibilities are invoked in the alternative explanation, a group that no doubt now includes most of us, are precisely those who would insist that the protection belongs primarily to the animals themselves, not merely to their own tender feelings. Indeed, it would be difficult even to account for the existence of such

2. Louis B. Schwartz, "Morals, Offenses and the Model Penal Code," *Columbia Law Review* 63 (1963): 673.
3. John Chipman Gray, *The Nature and Sources of the Law*, 2d ed. (Boston: Beacon Press, 1963), p. 43.

feelings in the absence of a belief that the animals deserve the protection in their own right and for their own sakes.

Even if we allow, as I think we must, that animals are the intended direct beneficiaries of legislation forbidding cruelty to animals, it does not follow directly that animals have legal rights, and Gray himself, for one,[4] refused to draw this further inference. Animals cannot have rights, he thought, for the same reason they cannot have duties, namely, that they are not genuine "moral agents." Now, it is relatively easy to see why animals cannot have duties, and this matter is largely beyond controversy. Animals cannot be "reasoned with" or instructed in their responsibilities; they are inflexible and unadaptable to future contingencies; they are subject to fits of instinctive passion which they are incapable of repressing or controlling, postponing or sublimating. Hence, they cannot enter into contractual agreements, or make promises; they cannot be trusted; and they cannot (except within very narrow limits and for purposes of conditioning) be blamed for what would be called "moral failures" in a human being. They are therefore incapable of being moral subjects, of acting rightly or wrongly in the moral sense, of having, discharging, or breeching duties and obligations.

But what is there about the intellectual incompetence of animals (which admittedly disqualifies them for duties) that makes them logically unsuitable for rights? The most common reply to this question is that animals are incapable of *claiming* rights on their own. They cannot make motion, on their own, to courts to have their claims recognized or enforced; they cannot initiate, on their own, any kind of legal proceedings; nor are they capable of even understanding when their rights are being violated, of distinguishing harm from wrongful injury, and responding with indignation and an outraged sense of justice instead of mere anger or fear.

No one can deny any of these allegations, but to the claim that they are the grounds for disqualification of rights of animals, philosophers on the other side of this controversy have made con-

---

4. And W. D. Ross for another. See *The Right and the Good* (Oxford: Clarendon Press, 1930), app. 1, pp. 48–56.

vincing rejoinders. It is simply not true, says W. D. Lamont,[5] that the ability to understand what a right is and the ability to set legal machinery in motion by one's own initiative are necessary for the possession of rights. If that were the case, then neither human idiots nor wee babies would have any legal rights at all. Yet it is manifest that both of these classes of intellectual incompetents have legal rights recognized and easily enforced by the courts. Children and idiots start legal proceedings, not on their own direct initiative, but rather through the actions of proxies or attorneys who are empowered to speak in their names. If there is no conceptual absurdity in this situation, why should there be in the case where a proxy makes a claim on behalf of an animal? People commonly enough make wills leaving money to trustees for the care of animals. Is it not natural to speak of the animal's right to his inheritance in cases of this kind? If a trustee embezzles money from the animal's account,[6] and a proxy speaking in the dumb brute's behalf presses the animal's claim, can he not be described as asserting the animal's *rights?* More exactly, the animal itself claims its rights through the vicarious actions of a human proxy speaking in its name and in its behalf. There appears to be no reason why we should require the animal to understand what is going on (so the argument concludes) as a condition for regarding it as a possessor of rights.

Some writers protest at this point that the legal relation between a principal and an agent cannot hold between animals and human beings. Between humans, the relation of agency can take two very different forms, depending upon the degree of discretion granted to the agent, and there is a continuum of combinations between the extremes. On the one hand, there is the agent who is the mere "mouthpiece" of his principal. He is a "tool" in much the same sense as is a typewriter or telephone; he simply transmits the instructions of his principal. Human beings could hardly be the agents or representatives of animals in this sense, since the dumb brutes could no more use human "tools" than mechanical ones.

5. W. D. Lamont, *Principles of Moral Judgment* (Oxford: Clarendon Press, 1946), pp. 83–85.
6. Cf. H. J. McCloskey, "Rights," *Philosophical Quarterly* 15 (1965): 121, 124.

On the other hand, an agent may be some sort of expert hired to exercise his professional judgment on behalf of, and in the name of, the principal. He may be given, within some limited area of expertise, complete independence to act as he deems best, binding his principal to all the beneficial or detrimental consequences. This is the role played by trustees, lawyers, and ghost-writers. This type of representation requires that the agent have great skill, but makes little or no demand upon the principal, who may leave everything to the judgment of his agent. Hence, there appears, at first, to be no reason why an animal cannot be a totally passive principal in this second kind of agency relationship.

There are still some important dissimilarities, however. In the typical instance of representation by an agent, even of the second, highly discretionary kind, the agent is hired by a principal who enters into an agreement or contract with him; the principal tells his agent that within certain carefully specified boundaries "You may speak for me," subject always to the principal's approval, his right to give new directions, or to cancel the whole arrangement. No dog or cat could possibly do any of those things. Moreover, if it is the assigned task of the agent to defend the principal's rights, the principal may often decide to release his claimee, or to waive his own rights, and instruct his agent accordingly. Again, no mute cow or horse can do that. But although the possibility of hiring, agreeing, contracting, approving, directing, canceling, releasing, waiving, and instructing is present in the typical (all-human) case of agency representation, there appears to be no reason of a logical or conceptual kind why that *must* be so, and indeed there are some special examples involving human principals where it is not in fact so. I have in mind legal rules, for example, that require that a defendant be represented at his trial by an attorney, and impose a state-appointed attorney upon reluctant defendants, or upon those tried *in absentia*, whether they like it or not. Moreover, small children and mentally deficient and deranged adults are commonly represented by trustees and attorneys, even though they are incapable of granting their own consent to the representation, or of entering into contracts, of giving directions, or waiving their rights. It may be that it is unwise to permit agents to represent principals without the latters' knowledge or consent. If so, then no one should ever be permitted to speak for an animal, at least in a legally binding way. But that is quite another thing than saying that such representation is logically incoherent or conceptually incongruous—the contention that is at issue.

H. J. McCloskey,[7] I believe, accepts the argument up to this point, but he presents a new and different reason for denying that animals can have legal rights. The ability to make claims, whether directly or through a representative, he implies, is essential to the possession of rights. Animals obviously cannot press their claims on their own, and so if they have rights, these rights must be assertable by agents. Animals, however, cannot be represented, McCloskey contends, and not for any of the reasons already discussed, but rather because representation, in the requisite sense, is always of interests, and animals (he says) are incapable of having interests.

Now, there is a very important insight expressed in the requirement that a being have interests if he is to be a logically proper subject of rights. This can be appreciated if we consider just why it is that mere things cannot have rights. Consider a very precious "mere thing"—a beautiful natural wilderness, or a complex and ornamental artifact, like the Taj Mahal. Such things ought to be cared for, because they would sink into decay if neglected, depriving some human beings, or perhaps even all human beings, of something of great value. Certain persons may even have as their own special job the care and protection of these valuable objects But we are not tempted in these cases to speak of "thing-rights" correlative to custodial duties, because, try as we might, we cannot think of mere things as possessing interests of their own. Some people may have a duty to preserve, maintain, or improve the Taj Mahal, but they can hardly have a duty to help or hurt it, benefit or aid it, succor or relieve it. Custodians may protect it for the sake of a nation's pride and art lovers' fancy; but they don't keep it in good repair for "its own sake," or for "its own true welfare," or "well-being." A mere thing, however valuable to others, has no good of its own. The explanation of that fact, I suspect, consists in the fact that mere things have no conative life: no conscious wishes, desires, and hopes; or urges and impulses; or unconscious drives, aims, and goals; or latent tendencies, direction of growth, and natural fulfillments. Interests must be compounded somehow

7. Ibid.

out of conations; hence mere things have no interests. *A fortiori*, they have no interests to be protected by legal or moral rules. Without interests a creature can have no "good" of its own, the achievement of which can be its due. Mere things are not loci of value in their own right, but rather their value consists entirely in their being objects of other beings' interests.

So far McCloskey is on solid ground, but one can quarrel with his denial that any animals but humans have interests. I should think that the trustee of funds willed to a dog or cat is more than a mere custodian of the animal he protects. Rather his job is to look out for the interests of the animal and make sure no one denies it its due. The animal itself is the beneficiary of his dutiful services. Many of the higher animals at least have appetites, conative urges, and rudimentary purposes, the integrated satisfaction of which constitutes their welfare or good. We can, of course, with consistency treat animals as mere pests and deny that they have any rights; for most animals, especially those of the lower orders, we have no choice but to do so. But it seems to me, nevertheless, that in general, animals *are* among the sorts of beings of whom rights can meaningfully be predicated and denied.

Now, if a person agrees with the conclusion of the argument thus far, that animals are the sorts of beings that *can* have rights, and further, if he accepts the moral judgment that we ought to be kind to animals, only one further premise is needed to yield the conclusion that some animals do in fact have rights. We must now ask ourselves for whose sake ought we to treat (some) animals with consideration and humaneness? If we conceive our duty to be one of obedience to authority, or to one's own conscience merely, or one of consideration for tender human sensibilities only, then we might still deny that animals have rights, even though we admit that they are the kinds of beings that *can* have rights. But if we hold not only that we ought to treat animals humanely but also that we should do so for the animals' own sake, that such treatment is something we owe animals as their due, something that can be claimed for them, something the withholding of which would be an injustice and a wrong, and not merely a harm, then it follows that we do ascribe rights to animals. I suspect that the moral judgments most of us make about animals do pass these phenomenological tests, so that most of us do believe that animals have rights, but are reluctant to say so because of the conceptual confusions about the notion of a right that I have attempted to dispel above.

Now we can extract from our discussion of animal rights a crucial principle for tentative use in the resolution of the other riddles about the applicability of the concept of a right, namely, that the sorts of beings who *can* have rights are precisely those who have (or can have) interests. I have come to this tentative conclusion for two reasons: (1) because a right holder must be capable of being represented and it is impossible to represent a being that has no interests, and (2) because a right holder must be capable of being a beneficiary in his own person, and a being without interests is a being that is incapable of being harmed or benefitted, having no good or "sake" of its own. Thus, a being without interests has no "behalf" to act in, and no "sake" to act for. My strategy now will be to apply the "interest principle," as we can call it, to the other puzzles about rights, while being prepared to modify it where necessary (but as little as possible), in the hope of separating in a consistent and intuitively satisfactory fashion the beings who can have rights from those which cannot.

VEGETABLES

It is clear that we ought not to mistreat certain plants, and indeed there are rules and regulations imposing duties on persons not to misbehave in respect to certain members of the vegetable kingdom. It is forbidden, for example, to pick wildflowers in the mountainous tundra areas of national parks, or to endanger trees by starting fires in dry forest areas. Members of Congress introduce bills designed, as they say, to "protect" rare redwood trees from commercial pillage. Given this background, it is surprising that no one[8] speaks of plants as having rights. Plants, after all, are not "mere things"; they are vital objects with inherited biological propensities determining their natural growth. Moreover, we do say that certain conditions are "good" or "bad" for plants, thereby suggesting that plants, unlike rocks, are capable of having a "good." (This is a case, however, where "what we say" should not be taken seriously: we also say that certain kinds of paint are good

8. Outside of Samuel Butler's *Erewhon.*

or bad for the internal walls of a house, and this does not commit us to a conception of walls as beings possessed of a good or welfare of their own.) Finally, we are capable of feeling a kind of affection for particular plants, though we rarely personalize them, as we do in the case of animals, by giving them proper names.

Still, all are agreed that plants are not the kinds of beings that can have rights. Plants are never plausibly understood to be the direct intended beneficiaries of rules designed to "protect" them. We wish to keep redwood groves in existence for the sake of human beings who can enjoy their serene beauty, and for the sake of generations of human beings yet unborn. Trees are not the sorts of beings who have their "own sakes," despite the fact that they have biological propensities. Having no conscious wants or goals of their own, trees cannot know satisfaction or frustration, pleasure or pain. Hence, there is no possibility of kind or cruel treatment of trees. In these morally crucial respects, trees differ from the higher species of animals.

Yet trees are not mere things like rocks. They grow and develop according to the laws of their own nature. Aristotle and Aquinas both took trees to have their own "natural ends." Why then do I deny them the status of beings with interests of their own? The reason is that an interest, however the concept is finally to be analyzed, presupposes at least rudimentary cognitive equipment. Interests are compounded out of *desires* and *aims*, both of which presuppose something like *belief*, or cognitive awareness. A desiring creature may want X because he seeks anything that is $\emptyset$, and X appears to be $\emptyset$ to him; or he may be seeking Y, and he believes, or expects, or hopes that X will be a means to Y. If he desires X in order to get Y, this implies that he believes that X will bring Y about, or at least that he has some sort of brute expectation that is a primitive correlate of belief. But what of the desire for $\emptyset$ (or for Y) itself? Perhaps a creature has such a "desire" as an ultimate set, as if he had come into existence all "wound up" to pursue $\emptyset$-ness or Y-ness, and his not to reason why. Such a propensity, I think, would not qualify as a desire. Mere brute longings unmediated by beliefs—longings for one knows not what—might perhaps be a primitive form of consciousness (I don't want to beg that question) but they are altogether different from the sort of thing we mean by "desire," especially when we speak of human beings.

If some such account as the above is correct, we can never have any grounds for attributing a desire or a want to a creature known to be incapable even of rudimentary beliefs; and if desires or wants are the materials interests are made of, mindless creatures have no interests of their own. The law, therefore, cannot have as its intention the protection of their interests, so that "protective legislation" has to be understood as legislation protecting the interests human beings may have in them.

Plant life might nevertheless be thought at first to constitute a hard case for the interest principle for two reasons. In the first place, plants no less than animals are said to have needs of their own. To be sure, we can speak even of mere things as having needs too, but such talk misleads no one into thinking of the need as belonging, in the final analysis, to the "mere thing" itself. If we were so deceived we would not be thinking of the mere thing as a "mere thing" after all. We say, for example, that John Doe's walls need painting, or that Richard Roe's car needs a washing, but we direct our attitudes of sympathy or reproach (as the case may be) to John and Richard, not to their possessions. It would be otherwise, if we observed that some child is in need of a good meal. Our sympathy and concern in that case would be directed at the child himself as the true possessor of the need in question.

The needs of plants might well seem closer to the needs of animals than to the pseudoneeds of mere things. An owner may need a plant (say, for its commercial value or as a potential meal), but the plant itself, it might appear, needs nutrition or cultivation. Our confusion about this matter may stem from language. It is a commonplace that the word *need* is ambiguous. To say that A needs X may be to say either: (1) X is necessary to the achievement of one of A's goals, or to the performance of one of its functions, or (2) X is good for A; its lack would harm A or be injurious or detrimental to him (or it). The first sort of need-statement is value-neutral, implying no comment on the value of the goal or function in question; whereas the second kind of statement about needs commits its maker to a value judgment about what is good or bad for A in the long run, that is, about what is in A's interests.

A being must have interests, therefore, to have needs in the second sense, but any kind of thing, vegetable or mineral, could have needs in the first sense. An automobile needs gas and oil to function, but it is no tragedy for it if it runs out—an empty tank does not hinder or retard its interests. Similarly, to say that a tree needs sunshine and water is to say that without them it cannot grow and survive; but unless the growth and survival of trees are matters of human concern, affecting human interests, practical or aesthetic, the needs of trees alone will not be the basis of any claim of what is "due" them in their own right. Plants may need things in order to discharge their functions, but their functions are assigned by human interests, not their own.

The second source of confusion derives from the fact that we commonly speak of plants as thriving and flourishing, or withering and languishing. One might be tempted to think of these states either as themselves consequences of the possession of interests so that even creatures without wants or beliefs can be said to have interests, or else as grounds independent of the possession of interests for the making of intelligible claims of rights. In either case, plants would be thought of as conceivable possessors of rights after all.

Consider what it means to speak of something as "flourishing." The verb *to flourish* apparently was applied originally and literally to plants only, and in its original sense it meant simply "to bear flowers: BLOSSOM"; but then by analogical extension of sense it came also to mean "to grow luxuriantly: increase, and enlarge," and then to "THRIVE" (generally), and finally, when extended to human beings, "to be prosperous," or to "increase in wealth, honor, comfort, happiness, or whatever is desirable."[9] Applied to human beings the term is, of course, a fixed metaphor. When a person flourishes, something happens to his interests analogous to what happens to a plant when it flowers, grows, and spreads. A person flourishes when his interests (whatever they may be) are progressing severally and collectively toward their harmonious fulfillment and spawning new interests along the way whose prospects are also good. To flourish is to glory in the advancement of one's interests, in short, to be happy.

Nothing is gained by twisting the botanical metaphor back

9. *Webster's Third New International Dictionary.*

from humans to plants. To speak of thriving human interests as if they were flowers is to speak naturally and well, and to mislead no one. But then to think of the flowers or plants as if they were interests (or the signs of interests) is to bring the metaphor back full circle for no good reason and in the teeth of our actual beliefs. Some of our talk about flourishing plants reveals quite clearly that the interests that thrive when plants flourish are human not "plant interests." For example, we sometimes make a flowering bush flourish by "frustrating" its own primary propensities. We pinch off dead flowers before seeds have formed, thus "encouraging" the plant to make new flowers in an effort to produce more seeds. It is not the plant's own natural propensity (to produce seeds) that is advanced, but rather the gardener's interest in the production of new flowers and the spectator's pleasure in aesthetic form, color, or scent. What we mean in such cases by saying that the plant flourishes is that our interest in the plant, not its own, is thriving. It is not always so clear that that is what we mean, for on other occasions there is a correspondence between our interests and the plant's natural propensities, a coinciding of what we want from nature and nature's own "intention." But the exceptions to this correspondence provide the clue to our real sense in speaking of a plant's good or welfare.[10] And even when there exists such a correspondence, it is often because we have actually remade the plant's nature so that our interests in it will flourish more "naturally" and effectively.

WHOLE SPECIES

The topic of whole species, whether of plants or animals, can be treated in much the same way as that of individual plants. A whole collection, as such, cannot have beliefs, expectations, wants, or desires, and can flourish or languish only in the human interest-

10. Sometimes, of course, the correspondence fails because what accords with the plant's natural propensities is not in our interests, rather than the other way round. I must concede that in cases of this kind we speak even of weeds flourishing, but I doubt that we mean to imply that a weed is a thing with a good of its own. Rather, this way of talking is a plain piece of irony, or else an animistic metaphor (thinking of the weeds in the way we think of prospering businessmen). In any case, when weeds thrive, usually no interests, human or otherwise, flourish.

related sense in which individual plants thrive and decay. Individual elephants can have interests, but the species elephant cannot. Even where individual elephants are not granted rights, human beings may have an interest—economic, scientific, or sentimental—in keeping the species from dying out, and *that* interest may be protected in various ways by law. But that is quite another matter from recognizing a right to survival belonging to the species itself. Still, the preservation of a whole species may quite properly seem to be a morally more important matter than the preservation of an individual animal. Individual animals can have rights but it is implausible to ascribe to them a right to life on the human model. Nor do we normally have duties to keep individual animals alive or even to abstain from killing them provided we do it humanely and nonwantonly in the promotion of legitimate human interests. On the other hand, we do have duties to protect threatened species, not duties to the species themselves as such, but rather duties to future human beings, duties derived from our housekeeping role as temporary inhabitants of this planet.

We commonly and very naturally speak of corporate entities, such as institutions, churches, and national states as having rights and duties, and an adequate analysis of the conditions for ownership of rights should account for that fact. A corporate entity, of course, is more than a mere collection of things that have some important traits in common. Unlike a biological species, an institution has a charter, or constitution, or bylaws, with rules defining offices and procedures, and it has human beings whose function it is to administer the rules and apply the procedures. When the institution has a duty to an outsider, there is always some determinant human being whose duty it is to do something for the outsider, and when the state, for example, has a right to collect taxes, there are always certain definite flesh and blood persons who have rights to demand tax money from other citizens. We have no reluctance to use the language of corporate rights and duties because we know that in the last analysis these are rights or duties of individual persons, acting in their "official capacities." And when individuals act in their official roles in accordance with valid empowering rules, their acts are imputable to the organization itself and become "acts of state." Thus, there is no need to posit any

individual superperson named by the expression "the State" (or
for that matter, "the company," "the club," or "the church.") Nor
is there any reason to take the rights of corporate entities to be
exceptions to the interest principle. The United States is not a
superperson with wants and beliefs of its own, but it is a corporate
entity with corporate interests that are, in turn, analyzable into the
interests of its numerous flesh and blood members.

DEAD PERSONS

So far we have refined the interest principle but we have not had
occasion to modify it. Applied to dead persons, however, it will
have to be stretched to near the breaking point if it is to explain
how our duty to honor commitments to the dead can be thought
to be linked to the rights of the dead against us. The case against
ascribing rights to dead men can be made very simply: a dead man
is a mere corpse, a piece of decaying organic matter. Mere inanimate things can have no interests, and what is incapable of having
interests is incapable of having rights. If, nevertheless, we grant
dead men rights against us, we would seem to be treating the interests they had while alive as somehow surviving their deaths.
There is the sound of paradox in this way of talking, but it may
be the least paradoxical way of describing our moral relations to
our predecessors. And if the idea of an interest's surviving its possessor's death is a kind of fiction, it is a fiction that most living men
have a real interest in preserving.

Most persons while still alive have certain desires about what is
to happen to their bodies, their property, or their reputations after
they are dead. For that reason, our legal system has developed
procedures to enable persons while still alive to determine whether
their bodies will be used for purposes of medical research or organic transplantation, and to whom their wealth (after taxes) is
to be transferred. Living men also take out life insurance policies
guaranteeing that the accumulated benefits be conferred upon
beneficiaries of their own choice. They also make private agreements, both contractual and informal, in which they receive promises that certain things will be done after their deaths in exchange for some present service or consideration. In all these cases
promises are made to living persons that their wishes will be

honored after they are dead. Like all other valid promises, they impose duties on the promisor and confer correlative rights on the promisee.

How does the situation change after the promisee has died? Surely the duties of the promisor do not suddenly become null and void. If that were the case, and known to be the case, there could be no confidence in promises regarding posthumous arrangements; no one would bother with wills or life insurance policies. Indeed the duties of courts and trustees to honor testamentary directions, and the duties of life insurance companies to pay benefits to survivors, are, in a sense, only conditional duties before a man dies. They come into existence as categorical demands for immediate action only upon the promisee's death. So the view that death renders them null and void has the truth exactly upside down.

The survival of the promisor's duty after the promisee's death does not prove that the promisee retains a right even after death, for we might prefer to conclude that there is one class of cases where duties to keep promises are not logically correlated with a promisee's right, namely, cases where the promisee has died. Still, a morally sensitive promisor is likely to think of his promised performance not only as a duty (i.e., a morally required action) but also as something owed to the deceased promisee as his due. Honoring such promises is a way of keeping faith with the dead. To be sure, the promisor will not think of his duty as something to be done for the promisee's "good," since the promisee, being dead, has no "good" of his own. We can think of certain of the deceased's interests, however, (including especially those enshrined in wills and protected by contracts and promises) as surviving their owner's death, and constituting claims against us that persist beyond the life of the claimant. Such claims can be represented by proxies just like the claims of animals. This way of speaking, I believe, reflects more accurately than any other an important fact about the human condition: we have an interest while alive that other interests of ours will continue to be recognized and served after we are dead. The whole practice of honoring wills and testaments, and the like, is thus for the sake of the living, just as a particular instance of it may be thought to be for the sake of one who is dead.

Conceptual sense, then, can be made of talk about dead men's rights; but it is still a wide open moral question whether dead men in fact have rights, and if so, what those rights are. In particular, commentators have disagreed over whether a man's interest in his reputation deserves to be protected from defamation even after his death. With only a few prominent exceptions, legal systems punish a libel on a dead man "only when its publication is in truth an attack upon the interests of living persons."[11] A widow or a son may be wounded, or embarrassed, or even injured economically, by a defamatory attack on the memory of their dead husband or father. In Utah defamation of the dead is a misdemeanor, and in Sweden a cause of action in tort. The law rarely presumes, however, that a dead man himself has any interests, representable by proxy, that can be injured by defamation, apparently because of the maxim that what a dead man doesn't know can't hurt him.

This presupposes, however, that the whole point of guarding the reputations even of living men, is to protect them from hurt feelings, or to protect some other interests, for example, economic ones, that do not survive death. A moment's thought, I think, will show that our interests are more complicated than that. If someone spreads a libelous description of me, without my knowledge, among hundreds of persons in a remote part of the country, so that I am, still without my knowledge, an object of general scorn and mockery in that group, I have been injured, even though I never learn what has happened. That is because I have an interest, so I believe, in having a good reputation *simpliciter*, in addition to my interest in avoiding hurt feelings, embarrassment, and economic injury. In the example, I do not know what is being said and believed about me, so my feelings are not hurt; but clearly if I did know, I would be enormously distressed. The distress would be the natural consequence of my belief that an interest other than my interest in avoiding distress had been damaged. How else can I account for the distress? If I had no interest in a good reputation as such, I would respond to news of harm to my reputation with indifference.

While it is true that a dead man cannot have his feelings hurt, it does not follow, therefore, that his claim to be thought of no worse than he deserves cannot survive his death. Almost every living person, I should think, would wish to have this interest

11. William Salmond, *Jurisprudence,* 12th ed., ed. P. J. Fitzgerald (London: Sweet and Maxwell, 1966), p. 304.

protected after his death, at least during the lifetimes of those persons who were his contemporaries. We can hardly expect the law to protect Julius Caesar from defamation in the history books. This might hamper historical research and restrict socially valuable forms of expression. Even interests that survive their owner's death are not immortal. Anyone should be permitted to say anything he wishes about George Washington or Abraham Lincoln, though perhaps not everything is morally permissible. Everyone ought to refrain from malicious lies even about Nero or King Tut, though not so much for those ancients' own sakes as for the sake of those who would now know the truth about the past. We owe it to the brothers Kennedy, however, as their due, not to tell damaging lies about them to those who were once their contemporaries. If the reader would deny that judgment, I can only urge him to ask himself whether he now wishes his own interest in reputation to be respected, along with his interest in determining the distribution of his wealth, after his death.

HUMAN VEGETABLES

Mentally deficient and deranged human beings are hardly ever so handicapped intellectually that they do not compare favorably with even the highest of the lower animals, though they are commonly so incompetent that they cannot be assigned duties or be held responsible for what they do. Since animals can have rights, then, it follows that human idiots and madmen can too. It would make good sense, for example, to ascribe to them a right to be cured whenever effective therapy is available at reasonable cost, and even those incurables who have been consigned to a sanatorium for permanent "warehousing" can claim (through a proxy) their right to decent treatment.

Human beings suffering extreme cases of mental illness, however, may be so utterly disoriented or insensitive as to compare quite unfavorably with the brightest cats and dogs. Those suffering from catatonic schizophrenia may be barely distinguishable in respect to those traits presupposed by the possession of interests from the lowliest vegetables. So long as we regard these patients as potentially curable, we may think of them as human beings with interests in their own restoration and treat them as possessors of rights. We may think of the patient as a genuine human person inside the vegetable casing struggling to get out, just as in the old fairy tales a pumpkin could be thought of as a beautiful maiden under a magic spell waiting only the proper words to be restored to her true self. Perhaps it is reasonable never to lose hope that a patient can be cured, and therefore to regard him always as a person "under a spell" with a permanent interest in his own recovery that is entitled to recognition and protection.

What if, nevertheless, we think of the catatonic schizophrenic and the vegetating patient with irreversible brain damage as absolutely incurable? Can we think of them at the same time as possessed of interests and rights too, or is this combination of traits a conceptual impossibility? Shocking as it may at first seem, I am driven unavoidably to the latter view. If redwood trees and rosebushes cannot have rights, neither can incorrigible human vegetables.[12] The trustees who are designated to administer funds for the care of these unfortunates are better understood as mere custodians than as representatives of their interests since these patients no longer have interests. It does not follow that they should not be kept alive as long as possible: that is an open moral question not foreclosed by conceptual analysis. Even if we have duties to keep human vegetables alive, however, they cannot be duties *to* them. We may be obliged to keep them alive to protect the sensibilities of others, or to foster humanitarian tendencies in ourselves, but we cannot keep them alive for their own good, for they are no longer capable of having a "good" of their own. Without awareness, expectation, belief, desire, aim, and purpose, a being can have no interests; without interests, he cannot be benefited; without the capacity to be a beneficiary, he can have no rights. But there may nevertheless be a dozen other reasons to treat him as if he did.

---

12. Unless, of course, the person in question, before he became a "vegetable," left testamentary directions about what was to be done with his body just in case he should ever become an incurable vegetable. He may have directed either that he be preserved alive as long as possible, or else that he be destroyed, whichever he preferred. There may, of course, be sound reasons of public policy why we should not honor such directions, but if we did promise to give legal effect to such wishes, we would have an example of a man's earlier interest in what is to happen to his body surviving his very competence as a person, in quite the same manner as that in which the express interest of a man now dead may continue to exert a claim on us.

FETUSES

If the interest principle is to permit us to ascribe rights to infants, fetuses, and generations yet unborn, it can only be on the grounds that interests can exert a claim upon us even before their possessors actually come into being, just the reverse of the situation respecting dead men where interests are respected even after their possessors have ceased to be. Newly born infants are surely noisier than mere vegetables, but they are just barely brighter. They come into existence, as Aristotle said, with the capacity to acquire concepts and dispositions, but in the beginning we suppose that their consciousness of the world is a "blooming, buzzing confusion." They do have a capacity, no doubt from the very beginning, to feel pain, and this alone may be sufficient ground for ascribing both an interest and a right to them. Apart from that, however, during the first few hours of their lives, at least, they may well lack even the rudimentary intellectual equipment necessary to the possession of interests. Of course, this induces no moral reservations whatever in adults. Children grow and mature almost visibly in the first few months so that those future interests that are so rapidly emerging from the unformed chaos of their earliest days seem unquestionably to be the basis of their present rights. Thus, we say of a newborn infant that he has a right now to live and grow into his adulthood, even though he lacks the conceptual equipment at this very moment to have this or any other desire. A new infant, in short, lacks the traits necessary for the possession of interests, but he has the capacity to acquire those traits, and his inherited potentialities are moving quickly toward actualization even as we watch him. Those proxies who make claims in behalf of infants, then, are more than mere custodians: they are (or can be) genuine representatives of the child's emerging interests, which may need protection even now if they are to be allowed to come into existence at all.

The same principle may be extended to "unborn persons." After all, the situation of fetuses one day before birth is not strikingly different from that a few hours after birth. The rights our law confers on the unborn child, both proprietary and personal, are for the most part, placeholders or reservations for the rights he shall inherit when he becomes a full-fledged interested being. The law protects a potential interest in these cases before it has even grown into actuality, as a garden fence protects newly seeded flower beds long before blooming flowers have emerged from them. The unborn child's present right to property, for example, is a legal protection offered now to his future interest, contingent upon his birth, and instantly voidable if he dies before birth. As Coke put it: "The law in many cases hath consideration of him in respect of the apparent expectation of his birth";[13] but this is quite another thing than recognizing a right actually to be born. Assuming that the child will be born, the law seems to say, various interests that he will come to have after birth must be protected from damage that they can incur even before birth. Thus prenatal injuries of a negligently inflicted kind can give the newly born child a right to sue for damages which he can exercise through a proxy-attorney and in his own name any time *after* he is born.

There are numerous other places, however, where our law seems to imply an unconditional right to be born, and surprisingly no one seems ever to have found that idea conceptually absurd. One interesting example comes from an article given the following headline by the *New York Times:* "Unborn Child's Right Upheld Over Religion."[14] A hospital patient in her eighth month of pregnancy refused to take a blood transfusion even though warned by her physician that "she might die at any minute and take the life of her child as well." The ground of her refusal was that blood transfusions are repugnant to the principles of her religion (Jehovah's Witnesses). The Supreme Court of New Jersey expressed uncertainty over the constitutional question of whether a non-pregnant adult might refuse on religious grounds a blood transfusion pronounced necessary to her own survival, but the court

13. As quoted by Salmond, *Jurisprudence,* p. 303. Simply as a matter of policy the potentiality of some future interests may be so remote as to make them seem unworthy of present support. A testator may leave property to his unborn child, for example, but not to his unborn grandchildren. To say of the potential person presently in his mother's womb that he owns property now is to say that certain property must be held for him until he is "real" or "mature" enough to possess it. "Yet the law is careful lest property should be too long withdrawn in this way from the uses of living men in favor of generations yet to come; and various restrictive rules have been established to this end. No testator could now direct his fortune to be accumulated for a hundred years and then distributed among his descendants"—Salmond, ibid.
14. *New York Times,* 17 June 1966, p. 1.

nevertheless ordered the patient in the present case to receive the transfusion on the grounds that "the unborn child is entitled to the law's protection."

It is important to reemphasize here that the questions of whether fetuses do or ought to have rights are substantive questions of law and morals open to argument and decision. The prior question of whether fetuses are the kind of beings that can have rights, however, is a conceptual, not a moral, question, amenable only to what is called "logical analysis," and irrelevant to moral judgment. The correct answer to the conceptual question, I believe, is that unborn children are among the sorts of beings of whom possession of rights can meaningfully be predicated, even though they are (temporarily) incapable of having interests, because their future interests can be protected now, and it does make sense to protect a potential interest even before it has grown into actuality. The interest principle, however, makes perplexing, at best, talk of a noncontingent fetal right to be born; for fetuses, lacking actual wants and beliefs, have no actual interest in being born, and it is difficult to think of any other reason for ascribing any rights to them other than on the assumption that they will in fact be born.[15]

FUTURE GENERATIONS

We have it in our power now to make the world a much less pleasant place for our descendants than the world we inherited from our ancestors. We can continue to proliferate in ever greater numbers, using up fertile soil at an even greater rate, dumping our wastes into rivers, lakes, and oceans, cutting down our forests, and polluting the atmosphere with noxious gases. All thoughtful people agree that we ought not to do these things. Most would say that we have a duty not to do these things, meaning not merely that conservation is morally required (as opposed to merely desirable) but also that it is something due our descendants, something to be done for their sakes. Surely we owe it to future genera-

---

15. In an essay entitled "Is There a Right to be Born?" I defend a negative answer to the question posed, but I allow that under certain very special conditions, there can be a "right *not* to be born." See *Abortion*, ed. J. Feinberg (Belmont, Calif.: Wadsworth, 1973).

tions to pass on a world that is not a used up garbage heap. Our remote descendants are not yet present to claim a livable world as their right, but there are plenty of proxies to speak now in their behalf. These spokesmen, far from being mere custodians, are genuine representatives of future interests.

Why then deny that the human beings of the future have rights which can be claimed against us now in their behalf? Some are inclined to deny them present rights out of a fear of falling into obscure metaphysics, by granting rights to remote and unidentifiable beings who are not yet even in existence. Our unborn great-great-grandchildren are in some sense "potential" persons, but they are far more remotely potential, it may seem, than fetuses. This, however, is not the real difficulty. Unborn generations are more remotely potential than fetuses in one sense, but not in another. A much greater period of time with a far greater number of causally necessary and important events must pass before their potentiality can be actualized, it is true; but our collective posterity is just as certain to come into existence "in the normal course of events" as is any given fetus now in its mother's womb. In that sense the existence of the distant human future is no more remotely potential than that of a particular child already on its way.

The real difficulty is not that we doubt whether our descendants will ever be actual, but rather that we don't know who they will be. It is not their temporal remoteness that troubles us so much as their indeterminacy—their present facelessness and namelessness. Five centuries from now men and women will be living where we live now. Any given one of them will have an interest in living space, fertile soil, fresh air, and the like, but that arbitrarily selected one has no other qualities we can presently envision very clearly. We don't even know who his parents, grandparents, or great-grandparents are, or even whether he is related to us. Still, whoever these human beings may turn out to be, and whatever they might reasonably be expected to be like, they will have interests that we can affect, for better or worse, right now. That much we can and do know about them. The identity of the owners of these interests is now necessarily obscure, but the fact of their interest-ownership is crystal clear, and that is all that is necessary to certify the coherence of present talk about their rights. We can tell, sometimes, that shadowy forms in the spatial distance belong to human beings, though we know not who or how many they are; and this imposes a duty on us not to throw bombs, for example, in their direction. In like manner, the vagueness of the human future does not weaken its claim on us in light of the nearly certain knowledge that it will, after all, be human.

Doubts about the existence of a right to be born transfer neatly to the question of a similar right to come into existence ascribed to future generations. The rights that future generations certainly have against us are contingent rights: the interests they are sure to have when they come into being (assuming of course that they will come into being) cry out for protection from invasions that can take place now. Yet there are no actual interests, presently existent, that future generations, presently nonexistent, have now. Hence, there is no actual interest that they have in simply coming into being, and I am at a loss to think of any other reason for claiming that they have a right to come into existence (though there may well be such a reason). Suppose then that all human beings at a given time voluntarily form a compact never again to produce children, thus leading within a few decades to the end of our species. This of course is a wildly improbable hypothetical example but a rather crucial one for the position I have been tentatively considering. And we can imagine, say, that the whole world is converted to a strange ascetic religion which absolutely requires sexual abstinence for everyone. Would this arrangement violate the rights of anyone? No one can complain on behalf of presently nonexistent future generations that their future interests which give them a contingent right of protection have been violated since they will never come into existence to be wronged. My inclination then is to conclude that the suicide of our species would be deplorable, lamentable, and a deeply moving tragedy, but that it would violate no one's rights. Indeed if, contrary to fact, all human beings could ever agree to such a thing, that very agreement would be a symptom of our species' biological unsuitability for survival anyway.

CONCLUSION

For several centuries now human beings have run roughshod over the lands of our planet, just as if the animals who do live there and the generations of humans who will live there had no claims on them whatever. Philosophers have not helped matters by arguing that animals and future generations are not the kinds of beings who can have rights now, that they don't presently qualify for membership, even "auxiliary membership," in our moral community. I have tried in this essay to dispel the conceptual confusions that make such conclusions possible. To acknowledge their rights is the very least we can do for members of endangered species (including our own). But that is something.

APPENDIX

The Paradoxes of Potentiality

Having conceded that rights can belong to beings in virtue of their merely potential interests, we find ourselves on a slippery slope; for it may seem at first sight that anything at all can have potential interests, or much more generally, that anything at all can be potentially almost anything else at all! Dehydrated orange powder is potentially orange juice, since if we add water to it, it will be orange juice. More remotely, however, it is also potentially lemonade, since it will become lemonade if we add a large quantity of lemon juice, sugar, and water. It is also a potentially poisonous brew (add water and arsenic), a potential orange cake (add flour, etc., and bake), a potential orange-colored building block (add cement and harden), and so on, *ad infinitum*. Similarly a two-celled embryo, too small to be seen by the unaided eye, is a potential human being; and so is an unfertilized ovum; and so is even an "uncapacitated" spermatozoan. Add the proper nutrition to an implanted embryo (under certain other necessary conditions) and it becomes a fetus and then a child. Looked at another way, however, the implanted embryo has been combined (under the same conditions) with the nutritive elements, which themselves are converted into a growing fetus and child. Is it then just as proper to say that food is a "potential child" as that an embryo is a potential child? If so, then what isn't a "potential child?" (Organic elements in the air and soil are "potentially food," and hence potentially people!)

Clearly, some sort of line will have to be drawn between direct or proximate potentialities and indirect or remote ones; and however we draw this line, there will be borderline cases whose classification will seem uncertain or even arbitrary. Even though any X can become a Y provided only that it is combined with the necessary additional elements, a, b, c, d, and so forth, we cannot say of any given X that it is a "potential Y" unless certain further—rather strict—conditions are met. (Otherwise the concept of potentiality, being universally and promiscuously applicable, will have no utility.) A number of possible criteria of proximate potentiality suggest themselves. The first is the criterion of causal importance. Orange powder is not properly called a potential building block because of those elements needed to transform it into a building block, the cement (as opposed to any of the qualities of the orange powder) is the causally crucial one. Similarly, any pauper might (misleadingly) be called a "potential millionaire" in the sense that all that need be added to any man to transform him into a millionaire is a great amount of money. The absolutely crucial element in the change, of course, is no quality of the man himself but rather the million dollars "added" to him.

What is causally "important" depends upon our purposes and interests and is therefore to some degree a relativistic matter. If we seek a standard, in turn, of "importance," we may posit such a criterion, for example, as that of the ease or difficulty (to some persons or other) of providing those missing elements which, when combined with the thing at hand, convert it into something else. It does seem quite natural, for example, to say that the orange powder is potentially orange juice, and that is because the missing element is merely common tap water, a substance conveniently near at hand to everyone; whereas it is less plausible to characterize the powder as potential cake since a variety of further elements, and not just one, are required, and some of these are not conveniently near at hand to many. Moreover, the process of combining the missing elements into a cake is rather more complicated than mere "addition." It is less plausible still to call orange powder a potential curbstone for the same kind of reason. The criterion of ease or difficulty of the acquisition and combination of additional elements explains all these variations.

Still another criterion of proximate potentiality closely related to the others is that of degree of deviation required from "the normal course of events." Given the intentions of its producers, distributors, sellers, and consumers, dehydrated orange juice will, in the normal course of events, become orange juice. Similarly, a human embryo securely imbedded in the wall of its mother's uterus will in the normal course of events become a human child. That is to say that if no one deliberately intervenes to prevent it happening, it will, in the vast majority of cases, happen. On the other hand, an unfertilized ovum will not become an embryo unless someone intervenes deliberately to make it happen. Without such intervention in the "normal" course of events, an ovum is a mere bit of protoplasm of very brief life expectancy. If we lived in a world in which virtually every biologically capable human female became pregnant once a year throughout her entire fertile period of life, then we would regard fertilization as something that happens to every ovum in "the natural course of events." Perhaps we would regard every unfertilized ovum, in such a world, as a potential person even possessed of rights corresponding to its future interests. It would perhaps make conceptual if not moral sense in such a world to regard deliberate nonfertilization as a kind of homicide.

It is important to notice, in summary, that words like *important*, *easy*, and *normal* have sense only in relation to human experiences, purposes, and techniques. As the latter change, so will our notions of what is important, difficult, and usual, and so will the concept of potentiality, or our application of it. If our purposes, understanding, and techniques continue to change in indicated directions, we may even one day come to think of inanimate things as possessed of "potential interests." In any case, we can expect the concept of a right to shift its logical boundaries with changes in our practical experience.

Human Duties and Animal Rights

Hardly anyone these days believes that morality permits us simply to have our way with animals and treat them in whatever manner suits our fancy or promotes our profit. That we do have duties of action and omission concerning animals is widely granted, but confusion over the ground and scope of those requirements, even when the duties are incorporated into law, is rife. Disagreements on these matters sometimes are derived from radically opposed basic attitudes toward animals or are rooted in clashing beliefs about such inaccessible facts as the nature of animal mental states, capacities, and vulnerabilities. (Some people disagree about whether fish feel much pain when hooks are stuck in their mouths, and among those who agree that fish *do* feel severe pain, some do, and some do not, care.) Other disagreements, however, are no doubt caused by misunderstandings of our moral vocabulary, which can be perplexing even in its application to all-human contexts, and becomes utterly bewildering in its extended applications to the nonhuman world. These conceptual confusions, while difficult, are somewhat more tractable than disagreements in basic attitude and in beliefs about animal psychology, and I shall attempt in this essay to dissipate some of them.

Insofar as a moral or legal system is rational there will be grounds for the various duties it imposes on those who are subject to its rules. Grounds for duties can be divided into two types. First, duties to treat other parties in certain ways may be derived from the prior claim of the other parties against us to be treated in those ways. Thus if *A* borrows ten dollars from *B* and promises to repay it by a certain date, then when that date arrives, A has a duty to pay B ten dollars, because B at that time has a valid claim against A, derived from A's promise, for ten dollars. The original transaction between the two parties gave B a right (valid claim) to repayment, and *in virtue of that right,* A has a duty to pay. If B were to waive his right, he would by that gesture destroy the ground for A's duty, and the duty would cease to exist. Similarly, human beings have valid claims conferred by moral principles and/or legal rules to noninterference in certain respects, and in virtue of these rights, other parties have a duty to respect their privacy, their property, and their persons.

Some of our duties, however, are based on a second type of ground. We have general moral duties—to be charitable and friendly, for example—that are not derived from the prior claims of any particular needy supplicant against us. Similarly, in some circumstances we have duties to obey the law even when no specific persons can claim our obedience as their own due. Moreover, our consciences can impose exacting moral requirements to act in heroic and self-sacrificing ways that could not plausibly be demanded or claimed from us as their due by those who benefit from them. The rule of *noblesse oblige* imposed duties on the nobility toward even those members of the lower classes thought to be undeserving of good treatment and thus in no position to claim it as their right.

There is then a variety of grounds for moral and legal duties other than the rights of those to whom the duty may be owed. We may have a duty to treat another in a certain way simply because he has a right or valid claim against us to that treatment, *or* simply because God, or conscience, or law, or self-ideal, or social role demands it of us, or because for some other reason it seems the decent or fitting thing to do, even in the absence of claims against us by our likely beneficiaries. Our duties to animals, I believe, are of both kinds. Some are correlated with valid moral claims of the animals themselves against us and thus require that we respect animal *rights;* others do not have that kind of support but are based on other reasons that are no less stringent.

I

According to a great many philosophers[1] and jurisprudents,[2] animals *do not* have rights for the simple reason that they are not the kinds of beings who *can* have rights. We can have duties *concerning* animals, these writers are often quick to add, but those duties are not owed to the animals as their due, and thus cannot be claimed against us as rights. Animals in this respect are like trees and rocks, automobiles and buildings, which are not the sorts of things of which it even makes sense to say they could have rights of their own. In respect to having rights, animals are more like pebbles and sunbeams than they are like full-fledged human beings. I believe that this view of the moral status of animals is radically mistaken, not because its distinguished proponents are somehow misinformed about the facts or insensitive in their attitudes, but rather because they misunderstand the basic terms of their own moral vocabulary even as applied to human beings.

To have a right is to have a claim against others to their action or omission in one's behalf and perhaps also against the state for enforcement of the claim against others. A claim is a right, properly speaking, when it is *valid*—that is, when it is recognized by legal or institutional rules or, in the case of moral rights, by the moral principles that inform an enlightened and sensitive conscience. Some claims, although based on good and relevant reasons, are in principle vulnerable to counterclaims. A valid claim, on the other hand, is a decisive case, invulnerable or conclusive. As such it is a morally sufficient title and an extremely valuable possession, neither dependent on nor derivative from the compassionate feelings, propriety, conscientiousness, or sense of *noblesse oblige* of others. It is a claim against another party in no way dependent for its incumbency on the love of the other party or the lovableness of its possessor. Hence, wicked, wretched, and odious human beings maintain certain rights against others, and the duties of others based on those rights are incumbent even on those who hate the claimants, and hate with good reason. A right is a matter of justice, and justice, while perhaps no more valuable than love, sympathy, and compassion, is nevertheless a moral notion distinct from them.

Because a right is a claim, it falls in neatly with a complex of claim-connected responses and attitudes. A claim-right, I have written elsewhere,[3] "can be urged, pressed, or rightly demanded against other persons. In appropriate circumstances the right-holder can urgently, peremptorily, or insistently call for his rights, or assert them authoritatively, confidently, unabashedly. Rights are not mere gifts or favors, motivated by love or pity, for which gratitude is the sole fitting response. A right is something a person can *stand* upon, something that can be demanded or insisted upon without embarrassment or shame. When that to which one has a right is not forthcoming, the appropriate reaction is indignation; when it is duly given there is no reason for gratitude, since it is simply one's own or one's due that one received."

When we think of others as claimants or right-holders against us, then, we think of them with a certain kind of *respect,* not merely with a feeling of duty or sympathy. The truest test of the existence of this respect is its steadfast persistence as an attitude of mind even toward the unlovable, the incapable, and the morally deficient, when these are otherwise qualified for it.

One would think that the conceptual suitability of animals for rights had been established once and for all by "cruelty to animals" statutes that seem to confer on animals at least legal rights to humane treatment. Still, it is always possible to say on the other side that such statutes were designed merely to protect public or private property or to protect human beings from corruption, or to protect the sensibilities of a minority of animal lovers who, as human beings, certainly do have rights. And there is little doubt that such reasons were the primary motives of the English legislators who originally passed animal protection bills. Edward Westermarck reports, for example, that "the bill for the abolition of bearbaiting and other cruel practices was expressly propounded on the ground that nothing was more conducive to crime than such sports, that they led the lower orders to gambling, that they educated them for thieves, that they gradually trained them up to bloodshed and murder."[4] Not a word about the pain and anguish of the animals! "Indifference to animal suffering," as Westermarck comments, "has been a characteristic of public opinion in European countries up to quite modern times."[5]

Whatever the motives of the original legislators, however, there can be little doubt now, in this final quarter of the twentieth century, that the directly intended beneficiaries of animal protection statutes are the protected animals themselves. Indeed, it is difficult even to invent plausible alternative rationales for the statutes. They cannot be designed wholly to protect property, for example, because mistreatment even of one's own chattels is forbidden. They cannot be designed exclusively to protect tender human sensibilities, because wholly private and unobserved mistreatment of animals is also prohibited. They could be intended to prevent the development of cruel habits that could eventually lead to violence against other human beings, I suppose, but why then are there so few statutes prohibiting the portrayal in literature and films of violence aimed *directly* at human victims? The simplest and least factitious account of the rationale of these laws is that they are intended, in the words of John Chipman Gray, "to preserve the dumb creatures from suffering."[6]

The fact that animals are the intended beneficiaries of protective legislation, however, does not yet prove that they have legal rights; and indeed the prevailing view of Anglo-American jurisprudence has been that animals do not, indeed cannot, have rights. Several reasons have been offered for this conclusion, but none can survive careful scrutiny. In the first place, it is commonly said that animals cannot have rights because they are not "moral agents."[7] Since they are incapable of having duties and responsibilities, they are not capable of being full-fledged members of our moral community, and thus they lack the moral "standing" to be right-holders. Since they cannot bear duties, they are not genuine moral subjects, and since they cannot be moral subjects, the argument concludes, they cannot be moral objects either. There are two possible replies to this argument. One is to deny the premise that animals are incapable of duties; the other is to deny the logic that deduces "no rights" from "no duties." To reply in the former way, I think, is to walk into a trap.

So far as we can know, no animals other than man have the intellectual equipment necessary for the reliable performance of duty and the discharge of responsibility. They cannot make promises or enter into contractual agreements. Nor can they even grasp the concept of a duty or a commitment. These failures of intellect and volition, I think, disqualify animals as genuine moral agents eligible for our trust and answerable for their failures.

One counterargument to these commonplace observations is that dogs and horses can be trained through instruction and discipline to bring their behavior up to a rather exacting standard. Dogs in particular are said even to manifest unmistakable signs of guilty conscience when they depart from the humanly assigned standard.[8] Here, again, the discussion of the moral status of animals can be snarled by an inadequate understanding or careless application of our ordinary moral concepts. Well-trained dogs sometimes let their masters down; they anticipate punishment or other manifestations of displeasure; they grovel and whimper, and they even make crude efforts at redress and reconciliation. But do they feel remorse and bad conscience? They have been conditioned to associate manifestations of displeasure with departures from a norm, and this is a useful way of keeping them in line, but they haven't the slightest inkling of the *reasons* for the norm. They don't *understand* why departures from the norm are wrong, or why their masters become angry or disappointed. They have a concept perhaps of the *mala prohibita*—the act that is wrong because it is prohibited, but they have no notion of the *mala in se*—the act that is prohibited because it is wrong. Even in respect to the *mala prohibita* their understanding is grossly deficient, for they have no conception of rightful authority. For dogs, the only basis of their master's "right" to be obeyed is his *de facto* power over them. Even when one master steals a beast from another, or when an original owner deprives it of its natural freedom in the wild, the animal will feel no moralized emotion, such as outraged propriety or indignation. These complex feelings involve cognitive elements beyond an animal's ken. Similarly, to suffer a guilty conscience is to be more than merely unhappy or anxious; it is to be in such a state because one has violated an "internalized standard," a principle of one's own, the rationale of which one can fully appreciate and the correctness of which one can, but in fact does not, doubt.

Punishment can be inflicted on animals to good effect. But unlike the genuine punishments inflicted on human criminals, it is not understood by a symbolic convention to express moral judgments on the offender or his past conduct. No animal could understand a moral judgment made about him in any language, natural or contrived. No animal could appreciate the morally blameworthy quality of his deviant act any more than it could appreciate the rational grounding of the violated rule. And no animal could be reasoned with by an appeal to commonly held ideals and convictions. That is why the full-fledged legal punishment of animals would be ludicrous, and that is why animals are not assigned legal duties and made legally answerable for their discharge.

Still another familiar way of describing this animal deficiency is to say that animals are not *persons*. As a friend and respecter of animals, I have no objection to this way of speaking, provided what is meant by a "person" is a being who is a conceptually appropriate subject of both rights and duties, for in that case one can deny that animals are persons on the grounds that they cannot have duties, while still keeping open the question whether they can have rights. On the other hand, if we follow John Chipman Gray[9] and take "person" to mean any being who can be a subject of *either* duties *or* rights, then we cannot deny that animals are persons without foreclosing analytically (to the animals' disadvantage) the question whether they can have rights. That is a good reason for rejecting Gray's usage, and it is reinforced by a consideration mentioned by Gray himself—namely, that in another very familiar, nontechnical sense, the word "person" is often used as a synonym for "human being," so it might seem unnecessarily paradoxical to assert that animals are persons. If we reject Gray's disjunctive criteria of personhood, however, then as respecters of animal rights, we have no reason to assert that animals *are* persons, and the appearance of paradox can be avoided.

Some friends of animals may be tempted to speak of them as persons for another reason. They overreact to the traditional practice of the common law of lumping animals in the same category as "mere things," with inanimate objects, plants, artifacts, and all the various objects that can be human property. (No one can deny, of course, that domesticated animals *are* property, but it *can* be denied that they *ought* to be property or that they are *merely* property.) These people then hastily assume that any being is either a person or a thing and opt for animal personhood. But in fact *animals are neither persons nor "mere things."* To treat them as mere things is to withhold from them even the possibility of right-ownership, but to treat them as persons, at least minimally on the same moral footing as human beings, may be to treat them even worse. We can have too high a regard for animals for the animals' own good, as evidenced by the bizarre practice of holding animals criminally responsible for the harms they cause to human beings, a custom that survived in Europe well into modern times.[10]

Overregard for beasts, oddly enough, is not so much a product of modern sophistication gone erratic as it is an essential ingredient of the primitive mind. The same habits of mind that inclined our prehistoric ancestors (and our primitive contemporaries) to ascribe humanlike minds to trees, winds, and mountains, led them to think of animals as humanlike spirits in eccentric guises, beings fully capable of honorable transactions as well as resentment, vindictiveness, and conspiracy:

> The savage, not only momentarily, while in a rage, but permanently and in cold blood, obliterates the boundaries between man and beast. He regards all animals as practically on a footing of equality with men. He believes that they are endowed with feelings and intelligence like men, that they are united into families and tribes like men, that they have various languages like human tribes, that they possess souls that survive the death of the bodies ... He tells of animals that have been the ancestors of men, of men that have become animals, of marriages that take place between men and beasts. He also believes that he who slays an animal will be exposed to the vengeance either of its disembodied spirit, or of all the other animals of the same species which, quite after human fashion, are bound to resent the injury done to one of their number. Is it not natural, then, that the savage should give like for like? If it is the duty of animals to take vengeance upon men, is it not equally the duty of men to take vengeance upon animals?[11]

When one considers the way men treat the other men who *are* their equals, when one ponders the sad chronicle of murders, vendettas, savage punishments, and holy wars, all accompanied by the swaggering self-righteousness that only human "persons" can achieve, and when one considers also the motives we have for treasuring our possessions, one is tempted to suggest that treating animals as mere things might on the whole be to treat them better than to treat them as the persons they are not. In any case, if it is the "friends" of animals who insist on their personhood, animals have little need for enemies....

II

Granted then that animals are the kinds of beings that *can* have rights, do they in fact have any, and if so, what rights do they have? Beginning with the relatively trivial, claims can be made on behalf of specific animals to goods that belong to them as a result of agreements made between human beings. Because of the intellectual incompetence of animals, it is impossible for a human being to make a promise to an animal or for the animal to reply with the promised *quid pro quo* required for a legal contract. But human beings can and do make promises to one another of which animals are the intended beneficiaries. I see no difference in principle between these arrangements and contractual agreements that confer rights on third-party human beneficiaries—for example, an agreement between a policyholder and an insurance company to pay a given sum to the policyholder's children in the event of his death. Upon the death of the insured, the children have a valid claim that can be pressed in their behalf against the insurance company in a court of law. This claim is valid even if the children had no knowledge or understanding of the contract that created it.

Similarly, human beings commonly make wills leaving money to trustees for the care of animals. Is it not natural to speak of the animal's *right* to his inheritance in such cases? If a trustee embezzles money from the animal's account,[16] and a proxy speaking in the mute beast's behalf presses the animal's claim, can the proxy not be described as asserting the animal's *rights?* Our legal tradition says not, but its reasons embody the confusions about the concept of a right that I have tried to dispel.

More important, there is no reason to deny that animals have general legal rights to noncruel treatment derived from statutes designed to protect them. These statutes are sometimes notoriously vague and, because of their escape clauses, very weak. In at least one case, however, a British act confers quite definite rights on animals—for example, the right to "complete anaesthesia" before being used in any "experiment calculated to give pain."[17] A proxy representative speaking for a rat might well seek an injunction on the animal's behalf to prevent a planned surgical operation without anaesthesia, or if such an operation is performed, criminal prosecution might be initiated for the violation of the rat's legal rights.

An even more fundamental right, one that is equally undeniable and is possessed by all creatures capable of suffering, is a general *moral right* not to be treated cruelly. What I mean by a moral right is a claim whose validity derives not (necessarily) from a legal or institutional rule, or a convention or agreement, but rather from a moral principle binding on the consciences of all moral agents. The underlying principle here is extremely simple. We condemn and conscientiously avoid inflicting unnecessary pain and suffering on other human beings simply because we regard pain and suffering as an *intrinsic evil.* That is, we judge pain and suffering to be evil simply because they *are* pain and suffering. In the case of human beings, at least, we never ask for any further reason that a given condition is evil and therefore to be avoided or corrected after we learn that it is a painful condition. The question "What's wrong with pain anyway?" is never allowed to arise.

We understand that some pain does more good than harm on balance, but what follows is that justifiable pain is a necessary evil, not that some pain is good in itself. If the essential character of pain and suffering themselves makes them evil—evil not for their consequences but in their intrinsic natures—then it follows that given magnitudes of pain and suffering are equally evil in themselves whenever and wherever they occur. An intense toothache is an evil in a young person or an old person, a man or a woman, a Caucasian or a Negro, a human being or a lion. A skeptic might deny that a toothache hurts a lion as much as it does a human being, but once one concedes that lion pain and human pain are equally pain—in the same sense and the same degree—then one cannot deny that they are equally evils in themselves. All this follows necessarily from the view that pain as such is an intrinsic evil, and not evil only because it tends to produce bad effects of other kinds.

The leading alternative to this argument for animal rights to humane treatment is the view that we owe our duties only to other human beings, not because human beings have some essential characteristic that animals lack, not because animals possess invulnerabilities to pain that humans lack, but only because the members of one species can have moral ties only to their own kind. This view holds that moral rules apply only to members of the human community, that animals are simply not in our club, and that the matter ends there. In this view, the chain of moral reasoning comes to an end at a different place, not at the self-evidence of the evil of pain as such, but rather at the exclusive loyalty of humans to their own kind. In the one view the only answer to the question "Why is pain evil?" is that it is pain. In the alternative view the only answer to the question "Why treat humans humanely but not animals?" is that they are humans.

It may therefore seem that the two views are on an equal footing morally, with nothing to choose between them, but that is not so. To be sure, all chains of reasoning must come to an end someplace, but it does not follow that all proposed stopping places are equally valid. The claim that all pain is evil in itself is a plausible candidate for a self-evident moral proposition, if only because no one can sincerely bring himself to doubt it in his own case. On the other hand, thousands of reflective persons have been led to wonder why the fact of humanity as such qualifies some living things for the right to humane treatment but not others. There is not a trace of self-evidence in the reply "Humans deserve good treatment simply and solely because they are humans and that's the end of reasoning about the matter." Moreover, to make loyalty to humanity the ultimate kind of "reason" in this manner is to make it no reason at all, but rather a piece of self-favoring arbitrariness antithetical to the character of all genuine moral reasoning. About this there is no gainsaying the late C. S. Lewis:

> If loyalty to our own species, preference for man simply because we are men, is not a sentiment, then what is? If mere sentiment justifies cruelty, why stop at sentiment for the whole human race? There is also a sentiment for a white man against the black, for Herrenvolk against the Non-Aryans.[18]

The exclusion of arbitrariness and favoritism is part of what we mean when we characterize judgments as "moral." This explains why we fall naturally into objective modes of speech when we ascribe moral rights. We decide whether or not to grant, recognize, or confer legal rights on classes of persons; as legislators, we discuss whether or not such conferrals would be good policy, useful, or fair. But when we ascribe moral rights, we speak not of deciding, but of discovering and reporting their existence. That is not because we believe they have already been conferred by some cosmic "moral legislature," and ours is not to reason why but simply to report them as discovered fact. Rather, it is because a right is a claim, and the basis of a claim is a reason, and when reasons are sufficiently cogent, they have a coercive effect on our judgments. When this is so, we feel that we have no more choice in making the judgment than we do when we report the findings of our senses about some matter of empirical fact (though surely moral judgments are not *about* some matter of empirical fact). Even in the legislative context, we may decide to create *legal* rights to X because we believe citizens "already have" *moral* rights to X—that is, claims against us to X based on objectively binding, principled reasons.

Among the rights that are often said (in the objective mode) to belong to persons already, prior to and independently of legislative enactment, are those called "human rights." It is interesting to note that the moral right to noncruel treatment satisfies one common definition of a human right—namely, a right held equally by all human beings, unconditionally and unalterably. If we define "cruel treatment" as behavior that inflicts *unnecessary* pain or torment on a creature capable of suffering—that is, pain for which there is no good or sufficient reason—then I should think everyone would agree that cruel treatment (so defined) *always* violates the rights of the being so treated and that those rights rest on no "condition" but the capacity to suffer and cannot ever be justifiably withdrawn or nullified. The one general right that animals most obviously have, then, is a "human right"!

In a narrower sense, of course, a human right is a moral right held unconditionally and unalterably by all and *only* human beings. The right to humane treatment is not peculiarly human in this sense, but there is at least one kind of absolute and unalterable right for which only human beings can qualify, and that is the right not to be degraded and exploited even in painless and humane ways. If we raised human beings for food, or treated them with tranquilizing drugs that rendered them compliant tools for our selfish purposes, or harnessed them like donkeys to carts or rickshaws, we would be violating a right we seldom think to ascribe to animals. We might yet treat them kindly, feed them well, and reward them with pats and sugar cubes instead of blows and angry words. Indeed, it would be good business practice to do so, since we could probably get more labor out of them in the long run for taking good care of them. But to convert humans into mechanical instruments in this way would be to humiliate, degrade, and utterly dehumanize them, even if we did it "humanely." It is difficult for me to conceive of animals being degraded in a similar sense; hence I doubt that the human right to a higher kind of respect, or an inviolate dignity, can properly be ascribed to them. Animals do make some claims against us, and by virtue of their capacity to be claimants and right-holders generally, they do qualify for a certain moral respect. But the higher kind of dignity that precludes even humane use as mere instruments requires a level of rational awareness that animals cannot achieve.

John Locke once wrote of the "natural rights" to "life, liberty, and property." Is it plausible to attribute any of that noble triad to animals? Animals do have claims against us to something like property and liberty, but these claims are clearly derivative from a more basic right to humane treatment. In some modern "animal factories" cattle are crowded so closely together that they have barely room to move their limbs. In mechanized farm buildings the new technology completely destroys the possibility of animal movement. Ruth Harrison writes:

> In some extreme systems the animal spends the major part of its life unable even to turn round in its pen, for example in most veal units, some barley beef units, sow stalls, and sow cubicles. These animals can only stretch their limbs when they are standing, and the bird in the battery cage is unable to stretch its neck fully within the cage or to spread its wings.[19]

These animals are deprived of liberty of movement in precisely the way prison cells deprive human beings of liberty. The rationale for condemning this practice, however, unlike that in the human case, rests on no principle other than that proclaiming the evil of suffering. The more elaborate argument for the value of human liberty as found, for example, in Mill's *On Liberty,* would hardly apply to animals. We need not concern ourselves that a given steer has no choice whether to live in Texas or Montana, or that this lack of ultimate control over the course of his life will stunt his intellectual and moral powers. Inability ever to move out of a narrow stall is another matter. The basis of the conditions in crowded animal factories is as clearly cruelty (actually a kind of "mental cruelty") as it would be in animal-baiting, or vivisection without anesthetic, as Harrison's example vividly shows:

> Lack of movement can lead to boredom, boredom to so-called "vices" such as tail-biting in pigs and featherpecking in birds. Rather than overhaul the system the producer then further deprives the animal, either of light to see its fellows clearly, or by mutilation—the hen of part of her beak or the pig of its tail.

Similarly, animal preserves might be likened to a kind of "property" owned by the various animals that occupy it. Poaching and other violent incursions by humans into the domain reserved for the animals then could be interpreted as a violation of the animal's "property right." But here too the right in question has a derivation different from its human counterpart. Without room to roam wild animals cannot flourish as wild; they become overly dependent on human support and vulnerable to new diseases; eventually they succumb painfully to droughts, famines, and the like. Ultimately, to deprive wild animals of their wilderness sanctuaries is to treat them cruelly, and for that reason, to violate their rights.

Whether or not there is a natural animal right to life is the most difficult and controversial question that can be raised about animal rights, and I can hardly do it justice here. It may be useful, however, to note that ascription of the right even to human beings is not altogether free of confusion and controversy. Those of us who regard human life as something precious in itself insist that all human beings have a claim against their fellows to be rescued when threatened with death and also a claim not to be killed. As a claim, the "right to life" is absolute. But a claim is not quite the same thing as a full-fledged right. Claims can come into conflict with other claims and can be outbalanced or overruled. Claims can differ in degree: some are stronger than others. Rights in a strict and proper sense do not differ in degree and cannot be in conflict with one another. Consider property rights, for example. Jones and Smith might both take to court what they think are valid titles to a given parcel of land. Each has a case to make or a claim to advance to ownership of the land. But ownership is the right to the *exclusive* control of the land. If Smith has a right to the land, then Jones has a duty to stay off it without Smith's consent, and if Jones has the right, then Smith has a duty to stay off. It would thus be contradictory to say that they both have a right and that the rights "conflict." If one has a right, then the other can have no more than an outweighed claim, for a right is a kind of trump card that cannot be outweighed.

Obviously, tragic circumstances may occur in which some can be saved only by killing (or risking death to) others. It cannot be the case, therefore, that all human beings in all circumstances have a right not to be killed or left to die. Indeed, in some circumstances we have the choice between conserving human lives and paying an enormous price in other values. We build roads and tunnels knowing full well that a certain number of workmen will be killed in unavoidable construction accidents, and we leave miners to die in underground cave-ins when the price of their rescue would be millions of dollars. So if our actual practice is an index of our attitudes, we allow even the claim to human life to be outbalanced by claims of other kinds. At most, then, all we can plausibly mean by an absolute human "right to life" is a *claim*, belonging to all human beings as such, to have very serious consideration always given to the value of their lives, not to be killed without cause, and, when endangered, to be rescued whenever this can be done at reasonable cost.

Once more, the cases in which animals most clearly have a claim against us to their lives are instances in which the claim is derivative from the more fundamental right not to be treated cruelly. When we kill a doe we leave her fawns without protection, and that is cruel to *them*. It is for that reason, not respect for animal life as such, that many laws grant a doe special protection against hunters. Even if an animal's life, like a person's, is of some value in itself, it would appear to be considerably less basic a consideration than its claim not to be treated cruelly. The British Cruelty to Animals Act of 1876, for example, seems to respond to a widespread (though not universal) element in the public conscience when it requires that an experimental animal be killed "before recovery from the anaesthetic, if it is in pain or seriously injured."[20] When we contrast this *duty* to kill animals with the great debate over whether there is even a *right* to kill humans deliberately in similar circumstances, it appears that the animal "right to life," if there is such a thing, is generally held to be a much weaker claim than its human counterpart.

The famous argument of Jeremy Bentham for humane treatment of animals, for which he has received much deserved praise from humanitarians over the years, implies or presupposes that there is no independent animal claim to life at all. The basis of all our duties to animals, Bentham thought, is the animal capacity for pain.[21] This imposes a strict duty on us not to cause them to suffer, but leaves us entirely free to kill animals when it is useful to us and not painful to them.

> If the being eaten were all, there is very good reason why we should be suffered to eat such of them as we like to eat: we are the better for it, and they are never the worse. They have none of those long-protracted anticipations of future misery that we have. The death they suffer in our hands commonly is, and always may be, a speedier, and by that means a less painful one, than that which would await them in the inevitable course of nature. If the being killed were all, there is very good reason why we should be suffered to kill such as molest us: we should be the worse for their living, and they are never the worse for being dead. But is there any reason why we should be suffered to torment them? Not any that I can see.[22]

It should be noted in passing that the Benthamite argument against an animal right to life would make the human right to life itself derivative from a more general right not to suffer pain, a result that could have drastic consequences for lonely but innocent humans who can be killed painlessly to no one's grief.

It is clear, I think, that animals have no general claim against humans to the protection of their lives in the state of nature where they must hunt, kill, and eat one another. Human intervention to save animal lives in the wild, in fact, would itself be a kind of cruelty to the animals whose instincts require them to kill. In short, if we respected animal claims to life as such in the same manner and to the same degree as we respect the human claim to life, our meddlings in nature would become even more officious and counterproductive than they are already.

If animals have any underivative claim to life, it would appear then so weak as to be outbalanced by almost any human purpose of a reasonably respectable sort with which it might come in conflict. We can kill animals for self-protection, for food, for skins, for purposes of sanitation and public health, or to protect still other animals from suffering. One might get carried away by this list, however, and extend it without limit. If an animal's life as such had no value, or if an animal had no claim whatever against us to the preservation of its life, then any human purpose (or even no purpose at all) would be sufficient justification for killing an animal if done in such a way as not to cause suffering. But in fact, to kill a horse, or a dog, or a lion just for one's idle amusement, when no contribution to the well-being of other animals is intended, would be to deny a very real claim without cause and hence to violate the animal's right, weak though it may generally be. Wholly wanton painless killing, even more obviously than killing for sport or amusement, would be an invasion of the rights of the victim.

If the conclusions about the animal "right to life" I have tentatively reached are correct, then at least two things need explaining: (1) why an animal should have any underivative claim to life-as-such at all and (2) why the animal claim to life is such a very weak claim compared with the human "right to life." In the space remaining I can only sketch the outlines of possible answers to these questions.

All animals, like all living things, are disposed by their inherited natures to remain in existence. This "impulse to self-preservation," like any other biological propensity, is something that can be respected and furthered or denied and hindered. One school of moral philosophy, whose chief spokesmen were

William James,[23] George Santayana,[24] and Ralph Barton Perry,[25] would make all conative urges, wants, impulses, even unconscious tendencies and directions of growth, worthy objects of moral respect. Any such state or tendency is a kind of "demand" for fulfillment, and other things being equal (which they never are), its satisfaction would be a thing of value. "The essence of value," James said, "is the satisfaction of demand."[26] So long as any demand whatever is frustrated, so long (as James put it somewhere) as "a single cockroach suffers the pangs of unrequited love," the world is not as good a place as it might be. Of course, not every demand for satisfaction is of equal value, and in our actual world it is necessary that many impulses to life be squelched if life itself is to flourish. Nevertheless, it is possible to hold that insofar as anything at all is the object of some "demand," it is, just so far, a thing of value. That would be a way of establishing at least some value for each animal life, however minimal.

An equally difficult question is why animal claims to life should be so much weaker than human claims. I should like to mention one rather quick way with this question, if only in passing. We should remind ourselves that a right is an addressed claim—that is, not only a claim to something, but a claim made against one or more specific persons. Now, an animal right to life could not be a claim against other animals, since animals are incapable of having duties and therefore of respecting the rights of others. Rather, an animal claim to life can be held only against human beings so that the animal claim is logically correlated with the human duty. Human duties to respect animal lives then are simply one part of the larger catalog of human duties of all kinds and must find their proper place in an order of priority. Generally speaking, our duties to persons close to ourselves in space and time, kind and relation, tend to have a greater stringency than our duties to creatures who are more remote in those respects. I have a greater duty to my immediate family than to my remote relatives, to my friends than to strangers, to countrymen than to foreigners. That might explain why the animal claims to life might rank well behind most claims of human beings, even on the assumption that animal life is as valuable a thing in itself as human life.

Our question assumes a more difficult shape, however, when

it requires us to justify the assumption that animal life is not as valuable as human life—the assumption most of us in fact make. How is it possible to hold consistently that any human life is a more precious thing in and of itself than any animal life? Recall the earlier argument about cruelty: If pain is an intrinsic evil, then it is an evil wherever and whenever it occurs, and degrees of intensity being equal, it is as great an evil in an animal as in a man. What are we to make of a similar argument applied to life? If human life is a good, intrinsically worth preserving for its own sake, then any life is equally a good, worth preserving for its own sake.

The parallel between the two arguments, I believe, is entirely superficial. Human pain seems self-evidently an evil to those who have known it quite simply because it is pain—because it hurts, and to be hurt is to suffer something evil in itself. Human life, however, seems a supreme good to those who treasure it, not because it is life, but because it is human. It is a truism, but one worth pondering, that one cannot be a human being and manifest whatever is precious in the human condition unless one is alive. Life, then, is a trivially obvious but necessary condition for the existence of any uniquely human properties that may have an intrinsic value. Abstracted from those properties, however, it is far from "self-evident" that life has any value in its own right at all, much less an invariant supreme value "wherever and whenever it occurs." I conclude therefore that it is possible to hold without inconsistency that an individual human life as such is a thing of far greater value than an individual animal life as such. If that judgment of relative worth is to escape the character of a mere sentiment of self-preference, however, it must be grounded in some properties that are present in human nature and missing in animal nature. If we cannot locate such properties and plausibly base the unique worth of human life on them, we may have to fall back ultimately to the Benthamite position that neither human nor animal life as such has an intrinsic value and that human life has a greater claim to protection only because of the greater human vulnerability to suffering from the deaths of others and from "protracted anticipations" of our own.

III

There is one kind of human duty toward animals that is not derived from any right of animals (or anyone else for that matter) against us, and yet honoring that duty may be even more important, morally speaking, than respecting animal rights. I refer to the duty to preserve *whole species* from extinction—certainly a more important matter morally than preserving the life of any single animal. Yet a species, unlike an individual animal, is not the kind of entity of which it even makes sense to say it can have rights. The name of a species is not that of some superentity distinct and emergent from the individual animals of which it is composed. Rather, it is simply the name of a collection of entities with certain defining characteristics in common. The species of elephant called *Loxodon africanus,* for example, is not an individual superelephant with wants and aims, feelings and beliefs. As a species, therefore, it has no interests of its own and is not even the kind of thing that could have a good of its own. It follows, if my analysis is correct, that a species is not the kind of being that could have a claim or a right.

We often speak of corporate rights and duties. The United States has a right to impose taxes and a duty to enforce laws. The General Motors Corporation has a duty to pay taxes and a right to issue stock. These statements, of course, are perfectly intelligible. A species, however, is quite a different kind of entity from a corporate institution. As a mere unorganized collection, it has no charter, no rules, no offices, no individuals empowered to act or be acted upon in its name.

Our duty to preserve African (not to mention Indian) elephants from extinction could be owed to our own posterity as *their* right. After all, our unborn descendants will have interests that can be represented by proxies now, so it makes good sense to speak of their rights to inherit a world of a certain kind and of our present duties to them to conserve that kind of world. But this can hardly be the whole ground of our duty to save the elephants (or even the major part of it). If the elephants disappear before our

great-great-grandchildren arrive, then our descendants will have
been deprived of something of value and can rightly complain
(over our graves) that we have invaded their interest in inheriting a
world that might have contained elephants. But how great a wrong
would that be to our descendants? Presumably they would feel
about elephants somewhat the way we feel about dinosaurs. It is a
shame that there aren't a few survivors, but we don't gnash our
teeth over the matter. The enormity of our wrongdoing in
permitting the extinction of elephants, however, would be out
of all proportion to the minor wrong done to our human descendants.

The duty we have as members of the human species to
preserve other species, then, cannot be explained wholly as the
consequence of anyone's rights against us. No explanation that a
philosopher can dream up will carry nearly the conviction that the
statement of the duty itself bears. My inclination is to seek an
explanation in terms of the requirements of our unique station as
rational custodians of the planet we temporarily occupy. We made
no decision individually or collectively to fill the role of superin-
tendents of nature. Like so many of the roles we occupy as individuals, this one was foisted on us by circumstances, and we
occupy it as if by default. But while it was not up to us whether to
assume responsibility for the care of our planet, it is entirely up to
us (as the ancient Stoics said so often) whether we do the job
sloppily or well. In the last analysis, our duty to preserve the other
species may be largely a matter of very human pride.

NOTES

1. A leading example is Immanuel Kant, *The Metaphysical Principles of Virtue* (Indianapolis: Bobs-Merrill, 1964), p. 106. See also W. D. Ross, *The Right and the Good* (Oxford: Clarendon Press, 1930), pp. 49ff.

2. For example, C. S. Kenny, *Outlines of the Criminal Law* (Cambridge: Cambridge University Press, 1958), pp. 171-172.

3. Joel Feinberg, *Social Philosophy* (Englewood Cliffs, N.J.: Prentice-Hall, 1972).

4. Edward Westermarck, *The Origin and Development of the Moral Ideas*, vol. 2 (London: Macmillan, 1917), p. 508.

5. *Ibid.*, p. 509.

6. John Chipman Gray, *The Nature and Sources of the Law*, 2nd ed. (Boston: Beacon Press, 1963), p. 43.

7. For example, W. D. Ross, *The Right and the Good.* For a forceful criticism of this view, see W. D. Lamont, *Principles of Moral Judgment* (Oxford: Clarendon Press, 1946), pp. 82-85.

8. See C. Lloyd Morgan, *Animal Life and Intelligence* (London: Arnold, 1890), p. 399.

9. Gray, *The Nature and Sources of the Law*, p. 27.
10. See Edward Evans, *The Criminal Prosecution and Capital Punishment of Animals* (London: Heinemann, 1906).
11. Westermarck, *The Origin and Development*, vol. 1, p. 258.
12. Gray, *The Nature and Sources of the Law*, p. 43.
13. *Ibid.*
14. For a development of this idea, see Joel Feinberg, "The Rights of Animals and Future Generations," in William Blackstone, ed., *Philosophy and the Environmental Crisis* (Athens, Ga.: University of Georgia Press, 1974).
15. *Ibid.*
16. The example is from H. J. McCloskey, "Rights." *Philosophical Quarterly* 15 (1965): 221.
17. British Cruelty to Animals Act of 1876, sections 2 and 3.
18. As quoted without reference to source by Richard Ryder, "Experiments on Animals," in *Animals, Men, and Morals,* ed. S. Godlovitch, R. Godlovitch, and J. Harris (London: Victor Gollancz, 1971), p. 81.
19. Ruth Harrison, "On Factory Farming," in *Animals, Men, and Morals,* ed. S. Godlovitch, R. Godlovitch, and J. Harris (London: Victor Gollancz, 1971), p. 17.
20. British Cruelty to Animals Act of 1876, section 3, part 4.
21. "The question is not Can they *reason?* nor Can they *talk?* but Can they *suffer?*"—Jeremy Bentham, *An Introduction to the Principles of Morals and Legislation* (New York: Hafner, 1948), p. 311n.
22. *Ibid.*
23. William James, "The Moral Philosopher and the Moral Life," in *Essays in Pragmatism* (New York: Hafner, 1948), pp. 65-87.
24. George Santayana, *Reason in Science* (New York: Scribner, 1905), ch. 8-10.
25. Ralph Barton Perry, *The General Theory of Value* (Cambridge, Mass.: Harvard University Press, 1926).
26. William James, "The Moral Philosopher," p. 77.

Is There a Right to Be Born?

If a person is told that voluntary sterilization is wicked and there-fore forbidden, he or she might cogently reply that what a person does with his own body is his own business, or a matter entirely between him and his physician, so that no one else has a right to interfere. Similarly, if a couple is told that the use of "mechanical" contraceptives is wicked and not to be permitted, they might reply with equal cogency that the decision whether or not to use contra-ceptives ought to be theirs alone, since no other parties have their interests directly involved. More exactly, the decision should ultimately be the woman's alone, since her will should reign sovereign on the question of what is to be done in or to her body.

Appeal to the right to determine the use of one's own body is also commonly made these days in support of the mother's right to abor-tion. But here the issue is much more complicated. Deciding whether or not to have a fetus removed from the womb does not at first sight seem quite the same sort of thing as deciding whether or not to have one's nose straightened, or one's gall bladder removed. Nor is a fetus a *part* of a woman's body in the same sense as that in which her vermi-form appendix is a part of her body. Opponents of legalized abortion point out that a fetus is not a constituent organ of the mother but an independent entity temporarily growing inside the mother, and to the question whose interests other than the mother's are involved in the decision whether to abort, these parties answer triumphantly that the fetus too has an interest in what is done to it. In fact, the fetus is said itself to have rights that command respect, one of which is the right to be born, violation of which is said to be as clearly murder as the deliberate killing of an innocent human being outside of the womb.

Now, from the fact that a fetus is not a "part," or a constitutive organ, of its mother's body it does not yet follow that it is a being possessed of claims against others to be treated in certain ways. Surely this minimal and negative characterization of the fetus (as a "nonorgan") leaves the question of its status as a right-holder entirely open. And yet this is the crucial question in the controversy over the legalization of abortion. If the fetus does have a right to be born, then we owe it *to it* not to prevent its birth; and a legal duty of noninterference might be imposed upon us *for the fetus's sake*. On the other hand, if the fetus has no right to be born, we owe no more to it than we do to a gall bladder or a wart or a contraceptive coil, and the mother's bodily sovereignty applies as much to this internal nonorgan as it does to her own genuine bodily parts.

I

Gall bladders and contraceptive coils, of course, are not the kinds of beings of which it even makes sense to say that they could have rights of their own. To ascribe rights to such things as bodily organs, rocks, stones, artifacts, machines, natural processes, and other "mere things" is to commit a kind of "category mistake" analogous to talk of home runs learning to tap dance or virtues having weight. It is absurd to say that *rocks* can have rights, for example, not because rocks are morally inferior things unworthy of rights (that statement makes no sense either), but because rocks belong to a category of entities of whom rights cannot meaningfully be predicated. That is not to say that there are no circumstances in which we ought to treat rocks carefully, but only that the rocks themselves cannot claim good treatment from us. Our first question about fetuses, then, should not be the normative one, "Do they have rights?," but rather the conceptual one, "Are they even the kinds of beings that *can* have rights?" Fetuses appear to fall somewhere between the clear cases of normal human beings, whose categorical suitability for right-ownership would be admitted even by extreme misanthropes who deny that anyone in fact has rights, and mere rocks, at the other extreme, to which the attribution of rights is conceptually impossible. Fetuses, then, are among a variety of bewildering borderline cases for the application of rights, which raise separate riddles of precisely the same form: Is it meaningful or conceptually possible to ascribe rights to individual animals? to whole species of animals? to plants? to idiots and madmen? to our dead ancestors? to generations yet unborn? Until we know how to settle these puzzling cases, we cannot claim fully to grasp the concept of a right or to know the shape of its logical boundaries.

In another paper[1] I have tried to answer all of these questions with one stroke by formulating a criterion for distinguishing the kinds of beings who can have rights from the kinds that cannot. I argued there

[1] Joel Feinberg "The Rights of Animals and Future Generations," *Philosophy and Environmental Crisis*, ed. by William Blackstone (Athens, Georgia: University of Georgia Press, 1974).

that only beings who have interests are conceptually suitable subjects for the attribution of rights. I came to that conclusion for two main reasons. First, interests are necessary for a being to be *represented* by proxies. Various kinds of incompetents, infants, insane and senile persons, even some of the higher animals, can be represented by guardians, or trustees, not in the sense in which a mere stand-in or mouthpiece represents the *will* of his principal, for these incompetents may have no will to be represented, but rather in the sense in which an attorney, for example, is delegated authority to represent his client's *interests* or to be his agent. Second, interests are essential to a creature's being the sort of thing that can have a *good of its own*, for to act for a creature's good simply *is* to act in its interest. It may seem at first sight as though even plants and "mere things," which most assuredly do not have interests of their own, might yet have a good or welfare that we can promote or retard. Certain kinds of fertilizer are "good for" lawns (as we say) and certain kinds of gasoline or oil are "good for" automobiles. But clearly all we can mean by these useful idioms is that the fertilizer or the gasoline and oil promotes *our* interest in the lawn or the automobile. Particularly in the case of the mere thing, where the absence of an interest of its own is certain, it is clear that the object, though it can *be* good or bad in a great variety or respects, can *have* no good of its own. "An automobile needs gasoline and oil to function, but it is no tragedy for *it* if it runs out—an empty tank does not hinder or retard *its* interests."[2]

This account, I think, explains why those who debate the question of animal rights often find it crucial to determine whether animals are the directly intended beneficiaries of protective legislation. To concede that animals can *be* beneficiaries (as the deniers of the possibility of animal rights were reluctant to do) is to acknowledge that they are the sorts of beings who can have interests and therefore a good of their own which can be represented by proxies and protected by guardians. Possession of interests by no means automatically confers any particular right or even any rights at all upon a being. What it does is show that the being in question is the kind of being to whom moral or legal rights can be ascribed without conceptual absurdity. To have a right, after all, is to have a claim, and to have a claim is to be in a legitimate position to make certain demands against others. A mute creature can make claims only by means of a vicarious representative

[2] *Ibid.* Cf. Aristotle's discussion of why we cannot be friends with inanimate objects, *Nicomachean Ethics*, Book VIII, Chap. 2: "We cannot wish for the good of such objects." And in a note: "It would be absurd, for example, for a man to wish his wine well. If he has any wish in the matter, it is that the wine may keep, so that he can taste the joys of possession." J.A.K. Thomson translation, Penguin Books (1953), p. 230.

speaking for it, but *if* it has no interests of its own it cannot be represented in this way, having *no "behalf" that another can speak in.* Moreover, if a creature has no interests of its own, it has no welfare or good of its own, and cannot be helped or hindered, benefited or aided, in which case, it has *no "sake" that one could act for.* In that event there could be no coherent reason for regarding any conduct of others as its due, and thus the concept of a right would simply not apply to it.

Applying the interest principle to the hard cases, I concluded that the higher animals *are* among the sorts of beings who *can* have rights, even though the rights they actually have are minimal, perhaps a general right not to be treated cruelly and rather rare specific rights derived from agreements between human beings. I denied that vegetables can have rights on the grounds that however interests are ultimately to be analyzed, they must be compounded somehow out of wants and purposes, both of which in turn presuppose something like expectation, belief, and cognitive awareness, which are presumably missing in vegetables (even in "human vegetables"). I hesitantly conceded, however, that dead persons can have rights against us, namely rights to the fulfillment of promises made to them when they were alive, and rights not to be falsely defamed to those who once knew and loved them. This admittedly paradoxical conclusion is supported by the idea that certain of a dead person's interests can be thought to survive their owner's death and constitute claims against us that persist beyond the life of the claimant. This in turn requires us to think of interests as fulfilled only by the coming into existence of that which is desired, and not simply as "satisfaction of desire" in the sense of contentment in the mind of the desirer when he believes that his desire has been fulfilled. It is too late, after all, for a dead man to experience contentment.

II

If the interest principle is to permit us to ascribe rights to fetuses and generations yet unborn, it can only be on the grounds that interests can exert a claim upon us even before their possessors actually come into being, just the reverse of the situation respecting dead men where interests are respected even after their possessors have ceased to be. The rights our law confers on the unborn child, both proprietary and personal, are for the most part placeholders or reservations for the rights he shall inherit when he becomes a full-fledged interested being. The law protects a potential interest in these cases before it has even grown into actuality, as a garden fence protects newly seeded flower beds long before blooming flowers have emerged from them. The unborn child's present right to property, for example, is a legal protection offered now to his future interest, contingent upon his birth, and instantly voidable if he dies before birth. As Coke put it: "The law in many cases hath consideration of him in respect of the apparent expectation of his birth";[3] but this is quite another thing than recognizing a right actually to be born. *Assuming* that the child will be born, the law seems to say, various interests that he will come to have after birth must be protected from damage that they can incur even before birth.

"There is nothing in law," says Salmond, "to prevent a man from owning property before he is born. His ownership is contingent, for he may never be born at all; but it is nonetheless a real and present ownership. A man may settle property on his wife and the children to be born of her. Or he may die intestate and his unborn child will inherit his estate."[4] To say of an unborn fetus that he has a right of ownership *now* is to say that funds have been left in trust for him on the expectation of his arrival. His right to use the funds is contingent upon his birth as a living human being. As Salmond puts it, "The legal personality attributed to him by way of anticipation falls away *ab initio* if he never takes his place among the living . . . A posthumous child, for example, may inherit; but if he dies in the womb, or is stillborn, his inheritance fails to take effect, and *no one can claim through him*, though it would be otherwise if he lived for an hour after his birth."[5] Even though it deviates from a certain technical legal usage, let us call the legal rights a fetus has in anticipation of his future postnatal interests, *contingent rights*, rights reserved for him on the expectation of his birth.

In recent years American jurisdictions have conferred another set of contingent rights upon fetuses—conditional (again) upon their eventually being born alive. I refer to rights to be free of bodily injury that will handicap them after they are born. With this contingent fetal right goes a corresponding postnatal right *ex delicto*, or right of action in tort, to sue for damages in compensation for injuries inflicted before he was born, a right which he can exercise through a proxy-attorney and in his own name any time *after* he is born. Thus, a child born with malformed limbs because a motorist negligently ran over his mother while he was in her womb is entitled to recover damages after he is born from the negligent motorist. If he dies *in utero*, however, no one can sue in his name, for his death. His prenatal legal rights than can be violated by another's negligence apparently do not include a right to be born alive, but only the conditional right *if* born alive, to be free of physical injury. (It is interesting to note paren-

---

[3] William Salmond, *Jurisprudence,* Twelfth Edition, ed. by P. J Fitzgerald (London: Sweet & Maxwell, 1966), p. 303.

[4] *Loc. cit.*

[5] *Ibid.*, p. 304.

thetically that the conduct that causes injury to the fetus for which it can recover after it is born may have occurred before it was even *conceived*. A pharmaceutical manufacturer who carelessly prepares medicine six months before an infant's conception will be answerable to a child fifteen months later, if the medicine taken by the mother damaged the embryo, and the fetus nevertheless survived until birth. Or consider the case where a blood transfusion to a mother gives her syphilis. One year later she conceives, and her child is subsequently born syphilitic. In an actual German case of a few years ago, the infant was able to recover damages from the hospital for its negligence in administering the blood transfusion to his mother almost two years before *he* was even born.)

Let me reiterate that these rights to sue, and the rights to be free of bodily injury that they presuppose, do *not* imply *unconditional* recognition of prenatal rights. The fetus's rights are recognized in Lord Coke's words "on condition only that it be born alive." If it dies *in utero* or is stillborn, then no person will exist to claim that he himself has been damaged; nor will anyone be able to represent the claimant, or derive any kind of rights by transmission from the fetus. There are certain older decisions that no longer have the force of precedent that awarded compensation to the fetus's estate for wrongful injuries suffered *in utero* resulting in stillbirth. Those decisions seemed to imply a noncontingent right of the fetus to be born alive, but they have now fallen out of our law.

There are numerous other places, however, where our law does seem to imply an unconditional legal right to be born, and very few commentators seem to have found that idea conceptually absurd. Of decisions that might be construed as recognizing the fetus's right while still a fetus to be born alive, two interesting ones can be mentioned here. The first is from the law governing treatment of condemned criminals: "A pregnant woman condemned to death is respited as of right, until she has been delivered of her child."[6] (The "as of right" mentioned in the quoted sentence must surely refer to a right of the fetus, not the mother, since the mother is denied the right to let her child die with her; that is, she is not given a discretionary right herself to decide the child's fate.)

The other interesting example of apparent judicial recognition of the right to be born comes from an article given the following headline by the *New York Times*: "Unborn Child's Right Upheld Over Religion." A hospital patient in her eighth month of pregnancy refused to take a blood transfusion even though warned by her physician that "she might die at any minute and take the life of her child as

[6] *Ibid.*, p. 303.

well." The ground of her refusal was that blood transfusions are repugnant to the principles of her (Jehovah's Witnesses) religion. The Supreme Court of New Jersey expressed uncertainty over the constitutional question of whether a nonpregnant adult might refuse, on religious grounds, a blood transfusion pronounced necessary to her own survival, but nevertheless ordered the patient in the present case to receive the transfusion, on the grounds that "the unborn child is entitled to the law's protection."[7]

It is important to reemphasize here that the questions of whether fetuses *do* or *ought to have* rights are substantive questions of laws and morals, open to argument and decision. The prior question of whether fetuses are the kinds of beings that *can have* rights, however, is a conceptual, not a moral, question, amenable only to what is called "logical analysis," and irrelevant to moral judgment. The correct answer to the conceptual question, I believe, is that unborn children *are* among the sorts of beings whom possession of rights can meaningfully be predicated, even though they are (temporarily) incapable of having interests, because their future interests can be protected now, and it does make sense to protect a potential interest even before it has grown into actuality. The interest-principle, however, makes perplexing, at best, talk of a noncontingent fetal right to be born; for fetuses, lacking actual wants and goals, have no actual interests in being born, and it is difficult to think of any other reason for ascribing any rights to them other than on the assumption that they will in fact be born.

I now turn to the difficult normative question of whether there are any noncontingent fetal rights.

III

To begin with, it does seem *morally* (though not "conceptually") *absurd* to claim that there is a general across-the-board right possessed by *all* human fetuses, simply as such, to be born. There may well be rights held by all human beings as such, for example, the rights not to be exploited, or degraded, or treated in cruel or inhumane ways. These of course are the claims we call "human rights," since one automatically acquires them simply by being born a human being. Most theorists formulate the basic human rights in such a way that they cannot, logically, conflict with one another, so that their claim upon others can be treated as absolute and unconditional. We have a human right, for example, not to be subjected to physical torture, which we think cannot be justly infringed in any circumstances. Whatever the tenability of this claim, it surely seems more plausible than a

---

[7] The *New York Times*, June 17, 1966, p. 1. The New Jersey Supreme Court denied the right of a nonpregnant adult to refuse a blood transfusion necessary to her survival in the later case. *John F. Kennedy Memorial Hospital v. Heston* (1971).

parallel claim on behalf of all fetuses that they enjoy a human or "fetal-human" right to be born that can *never* be justly infringed (or more narrowly redefined) even for the sake of those already alive. The latter claim would entail that fundamental interests of living persons are automatically to be forfeited whenever they conflict with a claim to be born made on behalf of an entity which is nothing more than a cluster of splitting cells still incapable of consciousness or desire, a judgment which seems utterly perverse.

The fetus, of course, has *future interests,* "contingent upon its being born" which can be protected in advance for it, on the expectation that it *will* be born. But it does not have an actual interest now that it be born later, because it is not yet capable of having *any* actual interests. That fact might tempt us to the view that a fetus *never* has a right to be born, that whatever rights it does have now are those "contingent rights" whose full statement has the form: "Assuming that the fetus *will* be born, we owe it to him now not to damage, or preclude the satisfaction of the interests he *will* have after his birth." This normative view tempts me very strongly. It does not, however, follow from the analytic view presented above. My position there was *not* that for every right there is a particular interest corresponding to it. That view is patently false, for at any given time I have rights to do many things that are *contrary* to my interests, and I may have interests that do not qualify or even deserve legal protection. My analytic conclusion, on the contrary, was only that it is a (conceptually) necessary condition for the possession of any rights at all that the possessor be the kind of being who is, was, or will be capable of having interests. I did not claim further that there need be a neat one-to-one correspondence between specific interests and specific rights. Therefore, without further premises, the fact that a given fetus at a given time does not have a specific actual interest in being born does not entail that he has no right, at that time, to be born. So the question is still open.

But now I wonder what *reasons* can be given in support of the normative judgment that a fetus has at least a general *claim* to be born even though that claim may be overridden in certain circumstances by stronger claims or rights. I should think that the fact that a being has an interest in X would be a very good reason, speaking generally, in support of the claim that he has a right to X, even though it is admittedly not, all by itself, a decisive reason; and similarly the fact that a being has no interest in X would at least put something of a heavier burden on the shoulders of the person who claims that that being has a right to X. For all I know there are reasons of still other kinds that have relevance to right-claims and particularly to prenatal right-claims, so I cannot be dogmatic. Some reasons clearly do not apply to fetuses. For example, it cannot be claimed that anyone has made a *promise* to a given fetus to bestow the so-called "gift of life" upon it. I should think that it is impossible to make a promise to a fetus. So the fact that a fetus has no actual interest in being born at any time before it is in fact born seems to me to be a very good reason (though not perhaps a conclusive one) for denying that it has an unconditional right to be born, even though it may be said to have contingent rights conditional upon its subsequent birth and the actualization of its future interests. I have some hesitation in endorsing this view, however, mainly because of the apparent examples, cited earlier, of legal acknowledgment of a right to be born.

One of these examples, that of the convicted pregnant murderess, raises some interesting questions. I find myself tempted in this case to the currently popular view that it should be the mother's exclusive right to decide whether or not her baby should be born, especially when there is no known father to be considered. To be sure, it fills me with horror to think of a conspicuously pregnant woman being hanged, unborn child and all; but that may be mainly because of the reprobative symbolism of the hanging ritual. Where the example is less complicated by guilt, the maternal prerogative principle is easier to apply. Imagine an impoverished, husbandless, pregnant lady dying of consumption in her hovel, amidst a brood of other illegitimate or else deserted children. It would seem utterly inhumane in this case to deny her the right to abort her child or otherwise prevent its birth, say, by dying with it still unborn. Indeed, if we did grant the right to decide the question of birth to the convicted murderess or the deserted consumptive, we might well expect them to exercise it, at least insofar as they are exclusively concerned with the welfare of the potential child they carry, by choosing abortion, unless, *mirabile dictu*, there is reason to think that the child would receive the parental love, family life, and economic necessities that would be its "birth right." Only in the latter case would a choice made on the ground of the infant's future welfare be a choice of birth rather than death.[8]

But now a new and startling possibility suggests itself. The conscientious mother will be determined to do her child justice, to make the right decision for *its* sake, to give it its due, and this seems to be another way of saying: *to honor its rights.* Whatever the circumstances may be, since the fetus has no actual interest, at the time, in being born, there is still no reason that I am sure of for ascribing to it a right to be born, though the existence of such a reason, as we have seen, is not logically precluded. But if the circumstances are very unhappy ones (for example prenatal damage, poverty, malnutrition, no father)

---

[8] Note a new interpretation of the idea of a birth-right suggested by this point: If you can't have that to which you have a birth-right then you are wronged if you are brought to birth.

there may very well be future interests of the child whose eventual fulfillment has already been blocked, so that if the child is allowed to be born, his rights to the protection of those interests will have *already* been violated, and that fact seems to me to be a very good reason for *not* permitting it to be born. Moreover, it seems a reason for saying that nonbirth is something we now owe it, that it is something that can now be claimed on its behalf as its due. Thus, even before we have been able to come to a strong conclusion about whether there is ever a right to be born, we seem to have stumbled onto an argument for the startling conclusion that there can be a *right not to be born.*

Here is a brief recapitulation of that argument:

1. The absence of an actual interest of a fetus in being born leaves open the question of whether there can ever be a right to be born.

2. The clearest cases of rights that a fetus does have, therefore, are rights to the present protection of future interests, *on the assumption* that he will be born. To say he has such a right to *x* is to say that *x* must be held for his arrival.

3. Thus, if the conditions for the eventual fulfillment of his future interests are destroyed before he is born, the child can claim, after he has been born, that his *rights* (his present rights) have been violated.

4. But if, before the child has been born, we know that the conditions for the fulfillment of his most basic interests have already been destroyed, and we permit him nevertheless to be born, we become a party to the violation of his rights.

5. In such circumstances, therefore, a proxy for the fetus might plausibly claim on its behalf, a *right not to be born.* That right is based on his future rather than his present interests (he has no actual present interests); but of course it is not contingent on his birth because he has it before birth, from the very moment that satisfaction of his most basic future interests is rendered impossible.

I am suggesting then that the only noncontingent rights fetuses ever have is the right not to be born (when all chance of fulfillment of birth-rights is already destroyed).

IV

Could a child then sue for damages on the ground that he was improperly allowed to be born? Surprisingly, this has already been done. And not only have infants sued defendants for "wrongful birth," so-called, they have in at least two cases sued defendants for wrongfully permitting them to be *conceived* in the first place! (Wrongful conception is what is implied by "wrongful birth" wherever abortion is illegal.) In *Williams v. State*[9] an infant girl sued the State of New

---

[9] *Williams v. State of New York,* 46 Misc. 2d 824, 260 N.Y.S. 2d 953 (Ct. Claims,

York for damages resulting from the state's negligent operation of a mental hospital. It seems that the infant's mother, a mentally deficient patient in the state institution, was sexually assaulted by an attendant, as a result of which the plaintiff was born out of wedlock to an incompetent mother. The suit, which charged the state with negligence in failing to protect the mother from the rape, met with success in the trial court, but was overturned on appeal. It was part of the plaintiff's pleading at the trial court that she had been "deprived of property rights; deprived of a normal childhood and home life; deprived of proper parental care, support and rearing; caused to bear the stigma of illegitimacy and has otherwise been greatly injured all to her damage in the sum of $100,000." From the philosophical point of view this bill of injuries would have been more interesting still had it included inherited mental retardation, genetically transmitted from the mother, and perhaps also an inherited tendency (say) to some chronically painful and incurable condition. In that (fictitious) case, the attorney for the plaintiff might have been in a stronger position to counter the argument that:

> What does disturb us is the nature of the new action and the related suits which would be encouraged. Encouragement would extend to all others born into the world under conditions they might regard as adverse. One might seek damages for being born of a certain color, another because of race; one for being born with a hereditary disease, another for inheriting unfortunate family characteristics; one for being born into a large and destitute family, another because a parent has an unsavory reputation . . .[10]

To this objection, from the opinion in *Zepeda v. Zepeda* cited by judge in the *Williams* case, the reply should be that not all interests of the newborn child should or can qualify for prenatal legal protection, but only those very basic ones whose satisfaction is indispensable to a decent life. The state cannot insure all or even many of its citizens against bad luck in the lottery of life. As the eventual Appeals Court opinion put it: "Being born under one set of circumstances rather than another or to one pair of parents rather than another is not a suable wrong that is cognizable in court." On the other hand, to be dealt feeble-mindedness or syphilis, or advanced heroin addition, or guaranteed malnutrition, or economic deprivation so far below a rea-

---

1965); *reversed,* 25 A.D. 2d 906, 269 N.Y.S. 2d 786 (App. Div. 1966); *reversal affirmed,* 18 N.Y.S. 2d 481, 233 N.E. 2d 343 (1966). I am grateful to Herbert Spiegelberg for calling this case to my attention.

10 From the opinion in a somewhat similar case, *Zepeda v. Zepeda,* 41 Ill. App. 2d 240, 190 N.E. 2d 849 (1963); *certiorari denied,* 379 U. S. 945, 85 S. Ct. 444, 13 L. Ed. 2d 545 (Dec. 1964); quoted by Judge Sidney Squire in *State v. Williams,* 260 N. Y. S. 2d 953.

sonable minimum as to be inescapably degrading and sordid, is not merely to have "bad luck." It is to be dealt a card from a stacked deck in a transaction that is not a "game" so much as a swindle.

The only reservations of the trial judge in allowing the case to be tried were that there was at the time no clear precedent for that kind of suit and that there was something approaching paradox in the idea that a tort can "be inflicted upon a being simultaneously with its conception."[11] He took neither of these misgivings seriously, but the second one proved to be the plaintiff's undoing at the appellate level. The Court of Appeals in its majority opinion held that the infant had no right to recover, "rejecting the idea that there could be an obligation of the State to a person not yet conceived." If my sketch of an argument above is correct, however, the court was too hasty. The obligation of the State, in my view, was not owed to some shadowy creature waiting in its metaphysical limbo to be born. Rather it was an obligation to its patient to protect her from assault, and as a consequence of its breach of duty to her, the rights of another human being, her daughter, which like most prenatal rights, are contingent upon later birth, were violated. Or perhaps the duty of the state can be characterized more felicitously still as a duty of care owed to anybody likely to be affected by its conduct, on analogy with the duty of a producer of canned baby food toward *all* eventual consumers of its product including some children yet unborn or even unconceived.

In a separate concurring opinion, Judge Kenneth Keating found another ground for ruling against the infant:

> Damages are awarded in tort cases on the basis of a comparison between the position the plaintiff would have been in, had the defendant not committed the acts causing injury, and the position in which the plaintiff presently finds herself. The damages sought by the plaintiff in the case at bar involve a determination as to whether nonexistence or nonlife is preferable to life as an illegitimate with all the hardship attendant thereon. It is impossible to make that choice.[12]

Now, it is perhaps true as a matter of law, that assessments of damages in tort cases (or at any rate, in all *other* kinds of tort cases) rest upon a hypothetical comparison of the plaintiff's condition after his injury with what his condition would have been had the defendant not affected it by his intentional or negligent wrong-doing; and of course that kind of comparison cannot be made when the alleged injury occurs at the very moment of conception, for it would have us consider the "condition" the plaintiff would have been in had he

[11] We have seen that it can be inflicted before conception or after conception and before birth.
[12] Judge Kenneth Keating in *Williams v. State*, 223 N.E. 2d 344.

never been conceived, which is a contradiction in terms. In this kind of case, then, assessments of damages would have to be made in some other way; but even if assessments were made on *admittedly arbitrary* grounds, they might better serve justice than if no damages are awarded at all. In any case, the question of damages aside, the grounds for charging that a wrongdoer has violated another's right not to be born do not include reference to a strange never-never land from which phantom beings are dragged struggling and kicking into their mothers' wombs and thence into existence as persons in the real world. Talk of a "right not to be born" is a compendious way of referring to the plausible moral requirement that no child be brought into the world unless certain very minimal conditions of well-being are assured, and certain basic "future interests" are protected in advance, at least in the sense that the *possibility* of his fulfilling those interests be kept open. When a child is brought into existence even though those requirements have not been observed, *he has been wronged* thereby; and that is not to say that any metaphysical interpretation, or any sense at all, can be given to the statement that he would have been better off had he never been born.

Now it might be asked why there should be such a striking asymmetry between a plausibly defensible right not to be born and its implausibly maintained counterpart, the alleged right of fetuses to be born. Just as we hurt a potential person when we *allow* him to be born in a condition such that he will have no chance to fulfill his most basic future interests, don't we also hurt a potential person when we *deny* him a chance to be born into a life quite sure to give him love and wealth and fulfillment? To be sure, there is no person around to complain that he himself was wronged or to sue for damages in the latter case, for the prospective plaintiff in that case is not in existence. But that doesn't prove that the fetus or potential person was not wronged in not being permitted to become an actual person. Perhaps, a proxy might have been permitted to seek an injunction on behalf of the unborn fetus with the promising future, so that there would be some parallel legal consequences in ascribing to it a right to be born, after all. There are other practical differences between the two cases, however. One is that the right not to be born is to be conferred only in those rare circumstances in which the fetus has no chance whatever of a decent life and we can know this with near certainty in advance. There could be no corresponding necessity or certainty in the case of the fetus with the especially promising future. Moreover, in the case where the right in question is violated, the fetus with no chance becomes a human being who gets badly hurt, but the fetus with the glittering future never learns what he is missing and never "knows what hits him." The main asymmetry between the two cases, however, derives from the differing moral statuses of harm and mere nonbenefit. It is generally much more plausible to make claim against others not to be harmed than to make the claim to be positively benefitted, contractual considerations aside. A claim not to be sunk into poverty is, in its very nature, easier to support than a claim to be kept in one's riches. The right not to be born is typical of a large and familiar class of rights *not to* be forced into a situation in which one's important interests are certain to be damaged. A general right *to be* born based on an exceptionally promising future would be an instance of a quite different sort of thing: a right to be permitted into a situation in which there is a good chance, as far as anyone can tell, that one's interests, basic and otherwise, will be advanced. In any case, when the right of a fetus not to be born is violated, there is an assignable living person who has been harmed. When a fetus with a promising future is aborted, neither he nor any other existing being is harmed by it (unless harm is confused with nonbenefit).

V

My doubts about the existence of a right to be born transfer neatly to the question of a similar right to come into existence ascribed to future generations. The rights that future generations certainly have against us are contingent rights: The interests they are sure to have when they come into being (assuming of course that they *will* come into being) cry out for protection from invasions that can take place *now*. Yet there are no actual interests, presently existent, that future generations, presently nonexistent, have *now*. Hence, there is no actual interest that they have in simply coming into being; and I am at a loss to think of any *other* reason for claiming that they have a right to come into existence (though there may well be such a reason). Suppose then that all human beings at a given time voluntarily form a compact never again to produce children, thus leading within a few decades to the end of our species. We can imagine, say, that the whole world is converted to a strange ascetic religion which absolutely requires sexual abstinence for everyone. Would this arrangement violate the rights of *anyone*? No one can complain on behalf of presently nonexistent future generations that their future interests which give them a contingent right of protection have been violated, since they will never come into existence to be wronged. My inclination then is to conclude that the suicide of our species would be deplorable, lamentable, and a deeply moving tragedy, but that it would violate no one's *rights*. Indeed, if, contrary to fact, all human beings could ever agree to such a thing, that very agreement would be a symptom of our species' biological unsuitability for survival anyway.[13]

[13] This paragraph is taken from my article "The Rights of Animals and Future Generations," *op. cit.*

Voluntary Euthanasia and the Inalienable Right to Life

It is surprising that in this bicentennial period we have not yet heard an argument that seems to bolster the case of opponents of voluntary euthanasia. The argument derives from an interpretation of Thomas Jefferson's famous words that all men "are endowed by their Creator with certain unalienable Rights, that among these are Life . . . ," and from similar passages in the writings of other founding fathers. To kill another person even with his consent or at his considered request, it might well be claimed, is to infringe his "Right to Life," a right the founders clearly held to be incapable of being waived or surrendered. Willfully to take one's own life or to permit another to take one's life, the argument continues, is in the relevant sense to *alienate* one's right to go on living; hence, suicide and voluntary euthanasia can both be viewed as efforts to alienate the inalienable, to give away what cannot properly be given away.

There is at least a superficial plausibility in this effort to invoke the authority of Jefferson as a basis for refusing legal sanction or denying moral legitimacy to such practices as suicide, aiding another's suicide, and voluntary euthanasia. The argument seems to present a dilemma for those of us who would defend a "right to die": either we must abandon our defense of what seem to us to be morally justifiable practices, or else we must reject the exalted eighteenth-century doctrine of in-

The 1977 Dean Obert Tanner Lecture in Moral Philosophy at the University of Michigan and Stanford University. Permission for publication is granted by the Tanner Lecture Trust. © 1977 by the Tanner Lecture Trust.

alienable rights, at least as it applies to the right to life. The former alternative seems inhumane and paternalistic, the latter seems virtually un-American. I have my doubts about the theory of inalienable rights in any case—doubts that will emerge in the following discussion —but my primary intention in this essay is to find a way between two alternatives by reconciling a right to die with the inalienability of the right to live, properly interpreted.

I. THE RIGHT TO LIFE

Just what kind of right is "the right to life"? Numerous distinctions can be made, of course, among the many types and categories of rights. While it is impossible here to work our way completely through the conceptual maze, it will be useful to clarify the right to life by placing it in relation to some of the more important of these distinctions. This will be in part a matter of stipulation, for the right to life is interpreted in different ways by different writers, and where there is disagreement or confusion, I can only try to make persuasive suggestions that one or another interpretation is more standard, useful, or important.

I propose, first of all, to interpret "the right to life" in a relatively narrow way, so that it refers to "the right not to be killed" and "the right to be rescued from impending death," but not to the broader conception, favored by many manifesto writers, of a "right to live decently." To be sure, as Hugo Bedau put it, ". . . the life to which we now think men are entitled as of right is not [merely] a right at the barest level sufficient to stave off an untimely death; rather it is a life sufficient for self-respect, relief from needless drudgery, and opportunity for the release of productive energy."[1] However, we can refer separately to the components of a right to live decently: a right to decent working conditions, a right to food, to clothing, to housing, to education, and so on. Another component right in this comprehensive package of rights is the right not to be killed or allowed to die. *This* is the right that is characteristically at issue in debates over euthanasia and suicide, not the various welfare rights enumerated in twentieth-

1. Hugo Bedau, "The Right to Life," *The Monist* 52 (1968): 567.

century manifestoes. It would ill serve clarity, therefore, to use the generic label when we are concerned only with the specific subspecies.

The right to life, in the second place, is generally thought, at least in our time, to be a *claim-right* as opposed to a right in the sense of mere liberty, privilege, or absence of duty to refrain. A claim-right is a more complex notion, and presumably a more valuable benefit, than a liberty. To say that John Doe is at liberty to do or have X is to say simply that he has no duty to refrain from or relinquish X. But that is not yet to say anything about anyone else's duties to Doe in respect to X. Doe may have a right (in the sense of liberty) to X even though everyone else is also at liberty to interfere with his efforts to do or possess X. If Doe's right to X, however, is a claim-right, then Doe is at liberty to do or have X, and his liberty is the ground of other people's duties either to grant him X or not to interfere with his doing or possessing X. A claim-right then is a liberty correlated with another person's duty (or *all* other persons' duties) not to interfere. If Doe has a claim-right to life, then those against whom he has the claim (presumably all the rest of us) have duties not to kill him or let him die when we can save him with no danger to ourselves. If, on the other hand, Doe's right to life were a mere liberty, it would amount to no more than the absence of a duty to kill or to fail to save himself, an absence that is perfectly consistent with the liberties and even the duties of others to kill him.

Even a "liberty-right" to life, while not as comfortable a protection as a claim-right, has some importance. Indeed, Thomas Hobbes interpreted the right to defend one's life as a "natural liberty," and made it the foundation of his political philosophy. In a state of nature there are no duties, hence everyone has complete liberty. The natural liberty to defend one's own life (that is, the absence of a duty to cooperate in one's own extinction) is so very important to everyone's natural interest and basic motivation, Hobbes thought, that no one in his right mind would ever agree to bargain it away in the negotiations that lead to the creation of civil society with its complex of new duties and claim-rights. Indeed, the strengthening of personal security is the essence of civil society, the "name of its game." Not even a prisoner convicted of a capital crime acquires a duty to cooperate with his executioner, though of course the latter will have the liberty, the duty, and the power to execute him in the name of the state.[2] The Hobbesian "natural liberty" guarantees that one can never have the duty to die; the "right to life" in the sense here being explained, in contrast, guarantees that (under normal conditions at least) others cannot be at liberty to kill you.

To have a right, then, is to have a claim against others, and claims can be further distinguished in terms of their *addressees*. The right to life, as we shall understand it here, is a *double-barreled* claim, addressed to two distinct sets of claimees. On the one hand, it is a right *in rem* holding against the "world at large," or all other private individuals or groups that might ever be in a position to kill or fail to save the claimant. On the other hand, it is (or ought to be) a claim that its possessor can make against the state for its legal enforcement. The former set of claims, being based on reasons derived from moral principles, are binding on the consciences of other persons and are the grounds of their duties to rescue or to forbear killing the claimant. As such, these claims can exist prior to or independently of their recognition by the state. Hence, they are, in the appropriate sense, *moral rights*. When they are recognized by the state they acquire support from reasons of an additional kind derived from legal rules and thus become legal claim-rights against one's fellow citizens, as well as moral rights. Enforcement-claims—which can have both a moral and a legal backing—obligate the state to require performance of the moral obligations that others have to me and to protect me by threat of punishment from wrongful interference. Valid laws often impose genuine obligations on the state (to refund excess tax payments, to provide trial by jury, to punish crimes, for example) and hence confer correlative rights of a legal kind on citizens as against the state. My (moral) right to life, however, would constitute a morally binding claim to enforcement against the state even in the fancifully hypothetical circumstance in which there were no laws against homicide. I

2. Stephen Becker's highly philosophical novel, *A Covenant With Death* (New York, 1965), tells of a relevant dilemma. A judge must decide the fate of a prisoner, wrongly convicted of murder, who kills the hangman lawfully attempting his execution. The judge decides to follow Hobbes and declares the prisoner not guilty of any crime.

would in that case have a powerful claim against the legislature to *make* laws against homicide so that the moral right to life would be converted into a legal right as well. In actual, prevailing circumstances, I have a moral (but not legal) claim-right against the Congress not to be victimized by the passage into law of invidious, though constitutional, legislation.

The right to life, as I shall understand it here, also belongs to that subclass of moral rights that are said, in virtue of their fundamentally important, indeed essential, connection with human well-being, to belong equally and unconditionally to all human beings, simply in virtue of their being human. It is, therefore, what the United Nations called a *human right*.[3] There is a controversy among philosophers whether all, or even any, human rights are *absolute rights*. That dispute is far too complicated to resolve here, but it will be useful to show in a sketchy way its bearing on the concept of a right to life. An absolute right (if there is such a thing) is a right that would remain in one's possession, fully effective as a ground for other people's duties to one, in all possible circumstances. If my right to X is absolute, then there are no circumstances in which it is "subject to legitimate limitation" or in which the correlated duties of others to me in respect to X are suspended. If the right is absolute, then I possess it, and others are bound to me in the appropriate ways in all circumstances *without exception.* This unqualified and exceptionless character of an absolute right implies (among other things) that it can never be in unresolved conflict with the absolute rights of other persons, whether those rights are of the same type (for example, rights to life) or of another type (say, rights to liberty or to property). If my right to life is absolute in this sense, and if my life can be saved only at the cost of taking your property, then your right to property cannot also be an absolute right, for it will be limited or suspended in this case of unavoidable conflict. In short, if conflicts occur between one person's absolute right and another person's right of another kind, the absolute right must always triumph. But it also follows that unavoidable conflict between one person's absolute right and another person's absolute right of the same type (for example, the right to life of two different persons) is

3. UNESCO, *Human Rights, a Symposium* (London and New York: Allan Wingate, 1949).

logically impossible in just the manner of a hypothetical conflict between an irresistible force and an immovable object. It simply cannot happen.

Since conflicts between rights do occur, it is implausible to maintain that *all* rights are absolute in the present sense. A more difficult question, indeed, is whether *any* rights at all can so qualify. In any event, it seems very doubtful that the right to life, as it is normally understood, can be absolute. A great many people who profess a belief in the right to life also support the killing of enemy combatants in war, capital punishment of convicted murderers, and killing of assailants and even "innocent aggressors" in self-defense. These people find no conflict in maintaining that everyone has a right not to be killed ("the right to life") while holding also that there are circumstances which limit the application of that right and require its suspension. The "right to life" that they believe in, therefore, cannot be absolute.

Nevertheless, it is hard to shed the intuitive conviction that there is somehow *something* that is "absolute" in the natural or human right to life (and the rights to liberty and property too, for that matter). There are at least three strategies that have governed the efforts of philosophers to isolate, specify, and strengthen that lingering intuition. Any one of the strategies would, if successful, be sufficient, but in theory they might also be used in various combinations. The first of these is the *method of presumptiveness*. One might conclude, with William Frankena, that certain human rights, including the right to life, are only prima facie rights.[1] That is, in every possible circumstance a person's right to life will be an actual right, commanding forbearance or performance from others, *except* where it is in unavoidable conflict with someone else's right to life (or to something else) which happens to be more stringent in the circumstances. In that unhappy situation the other party's actual right prevails and the presumption that one has one's normal right to life in *that situation*, as one does in most others, is overridden. But the presumptive right to life, as a presumption, always holds. It is the prima facie right that is absolute, not the actual right which may not be present in a rare instance of conflict. To declare that all persons have absolute prima

4. W. K. Frankena, "Natural and Inalienable Rights," *Philosophical Review* 64 (1955).

facie rights to life and other goods is "to say that interfering with [their] enjoyment of them always requires a moral justification."[5] There is *always* a presumption of the existence of the actual right, even though that presumption is not necessarily decisive in every possible situation. At least something, therefore, is constant and invariant in all circumstances.

This position may be expressed more clearly by employing the distinction between having a right and having a claim. To have a claim is to have reasons of some weight that put one in a position to make claim to something.[6] These reasons support the claim and lend it credence and cogency, even if, in the end, they should fail to *establish* the claim and compel its recognition. Unlike rights, claims can differ in degree: some are stronger than others. One very good kind of reason for denying that John Doe's admitted claim to X amounts to a right to X in the present circumstances is that Richard Roe also has a claim to X, and it is impossible for both Doe and Roe to do or have X. In that case, Roe (at most) has the right to X; nevertheless, it remains true that even in the circumstances that obtained, Doe did have a strong, but not decisive, *claim*. Using this terminology, a philosopher could affirm that *all persons always* have a powerful claim not to be killed even in those tragic circumstances where it is outweighed by a more powerful claim on the other side. If a judge or moral critic concedes the existence of the powerful claim while denying that it amounts to an actual right in the present circumstances, he thereby assumes the burden of showing how it is outweighed and overridden in the circumstances that prevail. Again *something* remains "absolute" and constant, namely the existence of the claim.

The second strategy for preserving an absolute element can be called, following Judith Thomson, the *method of full factual specification.*[7] A philosopher friendly to the idea of absolute human rights might argue that all simple and brief statements of (say) the right to life are of necessity mere abbreviations for an elaborately complex

5. Ibid., p. 228.

6. I have discussed this in Joel Feinberg, *Social Philosophy* (Englewood Cliffs, N.J., 1973), p. 68.

7. Judith J. Thomson, "Self-defense and Rights," *The Lindley Lecture*, University of Kansas, 1976.

statement defining a right that *is* absolute. The fuller statement would begin, presumably, by stating that all "human beings" (a phrase itself in need of detailed definition) have a right not to be killed. It would then proceed to explain what is to be understood by "killing" and which circumstances—described in a general, but not *too* general, way—constitute exceptions (this could lead to a discussion of war, capital punishment, and self-defense, among other topics). The statement would include a discussion of what priority rules are to be used for determining who has the right and who does not in situations of unavoidable conflict; again, these rules would be described in a general, but not too general, way. A similarly detailed statement would follow, describing the full extent, within carefully circumscribed limits, of the right to be rescued. Clearly such an enterprise would yield a book-length statement at the very least. Philosophers who prefer the method of presumptiveness are pessimistic about the plausibility of doing this, even in principle, and defenders of the method of full factual specification would have to admit that it has not yet been done in fact.

A more difficult problem comes from the inevitable loss of any semblance of Jefferson's self-evident truths in such a statement. Most of us would affirm without hesitation our belief in a human right to life, but any fully specified statement of that right, including the *correct* one (assuming that there is in principle *one* correct one), would divide us into a hundred quarreling sects disputing such questions as abortion, capital punishment, and the like. It is doubtful that *any* fully specified declaration of a right to life could ever win the unanimous assent of all those who believe that the existence of such a right is obvious. What is self-evident, according to this second view of the matter, can only be a bare "lowest common denominator" of a large number of contending moral systems, perhaps no more than what I have called, with deliberate vagueness, "an ideal directive to legislative aspiration commanding us to do our best for the cause of human life as we judge the various claims that may be before us in our roles as legislators, judges, and moral agents."[8] Or perhaps the common ground includes more precise and significant areas. Com-

8. Feinberg, *Social Philosophy*, p. 71.

mon to the moral systems of all who profess belief in a human right to life, after all, are such judgments as: it is always wrong to shoot a normal adult human being in the back of the head for the purpose of taking his money to buy luxuries for one's own enjoyment. When we include some of the circumstances in the description of the act, we can say that the right not to be the victim of such an action holds "in all possible circumstances." Beyond such examples, the method of full factual specification permits us to say that other human rights, fully specified, are absolute, but only at the cost of admitting that we do not really know, and cannot agree, which rights exactly these are.

The third strategy, which I shall call the method of *justified infringement*, can coexist with either of the other two. No matter how we separate out actual rights from prima facie or presumptive rights, rights from claims, abbreviated statements of rights that are unqualified and thus not absolute from fully expanded statements of rights that are exceptionless, we must face the possibility that some quite actual rights that are possessed by their owners in all situations can nevertheless be rightly infringed in certain unusual circumstances. As Bedau puts it, "A person's possessing a right is not always dispositive of the issue of how he ought to be treated."[9] If it can make sense to speak of the justified invasion of a genuine actual right, a "justified injustice" as it were, then it will be possible to speak of the proper infringement of an absolute right (that is, a right which is held by its possessor in all circumstances). In that case, the doctrine of absolute rights can be preserved even in the face of convincing examples of justified treatment contrary to what the right, considered alone, would require. Absolute rights, of course, are claim-rights and therefore logically correlated with the *duties* of other people to perform or forbear as the right, considered alone, requires. Thus a logical consequence of the view that sometimes one may justifiably infringe another's right is the proposition that on occasion one may justifiably fail to discharge one's duty.

At this point, it will be useful to borrow Judith Thomson's distinction between infringing and violating a person's right: ". . . we *violate* his right if and only if we do not merely infringe it, but more, are

9. Bedau, "The Right to Life," p. 569.

acting wrongly, unjustly, in doing so. Now the view that rights are 'absolute' in the sense I have in mind is the view that every infringing of a right is a violating of a right."[10] We can readily provide examples of rights that are *not* absolute in Thomson's sense. Perhaps the most plausible of these are property rights. Suppose that you are on a back-packing trip in the high mountain country when an unanticipated blizzard strikes the area with such ferocity that your life is imperiled. Fortunately, you stumble onto an unoccupied cabin, locked and boarded up for the winter, clearly somebody else's private property. You smash in a window, enter, and huddle in a corner for three days until the storm abates. During this period you help yourself to your unknown benefactor's food supply and burn his wooden furniture in the fireplace to keep warm. Surely you are justified in doing all these things, and yet you have infringed the clear rights of another person.

It will be argued, on the other side, that you have not infringed any-one's actual rights that were fully operative in the circumstances but only prima facie rights, the overturned presumption of rights, or inconclusive claims. It will be said, perhaps, that the undeniable right of the homeowner, when fully specified, excludes emergency circum-stances such as the ones that obtained, and thus he can have no grievance or counterclaim against you. It is, of course, possible to *say* these things, but only at the cost of rejecting the way most of us actu-ally understand the rights in question. We would not think it inappro-priate to express our gratitude to the homeowner, after the fact, and our regrets for the damage we have inflicted on his property. More importantly, almost everyone would agree that you owe *compensation* to the homeowner for the depletion of his larder, the breaking of his window, and the destruction of his furniture. One owes compensation here for the same reason one must repay a debt or return what one has borrowed. If the other had no right that was infringed in the first place, one could hardly have a duty to compensate him. Perhaps he would be an appropriate object of your sympathy or patronage or charity, but those are quite different from compensation. This is a case, then, of the infringement but not the violation of a property right.

10. Thomson, "Self-defense and Rights."

Not every case of justified killing infringes the victim's right to life. We may still have to resort to the presumptiveness strategy or the full specification strategy to explain why we do not infringe the victim's right to life in war killing, capital punishment, or self-defense. The other's right to life may not extend as far as these cases of justified killing and hence may not be involved at all. Surely, we acknowledge no duty of compensation to the heirs of an aggressor whom we killed in self-defense. On the other hand, there are some rare cases, as Thomson points out, of justified killing of innocents whose rights to life *are* thereby infringed—"If you are an innocent threat to my life (you threaten it through no fault of your own), and I can save my life only by killing you, and therefore do kill you, I think I do owe compensation, for I take your life to save mine."[11] One of Thomson's examples of an innocent threat is an "innocent shield," a child tied to the front of a tank driven by a malevolent aggressor whose intent is clearly to destroy me. There is no place for me to hide, but I happen to have an antitank gun, so to save my own life I blow up the tank, killing both the wicked aggressor and the innocent child. Self-defense presumably justifies me, and I have no duty afterwards to compensate the aggressor, but the child's right has been infringed, and I would have a strong obligation to set things straight somehow with her parents. In her case, I have infringed a right to life without violating it, so her right to life was not "absolute" in Thomson's sense, but the example does not show that her right was not absolute in our original sense, for the right continued to exist even in the circumstance where it was justifiably infringed. The "absolute" element in the *aggressor's* general right to life, however, if there is such a thing at all, must be demonstrated by one of the first two methods.

We may now tentatively conclude that by "the right to life" we can mean a right not to be killed or allowed to die which can be claimed against all other private individuals and groups for their forbearance and performance, and against the state for its enforcement. As a claim-right it signifies not merely the absence of a duty to cooperate in one's own death, but also the correlative duties of others toward one. It is a moral right in the sense that it is a claim rendered valid by

11. Ibid.

reasons derived from moral principle, and therefore can exist prior to and independently of legal recognition. It is presumably a human right since it is thought to be possessed equally by all human beings simply in virtue of their being human. Put simply and unqualifiedly as the right not to be killed or allowed to die, it is generally thought *not* to be an absolute right, since there are circumstances in which some human beings—soldiers, convicted murderers, homicidal aggressors—seem to be without it. Many philosophers, however, have tried by one method or another to isolate something that subsists through all the circumstances in which a human being with a right to life might find himself. Some locate the invariant element in a standing presumption of a right (a "prima facie right") or a constant but rebuttable claim to life. Others interpret the right to life in the bare minimal formulation given here as a mere abbreviation for a complex statement full of conditions and exceptions that does define an absolute right. Still others point out that in difficult circumstances some very basic rights can be infringed without being violated, and while this shows that they are not "absolute" in one sense (Thomson's), it is a way of showing the persistence of the right in some situations that might otherwise be thought to be inconsistent with its absoluteness in our present sense of context-invariance.

II. DISCRETIONARY AND MANDATORY RIGHTS

Up to this point the defining characteristics I have attributed to the right to life are either commonplace and uncontroversial or else technical and controverted only by abstract theorists. Now we come to a question about the right to life that is both controversial and directly relevant to our ulterior purposes. We must now ask how the distinction between "discretionary" and "mandatory" rights applies to the right to life. This is a familiar distinction which has borne a number of other names. Martin Golding has formulated it as well as any, using the terms "option-right" and "welfare-right."[12] A discretionary right, which

12. I have no quarrel with the label "option-right" and shall use it as an alternative way of referring to discretionary rights, but I find "welfare-rights" a misleading and even question-begging term insofar as it suggests that all of the rights we naturally associate with "welfare"—such as the right to a job, to medical care, to education—are necessarily what I call "mandatory rights."

Golding calls an option-right, is "an area of autonomy within which the right-holder alone is free to decide."[13] I have a discretionary right in respect to X when I have an *open option* to X or not to X correlated with the duties of others not to interfere with my choice. It is important to note that if I have a discretionary right to do X, it follows logically that I have a right also not to do X, if I should so choose. It cannot be the case that my right leaves me free to X but not free not to X. Any discretionary right to something is a right to take it or leave it, as one chooses. A mandatory right, in contrast, confers no discretion whatever on its possessor: only one way of exercising it is permitted. It leaves one path open to him but no genuine "option" between paths. It imposes a correlative duty on others to provide that path and leave it unobstructed, but it imposes no duty upon others of noninterference with deviance from the single permitted track. If I have a mandatory right to do X then it follows logically that I have—not a right not to do X—but rather a *duty* to do X. In the case of mandatory rights, duty and right are entirely coincident.

Golding cites the right to education as his chief example of a mandatory right. All children in a certain age group have a right to attend a school and receive instruction from teachers in it. At the same time, those children, since school attendance is required, have a *duty* to attend school. The right and the duty coincide; there is no free play for "discretion"; therefore, the right is mandatory.

Very likely there is no gainsaying Golding on his account of the right to education, but to those who find the very idea of a mandatory right intolerably paradoxical there is one possible way out. That is to interpret the right as a claim that each citizen has to live in an educated society. On this construction, each person has a right that all the *other* persons be educated, and in virtue of the right that the others have that *he* be educated, he has himself a duty to attend school. It is because of other people's rights that he has a duty to go to school, not because of his own. If he has no discretion in the matter, that is because the discretion theoretically lies with the others to release him or hold him to his duty. This is a perfectly coherent account of something to which "the right to education" might refer and, so interpreted,

13. Martin P. Golding, "Towards a Theory of Human Rights," *The Monist* 52 (1968), p. 546.

the right to education is not quite the same thing as a mandatory right. The only trouble with it is that it is not a very accurate account of what most of us mean in ordinary political discourse when we speak of "the right to education." We ordinarily have in mind, when we use that phrase, a claim that each child can make to his *own* education, not merely, or not only, a claim that he can make to be a member of an educated community.

Still, it is easy to understand why people should be uneasy with the very idea of a mandatory right. The theory behind the idea seems to be that there are certain undeniable benefits, such as education, health, welfare, to which we are all entitled, and that these benefits are so important that it cannot be in anybody's interest ever to forgo them. Opportunity to enjoy these benefits must be provided by others and not interfered with by others; because the benefits are undeniably advantageous whatever the beneficiary may think about the matter, the latter must not be free to forgo them. The concept of a mandatory right, in short, would seem to be a paternalistic notion, reasonably enough applied to children, but offensively demeaning when imposed on presumably autonomous adults. Perhaps that is why Golding's most plausible example of such a right, the right to education, is one thought by most of us to apply (at least in its mandatory aspect) to children only. Another perennial philosophical candidate for such a status is the "right to punishment" conferred by righteous moralizers on qualified wrongdoers in the same condescending spirit as that with which the nurse gives the reluctant child his evil-tasting medicine. ("*We* know that, unpleasant as it may seem, this treatment is bound to do you more good than harm in the long run. In fact, it is what you *need* if you are to get better, and you must take it if only for your own sake.") The contrast with option-rights, which we are free to exercise as we please, is striking in this respect. The primary benefit conferred by a discretionary right is a certain amount of guaranteed freedom; mandatory rights are guaranteed opportunities to secure goods of other kinds (education, moral regeneration, health) that are paid for by sacrifices of freedom.

The idea of a mandatory right, moreover, brings to mind some frightful sophistries. We recall the odious arguments used throughout history both by revolutionaries and reactionaries that there can be freedom to do good but not to do evil, to speak truth but not falsehood, to worship true but not false gods. "Freedom" to do evil, to speak falsehood, to commit religious error, is not freedom at all, it is said, but mere license. From this, it is but a short step to the view expressed in what Isaiah Berlin calls a typical statement made by a Jacobin club during the Terror: "No man is free in doing evil. To prevent him is to set him free."[14] Then if we guarantee a Jacobin "freedom" by imposing duties of noninterference on others enforced by the state, we have converted it into a "mandatory right."

Still, in all fairness, there is no necessity that any given mandatory right be enmeshed in such specious rhetoric. A mandatory right, after all, is a kind of duty looked at in a certain positive way, and there need be nothing sinister in the assignment of duties to people. Every duty trivially entails a liberty to do what duty requires. (A liberty to do X being defined as the *absence of a duty not* to do X.) When it is vitally important and essentially advantageous not only to the community in general but to the moral agent himself that his duty be discharged, we are likely to guarantee him, by the imposition of duties of noninterference on others, the opportunity to do his duty. Then the liberty trivially entailed by duty takes on the appearance of a claim-right against others. If the personal and social interest in the successful performance of the duty is great enough, opportunity to perform is guaranteed, opportunity to fail to perform is totally withdrawn, and, at this point, enforcible duty, treasured opportunity, and claim-right all coalesce into mandatory right. (All that is missing to the possessor is freedom.) Many duties are onerous burdens that, no matter how heavy, must be carried and many yield benefits to the bearer that he will surely wish to reap. Whether we describe these hybrids as duties or rights will depend on whether we wish to emphasize their character as hardships or benefits; on whether our aim is to threaten and entreat, or persuade and induce. Hegelian moralists describe the convicted criminal's duty to submit to punishment as a "right to be punished" when they wish to emphasize that punishment can provide

14. Sir Isaiah Berlin, *Four Essays on Liberty* (New York, 1969), p. 148 n.

the criminal with a unique opportunity for moral regeneration, a state of being that would be truly beneficial to him, whether he knows it now or not.

However, we do not have to think of duties that are hidden or of benefits that are unsuspected to appreciate the present point. Many of the most ordinary and often irksome political duties are easily conceived, without paradox, as genuine benefits; they are ardently pursued and demanded as rights by those who are not permitted to qualify for them. In Tolstoy's *Anna Karenina*, a group of country gentry discussing women's liberation come to an appreciation of the point quite naturally:

> Alexey Alexandrovitch expressed the idea that the education of women is apt to be confounded with the emancipation of women, and it is only so that it can be considered dangerous.

> "I consider, on the contrary, that the two questions are inseparably connected together," said Pestov; "it is a vicious circle. Woman is deprived of rights from lack of education, and the lack of education results from the absence of rights. We must not forget that the subjection of women is so complete, and dates from such ages back that we are often unwilling to recognize the gulf that separates them from us," said he.

> "You said rights," said Sergey Ivanovitch, waiting till Pestov had finished, "meaning the right of sitting on juries, of voting, of presiding at official meetings, the right of entering the civil service, of sitting in parliament . . ."

> "Undoubtedly."

> "But if women, as a rare exception, can occupy such positions, it seems to me you are wrong in using the expression 'rights.' It would be more correct to say 'duties.' Every man will agree that in doing the job of a juryman, a witness, a telegraph clerk, we feel we are performing duties. And therefore it would be correct to say that women are seeking duties, and quite legitimately. And one can but sympathize with this desire to assist in the general labor of man."

"Quite so," said Alexey Alexandrovitch. "The question, I imagine, is simply whether they are fitted for such duties."[15]

Jury service, whether in czarist Russia or in the United States, can be quite intelligibly described both as a duty *and* as a right, though it is more likely to be described as the former by a harrassed and annoyed citizen grudgingly performing the service, and as the latter by the victim of discrimination who is excluded from the process. The same can be said for many other irksome chores in the "general labor of man."

Indeed *any* duty can be thought of also as a right. As we have seen, the statement of a duty trivially entails the statement of a "liberty," not a liberty in the usual sense that implies a choice but a liberty only in the sense made familiar by the jurisprudence textbooks, namely that of "no duty not to."[16] "Jones must do X" entails that "Jones may do X," and if Jones is to be guaranteed an opportunity to do what he must and may do, then others must not prevent him from doing it. If doing his duty happens also to be something from which Jones himself will benefit and Jones wants very much to do it, he will view his "liberty" or "permission" to do it, together with his guaranteed opportunity to do it, as goods that he can *claim* from others, and/or the state. Its character as claim is precisely what his liberty shares with the more customary (discretionary) rights and warrants his use of the term "right" in claiming it.

We have a choice between two ways of viewing the right to life, and whichever way we choose will have profound normative consequences. On the one hand, we can think of the right to life as a discretionary right analogous to many of the rights we have in the categories of liberty and property. My right to freedom of movement, for example, entitles me to travel where I wish or not to travel at all. It's entirely

15. Leo Tolstoy, *Anna Karenina* (New York, 1966), Part 4, chap. 10.

16. The textbook sense of "liberty" (derived from Hohfeld) would be less misleadingly called a "half-liberty." In ordinary speech, to be at liberty to do x is to have no duty in respect to x, that is (a) to be free of the duty not to do x, and (b) to be free of the duty to do x. To be free of a duty not to do x is to have only a half-liberty with respect to x if one should at the same time have a duty to do x. One is deprived, in that case, of the other "half-liberty" that would add up to full liberty, or discretion to decide whether to do x or not.

up to me. I have a right to go to Boston, but I can happily *waive* that right and go to Chicago, or I can stay at home if I prefer. When it comes to such general questions of my movement, I am the boss, or as Golding says, I reign sovereign over these aspects of my life.[17] Similarly, I have a right to all the money in my wallet and in my bank account. To say that it is *mine* or belongs to me is precisely to say that I can do with it as I please: spend it on food or clothing or amusement, or not spend it at all, or simply give it away. I have a right, of course to keep it, but that is a right I cheerfully *waive* when I donate it instead to a charity. On this model, my life, too, is mine; it belongs to me; I am sovereign over it; in respect to living or dying insofar as that rests within my power, I am the boss. I have a right, of course, to stay alive as long as I can, but I can *waive* that right, if I honestly and voluntarily choose to do so, and choose to die instead.

Alternatively, we can think of the right to life as a mandatory right analogous to the child's right to education, the criminal's right (on the Hegelian view) to punishment, or even the citizen's right to serve on juries. In that case, it can be viewed from one side as primarily a duty, something incumbent on us whatever our wishes about the matter may be. The right to life, so viewed, is a duty to stay alive as long as one can or, at least, a duty not to take one's own life or not to cooperate with others in its taking. Since life is generally an extremely important benefit to a person, indeed a condition of almost all other benefits, it is generally important to him that he be protected in his ability to exercise that duty. That protection takes the form of an enforced claim against all others to their noninterference, and that claim is his right to life seen from another vantage point. But, unlike discretionary rights, it can never be waived, and can be "exercised" in only one way. On this view, even if life is a "gift," it is a gift that cannot ever be declined or given away.

III. The Concept of an Inalienable Right

Rights are not mere abstract concepts; they are instruments and devices that can be used by their possessors to *do* things. A full theory of the nature of rights, therefore, would explain how they can be

17. Golding, "Towards a Theory of Human Rights," p. 547.

reserved, waived, renounced, transferred, sold; surrendered, forfeited, prescribed (cf. "imprescriptible"); annulled or made void, withdrawn, canceled; overruled, overridden, outbalanced; invaded, infringed, violated; recognized, enforced, vindicated, respected; possessed, enjoyed, exercised, stood upon, acted on, abused; acquired, inherited, purchased. Indeed some categories of rights are defined in terms of the uses to which they may or may not be put. An inalienable right, for example, is a right that may not be alienated. To understand what a right in this category is or would be, we must first understand what it would be like to alienate a right. On this question there has been a great deal of confusion for two centuries largely because of a failure to distinguish alienating from two other things from the list of things that can be done with rights, namely, forfeiting and annulling, and also a failure to distinguish between two possible interpretations of alienating, namely, waiving and relinquishing. I shall take up these notions in turn.

Alienating vs. Forfeiting

It was an important part of the classic doctrine of natural rights as expounded by Locke and Blackstone that some natural rights at least (certainly including the right to life) can be forfeited but not alienated. The distinction is roughly that between losing a right through one's fault or error, on the one hand, and voluntarily giving the right away, on the other. To forfeit, says Webster's, is "to lose or lose the right to, by some *error, fault, offense,* or *crime*; to alienate the right to possess *by some neglect or crime*; to have to pay as forfeit; as, to forfeit an estate by treason; to forfeit reputation" (emphasis added). A forfeitable right, therefore, cannot be an absolute one in our original sense, for it is not possessed unconditionally in all circumstances. Rather it is a right that one must qualify for by meeting certain conditions of proper conduct. As soon as one's conduct falls below the qualifying standards one loses the right, whether one likes it or not. Sometimes the loss is thought to occur instantly and naturally—for example, at the moment a homicidal aggressor puts another's life in jeopardy, his own life is forfeit to his threatened victim; at the moment a murderer kills his victim, he has ipso facto lost his own right to life against the state. In other cases, when the possessor of a forfeitable right misbehaves, he disqualifies himself for continued possession and becomes liable to the annulment of the right at a later time at the pleasure of the state—for example, a negligent motorist may be deprived of his driver's license in a proceeding that occurs a week after his misconduct. Since the forfeited right in all cases was originally understood to be conditional on the possessor's continued proper conduct, it is often said that disqualification is something he has brought upon himself, not of course as part of his explicit intention or motive in acting, but rather as the predictable and avoidable consequence of his wrongdoing. A forfeited right is not one that has been arbitrarily canceled or withdrawn, nor is it one that has been voluntarily relinquished or transferred. Rather it is thought to be one whose possessor has carelessly, stupidly, or recklessly allowed it to get away from him.

There is at least one striking paradox in the traditional view that the right to life can be forfeited (by the condemned murderer where capital punishment is permitted by law) but not voluntarily alienated. The would-be suicide can lose the right to life he no longer wants only by murdering someone else and thereby forfeiting the right that keeps him from his desired death. The inalienability of his right to life permits him to shed that unwanted life only by taking the life of someone else and thereby forfeiting it. Those who believe in the inalienability of the right to life, therefore, might well think twice before endorsing its forfeitability. A *nonforfeitable right* is one that a person cannot lose through his own blundering or wrongdoing; an *inalienable right* is one that a person cannot give away or dispense with through his own deliberate choice. Whenever the right in question can be thought of as burdensome baggage, it cannot be made inalienable *and* forfeitable without encouraging wrongdoing—the pursuit of relief through "error, fault, offense, or crime."

Alienating vs. Annulling

The major source of confusion in criticisms of the doctrine of inalienable rights over the last century or so might have been obviated, as B. A. Richards suggests,[18] by consulting a good dictionary. Many commentators have assumed uncritically that the founding fathers

18. B.A. Richards, "Inalienable Rights: Recent Criticism and Old Doctrine," *Philosophy and Phenomenological Research* 29 (1969): 398 n.

meant by an "inalienable right" one that could not be canceled or withdrawn by the state. In fact, natural rights theorists tended to use the word "indefeasible" for a right that cannot be taken away from its possessor by others, and most of them, as we have seen, following Richards, explicitly denied that the natural rights with which "all men are endowed by their Creator" are indefeasible in this sense. Webster's gives two senses of "inalienable": (1) "indefeasible: incapable of being annulled or made void," (2) "incapable of being alienated, surrendered, or transferred to another." Almost certainly, it was the second of these two senses that was intended by the founding fathers. Most eighteenth-century manifestoes and constitutions state or imply that the natural rights they invoke are subject to legitimate limitation. This implication, together with numerous statements in correspondence and philosophical essays that natural rights can be "abridged or modified in their exercise," strongly suggests that the founding fathers did not think of those rights as "indefeasible." An inalienable right, in the sense most likely intended by such early American writers as Paine and Jefferson is (in Webster's words) a right that "one cannot give away or dispose of even if one wishes." An indefeasible right, in contrast, is a right that "one cannot be deprived of without one's consent."

It is, of course, possible to hold that some rights are both inalienable and indefeasible, and perhaps this was the actual view of *some* of the founding fathers. But, putting the question of abridgement and annulment aside, there is no doubt that the distinctive and emphatic aspect of the doctrine of inalienability upon which almost all the founders agreed is that an inalienable right cannot be voluntarily given up or given away by its possessor. A very clear and typical statement of this doctrine and its supporting reasons, quoted by Richards, is that of Samuel Adams in "The Rights of Colonists." He says there that it would be

> the greatest absurdity to suppose it in the power of one or any number of men at the entering into society, to renounce their essential natural rights, or the means of preserving those rights when the great end of civil government . . . is for the support, protection, and defence of those very rights: the principal of which . . . are

life, liberty, and property. If men through fear, fraud, or mistake,
should in terms renounce and give up any essential natural right,
the eternal law of reason . . . would absolutely vacate such renunciation; the right to freedom being the gift of God Almighty, it is
not in the power of Man to alienate this gift, and voluntarily become a slave.[19]

Several arguments are only vaguely suggested in the passage quoted,
but there is nothing vague about Adams' conclusion. Adams finds it
irrational for anyone to renounce a natural right and implies that
such renunciations must be prompted by "fear, fraud, or mistake,"
thereby failing to be wholly voluntary. But even if such a renunciation
were somehow made without mistake, fraud, or reason-numbing fear,
it would be invalid on the grounds that a "gift" from an all-powerful
Creator cannot, in the very nature of things, be refused or relinquished. Whatever we are to make of these arguments, there can be
no doubt what conclusion they are meant to support: the right to life,
like the other natural rights, "cannot be given away or disposed of,
even if one wishes."

Waiving vs. Relinquishing

Failure to distinguish between waiving exercise of a right that one
continues to possess and relinquishing one's very possession of the
right can leave the doctrine of inalienability ambiguous and uncertain
in its application to the problems of suicide and voluntary euthanasia.
What exactly is it that cannot be alienated when one has an inalienable right to X—X itself or the right to X? If it is X itself that cannot
be voluntarily alienated (abandoned, transferred, sold, and so on)
then the right to X is a mandatory right, and one has a duty to do X
or continue in possession of X. In that case, one is not at liberty to
waive his right to X in some circumstances while insisting on it in
others, at his discretion. If the right to life is inalienable in this strong
sense, then we have a duty to continue to live and forbear suicide that
we cannot waive, for it would not merely be our right to life that is
inalienable but our life itself. On the other hand, if it is the right
which is inalienable, as opposed to that to which it is a right, then it

19. Quoted by Richards, p. 398 n.

might yet be true that the right in question is a discretionary right (as is my right to move to Chicago or to read Joyce's *Ulysses* or to keep strangers off my land) which I can exercise or decline to exercise as I choose. To *waive* my discretionary right is to exercise my power to release others from correlative duties to me, to desist from claiming my right against them, as when I waive my right to exclusive enjoyment of my land by inviting in a stranger. To be sure, in other cases, such as moving to Chicago or reading *Ulysses*, failure to exercise a right is not called "waiving" it since the obligations of other parties are not affected in the appropriate way. But what is important for our present purposes is what "declining to exercise" and "waiving" have in common, namely the protected discretion to act or not as one chooses. It does not follow from the inalienability of the *right* to life, that I may not decline to exercise it positively or that I cannot waive it (by releasing others from their duties not to kill me or let me die) if I choose. If I decline to exercise the right in a positive way or else waive it, then it is my *life* that I alienate, not my right to life.

It will be useful at this point to illustrate this distinction by using it to generate two possible interpretations of the "inalienability" of the natural rights to property and liberty, as well as to life. Consider first the *right to* property. What would it be like to waive or decline to exercise the right, while keeping possession of it, that is, "reserving" it? One might sell all one's goods and then give away the money, and live thenceforth by begging. That would be to exercise one's right to property, interpreted as a discretionary right, in a negative way. So interpreted, one has a right to acquire property or not to acquire it, to "take it or leave it," as one chooses, just as one has a right to acquire as little or as much as one can. When I give all of my property away, I have not abandoned the discretionary right to acquire (or re-acquire) property; rather I have chosen to exercise that right in a particular, eccentric, way.

It is less clear what would be involved in relinquishing the right to property itself. Here we must imagine a constitutional order and a legal system in which the right to property itself is alienable. Perhaps under such a regime one could formally renounce one's right to acquire property in a legally binding way, thus relinquishing the right irrevocably (unless the system also provided some legal procedure for re-acquiring renounced rights). If one were thus permitted to relinquish the right permanently, one could possess objects and occupy places but never *own* them. One would be a member of a special lower order of citizenship in that respect, or perhaps a permanent member of a mendicant religious order whose vow of permanent poverty is now enforced by the state at his own original request.

Waiving one's right to all *liberty* for a period while continuing to possess the discretionary right to liberty is illustrated by a story that is somewhat more fanciful but no less coherent than the parallel story about the right to property. One might lock oneself in a room and throw away the key, having arranged to have one's food put in through the transom, and one's garbage hauled out daily until further notice. As a consequence, one would no longer be at liberty to come and go as one pleases except within the narrow and quite minimal confines of a small cell-like room. If contact with delivery and disposal men is scheduled daily at 9:00 A.M. and one finally decides to terminate the arrangement one morning at 10:00, then one will still have to go twenty-three more hours without one's natural liberty. But, in virtue of one's continued possession of the right to liberty throughout the period during which it is voluntarily waived, liberty itself can be re-acquired in time.

In contrast, if the legal system permitted one to alienate the right to liberty itself, and to do so permanently and irrevocably, then one's future enjoyment of liberty would be sporadic, limited, and entirely subject to the pleasure of other parties. The story illustrating this possibility is that of a person who formally contracts to become the permanent chattel-slave of another, in exchange for some initial "consideration," perhaps one million dollars to be paid in advance to a beneficiary or favorite cause of the contractor. Once he becomes a slave he is no longer free to come and go as *he* chooses, but only as commanded or permitted by his master.

When we turn from property and liberty to life, we discover an apparent asymmetry. Until now, we have been able to distinguish without much difficulty between alienating X and alienating the right to X and to give plausible illustrations of each. But where X stands for life there is an apparent difficulty. In the other cases, I could give up X, at least for a time, without relinquishing the right to X. I could give away my money, or throw away the key to my locked room without resigning my right to re-acquire property or liberty. But I cannot destroy my life for a period of time while maintaining my discretionary right to re-acquire life whenever I so choose. Thus, an illustration of the waiver or nonexercise of a maintained right to life cannot take the form of a story of a person who deliberately has himself killed. Nevertheless, despite this important difference from the other cases, the distinction between waiving and relinquishing can be applied, albeit in a distinctive way, to the right to life too.

An illustration of a temporary waiver of the right to life was suggested to me by Don E. Scheid. Imagine a community that has celebrated from time immemorial an annual spring rite. One of the traditional rituals is a kind of sporting contest in which all of the males of a certain age are encouraged, but not required, to participate. All the "players" are armed with knives, clubs, bows, and arrows, and then turned loose in a large forest. For an hour every man is both hunter and prey. For that period of time the normal right to life is suspended for all the voluntary participants. In effect, therefore, each has *waived* the protection of that right for a fixed period of time, with no possibility of repossessing it until the time is up and the game is over. Each player thus releases all of the other players from their normal obligation not to kill him. The object of the game is twofold: to stay alive oneself until the game is over and to kill as many of the others as one can. This is a fanciful but coherent illustration of a set of rules that confer on everyone a discretionary right to life and also the power to waive that right (thus exercising it negatively) while the right continues to remain in one's possession.

The example of the formal renunciation and irrevocable relinquishment of the right to life is closely similar to the corresponding cases of permanent abandonment of the rights to property and liberty. Now we must imagine a legal system so permissive that it allows one formally to contract with another, again for a sizable consideration paid to third parties in advance, to put one's life—one's continued existence—in the other's legal power. I consent, in this bizarre example, to the other's irrevocable right to kill me if or whenever *he* decides to do so. He may have no other legal control over me except that derived from the power of his threat to exercise his right to kill.

Technically, I am not his chattel or slave and am at liberty to accumulate property and move about at will, as long, of course, as I stay alive. I *might* stay alive indefinitely, even to the point of my natural death, provided my legitimate killer decides to be benevolent. But if he chooses to exercise his contractual right in another fashion, he may wipe me out, as he may swat a fly or squash a bug, since I have no more claim on his forbearance than does an insect.

The sense in which a right is "waived" in the example of the spring rite is not *very* different from that in which rights are "renounced" in the examples using slavery and a contract to kill. The difference is best understood as one of degree. In the contract examples, the right in question is renounced permanently and irrevocably; the renouncer can never get his right back simply by changing his mind. In the spring-rite example, the right is in effect irrevocably renounced for *a fixed period of time*; no change of mind during that period can restore the right to its original owner. But after the expiration of that interval, the right can be repossessed. "Waiving" a right in a second, weaker but more natural, sense is to give it up provisionally without relinquishing the right to change one's mind *at any point* and thereby nullify the transaction. "Waiving the right to life" by means of a "living will" would be waiving in this sense. In short, there are two senses of "waiving": a stronger sense, which is actually short-term renunciation, and a more familiar weak sense in which waiving is inherently revocable. Voluntary euthanasia involves waiving in the latter sense; the spring rite involves waiving in the former; the contract to kill involves permanently irrevocable "waiving," which is the same thing as unconditional nullification, or renunciation.

IV. A RIGHT TO DIE? THREE VIEWS

How could a person have a right to terminate his own life (by his own hand or the hand of another) if his right to life is inalienable? It would probably be wise here to treat suicide as a special case that should be put aside to enable us to focus more narrowly on voluntary euthanasia. That is because suicide directly raises an additional philosophical perplexity, the puzzle of reflexive moral relations. If it is conceptually possible to violate one's own right to life by committing suicide, it must be the case that one's right to life is a claim addressed inter alia to oneself. In that case, I could have a duty *to myself* not to kill myself from which I cannot release myself, a situation many writers, from Aristotle on, have found incoherent or paradoxical. The paradox is not mitigated simply by thinking of the right to life as a mandatory right. I might well have a mandatory right to life—that is, a *duty* not to kill myself—which is owed to other people. In that case the involved claims are addressed not to myself but to others, claims to provide me with the opportunity to live and not to interfere with my discharge of my duty to live. No paradox arises in that case because no claim is self-addressed. Not all proposed mandatory rights are non-controversially coherent and intelligible, but only those that are associated with duties which, being owed to others, escape the problem of reflexive moral relations.

Most people in normal circumstances do have a duty not to kill themselves that is derived from the rights of other people who rely or depend on them. That duty can be thought of as a mandatory right because in the circumstances in question, its discharge also happens to be importantly beneficial to the person who possesses it. Moreover, that person can *claim* the associated half-liberties necessary for its exercise. But it is not a paradoxical mandatory right, because its claims are addressed to others (not to interfere), and the duty at its core is owed to others. In these circumstances of interpersonal reliance, one's general right to life, even if it is discretionary and absolute in its own domain, is subject to "territorial" limitation. One's own personal autonomy ends where the rights of others begin, just as national sovereignty comes to a limit at the boundaries of another nation's territory. My life may be my property, but there are limits to the uses to which I can put anything I own, and I may not destroy what is mine if I thereby destroy or seriously harm what does not belong to me. So some suicides may violate the rights of *other* persons, though equally certainly some suicides do not.

But how could my suicide violate my *own* right to life? Is that right a claim against myself as well as against others? Do I treat myself unjustly if I deliberately end my life for what seem to me the best

reasons?[20] Am I my own victim in that case? Do I have a moral grievance against myself? Is suicide just another case of murder? Am I
really two persons for the purposes of moral judgment, one an evil
wrong-doer and the other the wronged victim of the first's evil deed?
Can one of me be blamed or punished without blaming or punishing
the other? Perhaps these questions make the head reel because they
raise interestingly novel moral possibilities. On the other hand, their
paradoxes may derive, as the predominant philosophical tradition
maintains, from the conceptual violence they do to the integrity of
the self and the way we understand the concept of a right.

In either case we would be well advised to confine our attention to
voluntary euthanasia and ask whether a person who accedes to an
ailing friend's urgent and deliberate request by painlessly killing him
or letting him die, has violated that person's inalienable right to life.
Here at least is a question that is conceptually open and difficult. The
distinctions explained above between discretionary and mandatory
rights, indefeasible and inalienable rights, and between waiving and
relinquishing rights will enable us to formulate three possible positions. It will then be clear, I hope, which of the three can plausibly be
attributed to the founding fathers.

The Paternalist

According to the first possible view, the right to life is a nonwaivable,
mandatory right. On this view there is no right to die but only a right
to live. Since there is no morally permitted alternative to the one prescribed path, following it is a duty, like the duty of children to attend
school and the duty of convicted felons to undergo punishment. But
since continued life itself is a benefit in all circumstances whatever
the person whose life it is may think about it, we may with propriety

20. St. Thomas Aquinas grants the point, on the authority of Aristotle, that
nobody can commit an injustice to himself, even by committing suicide. The
sinfulness of suicide, according to Aquinas, consists not in the fact that one
violates one's own rights (which Aquinas finds incoherent) but rather in that
(a) the suicide violates God's rights just as in killing a slave one violates the
rights of the slave's master; (b) the suicide violates his community's rights by
depriving it of one of its "parts"; (c) the suicide acts against the *charity* (not
the justice) that a person should have towards himself. Aquinas therefore would
agree that the suicide, sinful though he may be, does not violate his own "right
to life." See *Summa Theologica*, vol. II, Question 64, A5.

refer to it as a right. In this respect, too, the right to life is similar to the right to education and the right to punishment (as understood by Hegelians). The "right to life" is essentially a duty, but expressible in the language of rights because the derivative claims against others that they save or not kill one are *necessarily* beneficial—goods that one could not rationally forswear. The right therefore must always be "exercised" and can never be "waived." Anyone who could wish to waive it must simply be ignorant of what is good for him.

The Founding Fathers

The second position differs sharply from the first in that it takes the right to life to be a discretionary, not a mandatory right. In this respect that right is exactly like the most treasured specimens in the "right to liberty" and "right to property" categories. Just as we have rights to come or go as we choose, to read or not read, to speak or not speak, to worship or not worship, to buy, sell, or sit tight, as we please, so we have a right, within the boundaries of our own autonomy, to live or die, as we choose. The right to die is simply the other side of the coin of the right to live. The basic right underlying each is the right to be one's own master, to dispose of one's own lot as one chooses, subject of course to the limits imposed by the like rights of others. Just as my right to live imposes a duty on others not to kill me, so my right to die, which it entails, imposes a duty on others not to prevent me from implementing my choice of death, except for the purpose of determining whether that choice is genuinely voluntary, hence truly mine. When I choose to die by my own hand, I insist upon my claim to the noninterference of others. When I am unable to terminate my own life, I *waive* my right to live in exercising my right to die, which is one and the same thing as releasing at least one other person from his duty not to kill me. In exercising my own choice in these matters, I am not renouncing, abjuring, forswearing, resigning, or relinquishing my right to life; quite the contrary, I am *acting* on that right by exercising it one way or the other. I cannot relinquish or effectively renounce the right, for that would be to alienate what is not properly alienable. To alienate the right would be to abandon my discretion; to waive the right is to exercise that discretion. The right itself, as opposed to that to which I have the right, is inalienable.

The state can properly prohibit such sanguinary frolics as the spring rite described above without annulling the discretionary right to life, just as the state may limit the right to property by levying taxes, or the right to liberty by requiring passports or imposing speed limits. To limit discretion in the public interest is not to cancel it or withdraw it. The spring rite is forbidden, not because our lives are not our own to risk (what is more risky than mountain climbing or car racing?), but rather because: (a) it cannot be in the public interest to permit widespread carnage, to deprive the population of a substantial portion of its most vital youthful members, and leave large numbers of dependent widows and orphans and heartbroken friends and relations; and (b) the "voluntariness" of the participation in such a ritual, like that of the private duel to death, must be suspect, given the pressure of public opinion, the liability to disgrace by nonparticipation, and the perceived inequality of skills among the participants. These are reasons enough for a legal prohibition even in a community that recognizes an indefeasible discretionary right to life (and death).

The Extreme Antipaternalist

The third position springs from a profound and understandable aversion to the smug paternalism of the first view. Like the second view, it interprets the right to life as a discretionary right which we may exercise as we please within the limits imposed by the like rights of others and the public interest. So far, I suspect, Paine, Adams, and Jefferson would be in solid agreement, since the natural rights emphasized in their rhetoric and later incorporated in our Constitution were, for the most part, protected options, and these writers made constant appeal to personal autonomy in their arguments about particular political issues. But this third view goes well beyond anything the fathers contemplated, since it holds that not only is life alienable; the discretionary right to life is alienable too. This view, of course, cannot be reconciled with the explicit affirmations of inalienability made in most of the leading documents of the revolutionary period, thus it cannot be attributed to the founding fathers. But it would be a mistake to dismiss it too quickly, for paternalism is a hard doctrine to compromise with, and it rejects paternalism *totally*. According to this third view, a free and autonomous person can renounce and relinquish any right, *provided only that his choice is fully informed, well considered, and uncoerced,* that is to say, *fully voluntary.* It may well be, as I have argued elsewhere, that there is no practicable and reliable way of discovering whether a choice to abjure a natural right is fully voluntary.[21] The evidence of voluntariness which we can acquire may never be sufficiently strong to override the natural presumption that no one in his right mind, fully informed, would sell himself into permanent poverty or slavery or sell his discretionary right to life. On that ground the state might always refuse to sanction requests from citizens that they be permitted to alienate the right to life. But that ground is quite consistent with the acknowledgment that even the natural right to life is alienable *in principle,* though not in fact. At least such a consistent antipaternalistic strategy would keep us from resorting, like Sam Adams, to the peculiar idea of a "gift" that cannot be declined, given away, or returned, and would enable us to avoid the even more peculiar notion that the right to life of an autonomous person is not properly his own at all, but rather the property of his creator.

Whatever judgment we make of the third position, however, will be consistent with the primary theses of this essay: that the inalienable right to life can be interpreted in such a way that it is not infringed by voluntary euthanasia; that that interpretation (the second position above) is coherent and reasonably plausible; and that it is very likely the account that best renders the actual intentions of Jefferson and the other founding fathers.

21. See the discussion in Joel Feinberg, "Legal Paternalism," *Canadian Journal of Philosophy* 1 (1971): 105-124.

Duty and Obligation in the Non-Ideal World

THERE is no need to summarize the argument of this philosophical epic. In its basic outline it is sufficiently well known to the readers of this journal from Rawls's articles over the last twenty years. In this book Rawls has filled in gaps in the argument, answered numerous critical objections, applied his theory to problems of justice in politics, economics, education, and other important areas, and buttressed it with a theory of moral psychology and other argumentative reinforcement. The result is a remarkably thorough treatise which well deserves to be called a philosophical classic.

Rawls's primary aim, he tells us, is to provide a "workable and systematic moral conception" (viii) to oppose utilitarianism. Until now, the opponents of utilitarianism have been unable to provide an equally systematic alternative of their own, and have contented themselves with a series of *ad hoc* amendments and restrictions to utilitarianism designed to bring it into closer harmony with our spontaneous moral sentiments, at whatever cost in theoretical tidiness. They are likely to concede that *one* of the prime duties of social policy makers is to promote social utility, but then insist that one may not properly pursue that commendable goal by grinding the faces of the poor, framing and punishing the innocent, falsifying history, and so on. On the level of personal ethics, such moralists as W. D. Ross admit utilitarian duties of beneficence and nonmaleficence, but supplement them with quite nonutilitarian duties of veracity, fidelity, and the like, and there is no way of telling in advance which duty must trump the others when circumstances

seem to bring them into conflict. Similarly, on the level of social
policy, such theorists as Brian Barry (*Political Argument*) and
Nicholas Rescher (*Distributive Justice*) endorse utilitarian "aggregative principles" but insist that they be supplemented or limited
by equally valid equalitarian "distributive principles," and when
circumstances bring the principles of utility and equality into
opposition, there is no higher-order criterion to settle the conflict
or to provide in advance one uniquely correct set of weightings to
the conflicting principles. All pluralistic theories that do not provide rigid "priority rules" among principles require us to balance
conflicting considerations against one another on the particular
occasions of their conflict and "simply strike a balance by intuition,
by what seems to us most nearly right" (34). Rawls calls all theories
of this type "intuitionistic."

Rawls's main objection to intuitionism is its modesty. It doesn't
even try to provide us with a rigorously rational method of settling
hard problems in ethics; in cases of close conflict there are no
demonstrably correct results, and "the means of rational discussion have come to an end" (41). Perhaps no theory can do better,
Rawls concedes, but that is no reason why theorists shouldn't try;
for a pluralistic theory without rigid priority rules is but "half a
theory." Many intuitionists, however, will be inclined to reply, at
this early stage of the argument, that "half-theories" are the only
kind that can fit the facts of moral experience. Difficult moral decisions and judgments often (if not always) require balancing of
conflicting claims, deciding and choosing rather than calculating
and applying rules, committing oneself and legislating for others,
taking "existential leaps" in situations of "tragic surdity," and so
on. To most persons who have struggled with moral dilemmas, I
submit, the suggestion that Reason can provide a ready-made set of
priority rules is astonishing. Still, this observation is question-begging if intended as criticism. The question for the critic is whether
Rawls's theory itself has been able to dispense (convincingly) with
the balancing of coordinate considerations. If it has, it is an extraor-
dinary triumph over what would initially appear to be common
sense.

Rawls's objection to his other leading rival, utilitarianism, is the
familiar one that the theory in all its forms would justify too much,
in particular that it can justify sacrificing the interests of a few
for the sake of the greater total good shared by many. The complaint is not new, of course, but Rawls makes it with unexcelled
elegance and persuasiveness. Utilitarianism, however, is a slip-

pery target, and it is sometimes not clear whether arguments fatal to one of its forms have been aimed by Rawls at another form that has a relative immunity to them. There is some confusion, for example, between a utilitarian *analysis* of justice, as found, for example, in the final chapter of J. S. Mill's *Utilitarianism*, and a normative utilitarian theory of on-balance justification which can admit that utility is one thing and justice another, even admit that Rawls's analysis of justice is correct, and yet hold that, when they conflict, social utility has an invariant moral priority. A utilitarian *analysis* of justice will entail that justice, being "the name for certain social utilities which are vastly more important . . . than any others" [1] can never conflict with social utility. That implausible thesis is an easy target for Rawls. The utilitarian who will allow conceivable, though perhaps rare, conflicts between social utility (conceived in a sophisticated way) and justice, but stubbornly insists that social utility must win out in those cases, is a harder target, and the intuitionist who refuses to legislate in advance for all conceivable cases of conflict, a harder target still.

Rawls calls his own theory (the third horse in the race) "contractarianism," or "the contract theory," and traces its ancestry to the traditional theory of the social contract "as found, say, in Locke, Rousseau, and Kant" (11). This is a bit puzzling, for that part of Rawls's theory which is a direct rival to utilitarianism and intuitionism does not employ the idea of a *contract* at all. Depending on how the rival theories are interpreted, they are either statements of the ultimate principle (or principles) of right conduct generally or of social justice in particular. The principle Rawls proposes in opposition to them he takes to be a general test for the truth of specific principles (including priority rules) of social justice. A specific principle is correct, he argues, provided it would be chosen over any alternative that could be proposed to a hypothetical group of normally self-interested rational persons, each wearing an appropriate "veil of ignorance," gathered together in a state of nature for the specific purpose of designing afresh the institutions that will regulate their future lives. *That* criterion is neither utilitarian nor pluralistic, but neither does it make any reference to a "contract." Rawls holds that *any* rational person in the circumstances he describes would choose one definite set of principles over all others as the basic ground rules of the society he is to join, and that a collection of such persons, therefore, would choose those rules *unanimously*. In that case, in applying Rawls's ultimate cri-

[1] J. S. Mill, *Utilitarianism*, chapter v, final paragraph.

terion (that is, in employing his method for testing proposed principles of justice) we need consider only the reasoning processes of *one* hypothetical rational chooser. The concept of a conditional agreement sworn to by a number of parties and binding upon each on condition of promised performance or *quid pro quo* by the others does not enter the argument at all (at least at this stage). The traditional social-contract doctrine, as I understand it, was an answer to a different question from that answered by Rawls's "contractarianism." In its Hobbesian and Lockean forms, for example, it is not so much a general criterion for the truth of principles of social justice as a statement of the grounds and limits of *political obligation*; and the concept of a contract—tacitly actual or hypothetical, among subjects or between subjects and a sovereign—was essential to it. I shall discuss Rawls's own theory of political obligation, and the limited role that contract plays in it, below.

The "contract theory" as Rawls develops it, then, is a poorly named but genuine alternative to utilitarian and intuitionistic systems of ultimate justification (or "justicization," as the case may be). Like utilitarianism, contractarianism can be applied primarily to individual acts and policies or primarily to more general rules and institutions. Rawls did so much to clarify the distinction between acts and rules and to emphasize its importance in his famous early discussion of utilitarianism [2] that for several years he was thought by some to be working toward a rule-utilitarian theory himself. Instead, he was apparently setting the stage for his own rule-oriented brand of "contractarianism." "The primary subject of justice," as Rawls sees it, "is the basic structure of society" (7). By this he means that the principles of justice he has derived by the contractarian method are to be applied directly to the design or criticism of the major institutions—a political constitution, an economic system, and such basic social forms as the monogamous family. Institutions are defined by their constitutive rules which create offices and roles, regulate procedures, and assign rights and duties. Ultimately, then, the principles of justice apply to those rules, and only indirectly or derivatively to the acts and states of affairs that fall under the rules. A given pattern of wealth distribution is just, for example, whatever it be like, provided only it follows from the fair operation of a just economic practice as determined by the procedural rules of that practice. Distributive justice, in Rawls's own terminology, is an instance of "pure procedural

[2] John Rawls, "Two Concepts of Rules," *Philosophical Review*, LXIV, 1 January 1955): 3–32.

justice," insofar as there is no criterion of a just result independent of the fairness of the procedures followed to reach the result. The procedural rules themselves are part of the basic structure, which can be justified only by the principles of justice derived from the contractarian method.

As for the justice of particular economic transactions—"It is a mistake to . . . require that every change, considered as a single transaction viewed in isolation, be in itself just" (87/8). Rawls is not so much expressing his tolerance here for a certain amount of distributive injustice (despite his wording) as denying that a criterion of just arrangements can be found apart from the fairness of the procedures followed to reach them. (Note the parallel contention that could be made by a rule-utilitarian: "It is a mistake to require that every act considered in isolation from the practice that gives it its meaning be socially useful; it is sufficient that the rule-defined practice of which it is a part be socially useful.") The same point is made about legislation in a somewhat modified way: "Thus on many questions of social and economic policy we must fall back upon a notion of quasi-pure procedural justice: laws and policies are just provided that they lie within the allowed range, and the legislature, in ways authorized by a just constitution, has in fact enacted them" (201). The justice of a particular statute, then, is several steps removed from Rawls's initial contractarian criterion: the choice of hypothetical rational persons determines the basic principles of justice, which in turn determine the justice of a political constitution, which in turn determines the proper law-making procedures, which in turn partly determine the justice of a particular legislative outcome. At each stage, the fairness of a procedure (hypothetical or actual) largely determines the justice of a result. This general priority of fair procedures to just outcomes (in particular at the stage at which basic principles are chosen) leads Rawls to label his whole conception "Justice as Fairness."

Rawls makes one further qualification that is essential to an understanding of his theory. His book is an essay in what he calls "ideal theory" (as opposed to "non-ideal theory") or more specifically, "strict-compliance theory" (as opposed to "partial-compliance theory"). He presumes that his original choosers are to select principles that will regulate a "well-ordered society," that is, a society in which every one always acts justly, all laws are just, and all citizens always comply with them. (It is apparently also a society in which no one ever acts negligently and there are no automobile collisions, since Rawls consigns questions about compensatory justice to nonideal theory.) Rawls admits that the really pressing and important problems about justice belong to partial-compliance theory (e.g., questions in the theory of criminal justice, in tort law, in the theory of civil disobedience, and justice between nations) but "assumes" that the question of ideal theory is more fundamental since its answer will provide direction to our inquiries in non-ideal theory, and will be "the only basis for the systematic grasp of these more pressing problems" (8).

One of the ways the ideal theory helps with the real-life problems of the non-ideal world, according to Rawls, is by mediating our "natural duty" to promote just institutions. Insofar as our actual institutions depart from Rawls's basic principles of justice, we have a duty, he says, to work toward their reform. But in our actual imperfect world things are rarely that straightforward. For example, Sidgwick's paradox of "conservative justice" confronts us at every turn. Every reform of an imperfect practice or institution is likely to be unfair to someone or other. To change the rules in the middle of the game, even when those rules were not altogether fair, will disappoint the honest expectations of those whose prior commitments and life plans were made in genuine reliance on the continuance of the old rules. The propriety of changing the rules in a given case depends upon (*inter alia*) the degree of unfairness of the old rules and the extent and degree of the reliance placed upon them. Very often, when we consider reform, we must weigh quite legitimate incompatible claims against each other in circumstances such that whichever judgment is reached it will be unfair to someone or other. Rawls admits that intuitive balancing is unavoidable in dealing with problems of non-ideal theory, but I find very little acknowledgment (if any) that justice can be in *both* pans of the balance beam when claims are weighed. By and large, however, Rawls, in talking about non-ideal theory, makes large concessions to the skeptical intuitionist who insists on the necessity of claim-balancing. His sensitive treatment of the duty to obey an unjust law and its limits (350–355) is a good example of this. So is his grudging admission (on page 303) that in the more "extreme and tangled instances of nonideal theory" there will be a point where his rigid priority rules designed for ideal theory will fail, and there may be "no satisfactory answer at all."

Rawls's chapter devoted to civil disobedience and conscientious refusal is the one place in the book where political ties are analyzed, and so the one place where "social-contract theory," in a strict and traditional sense, might come into play. It is also worth discussing

here since it provides a usefully illustrative problem for the clash
between rule-contractarianism and act-contractarianism.

The problem of civil disobedience is primarily a problem in
individual ethics. To ask under what conditions, if any, an individual citizen is morally justified in engaging in a "public, non-
violent, conscientious yet political act contrary to law" (63) is to
ask a question very much like those about when an individual is
morally justified in telling lies, breaking promises, inflicting pain,
or otherwise acting contrary to normally binding moral rules. That
is because there is normally a presumption against disobeying the
law in a just, or near-just, society—not an unconditional moral
prohibition, but a kind of standing case that must be overridden
in a given instance by sufficient reasons. [Rawls does *not* hold the
discredited view, effectively attacked by Hugo Bedau, that there is
such a presumption in favor of obedience to "*any* law, however
instituted and enforced, whatever its provisions, and no matter
what would be the consequences of universal unswerving compliance with it." [3] His whole discussion of civil disobedience assumes
the special context of a near-just society with "legitimately established democratic authority" (63).] To solve the problem, it is not
sufficient to have a set of principles for determining the justice of
the basic structure of society; rather we need supplementary principles to guide the individual conscience in a society already assumed to have more or less just institutions.

Rawls derives his principles for individuals in the same rationalistic way he derived his principles of social justice. Once again, the
"contractarian method" is employed, and we must ask ourselves
which principles of right conduct would be chosen unanimously
by the rational and self-interested parties in the original position
after they have chosen the principles of social justice. These form a
relatively untidy miscellany, and as Rawls enumerates and clarifies
them, the reader is naturally reminded of Hobbes's "Laws of
Nature or Dictates of Reason." The main distinction Rawls draws
among them is between those which impose "natural duties" and
those which impose "obligations." Obligations arise from voluntary
acts, e.g., express or tacit promises, or accepting benefits; their content derives in part from the specifications of institutional rules;
they are owed to definite individuals, namely, those "cooperating
together to maintain the arrangement in question" (113). On the
other hand, such natural duties as the duty not to be cruel and the

[3] Hugo Bedau, review of Carl Cohen, *Civil Disobedience: Conscience, Taxes,
and the Law*, this JOURNAL, LXIX, 7 (April 6, 1972): 179–186, p. 185.

duty to help others in need "apply to us without regard to our voluntary acts . . . have no necessary connection with institutions or social practices . . . and hold between persons irrespective of their institutional relationships" (114 f). The principles imposing natural duties are irreducibly diverse, but all obligations ultimately are derived from a single principle which Rawls calls the "principle of fairness." This expresses the requirement that an individual "do his part as defined by the rules of an institution when . . . (1) the institution is just . . . and (2) one has voluntarily accepted the benefits of the arrangement or taken advantage of its opportunities" (111 f).

Insofar as the presumption in favor of obedience to law is grounded in the principle of fairness in Rawls's philosophy, his theory of political obligation falls squarely within the (or a) social-contract tradition. (Indeed, that interpretation of his theory is reminiscent of Socrates in his jail cell.) In fact, however, Rawls does not use the principle of fairness to provide much support for the presumption in favor of obedience. "There is . . . no political obligation strictly speaking," he says, "for citizens generally" (114). Those members of society whose "equal liberties" are worth very little because of economic deprivation, social discrimination, and exclusion from powerful offices (even under just and enlightened rules) and those whose "consent" to the governing institutional rules has been coerced by a kind of "extortion" are free of any genuine *obligation* to obey the law even in a society whose *institutions* (as opposed to policies and practices) are just. Society is not a "mutually advantageous venture" (343) for these citizens, and they do not "voluntarily" restrict their liberties under law in it. The principle of fairness, then, does not establish even the presumption of an obligation of obedience for them: "only the more favored members of society are likely to have a clear political obligation as opposed to a political duty" (376). Since the principles of natural duty "do not presuppose any act of consent, express or tacit, or indeed any voluntary act, in order to apply" (115), even this part of Rawls's system is not a "social-contract theory" except in a watered-down and untraditional sense.

The principle of natural duty that *does* account for the general presumption in favor of obedience in a just society is the principle imposing what Rawls calls the "duty to uphold justice." That principle, which Rawls argues would be acknowledged in the original position and is in that sense "derived from reason," requires individuals to "support and comply with" already existing just institutions and help bring about new just arrangements (115). It is *this* principle that binds people generally to their political institutions, and it is a "contractarian principle" only in the sense that it is derived by Rawls's so-called contractarian method.

Under what conditions can the presumption in favor of obedience be overridden? The problem of justifying civil disobedience, as Rawls conceives it, is a problem for individual choice, and "the difficulty is one of a conflict of [natural] duties": "At what point does the duty to comply with laws enacted by a legislative majority (or executive acts supported by such a majority) cease to be binding in view of . . . the duty to oppose injustice?" (363) (The latter, presumably, is another of the "natural duties.") If I understand Rawls correctly, the "intuitionism" that he rejected in his account of social principles is re-introduced here in his discussion of conflicting individual duties (though Rawls denies that he resorts to intuitionism even here). Intuitionism, as I understand Rawls's use of the term, is the view that there are no rigid priority rules assigning weights to normative principles that can conflict. Yet in his discussion of the conflict of duties that makes the problem of civil disobedience difficult, he cautions us that "Precise principles that straightway decide actual cases are clearly out of the question" (364). He modestly claims for his own discussion only that "it identifies the relevant considerations and helps us to assign them their correct weights in the more important instances," thus "clearing our vision" generally (364).

Rawls then lists a number of conditions whose satisfaction usually or generally (he calls them mere "presumptions") makes civil disobedience reasonable. First, it should be limited to the protest of wrongs that are "instances of substantial and clear injustice," in effect to "serious infringements of the principle of equal liberty" (373), that is to say, to denials of the basic political rights of citizenship. (It is worth noting in passing that this condition is not satisfied by civilly disobedient protests against cutting down sycamore trees to widen a city road, against busing pupils, over-severe marijuana laws, failure to install a traffic light at an intersection that is unsafe for children, or excessive air pollution. The weight Rawls assigns to the presumption for obedience is not easily outbalanced.) Second, civil disobedience is justified as, but only as, a last resort after legal means of redress have failed. Third, the case for civil disobedience weakens in proportion to the extent to which others have recently resorted to it or have as good a case for resorting to it, for "there is a limit to which civil disobedience can be engaged in without leading to a breakdown in the respect for law and the constitution" (374).

The question that divides both utilitarian and contractarian theories into "act" and "rule" varieties is the following: In choosing and justifying our actions, when may we appeal *directly* to an ethical first principle and when (if ever) must our appeal stop at some subordinate rule, itself justified by an ethical first principle? The act-utilitarian permits (indeed requires) each of us always to do the act that promises to produce the greatest gain in net utility. He admits, of course, that often (even usually) we can best maximize utility by conforming to rules and regulations that summarize the experience of many generations that acts of certain kinds tend to have bad consequences. He might even agree with G. E. Moore that some moral rules should be taken as absolutely binding, but only because the chances of a given murder, say, being optimific are always less than the chances that our predictions of optimificity are mistaken. Still he will hold, at least in principle, that we ought to violate any moral or legal rule whenever doing so will produce consequences that are better on the whole than the consequences of our obeying it. On the other hand, the philosopher who holds the view suggested by Rawls's "Two Concepts of Rules," which I have elsewhere called "Actual-Rule Utilitarianism," [4] will interpret our duties much more strictly. He may admit that some "moral rules" are mere "summaries," or rules of thumb, to be violated whenever the expected consequences of doing so are better than those of conformity (most "rules" of sexual ethics can be interpreted that way), but he will insist that valid legal rules and legal-like rules governing such practices as promising and punishing cannot rightly be broken merely to achieve a small gain in utility, but only to avoid a disastrous *loss* in utility. And he will support his strict legalism, paradoxically, by a kind of appeal of his own to utility. He will point out that it is conducive to social utility to have some rules (e.g., those pertaining to promising) that deprive persons, under certain conditions, of the right to appeal directly to the principle of utility in deciding what to do.

At first sight, it is not easy to see how a similar act-rule division would apply to contractarian theories, partly because it is difficult to say what corresponds to an "ethical first principle" in Rawls's system. It is implausible, I think, to take Rawls's statement of the contractarian method itself to fill the same role in his theory as

---

[4] "The Forms and Limits of Utilitarianism," *Philosophical Review*, LXXVI, 3 (July 1967): 368–381, p. 378.

the principle of utility does in utilitarianism. The principle that moral principles are correct if and only if they would be chosen by the parties in the original position is not itself an ultimate moral principle so much as a test of truth for proposed ultimate principles. The principles of social justice, though several in number, do have sufficient cohesion to play the role of a single ultimate principle in virtue of the strict priority rules that govern their application, but they are principles for the design of institutions and practices, not principles for individual actions. The most plausible candidate for a rival to the principle of utility as a standard of right conduct is the whole collection of principles assigning "natural duties" and obligations. However, these are *not* ordered by rigid priority rules and, thus, they lack the unity of their utilitarian counterpart. Still, the principle that imposes the "duty to uphold justice," directing us to obey the rules of established just practices and institutions, is very stringent and fundamental among these. So, for the sake of simplifying this discussion, we could consider *it* to be "the ethical first principle" for individuals in Rawls's system, at least for actions that fall within the ambit of already established near-just institutions. But we would have to remember that there are other natural duties that can conflict with the "duty to uphold justice" even for clearly rule-governed conduct. Some of these might very well have included the word 'justice' in *their* names; for surely the duties not to harm the innocent, not to disappoint reasonable expectations, not to assign arbitrarily heavy burdens, etc. have as much to do with justice as the duty to uphold just institutions has.

Now, one way of interpreting Rawls's rule-contractarianism is as follows. Normally we have the discretion, morally speaking, to appeal directly to the principles of natural duty in deciding what would be the right thing to do. Some actions, for example, are seen to be ineligible for our choice since they would violate the natural duty not to inflict harm upon the innocent. But when we are to act in our role as citizens in a fairly functioning democracy, when obedience to law is at issue, or when we occupy a special office such as juryman in a just institution, then we forfeit our right to appeal directly to the (other) first principles of natural duty, and the duty to uphold just institutions will normally trump. Thus, when the evidence establishes beyond a reasonable doubt that the defendant committed the crime with which he is charged, then we must find him guilty even though he is a morally innocent and admirable person charged under an odious but valid law. The example is an instance of "quasi-pure procedural justice," but it has elements of imperfect procedural justice too, since the fair procedures of a just institution, fairly followed, lead to a result which is unjust by a criterion that is independent of the institution itself. In a society whose basic structure is itself unjust or in an otherwise just society where a law has been created without proper regard to constitutionally specified procedures, the juryman's normal duty might be canceled. But the example in question is a case where there is a duty to perform an act (voting "guilty") that will have an unjust result. As such it is exactly parallel to the case under rule-utilitarianism where a person has a duty to perform an action with less than optimific consequences simply because he promised to perform that act and thus forfeited his right to appeal directly to considerations of utility in deciding what to do.

But suppose now that you are on a jury and the evidence establishes beyond a reasonable doubt that the ten-year-old defendant did steal turnips as charged and thereby committed a capital felony under duly established law. In this case the duty to uphold just institutions would have you commit not merely an unfortunate but routine injustice; rather it would have you become a party to a monstrous perversion of natural justice, a result so disastrously severe that the normally trumping effect of the duty to uphold just institutions would be nullified in this case. This example is exactly parallel to the case under rule-utilitarianism where a person must deliberately break his promise not because the net consequences of so doing are likely to be somewhat better on the whole than the consequences of keeping the promise (rule-utilitarianism would not permit that) but rather because breaking the promise is necessary to prevent some *severe* harm to third parties. The rules of promising themselves, having utilitarian grounding, would permit *that* kind of breach.

Violating one's oath as a juryman is an example more like conscientious refusal than like civil disobedience, but the principle involved is much the same. In both cases the natural duty to uphold just institutions conflicts with what can be called "the natural duty to oppose unjust laws, policies, and actions" (the latter a summary of all other natural duties that could well include the term 'justice' in their names). When the conflict is close, our natural duty on balance will be to try somehow to support just institutions and oppose injustice both, and civil disobedience, as Rawls conceives it, is a way of doing both these things at one stroke, since it is a way of "expressing disobedience to law within the limits of fidelity to law, although it is at the outer edge thereof" (366). In a nearly just society where the sense of justice is deeply entrenched, justified civil disobedience actually functions as "a final device to maintain the stability of a just constitution" (384). This is a welcome and ingenious idea, but one wonders whether an ideally just constitution will itself make some reference to civil disobedience and the conditions of its permissibility. If not, why not? If so, in what sense is civil disobedience "illegal"?

Rawls's theory of civil disobedience may well be the nearest thing we have yet to an adequate account of these subtle matters, but, for the reasons given above, I think that Rawls overestimates the role that contract and "pure procedural justice" play in it and in his theory of justice generally, and underestimates the extent of his own intuitionism.

Noncomparative Justice[1]

S UPPOSE a cautious, empirically minded philosopher who lacks any one central insight, or any one basic analytic principle, nevertheless undertakes to write a systematic treatise on the nature of justice. Such a person would naturally wish to get a preliminary idea of the lay of the land by searching through the data from which he must eventually extract his principles. What would he find? Without doubt, an enormous diversity of things. To begin with, there is a great variety of kinds of human activity in which questions of justice can arise: distributions of goods and evils, requitals of desert, compensation for loss, appraisals of worth, judgments of criticism, administration and enforcement of rules and regulations, games of amusement, settlements of disputes (by bargaining, voting, flipping coins), contracting, buying, selling, and more.

One way of imposing unity on the data of justice is to classify these diverse activities into more general kinds. Thus, from the Scholastic period on, philosophers have spoken of allocations, punishments, and exchanges under the rubrics "distributive," "retributive," and "commutative" justice, respectively. But from the point of view of theory, this classification does not cut very deep at all, and the inference from three general kinds of human activity to three distinct and theoretically interesting forms of justice would be a *non sequitur*. At best the traditional headings constitute a useful way of ordering a survey or dividing a book into chapters. An equally useful way of classifying the data of justice and one which promises more rewarding theoretical insights is that which divides injustices[2] into those that discriminate invid-

---

[1] I have profited from positive suggestions and sharp criticisms of earlier versions of this paper from Jonathan Bennett, Bernard Gert, T. Y. Henderson, Saul Kripke, Phillip Montague, Joshua Rabinowitz, Robert Richman, Arthur Schafer, Harry Silverstein, and especially David Lyons.

[2] As many writers have observed, it is much more convenient, when doing moral philosophy, to speak of injustice than to keep to the positive term, justice. That greater convenience is an undeniable fact, but I shall not speculate here whether it has any theoretical significance.

iously, those that exploit their victims, and those that wrong their victims by means of false derogatory judgments about them. This is a distinction among types of wrongs that are called injustices, and cuts across the distinctions among occasions or contexts of justice. Whatever the activity, whatever the institutional background, any injustice properly so called will be, I believe, a wrong of one of these three types.

A way of achieving still more unity is to separate the data of justice as neatly as possible into two categories. Perhaps this can be done in a variety of ways, but the one in which I am interested here sorts the various contexts, criteria, and principles of justice into those which essentially involve comparisons between various persons and those which do not. In all cases, of course, justice consists in giving a person his due, but in some cases one's due is determined independently of that of other people, while in other cases, a person's due is determinable *only* by reference to his relations to other persons. I shall refer to contexts, criteria, and principles of the former kind as *noncomparative*, and those of the latter sort as *comparative*. My aim in this paper will be to clarify the contrast between comparative and noncomparative justice, and also to investigate that which they might have in common, and in virtue of which the name of justice has come to apply to both.

I

In recent years, comparative justice has received far more attention than noncomparative justice, partly because writers have been able to agree about its general nature. Surprisingly many philosophers[3] have even gone so far as to claim that all justice *consists* (essentially) in the absence of arbitrary inequalities in the distribution of goods and evils, thus ignoring completely the many and diverse contexts for justice which are nondistributive

---

[3] E.g., Richard Brandt, *Ethical Theory* (Englewood Cliffs, N.J., 1959), p. 410; S.I. Benn and Richard Peters, *Social Principles and the Democratic State* (London, 1959), chs. 5 and 6; Chaim Perelman, *The Idea of Justice and the Problem of Argument* (New York, 1963), pp. 16 ff.; and Morris Ginsberg, *On Justice in Society* (Harmondsworth, Middlesex, 1965), p. 70 *et passim*.

in character. There is no denying, of course, that the problems of comparative justice are real and pressing; my concern here is only to correct the imbalance of emphasis resulting from the exclusive attention lavished upon them. Let us consider first, however, some typical occasions for comparative justice: (*i*) when competitive prizes are to be awarded, (*ii*) when burdens and benefits are to be distributed, and (*iii*) when general rules are to be made, administered, or enforced.

It is illustrative to notice how competitive prizes differ from grades and rewards. We can know that a grade or reward is improperly assigned without knowing anything about the claims or deserts of persons other than the assignee, whereas a prize, having the avowed purpose of selecting out the best in some competition (or, in the case of "booby prizes," the worst) or the exact ranking of contestants against one another, cannot be seen to be justly or unjustly awarded to one person prior to an examination of the credentials of all the others. Thus the awarding of prizes is an occasion for comparative justice, whereas the assigning of grades and rewards is typically noncomparative.

All comparative justice involves, in one way or another, equality in the treatment accorded all the members of a class; but whether that equality be absolute or "proportional," whether it be equality of share, equality of opportunity, or equality of consideration, depends on the nature of the goods and evils awarded or distributed, and the nature of the class in which the assignments and allocations take place. Comparative injustice consists in arbitrary and invidious discrimination of one kind or another: a departure from the requisite form of equal treatment without good reason. When the occasion for justice is the distribution of divisible but limited goods or the assignment of divisible but limited chores, *how much will be left for the others* is always pertinent to the question of how much it would be just for any particular individual to get. And where the occasion for justice is the application or enforcement of general rules, comparative justice requires that the judge or administrator give precisely the same treatment to each person who falls within a class specified by the rule.

These observations, of course, are by now boring and commonplace. My only purpose in making them here is to help make clear the contrast between comparative and noncomparative justice. Consider now the various noncomparative occasions for justice. When our problem is to make assignments, ascriptions, or awards in accordance with noncomparative justice, what is "due" the other person is not a share or portion of some divisible benefit or burden; hence it is not necessary for us to know what is due others in order to know what is due the person with whom we are dealing. *His* rights-or-deserts alone determine what is due him; and once we have come to a judgment of *his* due, that judgment cannot be logically affected by subsequent knowledge of the condition of other parties. We may decide, on the basis of information about other parties, to withhold from him his due; but no new data can upset our judgment of what in fact *is* his due. That judgment is based exclusively upon data about him and is incorrigible, as a judgment, by new information about others. When our task is to do noncomparative justice to each of a large number of individuals, we do not compare them with each other, but rather we compare each in turn with an objective standard and judge each (as we say) "on his merits." It follows that equality of treatment is no part of the concept of noncomparative justice, even though it is, of course, a central element in comparative justice. If we treat *everybody* unfairly, but equally and impartially so, we have done each an injustice that is, at best, only mitigated[4] by the equal injustice done all the others.

The clearest examples of noncomparative injustices are cases of unfair punishments and rewards, merit grading, and derogatory judgments. Of these three kinds of activities, the third seems the most basic from the point of view of justice, and since it has been largely neglected in recent discussions, it will be the main object of attention in the remainder of this essay. First, however, I shall briefly consider possible examples of noncomparative injustices in so-called commutative and retributive contexts. It might seem at first sight that when agreements, transactions, and transfers between free and equal bargainers are unfair, or when promises are wrongfully broken, the injustice is primarily noncomparative,

---

[4] "Mitigated" in the sense that its sting might not hurt as much in a given case, not in the sense that the degree of (noncomparative) injustice in a given case is actually reduced.

for in such cases the agreement reached or the promise breached is unjust because it denies one of the parties his due, quite apart from the way in which others are treated or have been treated by the actor in question or by other actors. A businessman to whom a commercial promise is made and then broken, for example, is treated unfairly not because of the contrast between his treatment and that of others (though, of course, when such a comparison is made it may serve to aggravate the sense of injury and show that there is a derivative injustice resting on another, comparative, ground); he is treated unfairly in any case, so it would seem, because his rights, determined independently of any such comparison, have been violated. If these cases are indeed instances of noncomparative injustice, however, they are not the clearest or purest examples. Not all cases of wrongful promise-breaking are instances of injustice of any kind (*pace* Hobbes). One can, after all, mistreat a person without being particularly unfair to him. Broken promises typically *are* unfair, however, because, like cheating and much lying, they are forms of *exploitation*, of one party taking advantage of another, or promoting his own gain wrongfully at the expense of his victim. When exploitation occurs, the balance of advantages is upset, and benefits and losses are redistributed. Injustice becomes manifest in these cases when a *comparison* is made between the resultant condition of the exploiter and that of his victim. The point applies a fortiori to bargains that are unfair in the first place.[5]

Purer cases of noncomparative injustice are encountered in retributive contexts. It should be obvious, for example, that to punish an innocent person or a lawbreaker who was not responsible for what he did is to commit an injustice to the one punished irrespective of similar treatment accorded all other offenders of his class. There is, to be sure, an element of comparative injustice in the situation where a guilty person goes free and an innocent one is punished for his crime, but punishment of the innocent person would be unjust to him even if the guilty party were also punished, or suffered a fate even worse than punishment.

The category of noncomparative justice to which I shall devote

---

[5] I discuss exploitation more fully below in Part III.

major attention I propose to call *the justice of judgments*. The importance of judgment in the theory has been insufficiently acknowledged, I think, by writers who (like Plato and Aristotle) concentrate on the *virtue* of justice or (like the modern utilitarians and their enemies) on the justice and injustice of *acts* and *rules*. The idea of judgmental injustice is familiar enough. In everyday discourse statements and the opinions and judgments they express are commonly called just or unjust. Sometimes one person's opinion of another may not "do him justice"; it may not be "fair to him," as we say. When judgments (as distinct from actions) are said to be unfair to the person judged, the injustice alleged is typically the noncomparative kind. When an innocent man is pronounced guilty, the record about him is falsified to the disadvantage of his reputation and to the detriment of the cause of truth. This is an injustice to him and remains so even if his sentence is suspended and no further hardship is imposed upon him. The injustice in this case consists precisely in the falsity of the derogatory allegation. It can also consist in the falsity of what is believed about the unjustly convicted man. Beliefs and opinions are often said to be unfair to those they are about, even if they are rarely voiced or disseminated to others. Similarly, if a book reviewer writes of a witty book that it is dull, or of a thorough discussion that it is superficial, or of a valid argument that it is invalid, he has not "done justice" to the book or its author. The injustice again is noncomparative. It can be discovered by anyone who reads the book in question, and depends in no way upon the other critical judgments that have been made by this and other critics about other books by this and other authors.

A hard case for the distinction between comparative and noncomparative justice is posed by judgments which are themselves comparative in form. For example, it is unfair to say that "*A* has more merit than *B*" when in fact *B* has more merit than *A*. So far, my definitional criteria are not precise enough to classify this injustice as either comparative or noncomparative. If a comparative injustice is an injustice that can be ascertained as such only after a comparison of *some kind or other* between the person unfairly treated and others, then of course the case at hand is comparative, for to establish the facts which would show the judgment in question to be true or false, *we must compare* the relevant traits of *A* with the relevant traits of *B*. On the other hand, the example differs from all the examples of comparative justice considered so far in a respect which is not without importance. All the other examples of comparative injustice require *comparisons of two kinds* —not only (*i*) comparison of the relevant characteristics, merits, or performances of the individual in question, which are the basis of his claim, with those of the relevant comparison group, but also (*ii*) comparison of consequent "treatments" (for example, prizes, grades, allocative shares, rewards, penalties, and, in this case, *judgments* about) accorded this individual claimant with the "treatments" (in this case, other judgments) made about relevant others. In all the cases of comparative justice considered thus far, a critic can find that justice was done when (as Aristotle might have said) the ratio between compared claims (in this case, merits) equals the ratio between compared treatments (in this case, judgments). But in the example at hand (the judgment "*A* has more merit than *B*") we can know that the judgment is unfair to *B* simply by learning that *it* is false—that is, by ascertaining that the relational fact it asserts does not hold in reality. We do not have to compare this judgment with *other judgments* about these or other persons, as we might in other contexts have to compare a present penalty, or prize, or allocative share with corresponding "treatments" (to use the generic term) of these or other persons. In short, the injustice is not like the comparative injustices already considered because it requires a critic to make only one, not two comparisons—a comparison of the merits of claimants but not a comparison of various treatments of (or judgments about) them.

This difference, I think, is sufficiently significant to warrant the classification of invidiously false comparative judgments as cases of noncomparative injustice. This can be done by simply appending an exceptive clause to our earlier definition, as follows. When the injustice done a person is noncomparative, no comparison of any kind is required to ascertain it *except* when the treatment in question consists of a *judgment* which is itself *comparative in form* so that a comparison of the claims (characteristics or past performances) of the person judged with those of others is required simply to confirm or disconfirm its truth. In contrast, when the treatment that is unjust to John Doe is unjust in the comparative sense, we must make two sorts of comparisons to ascertain it— namely, comparisons of Doe's claims with those of others, and comparison of this treatment of Doe with various treatments of others. When these two investigations uncover an Aristotelian "disproportion" between compared claims and treatments that is disadvantageous to Doe, then the treatment in question was unfair (in the comparative sense) to Doe.

A more thorough discussion of judgmental justice would have to distinguish between (*i*) the justice or injustice of the judgments themselves which, like their truth or falsity, are properties that belong to them quite independently of who comes to believe them (indeed, even if no one comes to believe them); (*ii*) the justice or injustice of the "mental act" of forming a judgment or of simply holding or believing the judgment; and (*iii*) the justice or injustice of expressing a judgment in language, or symbolically in one's conduct. It is admittedly very misleading to assimilate (*i*) or (*ii*) to the justice or injustice of treatments of persons, even when the word "treatment" is self-consciously draped in quotation marks. At best, only (*iii*), the actual communication of a derogatory judgment to an audience, could count as the treatment of a person in the same sense as that in which the awarding of a prize and the inflicting of a punishment clearly are treatments. This qualification, however, does not prevent me from reaching the conclusion that the justice or injustice of comparative judgments in cases (*i*) and (*ii*) as well as (*iii*), is best classified as belonging to the noncomparative category, because if there are no treatments of the usual kind in their case, then it cannot be true that treatments must be compared; and, furthermore, as we have seen, it is not necessary in their case that the judgments in question be compared with other judgments of their kind.

Still another kind of barrier in the way of a cut and dried application of the distinction between comparative and noncomparative justice is that which results from the complexity of our institutionalized practices themselves. The awarding of prizes, for example, often is a process that involves elements of grading and rewarding. Rewards, too, are often similarly complex. In the simpler cases, we reward people with gifts that they will presumably value quite apart from their symbolism as rewards. We do this as a way of expressing our appreciation or admiration for some good deed, but sometimes that deed is the manifesting of merit through winning a contest of skill. In that case, the distinction between reward and prize is blurred. In other cases, prizes have no value to the winners except through their symbolism as prizes. Thus a blue ribbon won at the pie-baking contest at the State Fair is a pure prize, with no element of reward, whereas ten thousand dollars given to the winner of a professional golf tournament is both a prize and a reward. Moreover, prizes are often assigned as a consequence of a process of grading and, like grades, can often be understood as expressions of judgments. Grades, moreover, can be valued by their recipients as much as prizes or rewards, a fact that tends to blur these distinctions further.

Now suppose that Mary wins the first prize (a blue ribbon) and Jane the second prize (a red ribbon) even though Jane's pie in fact was better than Mary's. Since mere ribbons have no value in themselves, there is hardly an element of reward, in any strict sense, in this situation. The awardings of the prizes, however, are expressions of judgments, in this case false comparative judgments, about the relative merits of the two pies. As such, they are unfair to Jane. As a case of judgmental injustice, pure and simple, the unfairness is noncomparative, since only one comparison (that between the two pies) is required to establish it. Still, in classifying the ribbon as a prize, and not *merely* the expression of a comparative judgment, we are ascribing to it a value that the mere public utterance of words would not have. Other ways of expressing judgments are relatively ephemeral; the prize is a judgment in the form of an enduring trophy that can be possessed and exhibited. It is not a reward because its value is not even partially independent of the judgment it symbolizes (as the value of a money prize would be); but, on the other hand, it is more than the judgment it embodies, having the character of a permanent tangible record or proof. Thus, the awarding of a prize *is* a kind of "treatment" of a person, as the mere making of a judgment is not, and in virtue of symbolic conventions, the blue-ribbon award is a better treatment than the red. Thus, injustice in the awarding of prizes can be established (only) by comparison of treatments as well as claim bases, and thereby qualifies as comparative injustice.

Before moving to the topic of *grades* as kinds of judgments, I shall obviate one important misunderstanding of the justice of judgments: noncomparative injustice is not done to a person by the expression of a judgment that treats him *better* than he deserves. The "injustice" done by undeservedly favorable criticism, for example, is injustice of another category: either indirect comparative injustice done to all other authors, invidiously aggravating the hurt done to the poorly reviewed ones and debasing the currency in which praise is given to the favorably reviewed ones, or else noncomparative injustice of a "Platonic" or other "cosmic" kind (of which I shall speak shortly). But such treatment is hardly an injustice to the lucky recipient of the undeserved praise. He has not been wronged; he has no personal grievance, no complaint coming.

Grading, too, can be subsumed under the "justice of judgments" rubric. When the object of a grading system is simply to assess as accurately as possible the degree to which a person has some talent, knowledge, or other estimable quality, then the fairness or unfairness of a given grade assessment is of the noncomparative sort. Indeed, the grade itself can be taken to express a *judgment* (or assessment, or appraisal) of a person, and thus is fair or unfair to him in precisely the same manner as other judgments. When grades come to be used as the basis for subsequent job assignments, opportunities, competitive honors, and other benefits, then an undeservedly low grade can cause a *further* injustice of a comparative kind, or of a different noncomparative kind analogous to the punishing of the innocent, or else, again, the "Platonic" injustice of preventing the square peg from entering the square hole it fits so well.

Sometimes, a grading system is understood to have a different aim. Instead of producing accurate assessments of each individual in a class, it may aim to stimulate a competition among the members of the class for positions of high rank relative to the other members of the class, as, for example, when students are "marked on a curve" so that it is a priori impossible that they all get high grades. The aim of such grading practices is to produce an accurate ranking of persons in respect to their possession of a given trait. The individual "curve grades," like all grades, are the expressions of judgments—in this case comparative judgments—and since the ascertainment of injustices requires only the limited single comparisons necessary for the confirmation or disconfirmation of the expressed assessments, unfair curve grades are unjust in the noncomparative sense. When, however, the avowed purpose of curve grading is to stimulate competition, and the curve restrictions are well known and consented to in advance, the graded performances resemble the elements of a rule-governed game or contest, with the higher grades taken as *prizes*. In that case, the injustices resemble those of the comparative kind since they deprive their victims of something like their "fair share" of a divisible good of limited supply—the highly prized, better grades.[6]

What I have called "Platonic justice" deserves just a word in

---

[6] The curve-grading situation, for similar reasons, has much in common with typical distributive contexts—for example, the dividing up of a pie. To give one person an undeservedly large portion is necessarily to deprive someone else of his proper share, so the just distributor will have to compare the claims of all the pie-eaters, and make the relation between his "treatments" (allocations) mirror the relation between their claims. Curve-grading is often more like prize-awarding than like pie-distributing, however, in that its treatments must mirror claims only in respect to their ranking order; the "size" of the grades cannot be modified to reflect close or wide differences between the strength of claims, whereas in principle one can make a piece of pie have any size at all short of the whole pie. In another respect, however, curve-grading is more like pie-distributing, for everybody gets assigned some "share" or other, whether it be an *A, B, C, D,* or *E.* To preserve a near-perfect analogy with prizes, we should have to interpret *every* grade as either a positive or negative prize, and each grade as a better prize than the one behind it and a worse prize than the one ahead of it in the ranking. At any rate, to the extent that grading is a kind of public exercise, with rule-determined risks and opportunities understood in advance by graders and those they grade alike, the curve-grading context is a comparative one, even though an individual grade as such is essentially an assessment—that is, the expression of a judgment. This is a complicated result, but I think there is no contradiction in it. We can say that in so far as *C*-minus is taken to be a judgment merely, even a comparative judgment, the injustice of its assignment when undeserved is noncomparative, and in so far as the assignment of *C*-minus to one of the better students in the class deprives him of the "prize" or "share" he deserves, and awards it (necessarily) to someone else instead, the injustice is comparative. "Double injustices," as I claim in Section II in the text, are frequent occurrences.

276 ESSAYS IN SOCIAL PHILOSOPHY

this place. (Otherwise I shall not have "done justice" to the subject.) I have no doubt that a conception of justice much like that of Plato and the pre-Socratics survives and lives side by side in our moral consciousness with its more prominent descendants. The Platonic notion, as I shall understand it, is a noncomparative one. When "functions," whether of an internal psychological kind, or a social kind, or a more general natural kind, are not performed by the thing or person best fitted by its (his) own nature to perform them, there is injustice done, at least from the cosmic point of view, whether or not any assignable individual is denied his due. The Greeks thought of all nature (as Plato thought of the state or all society) as a kind of organic system, on the model of a machine, or a living organism, in which the macroscopic functioning of the larger system is causally dependent on the proper discharging of the functions of the component subsystems and, to some extent, vice versa. Thus when a component "organ" or "mechanism" fails to function properly, the larger system of which it is a part is thrown out of kilter. (Combine this conception with the idea, also Greek in origin, that human beings have *moral* functions upon which the normal working of cosmic processes depends, and the Shakespearean notion of a foul murder throwing the universe "out of joint" becomes almost intelligible.) There is no point in trying to make this inherently vague conception more precise. My aim here is simply to point out that there is such a notion and that it is a noncomparative one, the perceived injustice not being suffered by those whose proper role is usurped (*that* injustice is the more common comparative kind) but rather by the badly used "function," and the organic cosmos in which it plays a part. "Cosmic injustice" is conceived as injustice suffered, *inter alia*, by the cosmos itself.[7]

---

[7] A quite different conception of cosmic injustice should be distinguished from the one described above. Cosmic injustice is sometimes conceived as injustice *caused* (as opposed to suffered) by the cosmos. When the best runner in the race fails to win the prize because he pulls up lame or suffers some other bad luck, a kind of injustice is done, but the unlucky runner has no grievance in that case against the judges or against his competitors. *They* have not done him wrong, and in fact his rights have not been infringed by any assignable person. If he nevertheless rails against his undeserved fate, he may conceive of his grievance as holding against the laws of nature, the fates, the gods, or

The noncomparative conception of injustice is sometimes implied, I think, in our talk of *states of affairs* as "not right." It is part of the conventional wisdom in Anglo-American analytic ethics that the distinction between "right" and "good" in ordinary language consists partly in the fact that "right" applies to actions only, whereas "good" is used more generally to appraise not only actions and things but any state of affairs.[8] On the contrary, we do sometimes speak of states of affairs as right or wrong, and when we do, we do not intend to say merely that they are good or bad in different but equivalent language. We say, "It is not right that such and such should be the case," and this is a stronger and sharper complaint than simply stating that it is not a good thing that such and such is the case. Moreover, we sometimes say with confidence that things are not right even when there is no individual we know to be especially wronged, and no other individual to be blamed, and even no actions known by us to have the quality or effect of injustice. "It's just not right and fitting that the President of this great country should be such a little man," we might complain, while ignorant of the identity of some bigger man who was wronged by the voters, or even while unwilling to blame the voters for their choice. When we determine that a state of affairs as such is not right, or that the universe of which it is a part is "out of joint" in something like the Platonic fashion, without reference to the claims of wronged parties, our judgment is noncomparative.

II

Applying the distinction between comparative and noncomparative justice to the real world is not easily done. The distinction

---

whatever. The conception of "cosmic injustice" which this suggests, unlike the one described in the text, is a comparative one: the winner's ability does not stand in the same "ratio" to the unlucky loser's ability as the winner's "treatment" (awarding him first prize) stands to the unlucky loser's treatment (awarding him a lesser prize or no prize at all).

[8] See, *inter alia*, W. D. Ross, *The Right and the Good* (Oxford, 1931), pp. 2-3, and Michael Stocker, "Rightness and Goodness: Is There a Difference?," *American Philosophical Quarterly*, 10 (1973), 93 *et passim*.

between concepts may be clear enough, but instances of each are rarely pure, any given example of one being likely also to have elements of the other. This contributes not only to conceptual confusion but also to moral perplexity. On many occasions for justice, both comparative and noncomparative principles apply. Comparative principles all share the form of the Aristotelian paradigm: justice requires that relevantly similar cases be treated similarly and relevantly dissimilar cases be treated dissimilarly in direct proportion to the relevant differences between them. Noncomparative principles, on the other hand, are irreducibly diverse in form as well as number. Some condemn punishment of the innocent or those who acted involuntarily; some require that reasonable expectations not be disappointed; others proscribe false derogatory judgments. When principles of both kinds apply to a particular case, often enough the duplication is benign, and what is just according to one principle is also the treatment prescribed by the other. On other occasions, the relevant comparative and noncomparative principles cut in opposite ways to the stupefaction of "the sense of justice."

To treat another person in contravention of both comparative and noncomparative principles when those principles coincide and reinforce one another is to inflict a kind of "double injustice" upon him. This is a point well appreciated by A. D. Woozley, who writes that "A man's getting less than he deserved for what he did [as remuneration for his labor] is doubly unjust if somebody else got more than he, but it would still be unjust if nobody else got more, even if nobody else was involved at all."[9] The underpayment of a worker, suggested by Woozley's example, does seem to be a double injustice to him, but it is not a clear example of the duplication of comparative and noncomparative principles. The principles of "commutative justice" which determine what is a "fair wage" might themselves be comparative principles, in which case Woozley's worker is treated unfairly on two grounds: he is paid less than his relevantly similar fellow worker at the same job, and he is paid less than a national "standard worker" at his trade, and therefore "less than he deserved." In that case, he is seen to

---

[9] A. D. Woozley, "Injustice," *American Philosophical Quarterly Monograph*, 7 (1973), 115-116.

be discriminated against when *compared* with a fellow worker in his own plant and also when *compared* with workers in relevantly similar jobs throughout the country, but no noncomparative principles seem to apply to his case at all. Perhaps, however, the commutative principles that determine a fair wage for a given job, like their counterparts in the area of retributive justice that determine a fair punishment for a given crime, are in part non-comparative. If beheading and disembowelment became the standard punishment for overtime parking, as the result of duly enacted statutes, the penalty as applied in a given case would be unjust (because too severe) even though it were applied uniformly and without discrimination to all offenders. Moreover, it would be unjust even if it were the mildest penalty in the whole system of criminal law, with more serious offenses punished with propor-tionately greater severity still (torture, punishment of the offender's family, and so forth). In short, it is possible for *every* punishment in a system of criminal law to be unjust because too severe, which shows that criminal desert is in part noncomparative. If the analogy between commutative and retributive justice holds in this respect, then it should be similarly conceivable that *all* of the wages in a hypothetical economy are too low, so that any given worker is getting less than he deserves, not as determined by a comparison between his wages and those of other workers, but rather as determined by the merits of his own case. The analogy seems to fail, however, in one respect. The underpaid workers are surely treated unfairly as *compared* to their employers whose *share* of the wealth produced must be disproportionately great if theirs is disproportionately small. (This is the respect in which all *exploi-tation* is a comparative injustice.)

There can nevertheless be an element of noncomparative in-justice in Woozley's example. Suppose, for example, that the case is one of racial bias, and the underpaid worker is discriminated against because he is black, though he is told (what is not true) that he is paid less because his work is inferior. On the one hand, this is unfair discrimination against one worker (or class of workers) among many, and thus is condemned by comparative principles. On the other hand, in so far as it is given the specious justification that it is based on assessments of ability, it can be taken to be an expression of nonrecognition of ability, a *judgment* that is unfair to the excluded worker who in fact has high ability, in which case, like all judgmental injustices, it is noncomparative.

When relevantly applicable comparative and noncomparative principles yield opposite judgments, there are, of course, two possibilities: what is condoned by the comparative principle is condemned by the noncomparative one, or what is endorsed by the noncomparative principle is declared unjust by the comparative one. Pure examples of the former kind are not easy to come by. The example of a slave society in which masters uniformly and impartially deprive their subjects of their due (as determined by the merits of their own cases) comes close, but even there the disparity between the resultant conditions of the privileged and deprived would be unjust on comparative grounds. A purer example is that suggested above of a system of criminal law, effectively and impartially administered, in which all penalties are disproportionate to actual culpability, for in that case (unlike the example of slavery) the judges, jurors, and jailers would not directly profit from the unjust treatments imposed on criminals; hence punishments would be unjust on noncomparative grounds, but not on comparative ones (at any rate, not if the punished offenders are compared only with each other). Even that example, however, is not perfectly pure, since comparisons of the excessive punishments of criminals may also be made to the nonpunishments of various noncriminals.

That the existence of comparative injustice is relative to the comparison class examined is a point whose importance is vividly shown by the perplexing case of a hypothetical system of criminal law in which people are punished even for involuntary infractions of rules. Imagine a system in which penalties are all exactly proportionate to moral guilt (whatever that might mean) or, in the case of "involuntary crimes," proportionate to the guilt that would have been involved had the infraction been voluntary. The courts in this imaginary system, with consistent impartiality, hold infants and insane people liable for crimes, and punish others for unavoidable accidents and innocent mistakes. These practices are, of course, grossly unfair to those who are punished, and the unfairness seems at least noncomparative. It might seem at first, however, that no element of comparative injustice need be involved at all, for none of these unfortunates would be in a position to complain of discrimination, prejudice, or favoritism in the enforcement of the law. Similar cases (involuntary wrongdoing) are rigorously treated, so it would seem, in similar ways (punished) so that the Aristotelian formula is satisfied. A quite different judgment results, however, when the comparison is made between different comparison classes. When all involuntary criminals are compared with each other in all relevant respects (their infraction of rules) and all voluntary noncriminals are compared with each other in all relevant respects (their compliance with rules), no invidious treatments can be discerned. But when all involuntary criminals are compared with all voluntary criminals of the same category, the result is quite different, for we soon discover that involuntary criminals are treated the same as voluntary ones even though they are *different in a morally relevant respect*—namely, that one group acted voluntarily and the other involuntarily. But why is voluntariness morally relevant? Simply because it is unfair to a person, any person, on noncomparative grounds, to punish him for his involuntary behavior. So this intriguing example illustrates another point of importance, that comparative and noncomparative principles can dovetail in such a way that they are conceptually linked. In the case at hand, a noncomparative principle of justice determines the criterion of relevance for the application of the otherwise formal principle of comparative justice for certain contexts.

The more common examples of genuine conflict are provided by instances of treatment condoned by noncomparative principles but condemned as unjust by comparative ones. Consider something like the Augustinian theory of salvation. No man considered entirely on his own merits, prior to or independently of Divine Grace, deserves to be saved, since all men by their very natures are totally depraved. In each case, then, noncomparative justice would be served by damnation and consignment to hell-fire. Nevertheless, God, out of His infinite mercy, exercises something like executive clemency, and allows His grace to touch the souls of an arbitrarily selected minority of men, permitting them to achieve their own (undeserved)[10] salvations. The others then *are* consigned to hell, but noncomparative principles, at least, allow them no just complaint, since they are sinners simply getting what they deserve according to the canons of retributive justice. Yet if they think about their equally sinful but luckier comrades, they are likely to feel at least somewhat aggrieved at what they can only take to be unjust discrimination in plain contravention of comparative principles.

The more we ponder cases of the above kind, the more confused we become; for justice and injustice seem alternately to flit in and out of focus like the pictures in an optical illusion, depending upon whether we consider comparative or noncomparative factors. And such cases are not confined to theological speculation. They arise whenever an authority makes an "example" or an "exception" of one or more out of a class of subjects whose individual deserts are alike. When all the students in a class or all the soldiers in a barracks are equally guilty and only one is punished (as a threat to the others) or only one is left unpunished (out of favoritism) then the punished ones have no grievance on noncomparative grounds, since they are guilty after all, but they can complain against discriminatory treatment.[11]

Cases of this general kind also include instances of gratuitous benefaction. No person has a right to another person's charity, and yet if a charitable benefactor distributes his largesse to nine persons in a group of ten, arbitrarily withholding it from the tenth for no good reason, his behavior seems in some important way unfair to the tenth. Still, the benefactor might reply to the charge of arbitrary exclusion with the reminder that, morally speaking, he did not *have to* contribute to any of the group, and that his aid to nine was a net gain above and beyond the call of duty. The

---

[10] One might choose to say "otherwise undeserved salvations" here to suggest that God confers on the elect not only their salvation, but also their desert of salvation. But this, I think, would render the concept of desert incoherent. Even though omnipotent, God can no more make the undeserving deserving *by fiat* than He can make $2 + 2 = 5$.

[11] Cf. A. M. Honoré: "If a rule forbids parking in a certain area, it is unfair to A who has parked in that area that he should be fined for doing so, whilst B, who has done the same thing is not punished" ("Social Justice," *McGill Law Journal*, 8 [1962], 67).

poor excluded beggar, his sense of justice confused, will feel aggrieved and unaggrieved in rapid alternation. There is no right to charity, or grace, or clemency, or any other form of gratuitous good treatment, and yet arbitrary inconsistency or favoritism in the distribution of these goods can seem unjust to those neglected or deprived of them.

A similar example of conflict between comparative and non-comparative principles is found in the case of the distribution of a *surplus* among a group of recipients after justice has already been done to each proper individual claim. According to Woozley: "If a father in the bequests which he makes to his sons *A* and *B* has fairly met their needs, he does no injustice to *B* if he leaves the whole of the rest of the estate to *A*—unless there is some further respect, other than need, in which the distinction between like cases is unjust."[12] Let us suppose, filling in Woozley's example, that *A* and *B* are roughly of the same age, size, health, appearance, abilities, beliefs, and ideals, that each has the same basic financial needs and that the bequests more than fulfill them in each case, but that the father leaves everything else after those basic needs have been met—say, one million unsuspected dollars—to *A*, simply because he likes *A* better (there being no other reason available).[13] We can suppose further that the existence of the "extra" one million dollars was totally unknown to the sons, so that neither of them had expectation or hope of inheriting any part of it. After individual claims based on needs, deserts, and "reasonable expectations" have been satisfied, injustice, by non-comparative standards at any rate, cannot be done. Yet comparative considerations might still properly agitate the sense of injustice (*pace* Woozley) of the "deprived" son.

The oppositions between comparative and noncomparative principles illustrated by these examples are not radical conflicts originating in the concept of justice itself of the kind that would render the very coherence of that concept suspect. I have given no examples where it is conceptually impossible to have justice

---

[12] Woozley, *op. cit.*, pp. 112-113.

[13] The import of the example would be changed, I think, if the father, preferring to have the whole (remaining) fortune in one set of hands than divided (and this for non-arbitrary reasons), selects *A* by flipping a coin.

both ways, cases in which satisfaction of a noncomparative principle requires violation of a comparative one, or vice versa.[14] All that the examples show is that it is sometimes possible to satisfy a principle of the one kind while violating a principle of the other kind. Such occasional and contingent opposition is one of the weaker senses in which principles can be said to conflict. In these cases of conflict, something less than perfect justice has been achieved, but that does not show that perfect justice is an impossible ideal. It is especially awkward sometimes to satisfy comparative principles, and we are tempted to take short cuts, for example, by punishing only some but not all members of a very large class of rule violators. In that event, we may choose for good reasons to compromise comparative justice for the sake of efficiency and convenience, and when we have already given noncomparative justice its due (that is, we have punished *only* the guilty) we might take our short cut with a relatively easy conscience. Still, we can easily *conceive* of what it would be like in cases of this kind to satisfy both comparative and noncomparative justice, so that the "conflict" between the two is by no means logically unavoidable. Since both noncomparative and comparative justice make valid claims on us, and since it is in principle possible for both to be satisfied, we must conclude that *in so far as a given act or arrangement fails to satisfy one or the other of the two kinds of principles, it is not as just as it could be.*

---

[14] There are easily imagined circumstances, on the other hand, in which it is *practically* impossible to do both comparative and noncomparative justice. E.g., suppose I owe A, B, C, and D each $100, but I have only $100 all together. If I pay $25 to each, there will be no comparative injustice (discrimination), but a "commutative injustice" will be done to each. But if I pay $100 to A and nothing to the others, then both comparative and noncomparative injustice is done to the others, but no injustice by any standard to A. Whatever I do, in this example, will have the effect of injustice *somewhere*.

It should be noted that I am concerned throughout this essay with the "effect" and not the "quality" of injustice. The distinction is Aristotle's. See the *Nicomachean Ethics*, V. For a convincing argument that justice in effect (justice *to* someone or other) is a more basic notion than justice as a quality of actions reflecting the virtue of the agent, see Josef Pieper, *Justice* (London, 1957). Pieper there paraphrases Aquinas: "in the realm of justice, good and evil are judged purely on the basis of the deed itself, regardless of the inner disposition of the doer; the point is not how the deed accords with the doer, but rather, how it affects 'the other person' " (pp. 36-37).

Another message to be inferred, I think, from our examples is that injustice by noncomparative standards tends to be a much more serious thing than comparative injustice. The right to be given one's due, where one's due is not merely an allotment or a share, but rather is determined (say) by prior agreements or by personal desert, is a more important right than the right not to be discriminated against. If a tyrant treats all his underlings "like dogs," then the injustice done underling John Doe is far more serious than he would suffer if he were given his due but everyone else were treated "like kings." Similarly, to be punished for a crime one did not commit is a greater outrage than to be punished for a crime one did commit while others who are equally guilty are let go. (The Dreyfus case was a greater injustice by far than the Calley case.)

Indeed, the superiority of the claims of noncomparative to comparative justice in some cases is so striking that one might well raise the question whether comparative justice, in those cases, makes any claims at all. Suppose an employer pays all his employees more than the prevailing scale in his industry, indeed more than any of them deserves by any reasonable noncomparative standard, but he pays Doe, a worker of only average skills and seniority, more than he pays Roe, a worker with superior skills and high seniority. If there is any injustice at all in this situation, it must consist entirely in the discriminatory character of the treatment. But where is the wrong in discrimination as such? In this example, no man is treated badly; in fact, each is getting more than his due. How then can Roe have *any* complaint? Why not describe the situation as one in which Roe is treated fairly but Doe gets *more* than his due? But to give a man more than his due is not to wrong him, and if no one is wronged, how can there be injustice? Much the same questions can be raised about the other examples considered above where noncomparative justice is satisfied and only discrimination remains to offend the sense of justice: punishment of the guilty when others equally guilty are let go, arbitrary exceptions to gratuitous benefactions, assignments of surplus goods after individual claims have been satisfied.[15]

---

[15] Still another example is that suggested by the biblical parable of the laborers in the vineyard, Ch. XX of the Gospel According to St. Matthew.

Still, there is no doubt that arbitrary discrimination as such, even in the absence of any other violated claims, strikes most of us as wrong, and not merely wrong, but unfair. The explanation of this near-universal reaction involves two elements. In the first place, as a matter of psychological fact, people are *hurt* by discriminatory treatment whether or not they are wronged according to some additional standard, and secondly, the hurt is perceived to be in some important way *"offensive to reason"*—absurd, arbitrary, disproportionate, or inconsistent. These two elements, I suspect, are sufficient to account for our use of the vocabulary of "unfairness," and the spontaneous offense to our sense of justice, in cases of the kind under consideration. That it hurts to be singled out or pointedly excluded by discriminatory treatment is a plain fact which itself calls for a full psychological explanation, but a plain fact still, however it is to be accounted for. The sting of discrimination is most painful in cases of double injustice where it adds salt to other moral wounds. When one is a member of an enslaved minority, for example, it is the enslavement that does one the greatest wrong, but the perceived contrast between one's own condition and that of others not enslaved, let us suppose only because of their race, while adding nothing to the primary wrong, tends to exacerbate its immediate effect. When nearly everyone is enslaved, and cruel rules are enforced equally across the board, then the element of having been selected out for special treatment is missing. That condition is no less unjust, but it will in most cases be less constantly before the mind, less pointed in its application, and less intensely resented. So powerful is the psychological tendency to resent discriminatory treatment that it manifests itself even in cases where the discrimination is the whole of the wrong suffered and is disadvantageous only in a relative way.

The more important part of the explanation why discrimination as such is unjust, however, consists in its absolute groundlessness,[16]

---

[16] There are contexts, of course, in which comparative justice is not only compatible with arbitrariness but actually requires it. Sometimes distributive justice calls for purely arbitrary—that is, random—procedures for allocating indivisible goods or burdens. (See David Lyons, *The Forms and Limits of Utilitarianism* [Oxford, 1965], pp. 161-177.) In these cases, however, there is an intelligible rationale for the procedure, whereas in the case of unjust discrimi-

or grounding on morally irrelevant criteria, and the characteristic sort of offensiveness these features engender, for the general characteristic this form of injustice shares with all the others is that, quite apart from any other harm, or hurt, or wrong it might bring to the one who suffers it, it offends against impersonal reason itself. As many writers have pointed out,[17] the principle that relevantly similar cases should be treated in similar ways, put in just that general way, is a principle of reason, in much the same way as Aristotle's principles of identity, contradiction, and excluded middle are "laws of thought." It is *absurd* to treat relevantly similar cases in dissimilar ways, to ascribe different geometrical properties to identical isosceles triangles, or to assign unequal wages to relevantly equal workers.[18] Individual triangles, however, have no feelings and no interests; they do not recognize pointedly selective treatment, or partiality, or exclusion; they cannot be hurt, or harmed, or treated in relatively disadvantageous ways. For those reasons discrimination among triangles is *merely* absurd, whereas discrimination that affects the balance of advantages among beings with interests and feelings is unfair.

The moral offensiveness of discrimination is *sui generis*. In particular, it is not wholly derived from consideration of the motives of the wrongdoer, though such consideration is capable of intensifying the irritation it produces. Often discriminatory treatment strikes its victim as having something "personal" in it, an element of malice, or unprovoked insult. In other cases, like exemplary punishment, the victim may feel badly used, a mere instrument for another's purposes. But when the personal and exploitative elements are clearly missing—as, for example, when one is deprived of a shared benefit not for a morally shady motive, but for no apparent motive at all—then invidious treatment can be even more maddening.

---

nation, there is either an irrelevant criterion employed, or else there is no "procedure" and no "rationale," but only arbitrariness through and through.

[17] E.g., Isaiah Berlin, "Equality as an Ideal," *Proceedings of the Aristotelian Society*, vol. LVI (1955-1956).

[18] It is, of course, even more absurd to assign unequal wages to relevantly unequal workers in *inverse* proportion to their relevant differences—that is, to pay more to the less deserving and less to the more deserving.

III

It is natural enough to respond to hurt with anger, but when the hurt seems to have been arbitrarily inflicted in the manner characteristic of unjust discrimination, anger is transmuted into moral indignation. Because the treatment is offensive to reason as well as hurtful, responsive anger borrows some of the authority of reason; it becomes righteous and impersonal, free of self-doubt, and yet disinterested and free of mere self-preference. This moralized anger is by no means peculiar to discrimination among the various modes of injustice. It is, in fact, the common element in reactions to all injustices, whether comparative or noncomparative, whether actions, rules, or judgments. Perhaps more than anything else, it distinguishes the apprehension of injustice from awareness of other kinds of wrong or harmful conduct. John Stuart Mill was perhaps the first important writer to make much of this distinctive emotion.[19] No analysis of the concept of justice is complete, he claimed, without a supplementary analysis of what he called the "sentiment of justice." Mill's own analysis, however, failed to account for the element of righteousness I have noted. He analyzed the sentiment of justice (more accurately, the sentiment of injustice) into an impulse to retaliate for injury, which he took to be a kind of animal instinct, plus a distinctively human feeling of sympathy that enables us to identify imaginatively with other victims of wrongdoing and respond angrily on their behalf as we would to our own injuries. Perhaps such elements *are* commonly part of the sentiment of injustice, but they would also be present, I should think, when we apprehend wrongdoing of other kinds, or even when we perceive harm caused to persons in an innocent or accidental way. Those elements peculiar to the sentiment of injustice that endow it with its uniquely righteous flavor have not been mentioned in Mill's account.

The sources of the sentiment of injustice are readily found in the experiences of childhood. Moral indignation in small children (in their own behalf, of course) is largely restricted, I think, to three kinds of contexts. In the first, outraged protest is directed

---

[19] J. S. Mill, *Utilitarianism*, Ch. V, pars. 16-24.

at what is taken to be *favoritism*. Its characteristic formulae are: "He got more than I did," or "You punished me but not him, and he did it too," or "Why does he have a privilege or benefit and not me?" Impelled originally by jealousy, children learn both to accuse others of special treatment, and to defend themselves from such charges, to find analogies and disanalogies between cases, to invoke precedents and appeal to consistency. In these exercises are found the roots of the sense of comparative justice. Personal anger directed at favoritism comes to be anger felt on behalf of, or from the perspective of, impartiality. When the feeling occasioned by hurt expands its target to include inconsistency, disproportion, anomaly, and other elements similarly offensive to reason, it becomes full-blown moral indignation, and not mere animal anger sympathetically projected.

A second source of the sentiment of injustice does not appear until the stage of peer-group orientation and co-operative play, starting at about age six.[20] A new object of juvenile wrath at that stage is *exploitation*—taking unfair advantage of another's handicaps or placing another at a disadvantage in competitive or co-operative undertakings. In competitive games, one player can secure unfair advantage over another either by exploiting natural inequalities inconsistent with the game's purpose—for example, larger size or greater age—or else by creating inequalities through cheating, bribing, or lying. In co-operative undertakings one can exploit a partner's trust by free-loading, betraying him for personal gain, or otherwise letting him down. Before the age of five or six, the child has no firm concept of a regulated competition for fun or gain in which "players" trust each other to obey the rules that are meant to nullify inappropriate influences on the outcome; nor does he have a firm concept of a joint undertaking by co-operative partners each of whom trusts all the others to do their share of the work that is necessary to their common gain. Once the child becomes preoccupied, however, with games of skill and chance, with team sports and "team spirit," and with group chores and quotas assigned by parents or teachers, the

---

[20] See Jean Piaget, *The Moral Judgment of the Child*, trans. by Marjorie Gabain (London, 1932).

streets echo with charges and rebuttals of unfairness not previously heard in the nursery.

Few six-year-olds have sufficient skill at abstract thinking to arrive at the philosophical views that will one day tempt most of them as adults: that all life is a competitive game or, alternatively, that all society is one large co-operative undertaking in which each and every partner has his assigned dues and his proper shares. The latter view is that of G. H. von Wright, who points to a respect in which *all* social wrongdoing is unjust in the manner of exploitation.[21] In von Wright's usage, escaping harm from others is the "share" which each member of a moral community has in the common good, whereas not harming others is the "price" one pays, or each member's "due share" of the price, for that good. Any time one member harms another, then, he tries to have his cake and eat it too—that is, to "have his share without paying his due," and this way of taking advantage of others, which is morally akin to cheating and free-loading, von Wright calls "the basic form of injustice."[22]

An interesting feature of von Wright's analysis in his suggestion of how exploitative injustice, too, contains an element that is offensive to reason:

One can ask questions like this: "What right have you got to put yourself in a privileged position? If you get your share without paying your due, then somebody else, who is equally anxious to get his share, will necessarily be without it. Don't you see that this is unfair?" One could almost call this appeal to a man's sense of justice an appeal to a man's sense of symmetry.[23]

The "asymmetry" referred to by von Wright is common to exploitation, distributive injustice, and discrimination. All create inequalities between relevantly equal cases, and all are offensive to reason in similar ways. Exploitation leads necessarily to unequal results that are in a way doubly unjust: the exploiter gets more

---

[21] G. H. von Wright, *The Varieties of Goodness* (London, 1963), Ch. X. Cf. also Herbert Morris, "Persons and Punishment," *The Monist*, vol. 52 (October, 1968).

[22] *Ibid.*, p. 208.

[23] *Ibid.*, p. 210.

than he deserves and his victim less. Like children on a seesaw, the one goes up by the same increment as the other goes down. The imbalance produced by exploitation rests on no correlated differences in which disinterested reason can find satisfaction. There are no relevant differences between the occupants of the up and down positions that underlie and justify the outcome. The crucial difference between them was a morally "irrelevant" one —worse, a morally inappropriate one; the gainer cheated or lied and the other did not.

Von Wright's bold claim that all social wrongdoing is essentially exploitative is an overstated insight. In the paradigm case of egregious exploitation that is apparently before his mind, *A* secures a gain for himself at the cost of a loss to *B*, and he does this by betraying *B*'s trust. This model fits far more cases than one might realize before reflecting, but it surely does not fit *all* cases of social wrongdoing. Some wrongs (for example, tax evasion) lack a determinate victim, or produce a trivial harm to "society" while producing a great gain to the wrongdoer. In other cases, *A* wrongfully harms *B* without any hope of gain for himself. In typical debauched or psychopathic crimes, nobody gains anything, and in cases of self-destructive malice, both parties lose. In still other cases, there need have been no prior trust relation between an aggressor and his victim. *A* and *B* may have been enemies constantly on the alert for the other's mischief. When their animosity erupts into combat one or the other of them is wrongfully injured. It is implausible to think of all these examples as instances of exploitation. Von Wright would probably insist, however, that in a great many cases of social wrongdoing that do not at first sight seem to involve duplicity, cheating, or free-loading, there is nevertheless an element, however attenuated, of exploitative injustice. Since the concept of injustice is somewhat diluted in this very general application, perhaps it would be wise to refer to "injustice in the weak sense." Then we can still ask how we can make out a contrast between those "unjust acts" which are also unjust in a specific stronger way and those which are not. My answer to that question is that the pointedly unjust acts (in the strong sense) are either those which are directly and obviously exploitative (for example, those involving cheating) or those which are invidiously discriminatory, or those expressive of derogatory falsehood. The "sentiment of injustice" in these cases is directed at the element of "asymmetry," "inconsistency," or "falsehood," all of which are, in a manner insufficiently appreciated by Mill, "offensive to reason."

IV

In a third kind of context for juvenile indignation, moral outrage stems neither from the awareness of exploitative "asymmetry" nor from the awareness of disadvantageous discrimination between like cases, for only one "case"—the child's own—may be involved. Rather the child reacts furiously to what he confidently believes to be a false judgment that is injurious to his esteem, or degrading to his status, or which simply misrepresents him in some respect that is important to him. Consider a typical example. An older child answers a parental question correctly. A younger sibling remarks that he too knew the answer, but that he did not have a chance to speak up in time. To this, the older child replies that the younger child did not know the answer and was silent only because of his ignorance. What a torrent of rage and frustration this will produce in the younger child if he *knows* that he knew the answer! In that case he has direct possession of the truth and cannot prove it to anyone. His rage, however, will not be merely an expression of his frustrated hope of presenting evidence. Nor will it be merely his reaction to the sting of an insult, for the imputation of specific ignorance in this context may not be very insulting, and much greater defamations (in the child's eyes) will not evoke the same response if they happen to be true. "You wet your bed last night," said accusingly by the older child, will, if true, evoke shame and humiliation. If false, it will produce the righteous anger characteristic of the outraged sense of (noncomparative) justice. What provides the special flavor in the child's response to the false allegation is the sense that not only he but *the truth itself* has been injured. His anger is righteous because it is not only in his own behalf; it is also and primarily in the name of the truth, or on behalf of *the way things really are*.

There is no doubt that an interest in the truth as such retains its central place in the moral outlook of adults. However we may disagree about other duties, all of us, upon reflection, will acknowledge a kind of transcendent and impersonal duty to the truth, and will also claim a kind of corresponding right to be truly ("fairly" here is a synonym of "truly") judged in matters that are relevant to our esteem. We do not insist with equal vehemence upon a right to be truly described in respects that are indifferent to esteem or to interest—for example, in respect to the color of our eyes or the shape of our fingerprints. If you describe my brown eyes as blue you will have said something false about me but not unfair to me.

The virtue of people who honor their duties of judgmental justice and respect the rights of others to be fairly appraised is called "fair-mindedness." Whatever job our voiced and written judgments may do, whatever changes they may effect in the world, they also form part of the human record, and all persons, or at least all fair-minded persons, have a double stake in that record. Everyone will wish to make his own record as good as possible, but all fair-minded persons will also wish the record itself to be accurate and untarnished, partly as a matter of common interest, but also, as we say, as *a matter of justice*, and justice in a quite basic and underivative sense. Nothing makes the head spin more than the death and burial of a known truth. Those who have read the passages about rewriting history in Orwell's *1984* will understand the "dizziness" which another writer, Albert Camus, cites as his response to "the absolute murder of a truth."[24] Our concern for the truth is also at the root of that feeling which is sometimes called "guilt" and is prominent in the consciousness of fair-minded people who sense that their own position in life implies a judgment of their merits that is too favorable, that they are therefore posing as something that they are not in fact. The moral principle behind these phenomena is that every person has a right to be treated and judged as the kind of being he is, and since this principle derives its persuasiveness and its impersonal authority from the alliance between interest and the objective truth, it also imposes a duty to

---

[24] Albert Camus, *The Fall*, trans. by Justine O'Brien (New York, 1956), p. 90.

accept no more favorable judgments from others than those that are in truth warranted. The alliance between personal interest and the truth may not always be present, and even where it exists, it may be short-lived, but the truth itself is timeless, and it is the truth's prestige that supports judgmental justice even when all connection with personal interests is severed. James Flexner writes that it is "unfair" to call George Washington a racist, given that he ardently and conscientiously opposed the institution of slavery.[25] Notice how the biographer naturally thinks of doing justice to his subject well after the subject, having long been dead, has any personal stake in the record.

Judgmental injustice is very commonly found to be an element of a complex injustice that includes as another element unde-servedly injurious treatment. Sometimes rather subtle analysis is required to separate out injustice to the truth (and to the victim's "double interest" in the truth) from undeserved damage to other interests of the victim. Suppose, for example, that the rules of my club "allow expulsion for cheating and I am expelled [for cheat-ing] without having cheated."[26] Note the two distinct ways in which the expulsion is unjust to me in these circumstances. On the one hand, it is an unwarranted deprivation of benefits, a hurt inflicted upon me that I have not deserved (though, of course, that deprivation, in itself, may not hurt very much if I do not particularly care for the club anyway); on the other hand the expulsion upholds, endorses, and affirms an unfair judgment—namely, the false charge that I have cheated. That affirmation would be unjust in itself even without the infliction of any further penalty.

Similarly, one player's cheating in a game may put his rival at an unfair competitive disadvantage, and that, of course, is a kind of injury to the rival's interests which may cause hurt and resent-ment, but the sense of injustice will be greatly magnified by the official judgment of the referee, or even the critical judgments of spectators and journalists, that there was no cheating in the first place. That judgment offends not only the player's interest in

---

[25] James Flexner, "Washington and Slavery," *New York Times*, Feb. 22, 1973, p. 39.
[26] The example is from Brian Barry, *Political Argument* (London, 1965), p. 99.

winning his match, but also it offends against the facts and involves the impersonal authority of truth as a reinforcement to the sense of merely private injury. This sort of phenomenon, which must surely provide for the philosopher one of his basic paradigms of injustice, finds a hundred illustrations in the official verdicts and decrees of courts and public tribunals. The Kent State murders, for example, angered and saddened most of us; yet the words "cruel" and "wanton" seem to describe those terrible events more naturally than the words "unjust" or "unfair" do. There was a different quality of responsive feeling, however, to the outrageous Ohio grand jury verdicts from that of the response to the actual primary happenings. Those official judgments added a new dimension of unfairness to the events they misrepresented, and thus rasped and rankled the sense of injustice as only the awareness of violated truth can.

V

Our legal system protects persons from the harm caused by certain kinds of false judgments by permitting them to sue their defamers for damages. But defamation (the generic legal term for libel and slander), while often involving judgmental injustice, is not simply to be identified with that moral category. It is useful to chart the differences between the two if only for the sake of getting clearer about what judgmental injustice is. Moreover, as so often happens when moral notions are compared with conceptual models drawn from the law,[27] we shall find that very precise questions can be raised within the framework of the law of defamation whose counterparts in the "natural" context of judgmental justice have no clear and easy answer. Some of these questions cannot simply be dismissed. In the interest of ultimate coherence, either precise answers should be stipulated for them through a reasoned process of "moral legislation," or else reasoned explanations should be given why such questions fail to make sense outside a narrow institutional setting.

Although defamation and judgmental injustice differ in crucial respects, there are several elements common to both. In the first

---

[27] See my *Doing and Deserving* (Princeton, 1970), Chs. 2-4.

place, both are propositional. Both essentially involve statements
or judgments about persons of a kind that could be either true or
false, but are in fact false. Prosser is especially emphatic in
restricting the scope of defamation to exclude insults:

The courts . . . have held that mere words of abuse, indicating that the
defendant dislikes the plaintiff and has a low opinion of him, but
without suggesting any specific charge against him, are not to be
treated as defamatory. A certain amount of vulgar name-calling is
tolerated on the theory that it will necessarily be understood to amount
to nothing more.[28]

Thus one can defame a man by calling him a drunkard, a wife-
beater, or a tax-evader, but not by calling him a rat, or a son of a
bitch. There may be elements of exploitative, distributive, or even
retributive injustice when a victim is made to suffer wrath or
humiliation by an unwarranted insult, but judgmental injustice
requires some judgment of fact, as opposed to the mere hurling
of epithets.

A second element, common to defamation and judgmental
injustice, is the derogatory character of the propositions
affirmed by each. The propositions involved are imputations of
fault, demerit, and responsibility for wrongdoing, of characteristics or actions that are somehow substandard. It is not defamatory
to print in a newspaper that a man is dead,[29] although it might
well seem to a living man that a widespread premature belief in
his death ill serves his interests. That belief, however, makes no
one think any the worse of him; a man's reputation will easily
survive him, if the report of his death carries no further information to his discredit. Similarly, the premature report of a person's
death may harm him (in some interest other than his interest in a
good reputation), but as a proposition simply, it can hardly be
unfair to him.

Defamation and judgmental injustice are also similar in that
they are primarily unjust to the persons they are about,

---

[28] William L. Prosser, *Handbook of the Law of Torts*, 2nd ed. (St. Paul, 1955),
p. 576.
[29] *Ibid.*, p. 574. See *Cohen* v. *New York Times Co.*, 1912, 153 App. Div. 242,
138 N.Y.S. 206, and *Lemmer* v. *The Tribune*, 1915, 50 Mont. 559, 148 P. 338.

not to listeners or readers who are led to have false opinions. The essence of judgmental injustice is not deception, not being lied to. Indeed, one can express an unfair judgment in all good faith with no intent to deceive. Unjust judgments are like some other unjust actions in this respect. The justice or injustice of their effect on others can be determined independently of the motive or intention with which they are made.[30] Of course, where one does deceive by lying, this may be a kind of exploitation of the listener and therefore unfair, on other grounds, to him, too.

The first of the distinguishing differences between defamation and judgmental injustice is that defamation requires communication. Indeed, defamation is a relation among at least three parties. It consists of a judgment made by one person about another person and communicated to at least one other person. A judgment, however, need not even be spoken or written to be unjust simply as a judgment. If someone comes to believe an unjust judgment, then he has an unjust belief, however blamelessly he comes to adopt it, however well supported it is by the evidence, however faithfully he keeps it entirely to himself. If John Doe has a belief that is unfair to Richard Roe and he voices it directly to Roe, then he expresses an unfair judgment, but he does not defame Roe, because he has not expressed that judgment to any third parties. Similarly, Doe may hold a belief that is unfair to himself, but even though he gives impulsive statement to that belief as he stares moodily at his image in the shaving mirror, he does not—indeed he cannot—defame himself.

A second difference has to do with the source of the injustice in the two cases. Although defamation usually (but not necessarily) commits judgmental injustice, the source of the legal wrong is not simply the unfairness of the communication but the harm it tends to cause. The harm in question must be suffered directly by the victim's reputation,[31] but a reputation itself may be valued for its

---

[30] Cf. Pieper, *op. cit.*, pp. 35-40.

[31] Prosser defines defamation as "an invasion of the interest in reputation and good name by communication to others which tends to diminish the esteem [elsewhere he writes 'respect,' 'good will,' or 'confidence'] in which the plaintiff is held, or to excite adverse feelings or opinions against him" (*op. cit.*, p. 572).

298   ESSAYS IN SOCIAL PHILOSOPHY

own sake or for the sake of some ulterior interest, social, professional, or pecuniary, and sometimes the law requires proof of
damage to one of these ulterior interests, too, before allowing
recovery. Harms to reputation and dependent interests may vary
in a large number of respects so that legal policies need to be
formulated for grading the relative seriousness of different dimensions. So, for example, a defamatory utterance may make a
major or a minor imputation of fault; the fault can be imputed
with emphatic certainty or tentative probability; the imputation
can be widely or narrowly disseminated; it can be communicated
to an important or unimportant audience (friends or strangers,
customers or creditors), and belief in its truth can threaten pocket-
book interests or interests of another kind. "He is a butcher,"
said of a surgeon, may affect his medical practice and lower his
income, whereas "He has syphilis," said about a rich playboy,
hurts almost exclusively his interest in seducing women. A court
of law can estimate pecuniary losses with reasonable exactitude
and assign a compensatory fee to injured plaintiffs in a non-
arbitrary way. Deciding on a fee to pay the playboy in compensation for his deprivation, on the other hand, requires a judgment
of the relative seriousness of this harm compared to harms that
carry non-arbitrary price tags, a comparison that is bound to be
inexact at best.

In contrast, the source of judgmental injustice as such is not
harm, but rather simple derogatory misrepresentation, harmful
or not. Most normal persons do have an interest in not being
thought worse of by others than they deserve. If only a half-dozen
widely scattered persons falsely believe that I am a wife-beater or
a plagiarizer, my interest in reputation is just to that extent
damaged, and in a perfectly intelligible sense I am harmed, even
though no other practical interest of mine is damaged as a
consequence. In the extreme case, where the public record is
forever falsified and everyone is convinced that I am (say) a
murderer, I am harmed to an extreme extent by the opinions and
judgments that are unfair to me. But those false opinions and
judgments would be unfair to me in any case even if they did not
cause me any harm.

Suppose a speaker stands up at a Harvard philosophical colloquium and accuses Professor Willard Van Orman Quine of being "the real and original Boston Strangler." I doubt whether this false derogatory judgment would do Professor Quine's reputation any harm. Nor would it be likely to distress him any. It is too patently absurd a judgment to have much of any effect at all, except perhaps to cause general amusement. And yet considered as a judgment simply, since it misrepresents the person it judges in a way that matters, it is unfair to him. Furthermore, if anyone were to come to believe it, then he would have a belief that is unfair to the person it is about.

I come finally to the differences between defamation and judgmental injustice that generate philosophical perplexities. These have to do with the nature of the standards employed in the two areas. Even within the law, there are disagreements over "the problem of the standard." "It has been held in England," Prosser tells us, "that the communication must tend to defame the plaintiff in the eyes of the community in general, or at least of a reasonable man, rather than in the opinion of any particular group or class."[32] The standard used in American courts, on the other hand, has been more realistic, "recognizing that the plaintiff may suffer real damage if he is lowered in the esteem of any substantial and respectable group, even though it be a minority one, with ideas that are not necessarily reasonable."[33] The class of persons whose esteem is lowered may be quite small, but not "so small as to be negligible." One plaintiff recovered damages as a consequence of a defendant's false public statement that her father was a murderer though clearly not many persons, and no reasonable persons, would think less of *her*, even if they believed the allegation about her father. On the other hand, no one today, not even a debutante, could recover damages for a false public allegation that her father was a coal miner or a factory worker. Hardly any person could admit without embarrassment that he thought less of her because of *that*. When the size of the group whose esteem is at issue is "substantial and respectable," however, its standards of value need not be reasonable at all. There have been many cases, in

---

[32] Prosser, *op. cit.*, p. 577.
[33] *Loc. cit.*

southern courts especially, for example, in which a white man has recovered damages for the assertion or insinuation, in print, that he is a Negro.[34] While the esteeming group need not be reasonable, however, it must be minimally "respectable." No professional criminal could sue successfully for defamation on the ground that he had been falsely described as a police informer, even though that allegation may have utterly smashed his reputation with other criminals.

Whatever the correct policy decision about the standard for determining defamation, there is no reason a priori to expect it to apply also to determinations of judgmental unfairness. Indeed, as we have seen in the example of the white man who was defamed by the insinuation that he was a Negro, a genuinely defamatory utterance need not be judgmentally unfair at all. What then is the standard for judgmental injustice as such? This is a question which we should handle gingerly, since we have no guarantee in advance that it can be answered in as clear and precise a fashion as its legal counterpart. The problem requires the choice among standards of three kinds. We can choose a *subjective standard* for judgmental injustice, an *objective standard*, or the *standard of actual truth*. And there are choices within these categories. Within the subjective category, we can allow judgmental unfairness to be determined by the evaluative standards of the person judging, the person judged about, or the audience (if any) to whom the judgment is communicated. The latter possibility, while plausible enough for the determination of defamation, will not do for judgmental injustice; since we are after a standard that will apply to any judgment, expressed or not, we could hardly settle for a standard that applies to a judgment only when it is expressed. Similarly, we can eliminate the standards of the person making the judgment, for that would leave us with an anarchically relativistic result. One and the same false proposition—say, that John Doe is a Communist—would be unfair to Doe when believed by one person—say, Richard Nixon—and not at all unfair when

---

[34] One of the more recent cases is *Natchez Times Publishing Co. v. Dunnigan*, Mississippi, 1954, 72 So. 2d 681. See also *Spencer v. Looney*, Virginia, 1914, 116 Va. 767, 82 S.E. 745, and *Jones v. R. L. Polk & Co.* Alabama, 1915, 190 Ala. 243, 67 So. 577.

believed by another—say, Angela Davis. This result cannot be ruled out dogmatically, but it does contradict a presupposition of our inquiry—namely, that propositions about persons can be unfair in themselves, just as they are true or false in themselves, quite independently of who believes, affirms, or asserts them. The most plausible of the subjective answers to our question is that the appropriate standard for judgmental injustice is the standard of the subject about whom the judgment is made. I shall return to it below.

Objective standards are not necessarily those that are actually employed by any given subject or group of subjects. Rather they are those that ought to be employed by any subjects, those that would be employed by all subjects if they were reasonable. Wherever the common law uses an objective standard, it refers therefore to the standard of "the reasonable man." If we had used an objective standard for defamation, as the English do, then Dunnigan should not have won his suit against the *Natchez Times* for insinuating falsely that he was a Negro, for surely he would not be lowered in the estimation of any reasonable man just for being thought to be a Negro. That is just another way of saying, of course, that racial prejudice is unreasonable. Applying objective criteria is not always that easy, especially if we permit our standard to be tailored somewhat to the circumstances, as indeed we often do in other contexts, when we consider that many of the evaluative standards of actual reasonable men do not correspond to those we would ascribe to a hypothetical ideal person whose values transcend the limitations of a particular culture at a particular time and place. With which human characteristics should we endow our hypothetical reasonable man if he is not to seem superhuman? Is he simply the normal man of average insight and sensitivity, like most of our neighbors? That is not a terribly attractive idea, but it may be a realistic one unless we wish to hold most of our neighbors themselves to a standard that is beyond their reach. Supposing we give the reasonable man standards of judgment that are a good deal closer to an ideal of correctness than the average, what other characteristics should we give him? Is he a reasonable Southerner or a reasonable Northerner? Does he know a lot of history, psychology, and economics, or is his knowledge defective in the manner of most of our neighbors in those respects?

When we are dealing with various purely legal matters including the question of defamation, we will often wish to soften an objective standard by bringing in certain subjective elements. So, for example, the law of negligence holds a blind man to the standard of a "reasonably careful and prudent blind man," not to the more elevated standard of a reasonable man with normal vision. Similarly in the law of criminal homicide, under some rules,[35] a defendant is entitled to the mitigating defense of "provocation" if he can show that he killed a man in circumstances that would have caused even a reasonable man to lose control of himself. Such rules attribute an emotional side to the reasonable man, and even a tendency in certain rare circumstances to very human passionate anger.[36] The introduction of softening elements into objective legal standards is a concession to common human frailties intended to prevent the unfairness of holding specific persons to standards they cannot meet. In the law of defamation the softening process increases the protection given to prospective plaintiffs, but toughens the requirements imposed on prospective defendants, for it permits some plaintiffs to collect

---

[35] E.g., Great Britain's Homicide Act (1957), Sec. 3: "Where on a charge of murder there is evidence on which the jury can find that the person charged was provoked (whether by things done or by things said or by both together) to lose his self-control, the question whether the provocation was enough to make a reasonable man do as he did shall be left to be determined by the jury."

[36] Such rules are by no means unanimously approved by legal commentators. Glanville Williams writes: "Surely the true view of provocation is that it is a concession to 'the frailty of human nature' in those exceptional cases where the legal prohibition fails of effect. It is a compromise, neither conceding the propriety of the act nor exacting the full penalty for it. This being so, how can it be admitted that that paragon of virtue, the reasonable man, gives way to provocation?" ("Provocation and the Reasonable Man," *Criminal Law Review* [1954], p. 742). The authors of the *Model Penal Code*, in their Comments on Tentative Draft No. 9 (1959), p. 47, argue that "To require, as the rule is sometimes stated, that the provocation be enough to make a reasonable man do as the defendant did is patently absurd; the reasonable man quite plainly does not kill. . . . But even the correct and the more common statement of the rule, that the provocative circumstances must be sufficient to deprive a reasonable or an ordinary man of self-control, leaves much to be desired since it totally excludes any attention to the special situation of the actor."

damages for false statements that would not diminish their stand-ing in the eyes of an ideal transcultural reasonable man, but would diminish the esteem of a reasonable man of deep southern background and affiliation, say, or of Orthodox Jewish religious commitment, or whatever. But when we apply a standard of judgmental unfairness quite outside of legal contexts, there are no "plaintiffs" or "defendants" to consider, nor even subjects or objects of spoken utterances or written statements to specific audiences in concrete circumstances. Here, we deal not with persons who might later complain of harsh treatment, but with *propositions* about people, and propositions have no human frail-ties to consider. Here if anywhere we should expect our standards to be as free as possible of subjective elements.

The most objective standard we could possibly employ would be that of actual truth: a false statement is unfair to a person if it is *truly derogatory* of him—that is, if it would lower the esteem of a hypothetical reasonable man who employed only correct evalu-ative standards. If we then ascribe to our ideally reasonable man complete empirical knowledge of all matters relevant to evalu-ations, we would be very close to identifying the reasonable man with God. In a way this is the easiest solution to our problem, for it allows us to evade difficult questions about the evaluation of human character. Unlike its alternative solutions to the problem of the standard for judgmental unfairness, this one is not merely partially but completely formal, needing to be filled in by a thorough account of what the true standards for admiring and disrespecting *are*—in short, by a long and systematic treatise in what Kant called *Tugendlehre*, or the theory of virtue.

Nonetheless, the standard of actual truth is prima facie the most plausible one for our limited purposes here. It seems to be the standard presupposed by our intuitions in clear cases, explaining, for example, why it is unfair to Quine to judge or believe him to be the Boston Strangler, even though there are few if any actual contexts in which the assertion of that proposition would defame him. An ideally reasonable man who employed only the correct principles of character appraisal would give Quine very low points indeed if he believed him to be a strangler. There may be possible if not actual cultures or subcultures which exercise such strong influences on their members that even generally reasonable men among them would think *more* of Quine for his extracurricular violence, but whatever the opinions of "reasonable *machos*" like that, our intuitions are unwavering: the proposition in question is unfair to Quine. Similarly, it would be false but not unfair to Quine to believe him to be a Negro, whatever the reaction of some hypothetically localized and humanized "reasonable man."

It would be satisfyingly simple, and superficially plausible, to leave the matter at that, but as usual in philosophy there are troublesome counterexamples and looming complications. Suppose we assume, merely for the sake of an example, that the analytic-synthetic distinction is perfectly sensible and that the arguments so far mustered against it are muddled one and all. On that assumption, would it be unfair to Quine to believe that he is a great *defender* of the analytic-synthetic distinction? If we communicated this belief to audiences of certain kinds, Quine would probably feel defamed, but that is at least partly because he believes the analytic-synthetic distinction to be untenable. Suppose, however, that an angel of the Lord comes to Quine near the end of his days and reveals to him the truth that the analytic-synthetic distinction is quite tenable, so that Quine is forced to change his mind about it. Even then, I suspect, Quine could hardly be content with the false judgment, communicated or not, that his career had been spent defending the tenability, now vindicated, of the distinction. Indeed, I should think he might even feel *wronged* by the judgment, though neither defamed, nor otherwise harmed, nor disparaged, nor belittled by it. To be misdescribed in a way that is very basic to one's conception of oneself, one might think, is to be judged or treated unfairly, even though not in any obvious way derogated or discredited.

There are better examples, often involving less controversial assumptions, that can be drawn from history's catalogue of lost causes. Those of us who are liberals might well understand how it is unfair to Bill Buckley to judge him to be a liberal, and even a doctrinaire socialist will appreciate the judgmental injustice in the false claim that T. S. Eliot was a socialist. It is unfair to any person who has conscientiously believed in a proposition, taken it to heart, advocated and campaigned for it, and in the extreme case even built his life upon it, to deny that he believed that proposition, even though in fact that proposition is false. Thus, even though God might think better of Bertrand Russell if He believed him to be a devout Christian, that belief about Russell would be unfair to him, and unfair even if atheism, his actual conviction, should be false.

The conclusion I draw from these examples is that the standard for judgmental injustice is necessarily disjunctive in form. A false judgment or belief about a person is unfair to that person if *either* it is truly derogatory of him *or else* it severely misrepresents him in a way which is fundamental to his own conception of himself. (Unfairness by the second criterion would have to be restricted to violations of self-conceptions that fall within wide limits of reasonableness. The sincere subjective standards respected by that criterion cannot be so highly eccentric as to be irrational.) A judgment or belief about a person is unfair to him according to the second criterion even though it misrepresents him in a way that would elevate his standing in the eyes of an ideally reasonable being.

The disjunctive criterion suggests that we have duties of at least two kinds in respect to our beliefs about other persons. Corresponding to the first disjunct is a duty to try to avoid believing objectively derogatory things about others in the absence of firm evidence. That is a duty to give others the benefit of one's doubts, to avoid thinking ill of them without warrant—in short, to be generous. The second duty, however, cuts the other way, for in some cases it would have us also be careful to avoid believing too well of a person in the absence of firm evidence, because of the danger that a false generous belief might misrepresent him in a respect which is crucial to his own conception of himself. To take this second duty seriously, then, would be to create a disposition that would tend to counterbalance that created by the first, at least for a certain class of cases.

The morality of belief and judgment is subtle enough to begin with, and this disjunctive criterion of judgmental injustice makes it even more difficult. That result, however, should not be alarming. Given that we run such complicated moral risks when we judge falsely about our fellows, we had better make all the more sure that our beliefs and judgments are true.

Wollaston and His Critics

The Rev. William Wollaston (1659–1724) was one of the most famous and highly esteemed writers of his time, and yet in the century following his death, his reputation fell into sharp decline until he became an object of disrespect in the writings of Hume, Price, Bentham, and others. A fair-minded contemporary reader, I think, will find that Wollaston did have something important and original to say, however confused his manner of saying it, so that is one reason for reexamining his major work, *The Religion of Nature Delineated* (1722).[1] I have still another reason. Elsewhere, I have found it useful to speak of the "symbolic aspect" of actions[2] and to claim even that some actions can "express judgments."[3] In all the modern history of moral philosophy, Wollaston is the writer who has taken these notions most seriously, so it might well be instructive to reconsider his views.

Wollaston's aim was to find an interpretation of that ancient Stoic formula about living "in accordance with nature" that would render it at once more intelligible and convincing as an account of the ultimate basis of morals. Immoral actions, Wollaston believed, have one thing in common: they somehow treat things *as if* they were other than they are in fact. In this way, all immoral actions offend against the truth. This ingenious idea depended upon a hazy theory that actions can somehow be declarative of propositions. This writer has suggested that *some* actions can be taken to express propositions, but Wollaston's view is more extreme, for he seems to make that claim for *all* actions. He then goes on to lay down as his "fundamental maxim":

whoever acts as if things were so, or not so, doth by his acts declare that they are so, or not so, as plainly as he could by words and with more reality. . . . [4]

Actions that do not correspond with the way things are, then, are like false statements, and as such provide an interpretation of what it is to act "out of accord with nature": it is to act in denial, not in affirmation, of the nature of things. "Truth is but a conformity to nature, and to follow nature cannot be to combat truth."[5]

The foundation of the theory is Wollaston's notion of declarative actions:

A true proposition may be denied, or things may be denied to be what they are, by deeds as well as by express words or another proposition. It is [for example] certain there is a meaning in many acts and gestures. Everybody understands weeping, laughing, shrugs, frowns, etc. These are a sort of universal language. . . . But these instances do not come up to my meaning. There are many

---

[1] I have used the eighth edition (1759) as edited and abridged by L. A. Selby-Bigge (Oxford, 1897). My citations will use Selby-Bigge paragraph numbers.

[2] *Doing and Deserving* (Princeton, 1970), 68–70, 98–105.

[3] "Non-comparative Justice," *Philosophical Review*, **83** (July 1974).

[4] *The Religion of Nature Delineated*, 1028. See note 2 above.

[5] *Ibid.*, 1030.

acts of other kinds, such as constitute the character of a man's conduct in life, which have in nature, and would be taken by any indifferent judge to have a signification and to imply some proposition as plainly to be understood as if it was declared in words, and therefore if what such acts declare to be is not, they must contradict truth, as much as any false proposition or assertion can. . . . [For example] a body of soldiers seeing another approach, fire upon him. Would not this action declare that they were enemies? And if they were not enemies, would not this military language declare what was false?[6]

Wollaston alternates a handful of different locutions, which are not necessarily equivalent in meaning, to express his view about the declarative function of actions. Actions are sometimes said to "express falsehood," to "imply falsehood," or "to declare something false concerning other things"; and agents are sometimes said to "act as if things were so when they are not," or to "treat things as what they are not," "to treat another as *if* he were what he is not," or more rhetorically, to "trespass upon truth" and "to live a lie."

In a discussion strikingly reminiscent of Hobbes's theory of the "absurdity" of injustice, Wollaston gives emphasis to the irrational character of falsely declarative conduct:

Designedly to treat things as being what they are not is the greatest possible absurdity. . . . To talk to a post, or otherwise treat it as if it were a man, would surely be reckoned an absurdity, if not distraction. Why? Because this is to treat it as being what it is not. And why should not the converse be reckoned as bad, that is to treat a man as a post, as if he had no sense and felt not injuries, which he doth feel; as if to him pain and sorrow were not pain, happiness not happiness. This is what the cruel and unjust often do.[7]

Unhappily, however, Wollaston cannot explain on the single ground of fidelity to truth why treating a post as if it were a man is not precisely as evil as treating a man as if he were a post. Both modes of conduct are absurd, declarative of falsehood, and out of accord with nature, *and equally so*. To judge one to be morally worse than the other, therefore, would require the introduction of a new and independent criterion of moral wrongdoing to supplement the one Wollaston employs. He does, later in the essay, try to make sense out of the idea of differences in the degree of truth-violating/wrong-doing, but that effort is totally unconvincing and limited in scope. Still elsewhere he distinguishes between truths in terms of their *importance,* but obviously this tactic requires him to introduce a new and different criterion of "importance" to reenforce his single criterion of fidelity to truth. Thus, despite much brave struggling and kicking, Wollaston seems committed to the paradoxical doctrine of the ancient Stoics that "all sins are equal."

I am no ardent admirer of Wollaston. His conclusions are not especially congenial to me, and his argumentation is undistinguished. But after discovering in various commentaries the amount of scorn and ridicule that have been heaped on his now forgotten theory, and the shocking misrepresentations and sophistries used in "refuting" it, I am moved (out of a simple sense of justice!) to set the record straight. Ninety-five percent of those who know of Wollaston know him only through David Hume's celebrated footnote containing the ribald

[6]*Ibid.,* 1026.   [7]*Ibid.,* 1034.

example of "liberties with my neighbor's wife," which makes Wollaston the butt of the joke.[8] Others may be familiar with the quick dismissals of Wollaston in Bentham[9] and Price,[10] or the mocking arguments in such histories as those of Leslie Stephen[11] and the latest in a long line of defamers of Wollaston, Alasdair MacIntyre.[12] I shall attempt to show here how dead wrong most of these standard criticisms of Wollaston have been, while indicating what is really wrong with Wollaston's view properly interpreted. I shall conclude, then, by suggesting a way in which Wollaston's one insight might yet have importance, however crudely he put it.

Hume gets off on the wrong foot right at the start of his discussion of Wollaston. In the passage in the main text leading up to the famous footnote, he writes:

'Tis certain that an action on many occasions may give rise to false conclusions in others, and that a person who through a window sees any lewd behavior of mine with my neighbor's wife may be so simple as to imagine she is certainly my own. In this respect my action resembles a lie or falsehood, only with this difference, which is material, that I perform not the action with any intention of giving rise to a false judgment in another, but merely to satisfy my lust and passion. It causes, however, a mistake and false judgment by accident; and the falsehood of its effects may be ascribed, by some odd figurative way of speaking, to the action itself. But still I can see no pretext of reason for asserting that the tendency to cause such an error is the first spring or original source of all immorality.[13]

Hume has simply misread Wollaston. Nowhere does Wollaston claim that the essence of all wrongdoing is telling a lie and thus deceiving others. Rather he holds that all wrongdoing is an offense against the truth, whether or not any observer is present to be deceived. What makes an act wrong, according to Wollaston, is not that it misleads others or causes false belief, but rather that it violates truth, which is quite another thing. I have already acknowledged that Wollaston's theory fails as an account of "the foundation of all morality," since at best it needs supplementation by criteria of relative "worth" and "importance," and also criteria of relevance for descriptions of actions and things represented or affected by actions. But the theory is no worse in this respect than the prevailing deist-stoic theory of "living according to nature," and is in fact what Wollaston intended it to be, an interpretation and partial clarification of that ancient theory. Wollaston holds with the Stoics that actions are wrong because they are "contrary to nature," not because they may have a tendency to deceive possible observers. Thus, Hume sets out to refute a theory Wollaston never held.

[8]*A Treatise of Human Nature* (Oxford, 1897), Bk. III, Pt. I, Sec. I, 461.

[9]*An Introduction to the Principles of Morals and Legislation* (London, 1823), Ch. II, Para. XIV, note. Wollaston is not mentioned by name, but example 8 in the footnote is a clear reference to him.

[10]*A Review of the Principal Questions in Morals* (London, 1787), reprinted in L. A. Selby-Bigge, *British Moralists, op. cit.,* Ch. VI, Para. 693.

[11]*English Thought in the Eighteenth Century* (London, 1876), Ch. IX, Pt. II, Para. 9, 10.

[12]*A Short History of Ethics* (New York, 1966), 170–71.   [13]*Op. cit.* (n. 8 above) 461.

There follows the famous footnote:

One might think it were entirely superfluous to prove this if a late author [Wollaston] who has had the good fortune to obtain some reputation had not seriously affirmed that such a falsehood is the foundation of all guilt and deformity. That we may discover the fallacy of his hypothesis, we need only consider that a false conclusion is drawn from an action only by means of an obscurity of natural principles which makes a cause be secretly interrupted in its operation by contrary causes, and renders the connection betwixt two objects uncertain and variable. Now, as a like uncertainty and variety of causes take place, even in natural objects, and produce a like error in our judgment, if that tendency to produce error were the very essence of vice and immorality, it should follow that even inanimate objects might be vicious and immoral.[14]

At this point I must interrupt Hume's argument to point out how sophistical it has become. It surely goes without saying that in order for an action to be "vicious and immoral," it must in fact *be* an action! Natural objects erupt, explode, tumble, and fall, but they do not act. *A fortiori,* they cannot act viciously and immorally. Wollaston's question was the same as that raised by all moral theorists, namely: What distinguishes the class of *human actions* that are morally wrong from the class of *human actions* that are not morally wrong? No answer to that question could possibly commit a theorist to the absurd consequence that inanimate objects sometimes act immorally. Hume's argument not only fails to touch the theory he wrongly ascribes to Wollaston, but it also can be directed just as well against any moral theory, including the utilitarian theory that Hume himself held, for if the production of pain and suffering is the basis of immorality, and natural objects by erupting, exploding, falling, and tumbling, cause pain, then it could be said to follow (by Hume's logic and on Hume's own moral theory) that inanimate objects can be vicious and immoral.

Hume seems to anticipate this reply, for he goes on to say that "'Tis in vain to urge, that inanimate objects act without liberty and choice,"[15] but no reason is given to show why this natural rejoinder is "in vain," but only the dogmatic reiteration that "If the tendency to cause error be the origin of immorality, that tendency and immorality would in every case be inseparable."[16] Later in the footnote Hume has a similar but even more egregious argument against the view he mistakenly ascribes to Wollaston:

'Tis well known that those who are squint-sighted do very readily cause mistakes in others and that we imagine that they salute or are talking to one person, while they address themselves to another. Are they on that account immoral?[17]

The answer, of course, is that they are not immoral; but this is no counterexample to the theory Hume attacks, for no more than any other theory of the foundation of morality does it entail that involuntary actions can be immoral. Again, this theory, like its rivals, is an effort to distinguish those voluntary actions that are immoral from those voluntary actions that are not. One might as well charge Bentham or Hume himself with holding that it is immoral even accidentally to cause another person pain, and that not only unlucky human beings but also wild animals, thunderstorms, and earthquakes are immoral.

But Hume has still more arguments in store. The lengthy footnote continues:

Add to this that if I had used the precaution of shutting the windows while I indulged myself in those liberties with my neighbor's wife, I should have been guilty of no immorality and that because my action, being perfectly concealed, would have no tendency to produce any false conclusions.[18]

This would be a convincing counterexample to Wollaston's view if only Wollaston had held that the criterion of wrong-doing is the production of false belief. Since Wollaston did not hold that view, the argument fails. Still, it does suggest other difficulties for Wollaston's theory of declarative action. Suppose Hume, to make things perfectly clear to his neighbor's wife, shuts the windows, pulls the blinds, and then announces: "I hereby declare that I am not your husband and you are not my wife, and that I am not about to treat you as if you were my wife, but rather I am going to act as if you are what you are in fact, namely, my mistress," and then proceeds to "take his liberties." It would be difficult to see in what way, then, Hume could be accused of acting "contrary to truth." Even if his lewd actions did have a tendency to imply or suggest that the woman was his wife (and I confess I don't understand how even that weak description of them could be true), surely that expressive tendency would be more than counterbalanced by the explicit statement *in language* that the woman is his mistress. Wollaston, I think, is right in holding that there are *some* actions that "bear such relations to other things as to be declaratory of something concerning them," but he goes wrong in assuming that every action, or every wrong action, or that most actions, or even typical actions fall into this category. Most actions suggest nothing at all beyond what an observer would be entitled to infer on the shakiest inductive grounds, which is to say they make no "declaration" whatever.

But now Hume, at last, as if by an afterthought, finds the real flaw in Wollaston (which shows that not even so great a philosopher as Hume can be wrong all the time):

Besides, we may easily observe, that in all those arguments [of Wollaston] there is an evident reasoning in a circle. A person who takes possession of *another's* goods and uses them as his *own* in a manner declares them to be his own, and this falsehood [sic] is the source of the immorality of injustice. But is property, or right, or obligation intelligible without an antecedent morality? . . . . A man that is ungrateful to his benefactor in a manner affirms that he never received favors from him. But in what manner? Is it because 'tis his duty to be grateful? But this supposes, that there is some antecedent rule of duty and morals. . . . [19]

Hume here makes the same kind of point against Wollaston that I have sketched above. At best Wollaston's single criterion of morality is merely formal or partially empty, presupposing some independent or "antecedent" criterion for its own application. What is of most interest, however, in the quoted passage from Hume is that he there accepts (at least for the sake of the argument) what I take to be the most suggestive point in Wollaston, namely, that certain actions can "in a manner declare or affirm" propositions.

Perhaps the lamest of all Hume's "refutations" of Wollaston is the one he saves for the end, and introduces with a grand flourish:

But what may suffice entirely to destroy this whimsical system is, that it leaves us under the same difficulty to give a reason why truth is virtuous and falshood vicious, as to account for the merit or turpitude of any other action. I shall allow, if you please, that all immorality is derived from this supposed falshood in action, provided you can give me any plausible reason, why such a falshood is immoral. If you consider rightly of the matter, you will find yourself in the same difficulty as at the beginning.[20]

This is precisely the challenge that can be leveled at a partisan of any first principle of morals, and of course, there is no conclusive way of meeting it. One cannot prove a first principle without assuming it in its own proof. Thus, one might challenge the hedonist to explain why it is wrong to cause pain, and the only cogent reply he can make is to question the ingenuousness of the query. The "falsehood principle" seemed as evident to Wollaston as the pain principle did to Bentham. "The truth," said Wollaston, "is *sacred*," and treating things as not the kinds of things they are is *absurd*. To ask why it is wrong to "trespass upon truth," to "breathe untruth," or to "live a lie," is to ask a question which neither has nor needs an answer.

Hume was not the last critic to treat Wollaston unfairly. The most recent in a distinguished line of commentators to misrepresent Wollaston is Alasdair MacIntyre, who erroneously attributes to Wollaston the following doctrines for which I can find no warrant in the text: that "all wrongdoing is a species of lying,"[21] that "lying is saying or representing what is false,"[22] and that "to call something wrong is simply to say that it is a lie."[23] MacIntyre then proceeds to endorse Hume's "demolition" of Wollaston's theory, and concludes by charging that "Wollaston, in any case, confused lying (which involves an intention to deceive) with simply saying what is in fact false."[24]

Wollaston surely understood the difference between lying and "simply saying what is false." His view was that all wrongdoing is false representing, not that all wrongdoing is lying. (The only place I could find where Wollaston makes his point in the language of lying is where he allows himself the rhetorical indulgence of speaking of the man who lives beyond his means as "living a lie," but even there Wollaston inserts the parenthetical phrase "if the propriety of language permits [us to] say.")[25] All morally wrong actions, on Wollaston's view, are (a) intentional and (b) expressive of falsehood, but it does not follow that they are all done with the intention of *expressing falsehood in order to deceive*. Wollaston's view is perfectly compatible with the common sense notion that lying is only one type of morally wrong action among numerous others.

The true defects in Wollaston's theory of violated truth as the essence of all

---

[20]*Loc. cit.*
[21]*Op. cit.* (n. 12 above), 170.   [22]*Loc. cit.*   [23]*Loc. cit.*   [24]*Ibid.,* 171.
[25]Wollaston, *op. cit.,* 1028.

immorality are the same as those of the ancient Stoic systems of which it is an explication. The theory cannot explain why some immoral acts are worse than others, and presupposes in still other ways antecedent moral principles that are irreducibly distinct from it. And the error in Wollaston's bold theory of declarative actions is simply that of uncritically extending a plausible account of the symbolic effect of *some* actions to cover the heterogenous class of *all* actions. If one man draws his sword and advances menacingly on another, he thereby *announces* his intent to do him harm. If one group of soldiers fires at another group, it *declares* thereby that they are enemies. If policemen throw a pedestrian into their paddywagon they strongly *imply* that he is a criminal. If a famous drama critic rises from his first row seat in the middle of the first act and stalks ostentatiously out of the theatre, he *suggests* to the audience that they are watching a poor play, and *affirms* quite plainly that he does not like the play. These are all plausible examples of the ways in which actions can have significance and thus be "involved" somehow with truth or falsehood. But one soon runs out of examples. For the most part, actions suggest propositions only in the very attenuated sense that they are performed in such contexts and in such a manner as to entitle an experienced observer to make highly tentative inferences to ulterior matters of fact. I see a stranger walking down the street with a tennis racket. I infer that he has just played a game of tennis. But perhaps he is on his way to play a game instead of returning from a game. Well, then, I infer that either he has just played or else is about to play. But perhaps he is simply returning a racket that he borrowed from a friend. Well, then, I weaken my inference and conclude that he is a man who plays tennis from time to time (though not necessarily today). But perhaps he is only returning the racket on behalf of a friend, or perhaps he works in a sports equipment store. The best hypothesis may yet be that he is a tennis player, but it would surely be stretching things to say that his action has that "implication," much less that it "declares" that proposition to the world. Another man walks down the street in a manner that is not particularly noteworthy. He wears ordinary clothes and carries nothing in his arms. He is surely acting voluntarily and he may even be acting wrongly, but what does he "declare" by his action? He seems to be a man bent on declaring as little as possible or nothing at all. It is otherwise when a man exploits (knowingly or unknowingly) the conventional symbolism of a *uniform* (to wear a backward collar is to declare oneself a priest), or uses implements that have a well-known single function (to walk on crutches is to "imply" that one has a broken or sprained limb), or makes a conventionally expressive gesture (a wink is a flirtatious ploy; a yawn can express boredom; a laugh, amusement).

Even though Wollaston's theory fails as a general account of (all) immorality and as a general account of the symbolism of actions, I think that part of it, at any rate, can be resurrected as an answer to a question different from those Wollaston tried to answer. Wollaston's one analytic insight was that *some* actions can be taken to express, imply, or declare propositions. When *those* actions declare to the world some proposition which is in fact false and defamatory, then the person defamed has been unfairly treated. Our shock and outrage at such treatment, which is characteristic of our reaction to perceived injustice generally, has a righteous and impersonal quality about it that is explained by our special allegiance to truth. The sense of violated justice in this case is one and the same as the sense of violated truth, hence its peculiar tone of impersonal objectivity, as if it were experienced on behalf of the truth itself. Not all wrongdoing commits injustice; and what the present point clarifies is not the basis of all morality (as Wollaston thought), but rather the basis of the distinction between certain unjust actions and actions that are morally wrong in ways that have little to do with justice. Sympathy with others makes us react with pity or anger to their sufferings; but when those sufferings are inflicted by words and actions that also offend against the truth, our anger or pity is refined by a wholly righteous ire into that toughened alloy which is the sense of injustice.

Index

Library of Congress Cataloging in Publication Data

Feinberg, Joel, 1926-
    Rights, justice, and the bounds of liberty.

    1. Civil rights—Addresses, essays, lectures.
2. Justice—Addresses, essays, lectures.   3. Liberty
—Addresses, essays, lectures.   I. Title.
JC571.F4   323.4'01   79-48024
ISBN 0-691-07254-X
ISBN 0-691-02012-4 (pbk.)